Microsoft® Exchange 2000 Infrastructure Design

Microsoft® Exchange 2000 Infrastructure Design

Co-existence, Migration, and Connectivity

Kieran McCorry
Donald Livengood

Digital Press
An imprint of Butterworth-Heinemann

Boston • Oxford • Auckland • Johannesburg • Melbourne • New Delhi

Digital Press™ is an imprint of Butterworth–Heinemann.

Recognizing the importance of preserving what has been written, Butterworth–Heinemann prints its books on acid-free paper whenever possible.

Library of Congress Cataloging-in-Publication Data

McCorry, Kieran, 1968–
Microsoft Exchange 2000 infrastructure design : co-existence,
migration, and connectivity / Kieran McCorry, Donald Livengood.
p. cm.
ISBN 1-55558-245-1 (pbk. : alk. paper)
1. Internet programming. 2. Web sites--Design. 3. Microsoft
Exchange server. I. Livengood, Donald. II. Title.
QA76.625 .M355 2001
005.7'13769--dc21
2001047402

British Library Cataloging-in-Publication Data

A catalogue record for this book is available from the British Library.

The publisher offers special discounts on bulk orders of this book.
For information, please contact:

Manager of Special Sales
Butterworth–Heinemann
225 Wildwood Avenue
Woburn, MA 01801-2041
Tel: 781-904-2500
Fax: 781-904-2620

For information on all Butterworth–Heinemann publications available, contact our World Wide Web home page at: http://www.bh.com.

10 9 8 7 6 5 4 3 2 1

Printed in the United States of America

To everyone who helped make our journey with
Exchange 2000 so fantastic, especially Maddog, Mooner, Popper,
Shark, and, of course, The Legend.

Contents

Foreword

The 1999 Microsoft Exchange Conference in Atlanta was the first time that we showed to the world the product that would become Exchange 2000 Server. Final release was still a year away, and installing it successfully was, to say the least, "challenging." I remember looking around the speakers' lounge at my esteemed Microsoft colleagues as they struggled to coerce early beta versions of Exchange 2000 to work on laptops—a technically audacious feat rivalled only by its complete irrelevance to the real world—and I thought "There's enough brainpower in this room to rewrite Exchange 2000 from scratch, but not to install it!"

Time has moved on, and installing Exchange has become a lot easier, even if it is probably not true that "A monkey could install Exchange" (as I was quoted—accurately, unfortunately—as saying in another book, an incident that should have taught me something about keeping my mouth shut around people writing books on Exchange). But as any inhabitant of The Real World knows, between running the Exchange 2000 setup program on a server machine, and saying that you have "a working Exchange 2000 system," is the frigid gulf that separates tidy theory from gritty reality.

This book is the boat you need to cross that gulf. It is about getting from point A to point B: it is about how to migrate from a working Exchange Server 5.5 installation to a working Exchange 2000 Server installation, and it is about how to get messages flowing through your system. These are two of the most basic questions that anybody contemplating a sizeable implementation of Exchange 2000 is ever going to face.

When I first heard that Kieran and Donald were writing a book, two thoughts came crashing through my head. The first was "Those reprobates are writing a book together?!?" The second was "This is going to be one hell of a book."

For the first thought I make no apologies. If you are ever lucky enough to meet them, as I have been countless times over the years, you will probably agree that they are two of the smartest, funniest, and most outrageous people with whom you could ever sit around a campfire. I hope that by the time you've read this book you'll agree with me about the second thought as well.

So how did I know it would be a hell of a book? For almost five years I have watched with awe the progress of the Compaq Exchange Academy, an initiative designed to train consultants and customers in how to build working Exchange 2000 installations. I watched as Kieran and Donald took what they learned in their day jobs as consultants for Compaq, and combined it with their considerable skills as teachers and presenters. I sweated as they berated me and my colleagues in the Exchange team to tell them how it all really worked under the hood. And now I smile as I get to see the end result.

Congratulations lads, and save me a place at the campfire!

Charles Eliot
August 2001

Preface

In the closing years of the twentieth century we have all been privy to some monumental and inspiring events. Veteran astronauts have returned to space, presidents have been impeached, sheep have been cloned, Prince got his name back, and the dreaded Y2K Bug passed by more or less unnoticed amid a barrage of low-flying champagne corks—well for some of us at least! While the world kept itself busy revolving and rotating, developers and program managers in Microsoft's Exchange 2000 product group worked diligently on the next version of Exchange: Exchange 2000. Not for one second might we suggest that the development, or indeed the release, of Exchange 2000 merits parity with any of these undoubtedly more significant events—Exchange is after all just a tool that helps you work harder—but there can be no doubt that Exchange 2000 represents a new departure in electronic messaging.

In times past, the demarcation line between messaging systems and operating systems was well defined. Messaging administrators could easily point fingers at system or network managers and say "they did it," when the e-mail service went down. And no doubt the fingers on the hands of those system and network managers were equally adept, and practiced, when it came to pointing right back at the messaging aficionados. Exchange 2000 is different, though. It signifies a new way of integrating a messaging system into the infrastructure and weaving links between accounts, mailboxes, directories, and transports.

A pervasive synergy now exists between all of those disciplines involved in designing a messaging environment based on Exchange 2000, from the network level, through Windows 2000 domain models, across DNS and WINS environments, right out to the desktop. No single line of expertise is immune to the reach of Exchange 2000. This new way of thinking about messaging has, not surprisingly, both its good points and its not so good points.

The tight integration of Exchange 2000 into the operating system facilitates the exploitation of a single directory, improves access via core Internet services, and offers improved performance. But, as ever, the scales require balancing, and on the other side of the coin we're faced with the prospect of increasingly sophisticated hardware configurations, more complex operating environments, and, of course, the challenge of migrating existing Exchange infrastructures to Exchange 2000 without incident.

What is this book about?

Deploying a messaging system is never straightforward. Deploying Exchange 2000 certainly does not contradict this maxim. In this book, we have outlined the important guidelines for a successful deployment. There's a focus on pure Exchange 2000 deployment issues, optimal Exchange 2000 routing models, coexistence with Exchange 5.5, and strategies for migrating from Exchange 5.5.

We know that we haven't described all possible routing configurations or every potential migration scenario. And, frankly, this book would be particularly boring if we had. What we do hope we've done is described enough of the Exchange 2000 technology so that you have a sound understanding of not just what Exchange does, but why it does it. Armed with this knowledge you should be well prepared to face head-on any curve ball that Exchange 2000 throws at you.

Intended audience

We, the authors of this book, are just like you: real people. As well as writing, we've also got full-time jobs working with companies putting Exchange 2000 into production. As much as possible we've tried to transfer that real-life knowledge onto the pages that follow.

If you're a messaging system designer, messaging administrator, or in any way responsible for the messaging infrastructure of your company or organization, this book should have something to interest you. In an ideal world, with the wind at your back and the planets in alignment, every chapter would have some relevance for you. However, the real world is rarely ideal, and accordingly, perhaps not every chapter of this book will be useful to you.

If you've already deployed Exchange 2000, or are in the process of doing so, we hope that this book might explain some aspects of Exchange 2000 that have hitherto been vague. And if something in the book encourages you to go back and refine your design or implementation, then we trust that you'll agree that your time spent flicking through these pages will have been time well spent indeed.

Acknowledgments

Although writing a book allows one to express oneself in many different ways, there is no part of a book that is more satisfying to write than that section where the author has the opportunity to thank those individuals who made a difference. In singling out particular individuals for praise, this by no means compromises the heartfelt gratitude that I have for everyone who helped in any way but whom I inadvertently omitted. If you fall into that category, then please accept my apologies and know that I am eternally grateful for your contribution.

One group of individuals, above all others, contributed more than they can ever know to my understanding of Exchange 2000. During 1999 and 2000, as Compaq prepared for and rolled out its Exchange 2000 Academy program worldwide, I had the honor of working alongside Pierre Bijaoui, Dung Hoang Khac, Kevin Laahs, my coauthor Donald Livengood, and, of course, Don Vickers (who is, by the way, actually very funny!). I have to say that our preparations for the Academy, our travels around the world, and those late nights working out the details of the next day's presentations in Don's room with only Kool Aid to sustain us were the best experiences that I've ever had in my professional life. And I'm serious about that! Thank you my dear friends.

A cast of very many others in Compaq was also involved in one way or another and helped me ultimately in the preparation of this book. Thanks are due to Karen Eber, Jerry Cochran, Tom Richer, Jeff Dunkelberger, Wendy Ferguson, Ken Hendel, Armelle Gara, Ian Burgess, Martin Simpson, Barry Hughes, Glenn Harm, Steve Atkins, Emer McKenna, Linda Gallagher, Marc van Hooste, Martin Rasmussen, Kurt Skjoedt Pedersen, Henrik Damslund, Micky Balladelli, Daragh Morrissey, Sharon Stafford, and Jan de Clercq. A separate expression of thanks is also due to those responsible for Compaq's own Windows 2000 and Exchange 2000 deployments, including Wook Lee and Dave Heuss and especially Stan Foster, who patiently answered my most trying and doubtless irritating questions. Several other individuals are worthy of mention, including Stephen Brown, Hans Uli Tittes, Derek Flint, William C. Minor, Oliver Kane, Michael McStay, Philip Robinson, and Greg Cope.

Particular thanks are due to members of the Exchange 2000 product group in Microsoft—namely, Geeman Yip, Erik Ashby, and Paul Bowden. They similarly took the time to either meet with me or answer my many questions, which I'm sure often served only as a distraction to them. Ken Ewert deserves a special word of thanks for answering all of my most tedious questions!

Jens Trier Rasmussen, Dave Lemson, and Gary Adams all deserve thanks for reviewing the manuscript and contributing to the book in many ways, and a special word of thanks is due to Charles Eliot for so kindly writing the Foreword to this book.

No book from the Compaq stable seems complete these days without a mention of Tony Redmond. I'm particularly indebted to Tony for all of his encouragement and support, especially in my writing, throughout the many years that I've had the pleasure of working with him. And, similarly, his and Don Vickers' indulgence of me as I completed this book with other work building up was most welcome.

Once again, the folks at Digital Press have been excellent. I very much appreciate the support and patience that they showed as deadlines came and went, again! Special thanks are due to Phil Sutherland, Pam Chester, and Theron Shreve.

And before closing I must extend particular thanks to Penton Media and especially Karen Nicholson. Much of the material in Chapters 1 through 7 has been adapted from material I've previously published in the *Exchange Administrator Newsletter* and *Windows 2000 Magazine*. It is with their kind permission that the material has been modified and reproduced in this book.

Finally, of course, a very special word of thanks to Catherine, who tolerated my self-obsession with this book and the rest of my job. Without your love and kindness I would not be who I am today.

Kieran McCorry
May 2001

"So, Donald, whaddya think about writing a book with me about Exchange 2000?" This is how it all started, with Kieran asking a simple question. With Tony Redmond and my other colleagues standing nearby, what was I to say other than "Sure, sounds like fun!" How naïve I was! What a load of work! Ultimately, it was fun in a sick, masochistic sort of way, but I really am glad for having done it. For the opportunity, I do want to thank Kieran.

As has been mentioned, the crew that helped me learn the most about this product were the guys who are all like brothers to me now: Kevin Laahs, Pierre Bijaoui, Kieran McCorry, Dung Hoang Khac, Don Vickers, and Tony Redmond. We started this journey with two intense weeks with the Exchange developers in 1999. When I say intense, I mean intense! We had those two weeks, plus four other weeks to learn the product, create presentations, create labs, and generally get our act together to deliver the first Exchange 2000 Academy to 110 of Compaq's messaging experts the week before MEC 99. Time was of the essence and so was teamwork. Fortunately we bonded like no other team I've ever seen, much less worked with. This closeness worked out well since we spent an incredible amount of time with each other in 2000 working our collective butts off! Amazingly, we managed to have some incredibly good times too (maybe too good) and the list of hotels we've nearly been thrown out of is long but distinguished. Cheers, guys!

I'd like to thank the other members of our group, too, who have also contributed in one way or another: Steve Atkins, Pat Baxter, Aric Bernard, Jerry Cochran (big time!), Jan De Clercq (can you say Security?), Olivier D'Hose (you rock!), John Featherly, Jean-Pierre Julaude, Alain Lissoir, Emer McKenna, and Barbara Moatz. I'd also like to thank Micky Balladelli.

Over the years I've heard many stories about Microsoft and Microsoft corporate people. You've heard them, too, I'm sure: "The Borg," "The Dark Side," "The Evil Empire," and so on. Well, I've got to say that I have been suitably impressed with the Exchange 2000 development team. From the first day that we showed up on site in Redmond, to the present, they have been very open and free with information, enabling us to be as accurate as possible with the information we present and write about. This willingness to help traversed the entire engineering team, from the general manager to the coders. It was a pleasant surprise to me and quite eye opening. The person providing me with the most help has been David Lemson. His willingness to explain routing to me (over and over) is most appreciated. I'm sure I was probably a pain in his neck, but he never failed to provide me with information and explanation. And, on top of that he also reviewed the manuscript and provided feedback. What a guy!

Some others at Microsoft I'd like to thank are Wayne Cranston and Paul Bowden, who assisted both directly and indirectly with information related to routing. To Charles Eliot I'd like to say thanks for writing the Foreword—and for regaling us with great stories and guitar playing! Excellent!

Within Compaq we do a great job of sharing experiences and information. It's always impressive to ask a question and get responses from around the world! I'd like to thank all of the folks who participated in this information sharing, as it has also contributed to the book. Some of the folks I'd like to tip my hat to are Ken Hendel, Glenn Harm, Brian Carter, Mike Daugherty, Tom Richer, Joe Neubauer, Marc Van Hooste, Susan McDonald, Evan Morris, David Wade, and Dave Banthorpe.

Some other folks I'd like to thank include Greg Williams, Fred Kastner, Rich Rocaberte, Donny Closson, John MacFarlane, Andrew MacFarlane, and Chris Fowler.

Specifically, I'd like to thank Hal Pryor, also of Compaq, for reviewing the book and providing excellent feedback, and correction, to my "product of Georgia public school education" writing skills. You da man!

And though I've mentioned Tony Redmond already, I'd like to thank him again. I've known Tony since 1986..., back in the days when we were both ALL-IN-1 kinda guys. In 1999 he asked me to join his team to, in his words, "do what I do." His is a tough act to follow and sets standards that push us pretty hard. It sometimes drives us crazy, but it does make us perform to a higher standard. Cheers, mate!

I'd also like to thank Don Vickers, whom I've literally known my entire professional career (since 1983), for all of his support during the writing of this book. Don is now my manager but over the years has been one of my mentors and a good friend. As managesr, I'd like to thank Don and Tony for their understanding and support during a very rough year for me personally.

This is my first attempt at writing a book, but the folks at Digital Press have stepped me through the process with aplomb. They have been fantastic and incredibly easy to work with. I'd like to thank Phil Sutherland for getting this project rolling. Theron Shreve took the reins and got us through it, and Pam Chester has been a gem.

Most importantly, I'd like to thank my daughter, Lexie, for putting up with my frequent distractions with regards to this book and work in general. You are the light of my life and I love you more than you'll ever know. I hope one day you can have a child as wonderful as you have been.

Donald Livengood
May 2001

If you've any comments or question on the material in this book, we'd be happy to hear from you. You can contact us at the following e-mail addresses:

Kieran.McCorry@compaq.com

Donald Livengood@compaq.com

1

Deploying Exchange 2000

1.1 Introduction

Exchange 2000 is radically different from Exchange 5.5 or any of its predecessors. Architecturally, it's a world away from the self-contained messaging system that is Exchange 5.5. Those components that are built into Exchange 5.5, such as the Directory Service, the SMTP service, and so on, are now separated out from Exchange itself and, in most cases, integrated into the underlying operating system. For Exchange 2000, that operating system is Windows 2000.

Exchange 2000 positively requires Windows 2000 in order to function. The Exchange 2000 executables don't run under any earlier operating system versions, and in order to have an Exchange 2000 mailbox, you must have a Windows 2000 account. Why is there such a dependency? Well, there are a variety of reasons, but one of the most important reasons is the Active Directory.

Exchange 5.5 has a reliable and distributable directory service built in. There is no directory service built into Exchange: Exchange 2000 relies completely on the Active Directory to store information about mailboxes, custom recipients, and distribution lists, although these Exchange 5.5 primitives are represented differently in Exchange 2000. Furthermore, all of the configuration information about Exchange servers that are held in the Configuration container of the Exchange 5.5 Directory Service, are now held in the Configuration Naming Context of the Active Directory with Exchange 2000. So what does all of this remodeling mean? First, it means that Exchange 2000 has a huge dependency on the Active Directory. Accordingly, you must get the design of your Active Directory totally correct if you want your Exchange 2000 deployment to be successful. By implication, this means that you must carefully plan and implement your whole Windows 2000 environment to provide a solid infrastructure for Exchange 2000.

1.2 Windows 2000 refresher

There are some factors that are critical for any Exchange 2000 deployment, irrespective of whether it is a green-field installation or a migration, to be successful. Getting the Windows 2000 infrastructure correct is the most important factor, so you must ensure that your Windows 2000 model is soundly in place. Windows 2000 brings with it many new phrases and terminology, so, as a refresher, let's quickly review some Windows 2000 terms that you'll meet again and again with respect to Exchange 2000.

1.2.1 Active Directory

The Active Directory replaces the flat-structured Windows NT4 SAM with an X.500-like hierarchical directory structure. Exchange 2000 uses the Active Directory extensively, because it no longer has a directory service of its own.

1.2.2 Active Directory schema

The schema, among other things, defines the objects that can be stored in the Active Directory. To store new object types, the schema must be modified to describe the structure of the new object, what attributes it may contain, where it may appear in the hierarchy, and so on.

1.2.3 Windows 2000 domain

A Windows 2000 domain is a collection of Windows 2000 computers and user accounts that share a common security boundary. A Windows 2000 domain may contain Windows 2000 and Windows NT4 computers as member servers or as Domain Controllers. A domain that contains both Windows 2000 computers and Windows NT4 computers as Domain Controllers is said to be in *mixed mode*. A domain that contains no Windows NT4 Domain Controllers is said to be in *native mode*.

1.2.4 Windows 2000 Domain Controller

When a user needs authentication within a domain, it contacts a Domain Controller. You may have multiple Domain Controllers within a domain and each Domain Controller holds a complete copy of the Domain Naming Context for the particular domain in which it resides. This means that it has knowledge of all other member servers, Domain Controllers, and users registered within that domain. A Domain Controller also holds a copy of the Configuration and Schema Naming Contexts for the whole forest. Domain Controllers listen on LDAP port 389 for local domain queries.

1.2.5 Windows 2000 forest

A forest is named after the first domain that is installed. The name that you use for the first domain is very important, since it potentially affects the naming structure for your entire organization. Many companies are initially using a placeholder domain to allow them to build a forest and thus reserve a neutral name for it. Any Domain Controllers within the forest share the same Configuration and Schema Naming Contexts. You can use the DCPROMO utility to join or leave domains in a forest. A forest is composed of a tree of domains, and a tree of domains in the same branch represents a contiguous name space.

1.2.6 Global Catalog server

The Global Catalog server holds the same information as a Domain Controller. However, the Global Catalog server also holds a read-only replica of every Domain Naming Context in the forest. Thus, a Domain Controller only knows about the objects in its domain, while a Global Catalog server knows about objects in its domain and every other domain. Although the Global Catalog server knows about all objects from every domain, it only has knowledge of a subset of the attributes for each object. The objects that are available for replication to a Global Catalog server are controlled by the Active Directory Schema Manager snap-in. By default, the first Domain Controller in a domain is a Global Catalog server. Global Catalog servers listen on port 3268 (using LDAP) for queries, as well as the standard LDAP port 389. A Domain Controller can be converted into a Global Catalog server by selecting the option from the Active Directory Sites and Services snap-in.

1.2.7 Operations Master

An Operations Master server is also known as a Flexible Single Master Operations (FSMO) server. There are five different master operations roles: schema, domain naming, PDC emulator, RID, and infrastructure. Only Domain Controllers can hold these roles. With respect to Exchange 2000, you need only be concerned with the Schema Operations Master. Although Windows 2000 supports multimaster replication of data, some forms of replication are single-master because conflicts would be impossible to resolve in the normal Active Directory last-writer-wins fashion. The Schema Operations Master is unique in the forest and it is responsible for making any modifications to the schema and distributing them to other Domain Controllers. When you first install Exchange 2000, you'll need to make modifications to the schema. This is performed against the Schema Operations Master server.

1.2.8 Windows 2000 site

This is similar to the definition of a site in Exchange 5.5 terms. It may also be considered as a collection of IP subnets, which are within an area of high-speed network connectivity such as a LAN. Sites may span domains, and, accordingly, domains may span sites. There is no direct correlation between a Windows 2000 domain and a Windows 2000 site.

1.3 Exchange 2000 and forests

Information about Exchange 2000 is rooted in the hierarchy of the Active Directory. In fact, information about your Exchange 2000 infrastructure is rooted in the Configuration Naming Context, and, since a Naming Context doesn't span forests, there should be no surprise when you learn that Exchange 2000 can't span forests either. If you have multiple forests in your Exchange 2000 deployment, say one per geographical area, then this means that you must have multiple Exchange 2000 organizations—essentially different Exchange 2000 implementations—so you need to plan for a homogeneous Windows 2000 infrastructure.

It's also important to note that you can't host multiple Exchange organizations within a single forest. This is not to say that you cannot host mailboxes from multiple organizations in a single Exchange 2000 organization. You can, but a full description of this is outside of the scope of this book. While this may not seem too important—you do want a single Exchange 2000 environment, after all—it is important if you consider what you do about test environments. If you want a separate Exchange 2000 implementation for testing purposes, then you'll have to root this in a separate forest.

Although no such tools are available with the first release of either Windows 2000 or Exchange 2000, you should expect to see forest management tools appearing with subsequent releases of Windows 2000 that will allow multiple forests to be merged together. We already see the beginnings of this kind of functionality in some of the third-party Windows 2000 management tools that are available (such as those from NetIQ, Bindview, and Fastlane), but you should expect to see even more improvements over time.

1.4 The importance of Domain Controllers and Global Catalog servers

1.4.1 User authentication

In the world of Exchange 5.5, sites are created on the basis of good network connectivity. The parameters you should look for are reasonable available bandwidth (where reasonable varies anywhere from 32 Kbps to 128 Kbps) and low latency. Although the concept of an Exchange site is no longer applicable with Exchange 2000, there is the concept of a Windows 2000 site to deal with. Technically, of course, a Windows 2000 site is a collection of IP subnets, but in practice, that often means that good bandwidth and low latency connectivity are available.

From a pure Windows 2000 design perspective, it's likely that Domain Controllers will be located near groups of users. The reason for this is straightforward. When a user logs on to a domain, the logon process contacts the Domain Controller for that domain to validate the user's credentials, so clearly it makes sense to locate a Domain Controller nearby for efficient logon performance. The logon process actually goes a little bit further than this, since logon requires not just access to a Domain Controller, but the Domain Controller requires access to a Global Catalog server. Although a Domain Controller can authenticate the credentials for the user in its domain, a user logon also requires a security token to be generated with details of every universal security group to which the user belongs. Of course, it's possible that the user may belong to a security group in a different domain, so a local Domain Controller would have no knowledge of such a "foreign" group. For this reason, the Domain Controller contacts a Global Catalog server to determine those groups to which the user belongs so that access control can be correctly enforced.

So, for every grouping of users, whether Exchange 2000 users or not, you should expect to see a Domain Controller and/or a Global Catalog server located nearby. Global Catalog servers are key because all Exchange 2000 configuration information is replicated to them.

1.4.2 Global Address List services

As well as servicing user logon requests, Global Catalog servers offer directory lookup functionality to Exchange 2000 clients. As I've mentioned earlier, Global Catalog servers hold a subset of the attributes from all objects within the forest, and, specifically, for Exchange 2000, they hold name and address information. This means that Exchange clients use information from the Global Catalog server in the same way that the Exchange 5.5 Directory Service offers a Global Address List (GAL). Different types of clients use Domain Controllers and Global Catalog servers in different ways to get access to the Global Address List.

Although access to GAL information is available from Global Catalog servers over LDAP on port 3268, MAPI clients do not use this mechanism. All MAPI client directory lookup is performed using the Name Service Provider Interface (NSPI) on a dynamically assigned port which is greater than 1024. (You can find more information about how to restrict the NSPI interface to a specific port number by consulting Technet article Q270836.) The NSPI interface is only available on Global Catalog servers, never on Domain Controllers.

1.4.3 The DSAccess And DSProxy components

DSAccess (implemented as DSACCESS.DLL) is an Exchange 2000 server component that provides an in-memory volatile cache of up to 50 MB of directory data. Essentially these directory data relate to user mailbox information, which is useful to Exchange 2000 server components, including the Store and the Message Categorizer. The cache is not used for client-based GAL lookups. Among other tasks, DSAccess is responsible for keeping a list of available, unavailable, in-synch, and slow (when response time is greater than five seconds) Domain Controllers and Global Catalog servers. (The DSADiag tool, which is used to display the contents of the DSAccess cache, is described in detail in Technet article Q279423.) It can be downloaded from http://www.exinternals.com/.

The DSProxy component (implemented as DSPROXY.DLL) allows MAPI clients such as Outlook to communicate with the Active Directory for directory lookups. DSProxy uses the cached list of Global Catalog servers (with Global Catalog servers from remote domains filtered out) that DSAccess maintains and either performs directory lookups to Global Catalog servers on behalf of MAPI clients or refers certain MAPI clients directly to Global Catalog servers to perform their own lookups. The list of servers that DSProxy maintains is updated by DSAccess as the state of servers in its cached list changes. If you wish to monitor the list of Global Catalog servers that DSProxy is currently using for either proxies or referrals, you can use the Event Log. Enable at least minimum diagnostics logging on the NSPI Proxy and the RFR Interface categories of the Exchange System Attendant on the appropriate Exchange 2000 server. (Select Properties of the server under appropriate Administrative Group of the Exchange System Manager.)

All Global Catalog server lookups using either DSProxy directly or by referred clients use the NSPI interface on the Global Catalog server: The LDAP protocol is not used because the overhead of conversion between LDAP and NSPI has too great an effect on performance. No caching is provided via DSProxy; accordingly, all lookup requests are serviced directly by GCs, but proxied connections and Global Catalog server referrals are round-robin load balanced between the servers that DSAccess makes DSProxy aware of. If your Exchange 2000 server is running on a Global Catalog server, then DSProxy detects this during Exchange 2000 startup and does not offer access to the Active Directory, as shown by the event log entry in Figure 1.1. Clients connected directly to that Exchange 2000 server for mailbox access have their directory lookups directed to the NSPI interface on the same server.

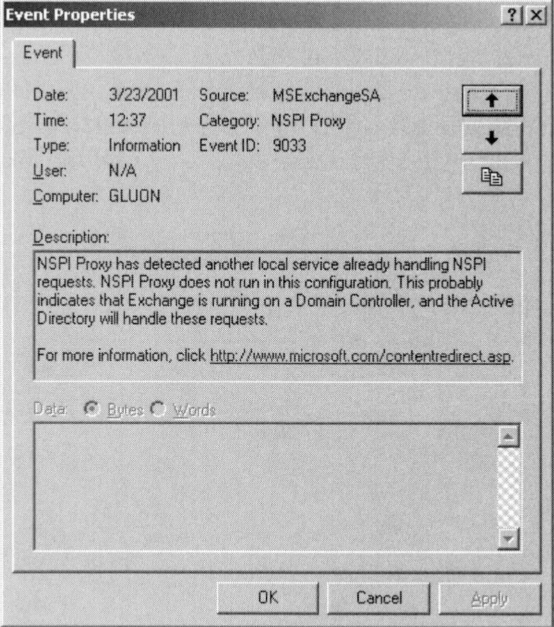

Figure 1.1 *Event log entry indicating NSPI proxy has not started.*

1.4.4 Client access to the directory service

As well as providing access to message stores, MAPI clients offer access to directory services that serve as a GAL. From Exchange 2000's perspective, MAPI clients come in two forms: pre-Outlook 2000 clients (i.e., Exchange 4.0 Client, Exchange 5.0 Client, Outlook 97, Outlook 98) and post-Outlook 2000 inclusive clients (i.e., Outlook 2000 itself and Outlook XP).

Pre-Outlook 2000 clients were designed to work with Exchange 5.5. Accordingly, when these clients connect to the Exchange 2000 server that hosts a user's mailbox, they expect a directory service to be available on the same server: This is always the case with Exchange 5.5. Since no directory service is present on the Exchange 2000 server, DSProxy services directory lookup requests from such clients instead. Figure 1.2 shows how DSProxy "proxys" directory lookups to a "nearby" Global Catalog server and returns directory information to the client. In this case, "nearby" means near the Exchange 2000 server, not necessarily near the client.

The situation is different for Outlook 2000 and Outlook XP clients. These "smart" clients were engineered while Exchange 2000 was being designed, and, as a result, they do not expect to access only a directory service on the Exchange 2000 mailbox server. (Service Release 2 for Outlook 98 allows it to behave as a "smart" client.)

Figure 1.3 illustrates the interaction between the smart clients and the Exchange 2000 and Global Catalog servers. When a smart client such as Outlook 2000 initially connects to an Exchange 2000 server, it requests a referral from DSProxy. DSProxy returns referral information, which specifies a nearby Global Catalog server to which Outlook 2000 should directly

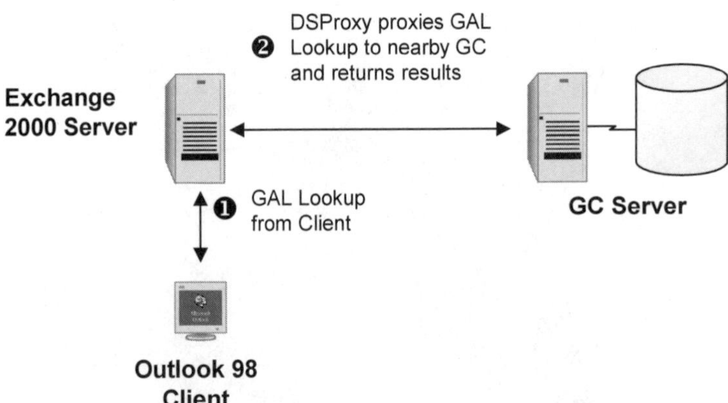

Figure 1.2 *DSProxy proxying GAL lookups to GC server.*

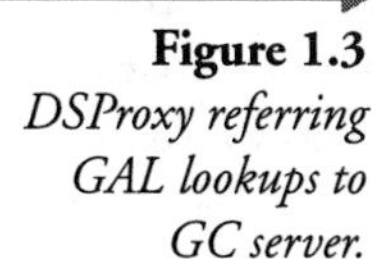

Figure 1.3
DSProxy referring GAL lookups to GC server.

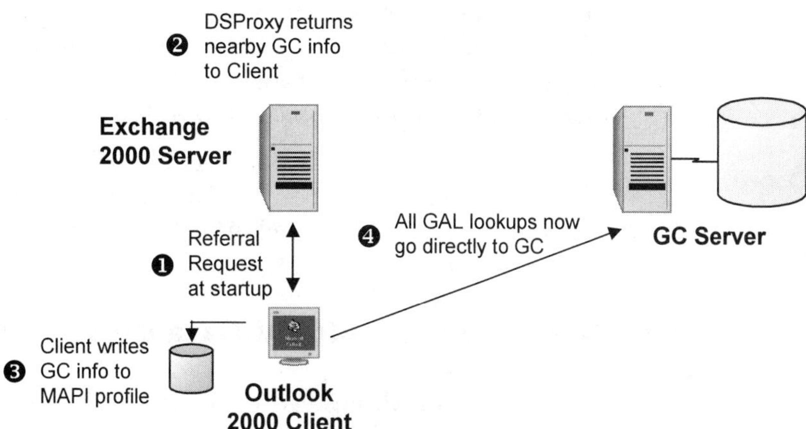

connect in future. Again, "nearby" in this case means near the Exchange 2000 server that performed the referral, not necessarily near the client. Traditional Outlook 2000 maintains this Global Catalog server referral by writing the information to its MAPI profile. The client writes the fully qualified domain name of the Global Catalog server into the following rather cumbersome registry location:

```
HKEY_CURRENT_USER\Software\Microsoft\Windows NT\
     CurrentVersion\Windows Messaging Subsystem\Profiles\
     <Profile Name>\dca740c8c042101ab4b908002b2fe182
Value name: 001e6602
Value type: STRING
Value data: <FQDN of the GC>
```

All directory lookup requests from this point on, even during the initial session, go directly to the Global Catalog server without any reference to the Exchange 2000 server. Subsequently, when Outlook 2000 next starts, it immediately attempts to access the Global Catalog server specified in the MAPI profile. If this Global Catalog server is unavailable, it requests a new referral from DSProxy.

This mechanism only allows Outlook 2000 to request a new Global Catalog server should its preferred choice be unavailable. To force Outlook 2000 to choose a new Global Catalog server you must delete the MAPI profile registry key. Additionally, Office 2000 Service Release 2C and Outlook XP clients implement a mechanism that allows a new Global Catalog server request every time the client starts. When these clients start, they ignore the Global Catalog server specified in the MAPI profile, request a new referral from DSProxy on their Exchange 2000 server, and then write this value to the MAPI profile to be used for the duration of the session. This dynamic allocation of Global Catalog servers offers improved support for load sharing, should new Global Catalog servers come on-line, whereas no such support is available with the persistent MAPI profile cache.

Other clients, such as Outlook Express, will make use of the Global Catalog server directly over LDAP and must be configured to point to a Global Catalog server directly. Outlook Web Access does not need to be configured for directory access.

1.4.5 Using Specific Global Catalog Servers

The nature of the clients that you use will determine the placement of Global Catalog servers. In the case of the proxy clients (e.g., Outlook 97 and Outlook 98), the clients themselves will have little requirement for Global Catalog servers to be located locally. Rather, adequate numbers of Global Catalog servers must be located near the Exchange 2000 servers. This generally implies one Global Catalog server to every four Exchange 2000 servers, but even when fewer than four Exchange 2000 servers are deployed, you should use at least two Global Catalog servers for redundancy purposes. The Global Catalog servers should be located on the same network segments as the Exchange 2000 servers and preferably in the same domain and/or site. This does not mean that users of proxy clients do not need to have Global Catalog servers nearby. On the contrary, they need to have Global Catalog servers nearby so that Windows 2000 logon can occur cleanly and efficiently. So, for these reasons you need to have Global Catalog servers placed near user workstations and near Exchange 2000 servers as well.

The same rules of thumb generally can and should be applied when using smart clients. When Exchange 2000 provides a referral back to the client, it is referring the client to a Global Catalog server that is near the Exchange 2000 server, not necessarily near the client. This is not ideal, since the local Global Catalog servers may be available to the clients via a WAN connection, and this is inherently inefficient, since directory lookups could be better serviced by Global Catalog servers nearer the clients. Truly local Global Catalog servers will be available in any event to service logons, so in an ideal world the client would be referred to one of these. While this form of Global Catalog server referral is not optimal, it is no worse than the proxy behavior or the behavior associated with Exchange 5.5.

It is possible to explicitly define the Global Catalog server that clients will use rather than relying on DSProxy to arbitrarily assign a Global Catalog server. For explicit proxying, you specify the fully qualified domain name of the Global Catalog server in the following registry key on the Exchange 2000 server:

```
HKEY_LOCAL_MACHINE\System\CurrentControlSet\Services\
     MSExchangeSA\Parameters
Value name: NSPI Target Server
Value type: STRING
Value data: <FQDN of the GC>
```

Similarly, for smart clients that use the referral mechanism, you can override DSProxy's Global Catalog server selection and specify the fully qualified domain name of a particular Global Catalog server to be used in the following registry key on the Exchange 2000 server:

```
HKEY_LOCAL_MACHINE\System\CurrentControlSet\Services\
     MSExchangeSA\Parameters
Value name: RFR Target Server
Value type: STRING
Value data: GC-server-name
```

If you do not wish to specify an explicit Global Catalog server for all clients that will receive referrals from this Exchange 2000 server, you can customize individual clients that are running Office SR2C or Outlook XP. Specify the fully qualified domain name of a particular Global Catalog server to be used in the following registry key on the Outlook client:

```
HKEY_CURRENT_USER\Software\Microsoft\Exchange\
     Exchange Provider
Value name: DS Server
Value type: STRING
Value data: GC-server-name
```

There's even another alternative. You can disable referrals altogether and force smart clients to use proxying. Set the following registry key on the Exchange 2000 server:

```
HKEY_LOCAL_MACHINE\System\CurrentControlSet\Services\
     MSExchangeSA\Parameters
Value name: No RFR Service
Value type: DWORD
Value data: 0x1
```

It's clear that there is a great dependency on the correct placement of Domain Controllers and especially Global Catalog servers in order to provide an efficient infrastructure for Exchange 2000 to run on top of.

1.4.6 Dealing with Global Catalog server failure

Neither proxy clients nor referral clients deal gracefully with the loss of a Global Catalog server. Normal connectivity from the client to the mailbox for access to mail messages and documents is still maintained, but directory lookup functionality is not. In the case of proxy clients, although the client maintains a connection to the Exchange 2000 server, which proxys the request to a specific Global Catalog server, the client address book provider (implemented as EMSABP32.DLL on the client PC) caches the Global Catalog server details locally. The caching is done so that the Exchange 2000 server always proxys the lookup request to the same Global Catalog server upon startup, thus maintaining consistency in the GAL presented to the client. However, should the Global Catalog server become unavailable, the client must restart (and accordingly clear the dynamic cache) before a new Global Catalog server can be used for the proxy requests.

A similar scenario holds true for the smart referral clients. While the Global Catalog server is available, a smart client will communicate with it directly. However, should the Global Catalog server become unavailable, the Outlook client must be restarted to request a new Global Catalog server. Under most circumstances the DSProxy component will provide the client with a new and available Global Catalog server, since DSAccess will inform DSProxy that the original Global Catalog server is down. However, real-life experience has shown that occasionally DSAccess does not update DSProxy in a timely manner, and the client may well be referred to the same Global Catalog server, which is still unavailable. Since DSProxy load balances its referrals, you can try restarting Outlook a few times to get a referral to an active Global Catalog server, but generally a single restart should suffice.

1.5 Choosing the right domain model

With Windows NT4 and Exchange 5.5 there are many restrictions on which domain model you can put in place. Typically, the restrictions relate to the maximum number of account objects that you can place in a domain or to management capabilities across different groups of administrators with different management interests or objectives. Using Windows NT4 and Exchange 5.5 usually results in an environment with one or more Master User Domains and one or more Resource Domains for Exchange 5.5 servers in all but the simplest environments (see Figure 1.4).

Using Windows 2000 we have an opportunity to build a streamlined domain model either for new environments or rationalized existing envi-

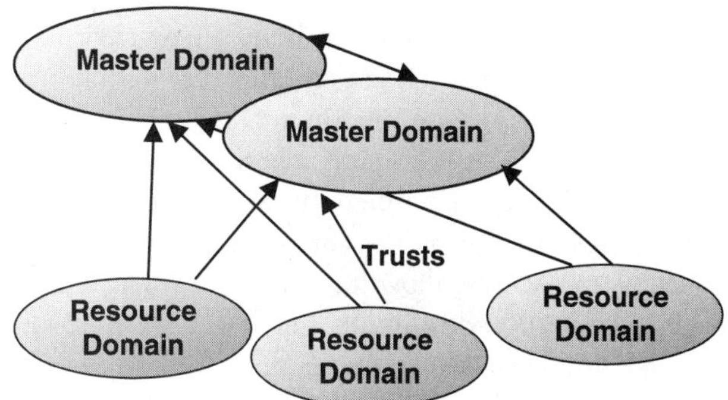

Figure 1.4 *Windows NT4 model suitable for Exchange 5.5.*

ronments. Ideally, a single domain model is the target for which you should aim. The ability to streamline to a single domain model using separate Organizational Units (OUs) where once you may have used a resource domain is a model that will be used by many organizations and becomes achievable with Windows 2000. Most importantly, because of the granular access controls, you can allow all objects to be hosted in a single domain, yet still finely control administration. (A preferred Windows 2000 domain model is shown in Figure 1.5.)

If you find yourself in a situation where you'll be migrating a Windows NT4 domain environment to Windows 2000, it makes sense to restructure, rather than upgrade that domain environment, if it's more than just a sim-

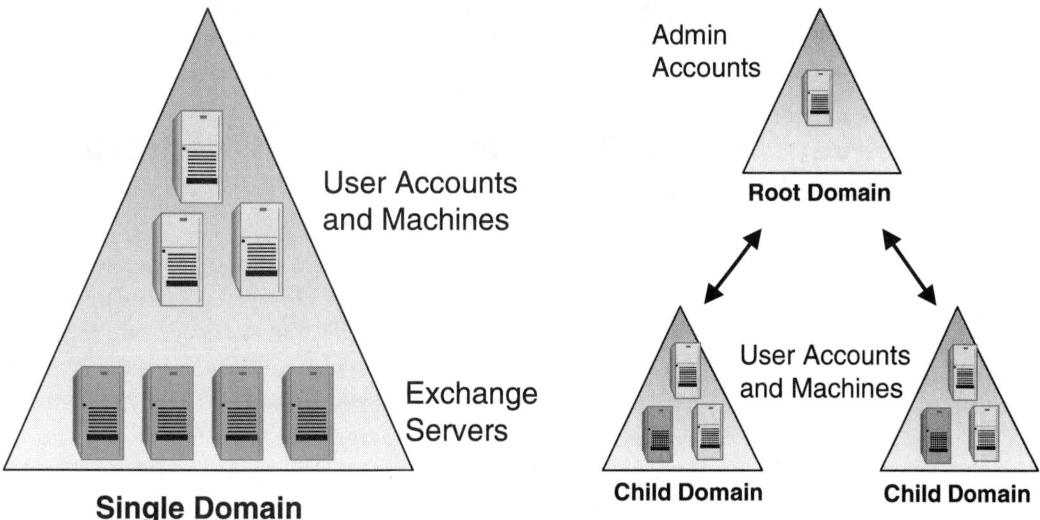

Figure 1.5 *Preferred Windows 2000 domain models.*

ple domain structure. As an alternative to just upgrading existing systems, a more innovative approach is to build a new environment alongside the old Windows NT4 environment and then use migration tools to transfer Windows NT4 account information into the newly built (restructured) domain. This approach is highly desirable because you get the opportunity to build a new streamlined environment and impact the existing user community as little as possible during the course of the migration. Most migration tools available today even allow for Windows NT4 passwords to be carried over to Windows 2000 during the user migration process. The result is an optimized Windows 2000 environment ready for Exchange 2000 and possibly reducing many hundreds of Windows NT4 domains to a handful of Windows 2000 domains. Figure 1.5 illustrates two approaches for a Windows 2000 domain structure. For simple environments, it's common to see a single domain model, which includes all user and machine accounts. In more complex environments, it's common to see a tiered domain approach, which typically uses just the root domain acting as a naming placeholder and holding just a handful of administrative accounts. The child domains typically hold all user and machine accounts, and it's usual to find one located near a major geographical area or business function.

You might take the Compaq environment as an example. The previous 13 Master Account Domains and over 1,700 Resource Domains that were used in the Windows NT4 environment have been reduced to just four Windows 2000 domains: One placeholder domain for CPQCORP.NET and three geographical domains, not so cryptically named AMERICAS.CPQCORP.NET, EMEA.CPQCORP.NET, and ASIAPACIFIC.CPQCORP.NET.

1.6 Universal Security Groups and mixed mode membership

Ideally, all of your domains should be in native mode before you start to either deploy or migrate to Exchange 2000. However, there is no explicit requirement for this to be the case and mixed mode domains can be used, if somewhat less effectively. In the scenario where you have Universal Security Groups in native mode domains there is no requirement that the membership be drawn from other native mode domains. This flexibility is useful, because it means that there's no restriction on the domain mode before you start to implement Exchange 2000. Having said that, as a matter of best practice you should complete the migration to Windows 2000 account domains before you begin to deploy Exchange 2000. In doing so, those account domains should be in native mode and the reasons for that are explained in the following text.

When a user logs on to a domain, the Global Catalog server is consulted so that the SIDs of any universal groups to which the user belongs are built into the user's security token. However, if the user is a member of a mixed mode domain, then those SIDs are not placed into the token, since the concept of Universal Security Groups is not supported in mixed mode domains—down-level Windows NT4 domains would not be able to parse them.

So clearly there is a problem, in so far as a user can be a member of a Universal Security Group, and, as we'll see later, you can use the Universal Security Group to permission Public Folders, but those permissions will not be adhered to if the user account is homed in a mixed mode domain and the user requests access to the permissioned Public Folder. At best, this will result in the user not being granted access to the Public Folder if the Universal Security Group has been used to identify those users who have access to the Public Folder. However, in the worst case, if Universal Security Groups have been used to enforce explicit deny access, then there is the possibility that users may be able to access Public Folder information, where ordinarily they would not.

1.7 Token Augmentation

Obviously, it's not appropriate to allow such a lapse in the Public Folder permissions model to exist in a production environment, so a technique called Token Augmentation is used to plug the gap.

This problem only exists if a user's account is homed in a mixed mode domain. (User accounts homed in native mode domains that are members of a Universal Security Group are not affected.) Windows 2000 provides a function that allows an application, Exchange 2000 in this case, to discover which Universal Security Groups a user is a member of and then add the SIDs of those Universal Security Groups into the user's token. This results in an augmented token that is used in subsequent access checks. This new function wasn't part of Windows 2000 RTM, but is available in a post-RTM hotfix and is bundled into Windows 2000 Service Pack 1.

In this way, Exchange 2000 offers the same functionality that you would expect to get with a native mode domain, although the user's domain is actually in mixed mode, with the complete token being built not at login time but deferred until later when the user tries to access the Exchange resource. Note that the token is only augmented on demand—that is, when the user requests access to the permissioned object. When the access is requested, Exchange 2000 only invokes the token augmentation code if the forest in which the domains are homed is not wholly in native mode. Exchange 2000 can determine if the user is from a mixed or a native mode domain, and the token is augmented once and then cached on the server that is attempting the access.

Token augmentation becomes more complex when you have to deal with trust relationships to Windows NT4 domains and to other Windows 2000 domains in different forests, as follows:

- Trust relationships to Windows NT4 domains may be used in conjunction with the Active Directory Connector (ADC) to create disabled user accounts in a new Windows 2000 domain and then assign mailbox rights back to that trusted Windows NT4 account. Since a trusted Windows NT4 account is being used, the token that is generated at logon time is based on the Windows NT4 account, yet any Universal Security Groups that you use to enforce access controls will be based on the disabled user object. In this case, Windows 2000 provides another set of function calls that allows Exchange 2000 to update the Windows NT4 token in the same way it updates the Windows 2000 user token.
- Trust relationships to domains in another forest use a special switch, setting `msExchAddGroupsToToken` to `TRUE`, to achieve the same effect.

Token augmentation is only implemented for certain client protocols—specifically, MAPI, Web-DAV, and OLE-DB covering the traditional Outlook-style clients, Web browser clients, and programmatic access. However, it is not available for ExIFS (access to Exchange via the M: drive), IMAP, NNTP, or POP3 clients, so the user capability may vary depending on the client that you're using at any particular time.

1.8 Preparing Windows 2000 domains for Exchange 2000

Since Exchange 2000 has such a huge dependency on Windows 2000, it's not surprising to learn that there are some explicit steps that you need to take to prepare the Windows 2000 environment for Exchange 2000. Two command-line options exist for the Exchange 2000 SETUP utility that allow administrators to prepare the environment. These options are collectively known as OrgPrep, but individually known as ForestPrep and DomainPrep.

Separating these forest and domain preparation tasks from the Exchange 2000 installation process proper makes a good deal of sense in larger and more complex environments. Any sizable organization may have different teams of administrators that are responsible for pure Windows 2000 administration, and preparing the forest and domain infrastructure is essentially a Windows 2000 administration task, which requires certain access rights. Allowing Windows 2000 administrators to do this means that you have the right group of people performing the task, rather than having to elevate the access rights of messaging system administrators.

1.8.1 Running ForestPrep

You run the ForestPrep utility by executing the `SETUP.EXE` from the Exchange 2000 installation CD-ROM with the `/FORESTPREP` qualifier.

Running ForestPrep performs a number of important functions. First, it extends the Active Directory Schema to add new definitions that Exchange 2000 uses. Windows 2000 has about 1,000 class definitions built into the Active Directory. These class definitions define the hierarchy of objects and the attributes that may be associated with any given object. But when Exchange 2000 comes into play, it needs to reference more attributes than just the standard ones that are in the base operating system definition. For example, Exchange 2000 needs to store extra information about your account, such as the Exchange 2000 server on which your mailbox is homed, which storage group your mailbox belongs to, and so on.

To do this, the ForestPrep tool adds some additional auxiliary classes that augment the object class definitions that are already present for user, contact, and group objects. The class definitions are loaded into the Active Directory as a set of LDIF commands. You can see the files that contain the commands in the `SETUP` directory on your Exchange 2000 installation CD-ROM named `SCHEMA0.LDF` through `SCHEMA9.LDF`.

When running ForestPrep, you need to run it in the domain that holds the Schema Operations Master, typically the root domain. To run ForestPrep you must use an account that is a member of the Domain Admins, Enterprise Admins, and the Schema Admins groups. In addition, you must ensure that the account you are installing with is also a member of the local server's built-in Administrators Group. Although the Active Directory offers multimaster replication, modifications to the schema, the very fabric of the directory, can only take place on the Schema Operations Master. If you have multiple domains in your Active Directory forest, you'll want to be sure that the schema extensions have successfully replicated to all Domain Controllers within the forest. It's important that you check that replication has completed if you have multiple domains or multiple Domain Controllers. If you try to install Exchange 2000 and the Domain Controller to which it connects during the install doesn't have the appropriate schema extensions in place, then the installation will terminate with errors.

As well as populating the Active Directory Schema with new class definitions, ForestPrep does some other work. It creates the Exchange Organization object in the Configuration Naming Context of the Active Directory and sets up the permissions structures, so you'll get prompted for an organization name that will be used for the Exchange 2000 Organization. Clearly the work that's carried on here requires the appropriate access rights, so you'll need to make sure that you are logged on to the domain with the appropriate privileges. You'll need to have Schema Admin privileges to make the changes to the Active Directory schema, and you'll also need Enterprise Admin privileges to create the configuration information.

If you intend to install an Exchange 2000 server into an existing Exchange 5.5 site, then you'll also need to have at least read-only rights in the Exchange 5.5 Directory Service. In this case, you won't be prompted to enter the organization name; instead, you'll be prompted to enter the name of an existing Exchange 5.5 server. ForestPrep will contact the Exchange 5.5 server and interrogate the Exchange 5.5 Directory Service to get organization and site naming information that will then be configured into the Active Directory. This configuration information is obtained by using a special type of Connection Agreement (CA) known as a Configuration Connection Agreement (ConfigCA). The creation of the ConfigCA requires that the ADC be already installed.

1.8.2 Running DomainPrep

As well as running ForestPrep, which serves to perform some configuration that's required across the whole Active Directory environment, you will also need to run DomainPrep in every domain where Exchange 2000 will be installed or where Exchange 2000 users will be located. You must also run DomainPrep in the domain in which you've previously run ForestPrep. It's run the same way as ForestPrep; just execute `SETUP.EXE` from the Exchange 2000 installation CD with the `/DOMAINPREP` qualifier.

DomainPrep performs tasks such as creating the required security groups for Exchange 2000 administration and Exchange 2000 service access to the Active Directory, and, similarly, you'll need to be logged on with Domain Admin privilege, in order to run this utility. Also make sure that the account that you are installing from is a member of the local server's built-in administrators group. Running DomainPrep creates the Domain Ex Servers group and the All Exchange Servers group.

1.8.3 How do you know if your schema needs upgrading?

If you take a look at the end of the SCHEMA9.LDF file, you'll find an attribute called ms-Exch-Schema-Version-Pt. For example, with the RTM build of Exchange 2000, build 4417.5, the attribute settings in the file read:

```
dn: CN=ms-Exch-Schema-Version-Pt,<SchemaContainerDN>
changetype: modify
replace: rangeUpper
rangeUpper: 4197
```

During installation, Setup checks the value of this attribute in the SCHEMA9.LDF file against the actual value in the Active Directory and determines whether or not the schema needs to be upgraded.

Obviously, you can check the attribute settings as well, using a tool such as ADSI Edit (more information in ADSI Edit later) to see the value of the Active Directory object's attribute.

1.8.4 Best practices you should observe when preparing for Exchange 2000

Running the OrgPrep tools against your Active Directory infrastructure is not a task that should be performed without proper planning and preparation. You are making real changes to the very definition of the Active Directory, and, as such, any change should be properly evaluated. It makes a great deal of sense to establish a process of schema extension review (for the Exchange 2000 extensions and any other extensions you might make to tailor your Active Directory).

Furthermore, once the schema extensions have been applied to the Schema Operations Master, don't just rush off and try to install Exchange 2000 immediately. Give the Active Directory time to replicate the changes around your organization. Visit each Domain Controller (logically, of course) and verify that replication has indeed taken place. Experience gained on other large-scale Active Directory and Exchange 2000 deployments has always indicated the absolute importance of a functioning Active Directory replication infrastructure. Bear in mind that running ForestPrep creates attributes that will be replicated to all Global Catalog servers, so significant replication should be planned for.

1.9 Installing Exchange 2000

Having prepared the way for Exchange 2000 using the OrgPrep tools, all that remains is to go ahead and install the software. Installation of Exchange 2000 uses a completely different user interface, shown in Figure 1.6, from that used with previous versions of the product. The existing installation process was more than eight years old, and although it served well for previous versions of Exchange, it is no longer suitable for use with a more complex installation process such as Exchange 2000.

The new installation process uses a COM-based model for installing components that offers a common look and feel across all of the BackOffice applications. (It should be noted that there is no support for MSI with Exchange 2000.)

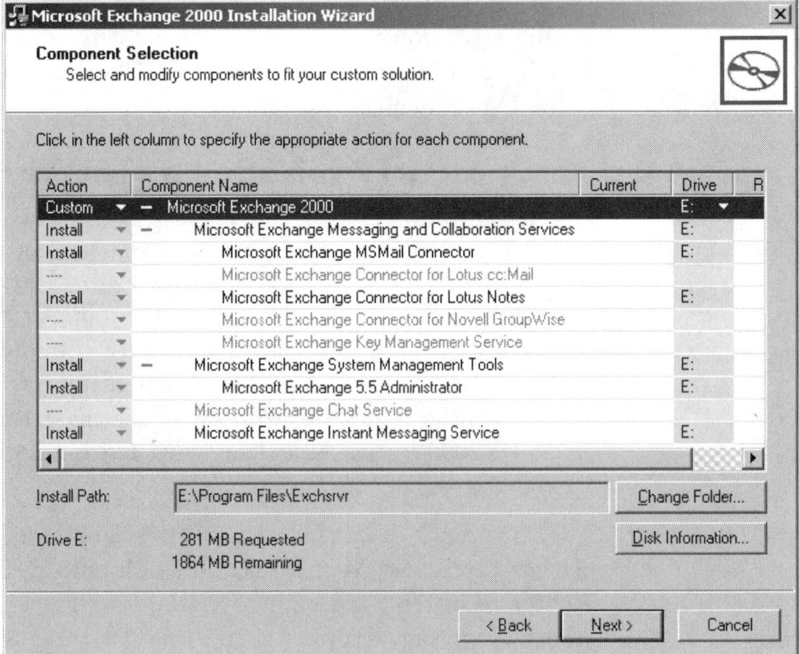

Figure 1.6 *Exchange 2000 installation user interface.*

The installation process is more or less consistent with other types of installations—specifically, installing Exchange 2000 on a cluster. Although a cluster installation puts down essentially the same code, there are some cluster-specific files that get installed for cluster operation. In fact, an Exchange 2000 cluster uses its own resource DLL, which offers finer control for fail-over handling. All nodes in a cluster must receive Exchange 2000: You can't just have a few nodes in the cluster running the software.

As well as an arguably improved Graphical User Interface (GUI), the installation process offers improved support for unattended installations.

1.10 Summary

Preparation truly is everything when it comes to deploying Exchange 2000. More than ever before, the messaging systems relies completely on the underlying operating system, and it is absolutely critical that you invest appropriate time and effort to building an infrastructure on which to deploy Exchange. The key components you should bear in mind relate to the Active Directory. Plan your domain model and strive for as much simplicity as possible, reducing domains where appropriate. Deploy Domain Controllers and especially Global Catalog servers with generosity. Make sure that everywhere you deploy Exchange 2000 servers or have populations of Exchange 2000 clients, you have Global Catalog servers nearby.

2

Synchronization with the Active Directory Connector

2.1 Introduction

The Active Directory Connector (ADC) is one of the most powerful tools available to the messaging consultant. You already know that Exchange 2000 doesn't have its own built-in directory service but instead uses the Active Directory. During a migration project from Exchange 5.5 to Exchange 2000, one of the most important aspects of coexistence is that of synchronizing directory information between the Exchange 5.5 Directory Service and the Windows 2000 Active Directory. The ADC does just that: It maps the Exchange 5.5 Directory Service object to corresponding objects in the Active Directory and vice versa.

In this chapter, we'll explore some of the ADC's dark secrets and, hopefully, by the time you've read about ADC, you'll be prepared to give it the respect it deserves when you go to deploy it.

2.2 ADC core technology description

There are many aspects of the ADC's operation that merit broad and comprehensive discussion. In the simplest of cases you can look at its operation in the simplest of environments. In such a case, you need to be concerned with how the ADC takes information from the Exchange 5.5 Directory Service and synchronizes it into the Active Directory. Of course, in this simple case, you must also be concerned with the reciprocal process—how the ADC synchronizes information from Active Directory into Exchange 5.5 Directory Service.

This defines the basic behavior of the ADC, and, while it appears reasonably straightforward, there is a lot of work taking place under the covers to make it function correctly. The following text describes in some detail the inner workings of the ADC. Armed with this knowledge, based on a simple environment, you should be able to use the ADC in somewhat more complex environments.

2.2.1 What is the ADC?

In any environment where interoperability between mail systems is required, there is typically a requirement to exchange directory information. The coexistence environment between Exchange 5.5 and Exchange 2000 is no exception to this rule. The ADC runs on a Windows 2000 server computer, and its installation process performs a number of different tasks, including installing the ADC binaries, the management interface, and potentially some extensions to the Active Directory schema.

The purpose of the ADC is to synchronize information between the Exchange 5.5 Directory Service and the Windows 2000 Active Directory. The ADC provides multimaster and bidirectional synchronization of data between the Exchange 5.5 Directory Service and the Active Directory using the LDAP protocol. ADC synchronization can take place unidirectionally if required, and in some instances this can be desirable. The ADC operation is based on the replication model that the Exchange 5.5 Directory Service uses—that is, the object-based replication model the Exchange 5.5 Directory Service uses—in contrast to the attribute-based replication model the Active Directory uses.

As you move users from the Exchange 5.5 environment to the Exchange 2000 environment, it is imperative that you provide a consistent directory for both groups of users. The issue here, of course, is that when an Exchange 5.5 mailbox becomes an Exchange 2000 mailbox, the representation of that user in the directory moves from the Exchange 5.5 Directory Service to the Active Directory. Since we'll have a period of time when we have a mix of both types of users, we need a mechanism to represent the new Exchange 2000 users in the old Exchange 5.5 directory and, similarly, a mechanism to represent the old Exchange 5.5 users in the new Active Directory (Exchange 2000 directory).

2.2.2 Is there more than one ADC?

The simple answer to this question is: Yes, two! You'll find a version of the ADC on the Windows 2000 CD-ROM, so obviously the ADC has been around for as long as Windows 2000 has been around. Many companies that have been experimenting with Windows 2000 since its beta days have also taken the time to play with the Windows 2000 ADC and have been synchronizing information from the Exchange 5.5 Directory Service into the Active Directory.

You'll find another version of the ADC on the Exchange 2000 CD-ROM, and this is the one that you should really be using when Exchange 2000 itself comes into the picture. The Windows 2000 ADC is functional insofar as it allows you to synchronize recipient information (mailboxes, custom recipients, and distribution lists) between the Exchange 5.5 Directory Service and the Active Directory, but the Exchange 2000 ADC goes further. As well as having the capability to synchronize recipient information, this version of the ADC can also deal with Exchange 5.5 configuration information.

For most companies, making the move from Exchange 5.5 to Exchange 2000 will probably result in some form of coexistence between the old Exchange environment and the new one. This kind of coexistence implies mail interoperability, where Exchange 2000 servers can use RPCs to deliver messages natively to Exchange 5.5 servers. To do this, Exchange 2000 needs to have information about the Exchange 5.5 environment, and it does this by using information that's held in the Configuration container of the Exchange 5.5 Directory Service. The Exchange 2000 ADC creates a special

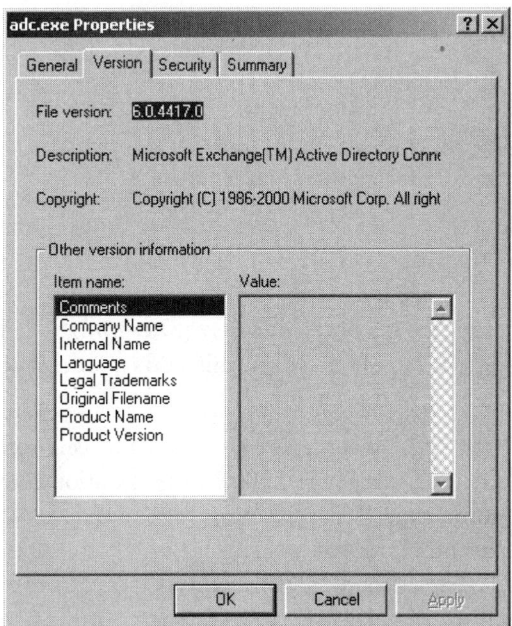

Figure 2.1 *The ADC Properties tab showing version number.*

type of Connection Agreement (CA), which defines an instance of synchronization called a Configuration Connection Agreement (ConfigCA). The role of the ConfigCA is to synchronize Configuration container information with the Configuration Naming Context of the Active Directory. The Configuration Naming Context holds all of the configuration information about the Exchange 2000 environment that Exchange 2000 servers require.

You shouldn't be too concerned with the management of ConfigCAs. Exchange 2000 automatically creates them on your behalf when you upgrade an Exchange 5.5 server to Exchange 2000 or when you install an Exchange 2000 server into an existing Exchange 5.5 site. But for this to work, you do need to make sure that you've got the correct variant of the ADC already installed: You must use the Exchange 2000 ADC, not the Windows 2000 ADC.

You can tell which version of the ADC you're using by looking at the version number on the Properties tab of the file `ADC.EXE`. On a Windows 2000 ADC, you'll see that the version number is 6.0.3939.7, whereas on the Exchange 2000 ADC, it'll be much higher. As you can see in Figure 2.1, the version number associated with the ADC from the Exchange 2000 RTM kit is 6.0.4417.0.

2.2.3 ADC operation overview

The ADC uses the LDAP protocol to provide synchronization of data between the Exchange 5.5 Directory Service and the Active Directory. In general, you'll want to provide directory synchronization in both directions, but characteristics of the environment may mandate that you only perform synchronization in one direction, and the ADC can do this if required.

Exchange 5.5 Directory Service object replication works using Update Sequence Numbers (USNs), which are associated with every object. When an object is changed, its USN is updated, and this change in the USN indicates that a local copy of the object requires updating. The ADC synchronization engine is loosely based on this USN model, and we'll discuss this in more detail later in this chapter.

While the ADC is termed a *connector*, this isn't some special add-on to, or component of, Exchange 2000 in the traditional Exchange 5.5 sense of the term connector. The ADC runs as a standalone Windows 2000 service just like any other service, named MSADC, and you can control it using the MMC Services snap-in. Alternatively, you can control it from the command window using the `net start msadc` or the `net stop msadc` commands, if you like that sort of command-line retro thing.

You'll need to have a Windows 2000 server available on which to run the ADC, but you don't need to run it on a special Windows 2000 server such as a Global Catalog server or a Domain Controller. A simple Windows 2000 member server will be more than adequate to run the ADC components, but, of course, you do need to make sure that this server can contact an Exchange 5.5 server and a Global Catalog server, since these provide directory services and the data sources for the synchronization. Using a dedicated ADC server is not mandatory, but for larger deployments it certainly does make sense to host the ADC on a separate system, rather than bundling it on a system that serves other functions.

2.2.4 Ports and protocols

The ADC uses LDAP more or less exclusively for all of its operations. (A few types of operations will use RPC connections, and one such instance is described later in this section.) In the first instance, a CA accesses the Exchange 5.5 Directory Service using the LDAP protocol on port 389.

Exchange 5.5 supports the LDAP protocol as a feature of the Directory Service, and it is enabled by default. However, if you are intending to run Exchange 5.5 on a Windows 2000 Domain Controller or Global Catalog server and you need to get to the Exchange 5.5 LDAP service on such a server, then you must make some modifications to the Exchange 5.5 LDAP protocol configuration. Domain Controllers or Global Catalog servers also use the LDAP protocol natively and during startup; they register their LDAP service against port 389. By the time the Exchange 5.5 Directory Service starts up and tries to use port 389, it is no longer available. So, in a situation such as this, you'll need to modify the protocol settings on the Exchange 5.5 server to use a different port; port 390 is the usual alternative port number to use, but any port will do. Having performed the Exchange 5.5 LDAP protocol reconfiguration, you must restart the Exchange 5.5 Directory Service for the service to be available.

The ADC configuration takes this into account and you can see from Figure 2.2 that you can modify the port number on which to access the Exchange 5.5 Directory Service using LDAP.

You should also notice from Figure 2.2 that it is only possible to change the port number for the connection to the Exchange 5.5 Directory Service: You cannot change any settings for the Active Directory server. The reason for this is simple: The ADC will always connect to the Active Directory via a Global Catalog server using port 3268. Although Domain Controllers use LDAP over port 389, the nature of ADC operation means that you should

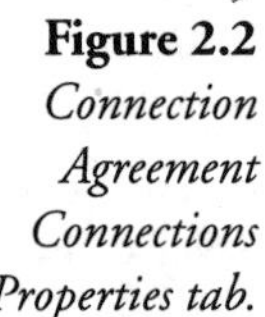

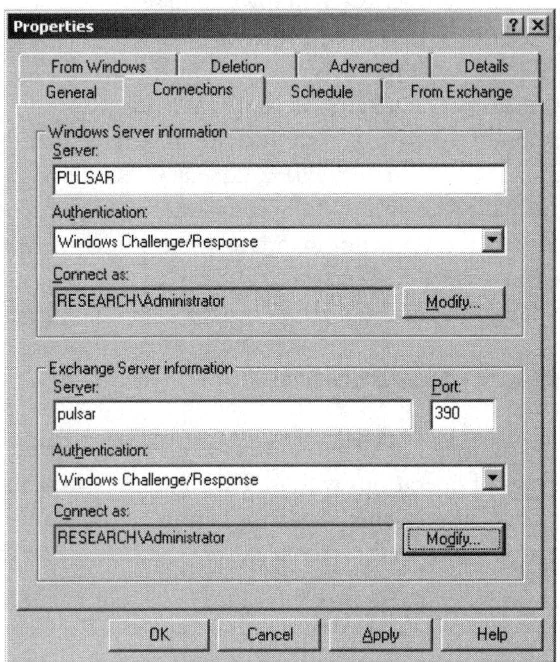

Figure 2.2 *Connection Agreement Connections Properties tab.*

always point a CA to a Global Catalog server: A Domain Controller can be used, but you will incur a performance penalty since the CA must check with a Global Catalog server anyway.

Under normal circumstances, all network communication that the ADC generates relies on the LDAP protocol and is limited to ports 389 (or your specified alternative) and 3268, but there is at least one exception to this rule. It is possible to use the Active Directory Users and Computers tool to create a new Windows 2000 user object and have an Exchange 5.5 mailbox created for the object. When you do this, although the user object is created in Windows 2000 immediately, the mailbox doesn't get created until the next time the ADC runs the CA that deals with the particular location in the Active Directory where the user object is located.

As the CA executes and the Exchange 5.5 mailbox is created, proxy addresses get generated for the new mailbox. To do this, the Proxy Address Generator gets called, and, unfortunately, this component of Exchange 5.5 can only be called using RPCs. In this circumstance, you'll see network activity take place against port 1026.

2.3 Connection Agreements

A CA defines an instance of synchronization between the Exchange 5.5 Directory Service and the Active Directory. Such a CA runs on the ADC and points to both directory services. One end of the CA points to a Windows 2000 Global Catalog server, while the other end points to an Exchange 5.5 Directory Service (with SP3 or SP4) running the LDAP protocol.

Technically you do not need to direct the Windows 2000 end point of CA to a Global Catalog server. You can just direct the end point to a regular Domain Controller. However, since the ADC requires access to information held in the Global Catalog server, merely directing the end point to a Domain Controller is inefficient. When CA end points are directed to a Domain Controller, some search operations are repeated, because the ADC first attempts to locate the information on the Domain Controller but must then expand the search to a Global Catalog server. Such activity takes place whenever the CA is attempting to match or create a new object in the Active Directory. A Global Catalog server must be queried to determine if the object has already been synchronized to another domain The ADC will automatically locate and connect to Global Catalog servers as required, but the repetition of the search operation is inefficient and places unnecessary overhead on the ADC server and the Active Directory itself.

A single CA does not necessarily define the complete synchronization of the two directories, but it is more likely that it defines the synchronization of a small part. In doing so, you'll probably have many CAs that collectively synchronize the whole of your two directories' environments.

A CA, as with most other Windows 2000 objects, is represented in the Active Directory. For example, in my lab environment I have a CA identified as:

```
cn=Ex 5.5 to AD, cn=Active Directory Connections, -
cn=Microsoft Exchange, cn=Services, cn=Configuration, -
cn=compaq, cn=com
```

You can use a tool such as ADSI Edit or the Active Directory Administration Tool (LDP) to locate the CA objects in the Active Directory and view or manipulate them. (Both of these tools are available on the Windows 2000 Support Tools kit on the Windows 2000 CD.)

But, of course, directly editing the attributes in the Active Directory is not the preferred method for configuring CAs. It's best to use the ADC

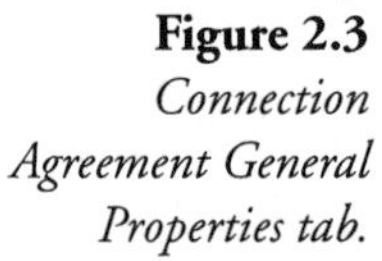

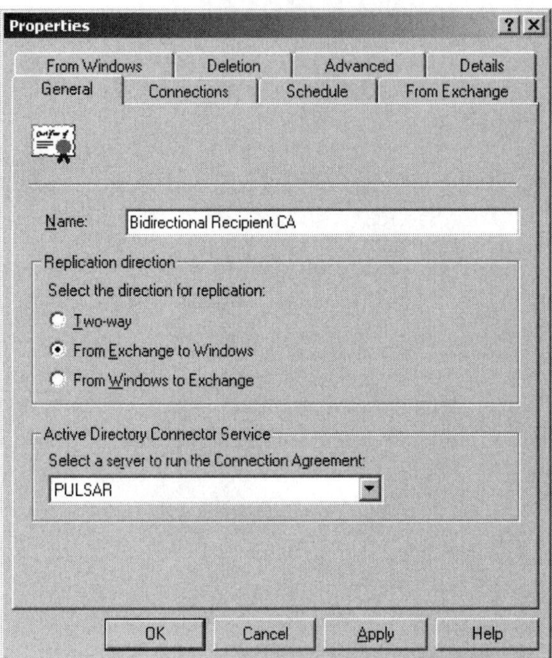

Figure 2.3 *Connection Agreement General Properties tab.*

Administrator snap-in for this purpose. Defining an instance of synchronization involves setting many different characteristics of the CA. These characteristics basically define the names of the servers that will take part in the synchronization, the names of the containers or OUs that represent the source and target of synchronization, a schedule, and authorization.

On the General Properties page, as shown in Figure 2.3, you can define the direction of a CA. CAs may be unidirectional, either From Exchange or From Windows—that is, from the Exchange 5.5 Directory Service or from the Windows 2000 Active Directory.

Alternatively, CAs may be bidirectional or two-way in operation, where you specify information to be exchanged in both directions.

A single ADC server can host one or more CAs. There's no real architectural limit on the number of CAs that an ADC can support, but it's related more to performance than anything else. Popular opinion and sources close to Microsoft suggest that around 70 or 75 CAs is a reasonable upper working limit to have on a single ADC server. Your environment may never even require that many CAs, but it's useful to know just what the limits are. The actual load on an ADC server isn't that great from hosting multiple CAs, but you will begin to see some load should all of the CAs be scheduled to execute at the same time. Similarly, you'll see load at either end of the CA as the LDAP operations execute in the respective directory services.

Homing a CA on a particular ADC server is a relatively easy process. On the General Properties page you can specify which server a particular CA should run on. So, if you find that you've got too many CAs on a particular server, it's easy to change some of them to be homed elsewhere. We'll discuss when it makes sense to have multiple CAs and multiple ADCs later in this chapter.

2.3.1 Using real two-way Connection Agreements

When you configure a CA, you have the option of specifying the direction in which you want it to operate, as described previously. As well as just specifying the direction, you need to specify which subtrees of the directory services you want to participate in the synchronization. Take a look at the settings shown in Figure 2.4 for the two-way CA.

From the screen capture, you can see that any Exchange 5.5 objects that exist in containers called DirSynced Objects, External People, and Recipi-

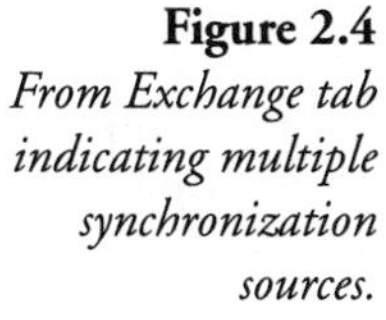

Figure 2.4
From Exchange tab indicating multiple synchronization sources.

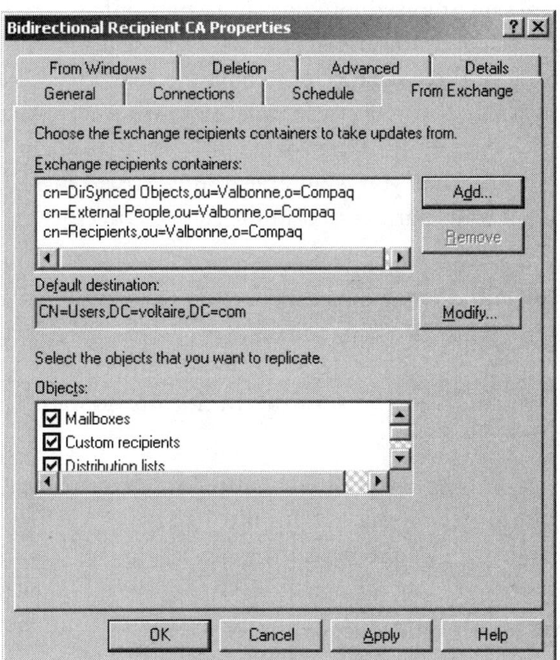

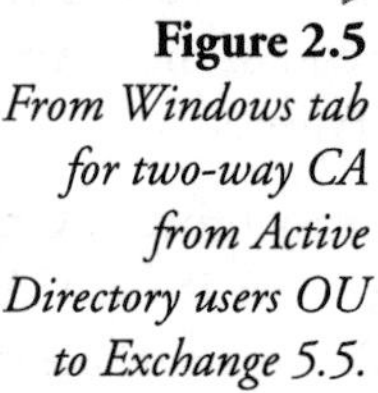

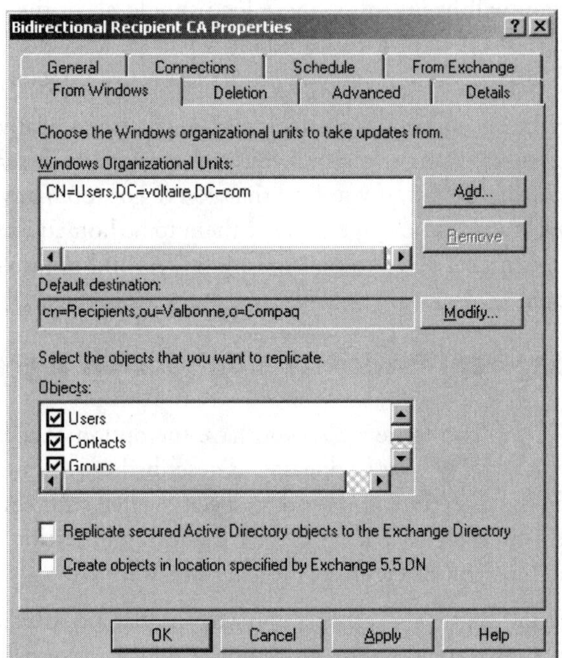

Figure 2.5 *From Windows tab for two-way CA from Active Directory users OU to Exchange 5.5.*

ents are synchronized into one single part of the Active Directory, the Users OU. This is a fine example of a CA, because it shows the many-to-one characteristic of the Exchange 5.5 container to Active Directory OU mapping. If you wanted to reflect the same separation of objects into multiple containers in the Active Directory, similar to that in the Exchange 5.5 Directory Service, then you would need three CAs: One CA to map each source container to its partner OU in the Active Directory.

In this environment, there are settings on the From Windows tab that represents the other direction for the two-way CA. You can see these settings in Figure 2.5, where the CA properties specify that objects created or changed in the Users OU of the Active Directory will have their modifications synchronized back to the Recipients container in the Exchange 5.5 Directory Service.

Now, you need to think about the subtlety associated with this CA configuration. A two-way CA is only a two-way CA if you explicitly map an Exchange 5.5 source container, say it's named FOO, to a target Active Directory OU, say it's named BAR, and you explicitly provide a mapping back from the target OU, BAR, to the source container, FOO.

In this example, the only real two-way part of this CA is between the Exchange 5.5 Recipients container and the Active Directory Users OU. Objects from the Recipients container will get synchronized into the Active Directory, and if you make any changes to the synchronized objects in the Active Directory, possibly using the Active Directory Users and Computers tool, these changes will get synchronized back to the source object, because an explicit synchronization path exists from the Users OU back to the Recipients container.

Unfortunately, the same is not true for the two other Exchange 5.5 containers, Dirsynced Objects and External People. There's no explicit synchronization path back from the Users OU to their respective Exchange 5.5 containers, so any changes that are made to these objects in the Active Directory are not synchronized back to the Exchange 5.5 Directory Service.

Each Exchange 5.5 site requires its own CA to support centralized management of both Exchange 5.5 Directory Service objects and Active Directory objects from the Active Directory Users and Computers snap-in. You need at least one CA per site so that the CA can write changes back to objects in the Exchange 5.5 Directory Service: in Exchange 5.5, objects outside their home site are read-only.

2.3.2 Configuration Connection Agreements

So far when I've described CAs I've really been concerned with the synchronization of recipient container information between the Exchange 5.5 Directory Service and the Active Directory. However, you also need to be familiar with behavior of the Configuration Connection Agreement, or ConfigCA.

As well as synchronizing recipient information, cooperation between Exchange 5.5 and Exchange 2000 servers means that configuration information must be exchanged too. Information from the Exchange 5.5 Directory Service Configuration container is synchronized into the Configuration Naming Context of the Active Directory using a ConfigCA. ConfigCAs are created automatically when an Exchange 5.5 server is upgraded to Exchange 2000 or when an Exchange 2000 server is installed into an Exchange 5.5 site, so there's no manual intervention required to set them up. There's little more that needs to be covered. ConfigCAs should operate with the least amount of intervention, and you should not need to touch their configuration.

2.4 ADC schema modifications

I've already described how installing Exchange 2000 extends the Active Directory schema and the reasons for doing so. The ADC comes with its own complement of schema extensions, but these are actually a subset of the Exchange 2000 schema extensions. The Exchange 2000 schema extensions comprise some 1,000+ modifications to the Active Directory, while the ADC schema extensions only make 188 modifications to the Active Directory.

It's common to find organizations wishing to deploy the ADC early in their migration plans so that the initial flood of network traffic associated with Exchange 5.5 Directory Service to Active Directory synchronization is completed up front. If you intend to use the ADC to provide directory synchronization between Exchange 5.5 Directory Service and the Active Directory for Exchange 2000 servers in the same organization, then you must install the ADC and its extensions first before you attempt to run Exchange 2000 setup with the ForestPrep option.

This may seem counterintuitive given that the ADC extensions are actually a subset of the Exchange 2000 schema extensions. It may seem logical that if you run ForestPrep, all of the schema extensions, including the ADC extensions, will be applied to the Active Directory. While this does indeed seem logical, the problem lies with how ForestPrep executes. As well as simply adding the schema extensions, running ForestPrep and choosing the option to integrate with an existing Exchange 5.5 organization brings up Exchange 5.5 configuration information. To perform this configuration import, ForestPrep uses a ConfigCA. Critically, the need to create the ConfigCA takes place before ForestPrep can install its schema extensions; to create the ConfigCA, some ADC schema extensions must be in place in addition to a server on which to temporarily host the ConfigCA. Hence, the requirement to install the ADC before running ForestPrep.

It is possible to install just the schema extensions when you install the ADC. You can omit the ADC management components and ADC replication engine and install only the extensions using the `SETUP.EXE /SCHEMAONLY` option.

This unfortunate sequencing results in a hefty amount of unnecessary Active Directory replication. Some of the ADC schema extensions include new attribute definitions, which are globally replicated to all Global Catalog servers in the forest in the same way that ForestPrep's schema extensions include such attributes. As with the ForestPrep extensions, adding a new attribute to the global replica set implies that all global attributes must be rereplicated; thus, two waves of replication take place. Perhaps Microsoft may have done better if the ADC contained a complete set of all attributes required by the ADC and Exchange 2000 rather than implementing this subset approach. Doing so would have caused just one wave of replication and a significantly more straightforward model for the average messaging system design to grapple with.

2.5 Determining which directory objects to synchronize

The ADC uses USNs to control synchronization between the Exchange 5.5 Directory Service and the Active Directory in much the same way that Exchange 5.5 uses USNs to control both intrasite and intersite replication. Each CA uses the value of two attributes: `msExchServer1HighestUSN` and `msExchServer2HighestUSN` to control synchronization from the Active Directory to the Exchange 5.5 Directory Service and from the Exchange 5.5 Directory Service to the Active Directory, respectively. I'll describe the use of these attributes in more detail later.

Each CA has its own signature, which is defined during the configuration of the CA. As the ADC synchronizes Active Directory objects into the Exchange 5.5 Directory Service, it stamps the CA signature into the `Replication-Signature` attribute on the newly created Exchange 5.5 Directory Service object. Additionally, as objects are written to the Exchange 5.5 Directory Service, the `Object-Version` attribute of the Exchange 5.5 object is modified. This attribute is set to 1 if the object is being newly created or incremented by one if a modification is being applied to it. The value of the `Object-Version` attribute is then written into the `Replicated-Object-Version`. Therefore, if the ADC has just modified an object in the Exchange 5.5 Directory Service, the value of both the `Object-Version` and the `Replicated-Object-Version` attributes will be identical.

Let's look at the synchronization from the Exchange 5.5 Directory Service to the Active Directory. When a CA is activated, it obtains the value of the `msExchServer2HighestUSN` associated with that CA. The `msExchServer2HighestUSN` will have been set during the last synchronization cycle to the value of the highest USN that was encountered on an object in the source Exchange 5.5 Directory Service. If this is the first time that the CA has been activated, then the value of `msExchServer2HighestUSN` will be set to 0. The ADC then searches the Exchange 5.5 Directory Service for all objects that have a `USN-Changed` attribute with a value higher than the current value of `msExch-Server2HighestUSN`. Thus, all objects that have changed since the last synchronization cycle are selected for synchronization. When the objects have been synchronized, the highest `USN-Changed` value encountered will be written to the `msExchServer2HighestUSN` attribute and this will define the high watermark for the next synchronization cycle.

Another check is performed in addition to simply looking for any changed objects. The CA excludes any changed objects that have a `Repli-cation-Signature` attribute value identical to the signature of the CA. This prevents the ADC from unnecessarily resynchronizing back to the Active Directory any objects that it synchronized in the first place. However, using this filter alone would ignore any objects that had been legitimately changed in the Exchange 5.5 Directory Service and that should be synchronized back to the Active Directory across a two-way CA. Therefore, the object is only excluded if the `Replication-Signature` matches the CA's signature and the value of the `Object-Version` attribute is not greater than the value of the `Replicated-Object-Version` attribute.

The same process takes place in the opposite direction from the Active Directory to the Exchange 5.5 Directory Service, since Active Directory objects use USN values to perform intrasite and intersite Active Directory replication. It is slightly more complicated in this instance, because the Active Directory uses attribute-based replication rather than object-based replication. Therefore, in addition to using the USN values on the object, the sum of the attribute versions of each Active Directory object is used. However, from Active Directory to Exchange 5.5 Directory Service synchronization the `msExchServer1HighestUSN` attribute is used to store the highest USN of the object synchronized.

2.6 ADC block searching

During an initial synchronization between directory services, it is possible that the ADC may select many thousands of objects to be synchronized. This, of course, depends on the number of objects defined in the directory services.

Take, for example, a large Active Directory instance that has some 100,000 objects defined. If this is the first time that synchronization is to take place, or a complete resynchronization is to take place, all of the 100,000 objects will have to be synchronized. While the synchronization process is under way, it is possible that some external factor, such as a network link failure or a power failure on the remote system, may occur. When the synchronization process restarts, it must perform the synchronization from the beginning again. While this is tolerable if the failure occurred during the early part of the synchronization process, it is less acceptable if the failure occurs toward the end.

To avoid the unnecessary resynchronization of data, the ADC only processes objects in bands of 10,000. A search is performed against the Exchange 5.5 Directory Service and the value of the highest `USN-Changed` is determined. The first synchronization attempt only processes objects whose `USN-Changed` attribute has the value between the current value of `msExchServer1HighestUSN` and `msExchServer1HighestUSN` +10,000 (or the highest `USN-Changed` value determined if this is less than `msExchServer1HighestUSN` +10,000). Once the changed objects in this range have been processed and committed to the Exchange 5.5 Directory Service, the `msExchServer1HighestUSN` is incremented by 10,000. If the new value of `msExchServer1HighestUSN` is less than the highest `USN-Changed` value determined, processing of the next batch of Active Directory objects is performed. This process continues until all eligible objects have been processed, and subsequently the highest `USN-Changed` value is written to the `msExchServer1HighestUSN` attribute. The same process takes place in the reverse direction using the `msExchServer2HighestUSN` attribute.

2.7 How the ADC uses the Active Directory

The ADC caches significant amounts of information to improve performance. Specifically, the `msExchServer1HighestUSN` and `msExchServer2HighestUSN` is cached in memory and only written directly to the Active Directory occasionally. When I described previously the updates that were applied to these attributes after a synchronization cycle or a search block, you should know that the updates are applied only to the memory resident versions.

In general, the `msExchServer1HighestUSN` and `msExchServer2HighestUSN` values are written to the Active Directory every 24 hours; but for new CAs, updates to these attributes are committed to the Active Directory every 30 minutes. A new CA is a CA that is executing its first synchronization cycle. Typically this can take an extended period of time and is influenced by factors such as network bandwidth and the performance of the Exchange 5.5 Directory Service and Active Directory systems. New CAs have these attributes committed with a higher frequency because of the typically large amounts of data that are synchronized shortly after a CA is configured. Should a system failure occur on the ADC server, the maximum of resynchronization that will take place will be limited to 30 minutes.

Immediate updates to Active Directory are also performed under three other circumstances, as follows:

1. When the ADC service is stopped
2. At the end of the first synchronization cycle of a new CA
3. When a CA is moved from one ADC server to another

Some other attributes of a CA are of interest. The `msExchServer2HighestUSNVector` attribute is not used, but the `msExchServer1HighestUSNVector` is populated. The vector attribute is multivalued and is only relevant to Windows 2000 servers. This attribute holds the highest committed USN for any Domain Controllers that have been contacted during a CA's lifetime. For example, if you had previously configured a CA to synchronize from a Domain Controller named GEORGE and then modified the configuration so that synchronization occurred now from a Domain Controller named JERRY, you would see two values set for this attribute: one relating to the highest USN committed on GEORGE and the other for the highest USN committed on JERRY. The ADC stores this information so that no objects are missed when a CA is rehomed to another ADC.

2.8 Mailbox-enabled and mail-enabled objects

It's important to understand the difference between mail-enabled and mailbox-enabled objects. Mail-enabled objects are those users that have the mail-recipient auxiliary class associated with them. This means that such objects are capable of having e-mail directed to them, because they have an Exchange-style e-mail address. Mailbox-enabled objects are a special case of mail-enabled objects, because they not only have the mail-recipient class, but they also have the mail-storage class associated with them. Mailbox-enabled objects always have an Exchange mailbox associated with their account.

2.9 Object class mapping from Exchange 5.5 to Active Directory

Exchange 5.5 objects get replicated to the Active Directory and are represented as object types that depend on which object type they are in the

Exchange 5.5 Directory Service. In all cases of replication, attributes associated with the source object are replicated to the destination object.

2.9.1 Mailbox replication

An Exchange 5.5 mailbox that's associated with a Windows NT4 account can be mapped to a mail-enabled contact, a mailbox-enabled user, or a disabled mailbox-enabled user. You decide whether objects should be mapped to contacts or user objects, but typically the overall migration process is much simpler if mappings are made to either live or disabled users. However, if you've already migrated the Windows NT4 account over to Windows 2000 and the Exchange 5.5 mailbox is associated with this user account, then the mapping behavior is different. A Windows 2000 account already associated with an Exchange 5.5 mailbox always gets mapped across to a mailbox-enabled user in the Active Directory. When a user object already exists in the Active Directory and the ADC matches with it, attribute information from the source object is merged into the existing Active Directory user object.

When the ADC has matched an Exchange 5.5 mailbox object with an Active Directory user object or has created a new Active Directory user object, the user object has a number of specific attributes set that correspond to characteristics of the Exchange 5.5 mailbox. Specifically, they are as follows:

- The `legacyExchangeDN` attribute is set to correspond to the Distingushed Name (DN) of the Exchange 5.5 mailbox. This should be something in the form of `/o=Org/ou=Site/cn=Recipients/cn=RDN`.
- The `msExchHomeServerName` attribute is set to correspond to the Exchange 5.5 server `/o=Org/ou=Site/cn=Configuration/cn=Servers/cn=Server-Name`.
- The `replicationSignature` attribute is set to correspond to the unique signature on the CA that replicates this object.

2.9.2 Custom recipients and mailbox agents

Exchange 5.5 objects such as custom recipients and mailbox agents (e.g., the Schedule+ Free/Busy Connector) are represented by objects of the same class in the Active Directory target container. A custom recipient is created in the Active Directory as a mail-enabled contact object, and the E-Mail address field of the contact is set to the SMTP proxy address of the source object, even if it is a non-SMTP custom recipient. (The SMTP proxy address will always get created based on the site addressing properties.)

2.9.3 Distribution lists

Mapping Exchange 5.5 distribution lists across to corresponding primitive objects in Active Directory—namely distribution groups—is more complicated than it might seem. By default, the ADC will always map an Exchange 5.5 distribution list across to a Universal Distribution Group in the Active Directory. Let's take a moment to refresh our memories on the different types of group scope that you might encounter. They include the following:

- Domain Local Groups can have membership from anywhere in the forest, but the group only has local domain scope.
- Domain Global Groups can only have membership drawn from the local domain, but the group has global scope.
- Universal Groups can have membership drawn from anywhere in the forest, and the group has global use.

Universal Distribution Groups have the membership and scope that Exchange 2000 requires and they can exist in mixed-mode domains, so, for the purposes of mail distribution, such groups work very well.

However, many Exchange 5.5 installations use distribution lists for more than just mail expansion. Specifically, where Public Folders are used, it's not uncommon to find users bundled into distribution lists and have Public Folder Access Control Lists (ACLs) put in place using distribution lists. In the Active Directory, ACLs cannot be used with any form of distribution group.

While Universal Distribution Groups can't be used to enforce access controls in the Active Directory, Universal Security Groups can be, and, in fact, must be used if you wish to use a group of any kind to set ACLs on an Exchange 2000 Public Folder hierarchy. There are some characteristics of Universal Security Groups that are of concern to you with respect to Exchange 5.5 interoperability. Universal Security Groups can only exist in native-mode Windows 2000 domains, but they can contain members that exist in mixed-mode domains. This gives rise to the use of Token Augmentation, which was described earlier.

Although the ADC will never create Universal Security Groups directly, it will always create Universal Distribution Groups, which, if they are homed in a native mode domain, may get converted to Universal Security Groups at a later stage by one of several methods, which will be discussed in Chapter 5. For this reason alone, you can see the importance of getting Windows 2000 native mode domains in place as soon as possible.

2.9.4 Distribution lists and synchronization latency

Under certain circumstances, you may find that Exchange 5.5 distribution list objects can get synchronized before the discrete objects that make up their membership are synchronized to the Active Directory. For example, you may find that you are using one CA to synchronize a distribution list that's newly created, and the schedule for this has its synchronization running before another CA that synchronizes mailbox object membership. If the distribution list has membership objects that reference user objects that are not yet created in the Active Directory, then the Universal Distribution Group could not populate its membership for those phantom objects. This is a referential integrity feature of the Active Directory.

In this case, and if no other precautions were in place, when the Connection Agreement that controls synchronization in the reverse direction would run later, there is a risk that this partial Active Directory Universal Distribution Group would force the original Exchange 5.5 distribution list to have its membership altered, thus removing perfectly good membership information.

However, the ADC and the Active Directory avoid this problem by using a special Active Directory attribute called `unmergedAtts`. During the first synchronization run, if objects can't be added to the `member` attribute of the Active Directory Universal Distribution Group because those membership objects don't yet exist, they're added to the multivalued `unmergedAtts` attribute of the Universal Distribution Group. This attribute is used on the subsequent back synchronization to ensure that no membership information is lost.

This is not a problem in the reverse direction. There is no restriction on the membership of an Exchange 5.5 distribution list that enforces the existence of a particular Exchange 5.5 Directory Service object before the DN for that object is added to the `Members` attribute of an Exchange 5.5 distribution list. Therefore, there is no need to use an `unmergedAtts` attribute with Exchange 5.5 distribution lists.

2.10 Object class mapping from Active Directory to Exchange 5.5

In the same way that the ADC replicates objects from the Exchange 5.5 Directory Service to the Active Directory, a similar process takes place in the opposite direction, although it is more straightforward.

Mailbox-enabled user objects in the Active Directory are replicated as mailboxes in the Exchange 5.5 Directory Service, while mail-enabled user objects get replicated as custom recipients. Mail-enabled contacts from the Active Directory get replicated to the Exchange 5.5 Directory Service as custom recipients. Similarly, mail-enabled groups (both distribution and security) get replicated as distribution lists.

If you look carefully at Figure 2.5, you'll see a checkbox at the bottom of the dialog box that says: Create objects in location specified by Exchange 5.5 DN. In general, the ADC will create replicated Exchange 5.5 Directory Service objects in the location specified by the Exchange 5.5 container in the CA; however, this can be overridden by the value of the `legacyExchangeDN` attribute.

When an Active Directory object is mail-enabled (by right-clicking the object from within the Active Directory Users and Computers tool and selecting Exchange Tasks, Establish Exchange Mail Addresses), you can associate an Exchange 5.5 site or Exchange 2000 Administrative Group with that object. Similarly, when you mailbox enable a Windows 2000 user object, you implicitly associate it with an Exchange 2000 Administrative

Table 2.1 *Object Mapping from Exchange 5.5 Directory Service to Active Directory*

Exchange 5.5 Object Type	Active Directory Object Type
Mailbox and Windows NT4 Account	Mail-enabled, User Object
	Mail-enabled, disabled User Object
	Mail-enabled, Contact
Mailbox and Windows 2000 Account	Mailbox-enabled, User Object
Custom Recipient	Mail-enabled Contact
Distribution List	Universal Distribution Group
Distribution List (used for Access Control)	Universal Distribution Group initially, but converted later to Universal Security Group

Group. This sets the legacyExchangeDN attribute. With the Create objects in location specified by Exchange 5.5 DN checkbox checked, the ADC will create the replicated object in an Exchange 5.5 Directory Service container as specified by this attribute.

Exchange 5.5 objects affected by the ADC will also contain some new or changed attributes, including the following:

- The ADC-Global-Names attribute, which is blank by default for replicated objects in the Exchange 5.5 Directory Service and gets populated only when an Exchange 5.5 object is being replicated to the Active Directory. (This is a new attribute.)
- The DSA-Signature attribute, which is set to the Invocation-ID of the Exchange 5.5 bridgehead server specified in the CA. (This is a modified attribute.)
- The Object-GUID attribute, which is set to the value of the object-GUID attribute present on the source object in the Active Directory. (This is a new attribute.)
- The Object-Version attribute, which gets incremented by one after the initial replication. (This is a modified attribute.)
- The Replication-Signature attribute, which is set to the unique signature of the CA that made the last modification to the replicated object. (This is a new attribute.)
- The Replicated-Object-Version attribute, which matches the Object-Version attribute since the ADC made the last change to the replicated object. (This is a new attribute.)

Table 2.1 defines how the ADC maps objects from the Exchange 5.5 Directory Service and the Active Directory, while Table 2.2 defines the mappings from the Active Directory to the Exchange 5.5 Directory Service.

Table 2.2 *Object Mapping from Active Directory to Exchange 5.5 DS*

Active Directory Object Type	Exchange 5.5 Object Type
Mailbox-enabled User Object	Mailbox
Mail-enabled User Object	Custom Recipient
Mail-enabled Contact	Custom Recipient
Mail-enabled Group (any scope, either distribution or security)	Distribution List

2.11 Synchronizing hidden objects

Objects in the Exchange 5.5 Directory Service that are hidden from the Address Book have their `Hide-From-Address-Book` attribute set to 1. You control whether an object is displayed in the Exchange 5.5 GAL by checking the Hide from Address book box on the Advanced tab of the mailbox properties when using the Exchange 5.5 Administrator program. By default the hidden objects are not displayed in recipient containers within the Administrator program unless you choose the Hidden Objects option from the View menu.

The ADC will synchronize hidden objects into the Active Directory, but unlike the behavior in Exchange 5.5, they are visible by default from Active Directory Users and Computers when browsing through an OU. However, a careful look at the Hide from Exchange address book on the Exchange Advanced tab will indicate that the object is indeed hidden. (Make sure that you've selected Advanced Features from the View drop-down menu from the snap-in in order to see the Exchange Advanced tab.) Exchange 2000 users will not see Active Directory objects (users, contacts, or groups) that have this box checked displayed in the GAL.

The Hide from Exchange address book checkbox on Active Directory objects implies that the `msExchHideFromAddressLists` attribute is set to TRUE. Similarly, when synchronizing a hidden object from the Active Directory to the Exchange 5.5 Directory Service, the object is hidden in the Exchange 5.5 GAL.

2.12 Dealing with hidden distribution list membership

In Exchange 5.5 you can control whether or not membership information of a particular distribution list is displayed to a client by checking the Hide membership from address book checkbox on the Advanced tab of the distribution list properties when using the Exchange 5.5 Administrator program.

When the ADC synchronizes a DL from the Exchange 5.5 DS, it reads the `Hide-DL-Membership` attribute and accordingly sets the `hideDLMembership` attribute on the synchronized object in the Active Directory. This effectively applies a set of Access Control Entities (ACE) on the group in the Active Directory to deny access. Although the ACE prevents Exchange 2000 users from enumerating the group membership, some security principals do need to have access to the membership list: Exchange 2000 itself, for example, needs to enumerate the membership in order to send mail to the group's members. The ADC reads the `msExchServerGlobalGroups` attribute from the Organization container entry in the Active Directory. This attribute contains the list of Exchange 2000 servers in the organization that must have access to the membership. Actually, it is the Exchange Enterprise Servers and Exchange Domain Servers groups, created when a CA is configured, that are granted access to membership of the group. But by default, Exchange 2000 servers are members of these groups.

In Exchange 2000, if you subsequently add a new Windows 2000 domain that includes Exchange 2000 servers, the Recipient Update Service will detect this and it will update all groups with `hideDLMembership` set to `TRUE` with the security principals of the new Exchange Domain Servers group.

Synchronizing in the reverse direction, from the Active Directory to the Exchange 5.5 Directory Service, the ADC checks the value of the `hideDLMembership` attribute and sets the `Hide-DL-Membership` attribute on the Exchange 5.5 distribution list. You can use the Active Directory Users and Computers tool to control whether membership of an Active Directory group is displayed or not by right-clicking on the group and selecting Exchange Tasks and Hide Membership.

2.13 Object deletion

When you create a CA, you can define the behavior of the ADC with respect to deleting objects from both the Exchange 5.5 Directory Service and the Active Directory. The settings on the Deletion tab apply to both directions. Setting the CA to delete objects implies that when an object is deleted in the Exchange 5.5 Directory Service (perhaps using the Exchange 5.5 Administrator program), it is automatically deleted in the Active Directory. The same behavior is true in the reverse direction.

If you elect not to perform directory deletions immediately, the ADC writes non-replicated deletions to a temporary file located on the ADC server. Deletions that occurred in the Exchange 5.5 Directory Service are staged to a file named `WIN2000.LDF`, while deletions that occurred in the Active Directory are staged to a file named `EX55.CSV`. By default, these files are located in the following location: `<ADC Path>\MSADC\<CA Name>\`

If you wish, you can override this default location by setting the following registry key:

```
HKEY_LOCAL_MACHINE\System\CurrentControlSet\Services\
     MSADC\Parameters
Value name: Transaction Directory
Value type: STRING
Value data: <Full Directory Path, e.g., C:\ADCLogs>
```

Setting this registry key creates a parent directory for the deletion logs. Each CA will create its own subdirectory under this parent directory and will write a file named `MSADC.INF` to the directory, which contains the name and GUID of the CA that is associated with the directory.

You can apply these LDF files to the Active Directory and CSV files to the Exchange 5.5 Directory Service using the LDIFDE and ADMIN /I tools, respectively.

2.14 Connection Agreements and authentication

For a CA to read or write object information from either the Exchange 5.5 Directory Service or the Active Directory, it must make an authenticated connection to both directory services over LDAP. You can specify the credentials you will use for the connection on the Connection Properties tab, as shown in Figure 2.6.

You should think carefully about the accounts that you use to access the directory services. The accounts specified must have the appropriate read and/or write access to the respective directory containers or OUs that you specify. It is inadvisable to use an Administrator account. It suffers from the same restrictions that you would come across if you tried to use the Administrator account as the Site Services Account in the Exchange 5.5 world, such as changing the Administrator password and then slowly finding out later that services fail to start after the next reboot. In the same way, you'd expect to see ADC synchronization fail to operate and the cause may not be immediately obvious. So for this reason alone, it makes better sense to separate authentication functionality and use a dedicated account—perhaps the Exchange Site Services Account when connecting to the Exchange 5.5 Directory Service, and, since there's no Site Services Account used in the Exchange 2000 world, a dedicated account, which in the example shown in Figure 2.6, is the ADCService account.

The ADC stores the credentials for the accounts used to access the Active Directory and the Exchange 5.5 Directory Service in the Local Secu-

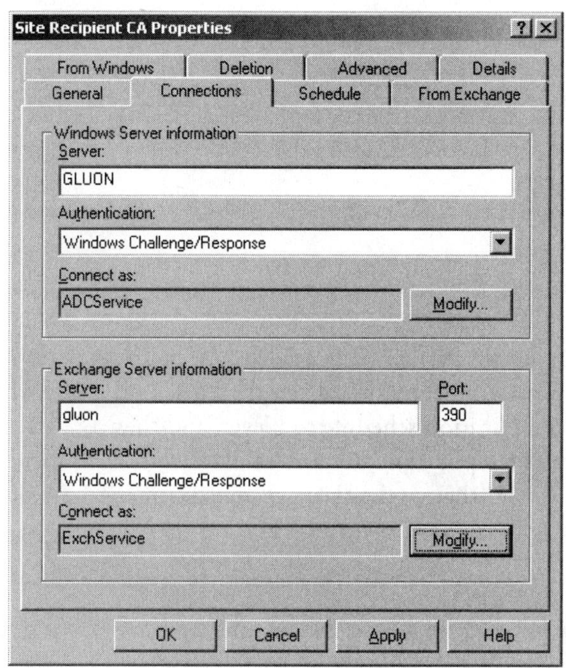

Figure 2.6 *Connection agreement connections and authentications.*

rity Authority (LSA). (You find more information about the LSA in the book *Mission-Critical Active Directory* by Jan de Clercq and Micky Balladelli.) When you create a new CA, the ADC Manager snap-in performs an RPC call to the ADC service and requests storage for the credentials on the local ADC server. The password associated with the credentials stored in the LSA can only be read by the ADC service, not by the MMC interface. Therefore, when you modify a CA, changing either source or target containers or rehoming the CA, you must reenter the password. If you use the same set of credentials for multiple CAs, only one set of credentials is stored in the LSA to conserve space. This also saves time should you need to change the password associated with an account being used for the CA. Changing the password on one CA changes it for all other CAs that use the same credentials.

Whenever you modify the credentials using the ADC Manager snap-in a timestamp for that entry in the LSA is updated with the current time. Similarly, when the ADC reads the password during a synchronization operation and the timestamp is older than seven days, it is updated again with the current time. The LSA has limited space and the ADC service is allocated only 64 KB on a given ADC server. When space begins to run out, the oldest nonused credentials are removed.

Table 2.3 *Expiration Limits Associated with ADC Credentials Stored in the LSA*

Total Credentials Stored	Expiry Limit (Days)
1 to 15	180
16 to 31	120
32 to 127	90
More than 128	60

As shown in Table 2.3, credentials that haven't been used within the last 180 days will be removed from the LSA. In the case where you create a CA, set its replication schedule to Never, and then 181 days later force it to replicate, the replication attempt will fail. You can control the minimum number of days that credentials can remain in the LSA by using the following registry key:

```
HKEY_LOCAL_MACHINE\System\CurrentControlSet\Services\
      MSADC\Parameters
Value name: Password Expiration
Value type: DWORD
Value data: <Minimum No. of Days to remain in LSA>
```

Connection agreements that have replication schedules set to Selected times or Always will never expire.

It's also important to note that you can specify the port number for the connection to the Exchange 5.5 Directory Service. Connections to the Active Directory always take place against a Global Catalog server on port 3268, but on both a Global Catalog server and a Windows 2000 Domain Controller, port 389 is also used for general domain scope LDAP queries. If you're running Exchange 5.5 on a Windows 2000 Domain Controller and you have enabled the LDAP protocol from within the Exchange 5.5 Directory Service, then it can't use port 389 because it has already been allocated to Windows 2000. In this case, you need to modify the port. It's common to change the port number to 390, since this is not used by any other applications, but remember to then modify the port to connect on in the Connections tab.

2.15 Controlling the synchronization schedule

The ADC uses a polling-based mechanism to request changes from the Exchange 5.5 Directory Service and the Active Directory. Each request for

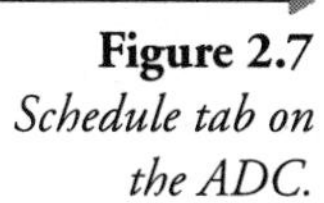

Figure 2.7 *Schedule tab on the ADC.*

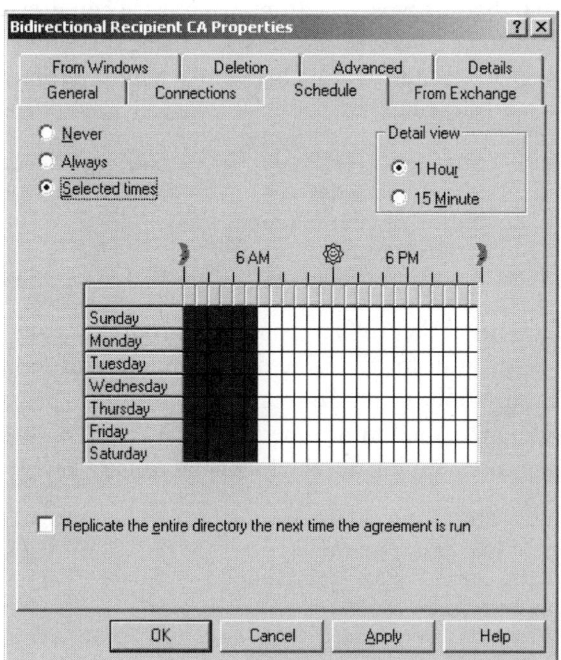

changes and any subsequent replication activity represents a synchronization cycle. With a two-way CA the first stage in the cycle checks for changes in the Exchange 5.5 Directory Service and then in the Active Directory. On the Schedule tab you can elect to have replication take place at Always, Selected Times, or Never (see Figure 2.7). This schedule tab looks almost identical to the Schedule tab associated with the Exchange 5.5 Directory Replication Connector. On an Exchange 5.5 Directory Replication Connector, when you set the schedule to Always, that actually translates as: Try to do some replication every 15 minutes. However, on the ADC, setting the schedule to Always means: Try to do some synchronization every 5 minutes.

If you select Selected Times, you can specify times with either a 15-minute or one-hour granularity. For each box on the schedule grid that you check, this instructs the ADC to start polling at that moment, but it does not necessarily imply that the cycle will last for exactly 15 minutes or one hour. When the cycle commences at the indicated time, it will continue to run until it is finished. If this is less than 15 minutes or one hour, the ADC will not attempt to start another synchronization cycle until the next indicated start time on the schedule.

You can fine-tune the synchronization behavior. For example, if the ADC is processing a very large number of modifications for objects, it is possible that a single synchronization cycle could extend for many hours. You can force interruptions to such a single cycle by selecting the default number of seconds to wait between synchronization cycles by setting the following registry key:

```
HKEY_LOCAL_MACHINE\System\CurrentControlSet\Services
     \MSADC\Parameters
Value name: Synch Sleep Delay
Value type: DWORD
Value data: <number of seconds to wait between cycles>
```

This causes the ADC to pause synchronization after the defined number of seconds, wait for the same defined number of seconds, and then restart synchronization again. You can customize this behavior even further by extending the amount of time for which the ADC will synchronize objects without interruption. Set the following registry key:

```
HKEY_LOCAL_MACHINE\System\CurrentControlSet\Services
     \MSADC\Parameters
Value name: Max Continuous Sync
Value type: DWORD
Value data: <number of seconds that sync takes place
without interruption >
```

The ADC uses LDAP to get access to both the Exchange 5.5 Directory Service and the Active Directory, and, as it checks to see if objects are to be synchronized, it executes an LDAP search based on the container and OU information that you've specified elsewhere on the CA. LDAP operations are pretty costly in terms of system resources, and they impose a significant amount of load on the CPU of the systems on which the searches are being executed. Executing these LDAP searches very frequently will affect the performance of the Exchange 5.5 servers and Active Directory servers that are hosting the ends of the CA.

If you really want synchronization to occur very frequently, then you should consider having dedicated systems to host the ends of the CA. In the case of a dedicated Exchange 5.5 server in every site where CAs get terminated, hosting no mailboxes would be a good idea. You could use existing servers: maybe your current site bridgeheads or connector servers? Similarly, you should apply the same logic to the Active Directory servers, but you only need one such dedicated server here, since Active Directory information is read-writeable anywhere in the forest, unlike Exchange 5.5 where Directory Service containers are read-only outside their home site. Of course, the topology and complexity of your environment will ultimately define how many servers you will need.

Getting the scheduling of your CAs right is pretty important. You should arrange to have CA synchronization take place after you perform any moves or updates to objects in either directory. So if you intend to migrate users from Exchange 5.5 servers to Exchange 2000 servers overnight, you should be sure to run the CA immediately after those moves have taken place; you can use the Selected Times option for this. If you are moving user accounts generally at any time, then you'll probably want to set the schedule to Always.

You'll notice another box on the Properties tab in Figure 2.7: Replicate the entire directory the next time the agreement is run. Ordinarily, a full replication only takes place the first time that the CA is executed. Checking this box forces all directory objects to be checked for consistency, and if there are any discrepancies between the directories, objects will be replaced. If objects are found to be consistent, they will not be replicated.

You can force a full replication from Exchange 5.5 to Active Directory by setting the `msExchServer2HighestUSN` to 0 and a full replication from Active Directory to Exchange 5.5 by setting the `msExchServer1HighestUSN` to 0.

Setting `msExchDoFullReplication` to `TRUE` forces a full replication in both directions.

2.16 Connection Agreement advanced parameters

There are a number of specific settings you can define on a CA that will result in either improved performance during synchronization or significant modifications to behavior. Advanced settings are shown in Figure 2.8.

2.16.1 Paged results

You can specify the size of a page that the ADC expects to receive as the result of an LDAP search. Set the values for the Windows Server entries per page and Exchange Server entries per page to reflect the page size for the Active Directory and the Exchange 5.5 Directory Service, respectively. Both of these settings are available on a two-way CA, but for one-way CAs only the appropriate setting can be set.

Paging offers an improvement to performance by grouping together objects that are being synchronized. Larger page sizes have more entries in the page and, accordingly, result in fewer requests to the directory service. However, large pages require more memory during processing.

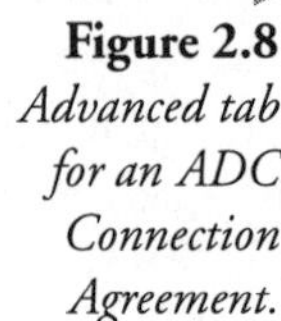

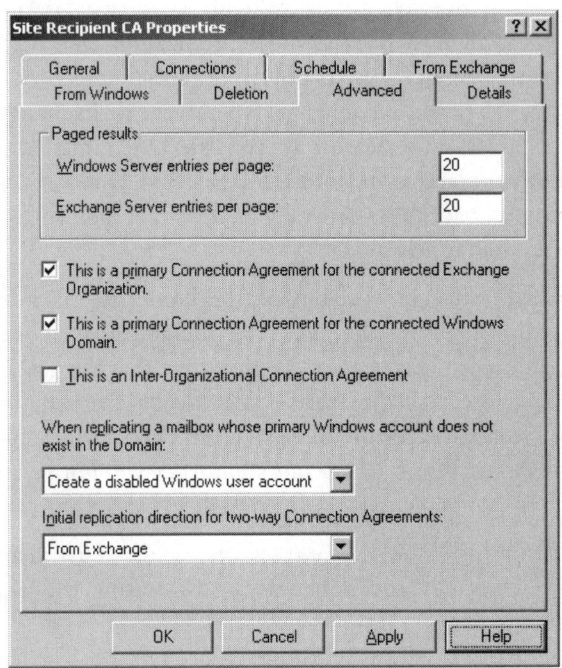

Figure 2.8 *Advanced tab for an ADC Connection Agreement.*

The default page size settings for the ADC are set to 20 entries per page. The corresponding directory service must be configured to return pages in line with these settings. In the default case, while the directory service can return pages with more than 20 entries per page, it should not be configured to return pages with fewer than 20 entries per page if the ADC still expects 20. Such a setting will result in synchronization errors.

By default the Exchange 5.5 LDAP service returns 100 entries per page, although you can modify this by setting the appropriate value on the Search tab of the LDAP Protocol properties on either the Exchange 5.5 Site defaults on or a specific server, as shown in Figure 2.9.

By default, Active Directory servers return 1,000 entries in an LDAP page. Modifying the LDAP page size on the Active Directory can be done using the NTDSUTIL utility and the following sequence of commands from a Windows 2000 command window:

```
ntdsutil.exe
ntdsutil: ldap policies
ldap policy: connections
server connections: connect to domain <domain name>
server connections: quit
ldap policy: show values
```

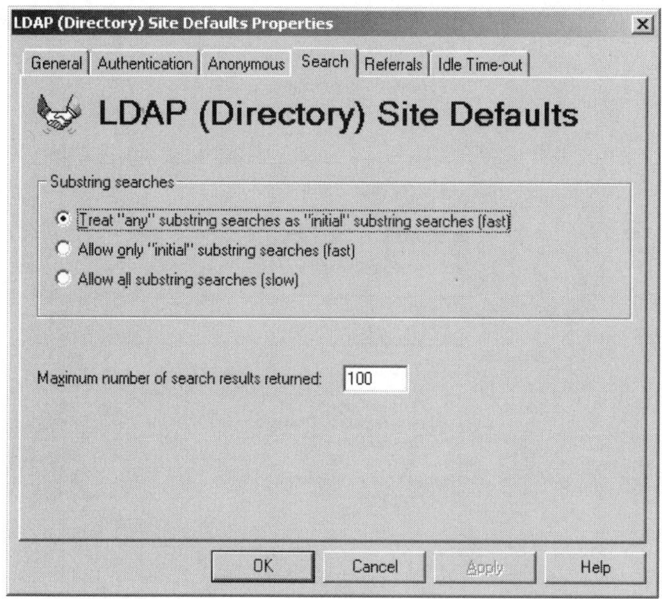

Figure 2.9 *Exchange 5.5 LDAP protocol search settings.*

```
ldap policy: set maxpagesize to <value>
ldap policy: commit changes
ldap policy: quit
ntdsutil: quit>
```

This updates the `LDAPAdminLimits` attribute on the Default Query Policy of the Active Directory. You can see the attribute value using ADSI Edit (shown in Figure 2.10) below the Configuration Naming Context/Services/Windows NT/Directory Service/Query-Policies.

Under normal circumstances you shouldn't need to make any modifications to LDAP page settings: The default settings should be sufficient. However, as you can see, without making any modifications to the source directory systems you could change the ADC settings to process 100 entries from the Exchange 5.5 LDAP service and 1,000 entries from the Active Directory to glean a small performance improvement.

2.16.2 Primary and nonprimary Connection Agreements

CAs may be either primary or nonprimary. Primary CAs can create objects in the target container or OU, while nonprimary CAs can only modify an existing object in the target container or OU. You should have only one primary CA for any given group of recipients, although you may have nonpri-

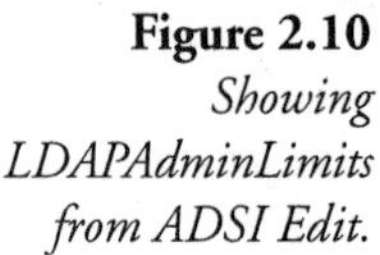

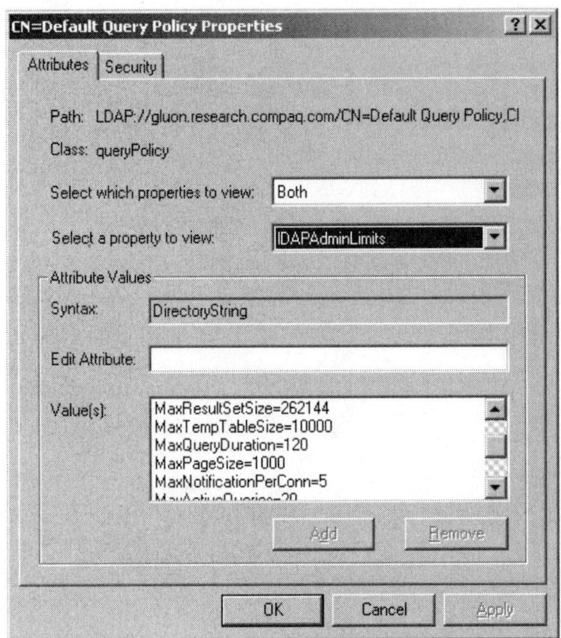

Figure 2.10 *Showing LDAPAdminLimits from ADSI Edit.*

mary CAs for those same recipients and target containers, especially if you have a large environment and you want to put overlapping CAs in place. Overlapping CAs should be avoided if at all possible, but they can be useful for those environments where an object may be moved from one location in the source directory to another and you want to retain the ability to synchronize it irrespective of its location.

Setting the Primary Connection Agreement flag on more than one CA having the same source and target should really only be done if different object classes are synchronized by each CA. Incorrectly using this setting will result in duplicate objects in the target directory. Those primary or nonprimary CAs can be either in the direction of Exchange 5.5, the Active Directory, or both. You can see the settings in Figure 2.8.

As a matter of best practice, it's much better to have a single point of synchronization and have your Exchange 5.5 Directory Service and Active Directory replication schedules set to minimize latency.

2.16.3 Interorganizational Connection Agreements

You'll notice a checkbox in Figure 2.9 that reads: This is an Interorganizational Connection Agreement. Setting this option essentially turns the CA into a general-purpose synchronization tool between two different

Exchange 5.5 and Exchange 2000 organizations. That is, the organization names for Exchange environments are different.

When you check this box, the CA is prevented from creating mailbox-enabled users in the Active Directory; Exchange 5.5 mailboxes get represented as mail-enabled contacts in the Active Directory and, similarly, in the Exchange 5.5 Directory Service custom recipients are always created for Exchange 2000 mailbox-enabled users. Custom recipients, contacts, distribution lists, and distribution and security groups are also supported over an interorganizational CA.

Exchange 2000 Service Pack 1 provides some additional functionality in this area. As well as allowing Exchange 5.5 mailboxes from one organization to be represented as mail-enabled contacts in the Active Directory of another Exchange 2000 organization, the SP1 ADC will allow mail-enabled user objects to be created. This functionality is designed to work hand-in-hand with the SP1 Exchange Migration wizard, which allows mailboxes from one Exchange 5.5 organization to be moved to a different Exchange 2000 organization. Rather than only allow the creation of mail-enabled contacts, which the Exchange Migration wizard would have to transform into a user object, the SP1 ADC allows user objects to be created initially and subsequently matched with the wizard.

2.17 Exchange 5.5 mailboxes and multiple Windows NT accounts

In Exchange 5.5 it is possible to associate multiple mailboxes with a single Windows NT4 account. However, with Exchange 2000, a mailbox is a property of an Active Directory user object, and subsequently there is a one-to-one relationship between Exchange 2000 mailboxes and Active Directory user accounts.

Let's assume that we have an Exchange 5.5 resource mailbox with an alias name of CONFROOM. This CONFROOM mailbox is associated with the Windows NT account BARRYF. However, this is not the primary mailbox associated with the BARRYF account: The primary mailbox for this account actually has an Exchange alias of BARRYF. As the ADC processes mailboxes for the first time, it attempts to match against an Active Directory user account or create a new Active Directory object if no match can be found. If the ADC processes the CONFROOM mailbox before it processes the BARRYF mailbox, it will either match with an existing object (based on SID or SID history) or create a new object in the Active Directory for the CONFROOM mailbox and associate it with the BARRYF

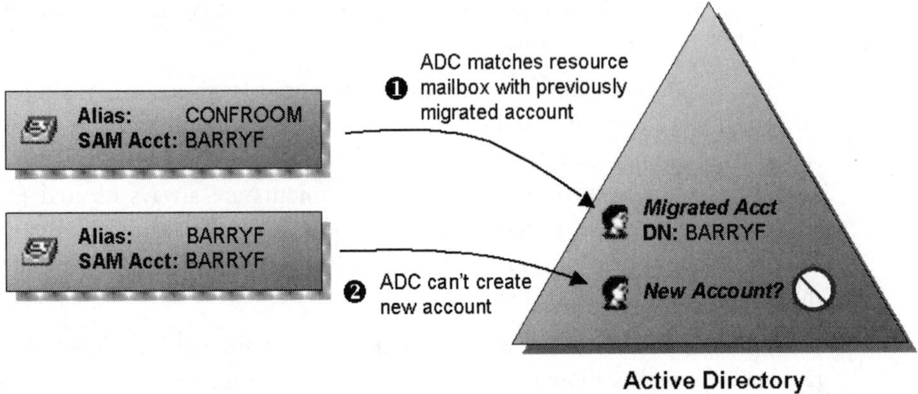

Figure 2.11 *ADC behavior when two Exchange 5.5 mailboxes share Windows NT4 account.*

Windows NT4 account. (This is shown in Figure 2.11.) Either way this is a problem, since the wrong attributes (from the CONFROOM mailbox) are associated with the Active Directory user account; the correct attributes should come from the BARRYF mailbox.

As the ADC processes the BARRYF mailbox, it will attempt to create a disabled user object. Although this seems as if it should work, the situation is far from correct. As the ADC attempts to create this new Active Directory user object, it attempts to set the `msExchMasterAccountSID` attribute to the SID of the primary Windows NT4 account associated with the mailbox. This value is identical for both Exchange 5.5 mailboxes, but Active Directory objects must have unique values for `msExchMasterAccountSID`. Accordingly, in our example, the new Active Directory user object cannot be created, and we end up with the wrong mailbox associated with the Active Directory user object. (The ADC generates Event 8281 in the Event Log to indicate that the `msExchMasterAccountSID` could not be replicated because the value exists on another Active Directory object.)

In such cases it is desirable to mark resource mailboxes so that they are not processed by the ADC. This can be done in one of several ways. You can use an LDAP search filter or use the NTDSNoMatch utility. Ideally, you should analyze your existing Exchange 5.5 mailbox and Windows NT4 account mappings and ensure that you have a separate Windows NT4 account for each and every Exchange 5.5 resource mailbox.

Similar problems occur if you have a Windows NT4 group associated with an Exchange 5.5 mailbox and you try to replicate this to the Active Directory. Ideally, you should identify such mailboxes and exclude them from processing by the ADC until you can modify them so that the mailbox is associated with a user object, not a group. Groups cannot be mailbox enabled in the Active Directory, and, accordingly, there is no corresponding relationship between an Exchange 2000 mailbox and an Active Directory Group.

If such mailboxes are processed by the ADC you can expect to see the following behavior:

- If the Exchange 5.5 mailbox is associated with a Windows NT4 group (as its primary Windows NT account), then the ADC will by default attempt to match or create this mailbox with a user object in the Active Directory. The user object's DN will be based on the Display Name of the mailbox and the SID of the Windows NT4 group. If no such group has already been migrated into the Active Directory, then this user object creation will be successful. However, if you have already migrated the Windows NT4 group to a security group in the Active Directory, the user object creation will fail when it attempts to assign the SID to the `msExchMasterAccountSID`, in the same way as described previously.
- If the Exchange 5.5 mailbox is associated with a Windows 2000 security group, then the same problem occurs, attempting to assign the same SID to the new user object.

2.18 Mailbox delegate access

In the Exchange 5.5 Directory Service, the Can send on behalf of attribute (the LDAP `Public-Delegates` attribute) holds the Exchange 5.5 DNs of any other Exchange 5.5 users that have delegated access to a specific user's mailbox. For example, Figure 2.12 shows two Exchange 5.5 mailboxes that have delegate access to Kate Scott's mailbox.

Since this is just another attribute of an Exchange 5.5 mailbox, it should come as no surprise that the ADC synchronizes it to a similar attribute of the Active Directory user object. Figure 2.13 shows the Active Directory `publicDelegates` attribute of Kate Scott's Active Directory user object.

Thus, delegate access to mailboxes is preserved in a coexistent environment using the ADC. Note that if either of the two delegates shown in Figure 2.12 haven't already been synchronized into the Active Directory, they will not appear in the `publicDelegates` attribute. Only when they, as Exchange 5.5 mailbox objects, have been synchronized into the Active Directory in their own right can they be established as delegated user objects.

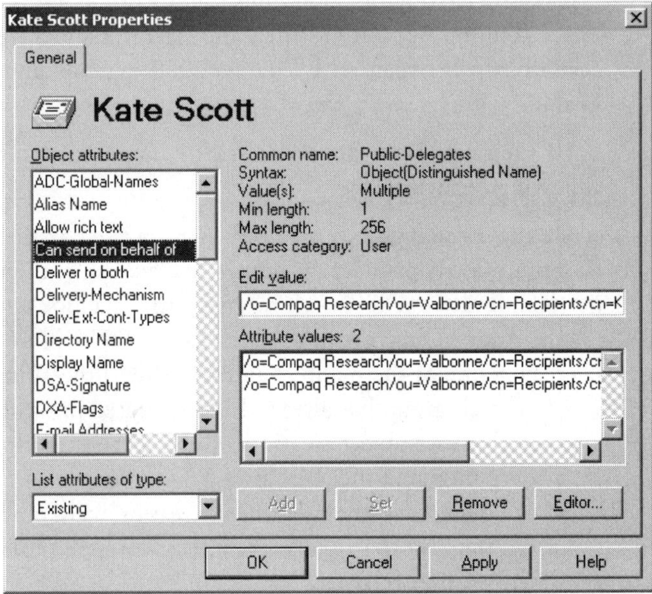

Figure 2.12 *Raw properties showing delegated mailbox access.*

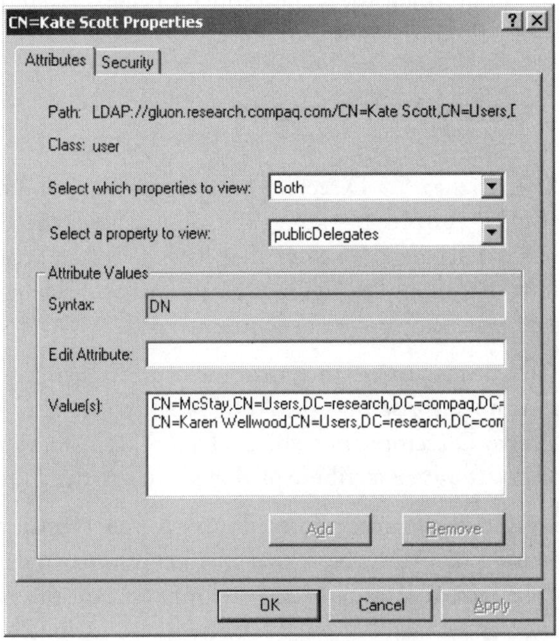

Figure 2.13 *ADSI edit view of publicDelegates of Active Directory user object.*

The following delegated access models are all supported with a mixed Exchange 5.5/Exchange 2000 environment with the ADC:

- Exchange 5.5 mailbox with another Exchange 5.5 mailbox as a delegated user.
- Exchange 5.5 mailbox moved to Exchange 2000 mailbox with another Exchange 5.5 mailbox as a delegated user.
- Exchange 5.5 mailbox with another Exchange 5.5 mailbox moved to Exchange 2000 mailbox as a delegated user.
- Exchange 5.5 mailbox moved to Exchange 2000 mailbox in a particular storage group on a particular database with another Exchange 5.5 mailbox moved to the same storage group but a different database as a delegated user.
- Exchange 5.5 mailbox moved to Exchange 2000 mailbox in particular storage group on a particular database with another Exchange 5.5 mailbox moved to a different storage group and different database as a delegated user.

2.19 Troubleshooting ADC synchronization problems

After configuring the appropriate CAs, you should expect to see mail-enabled objects replicating between the Exchange 5.5 Directory Service and the Active Directory.

Should objects not be synchronized, there are a number of checks you can make to determine the cause. First, some basic checks, as follows:

1. Check that the ADC process is running. Look for the service called `MSADC`.
2. Check that a CA exists for the source and destination containers that you need to synchronize the object from/to.
3. Check that the schedule is set on the CA so that objects are actually being synchronized. You should check that the schedule is set to Always or Selected Times. If set to Selected Times, wait until the activation time passes before expecting to see the object synchronized. If the schedule is set to Never, you should not expect synchronization to occur. You can also select the appropriate CA, right-click on it, and select Replicate Now from the pop-up menu.

4. Check that the Exchange 5.5 Directory Service is up and running on the source computer.
5. Check that the LDAP protocol is enabled on the source computer.
6. Check that the Active Directory is available on the target computer.
7. On the CA, check that you've selected the appropriate object classes for synchronization. For example, if you've only selected mailboxes for replication, you should not expect to see custom recipients synchronized.
8. Check that the credentials that you have associated with the CA are valid.
9. If you have created a new object in the source directory and it is not being created in the target directory, check that the CA is a primary CA.
10. If you are waiting on a newly created object to be synchronized from the source directory to the target directory, ensure that latency issues in the source environment are not to blame. For example, if you've just created a new object in one Exchange 5.5 site, but your CA points to a different Exchange 5.5 site, you'll have to wait for intersite directory replication to occur before you should expect to see the object replicated. This will take at least 15 minutes, or more, depending on the schedule of your Directory Replication Connector. Even with intrasite replication, if you create an object on one server, it can take up to five minutes before the object is replicated within the site. Also, be aware of latency delays within the Active Directory. Quoting a colleague of mine from Compaq in charge of Compaq's worldwide Exchange 2000 deployment, "Latency is everywhere." You have been warned!
11. Finally, check the Application Event Log on the ADC server for telltale errors.

If these checks reveal no insight into the problem, there are some other investigations you can perform to explain objects not being synchronized. These are as follows:

1. If you have previously synchronized an object from the source directory to the target directory and you have deleted the synchronized copy of the object in the target directory, the ADC will

not recreate the synchronized object when it is next activated. (This assumes that you are not propagating deletions with a two-way Connection Agreement.)

2. If you have previously synchronized an object from the source directory to the target directory but you have subsequently moved the source or target object to a location in its respective directory where the ADC does not have read/write access, it will not synchronize changes associated with the object.

3. If the ADC is not creating objects with the object class that you expect (e.g., the ADC creates an Active Directory contact for an Exchange 5.5 mailbox), check that the Connection Agreement is set to intraorganization.

4. If you have created an object in the Active Directory and it is not being replicated to the Exchange 5.5 Directory Service, check that the object is mail enabled. (Ensure that at least one of the following attributes are set: mail, `legacyExchangeDN`, `textEncoded-ORAddress`, `proxyAddresses`, or `msExchHomeServerName`. Objects in the Exchange 5.5 Directory Service are mail enabled by definition.)

5. Check that any matching rules or LDAP search filters are not preventing synchronization.

2.20 Summary

The ADC is a powerful tool that does a great job of facilitating coexistence between Exchange 5.5 and Exchange 2000. As well as that, it can be used in other innovative ways to provide interorganizational directory synchronization and more advanced forms of filtering, object matching, and data manipulation, which we'll discuss in the next chapter.

However, the ADC is not a straightforward tool. Its power stems from its sophistication, and that sophistication means that you have to fully understand its operation in order to put it to good use. If you want a successful deployment of Exchange 2000, you must get to know exactly how the ADC works. Build a test lab that mirrors your production environment and keep on testing and retesting until everything makes sense to you.

3

Advanced Active Directory Connector Configuration

3.1 Introduction

At this point, you should be familiar with the basic operation of the ADC. To summarize: It is a utility that uses CAs to define instances of synchronization between the Exchange 5.5 Directory Service and the Active Directory. At first glance, its granularity of operation seems limited. From the Exchange 5.5 Directory Service you can select the contents of one or more recipient containers to be synchronized into a single OU in the Active Directory. Similarly, from Active Directory, you select the contents of one or more OUs to be synchronized into a single recipient container in the Exchange 5.5 Directory Service.

Let's explore synchronizing from the Exchange 5.5 Directory Service. In general, if the source recipient container contains only mailbox entries, you must synchronize all of those mailbox entries; if the source recipient container contains only custom recipients, you must synchronize all of those custom recipients. This also pertains to distribution lists. In general, if the source OU contains only user objects, you must synchronize all of those user objects; if the source OU contains only contacts, you must synchronize all of those contacts; and, again, the same is true for groups. However, it is often desirable to synchronize just a subset of the objects from within a recipient container, when synchronizing to the Active Directory, an OU, or the Exchange 5.5 Directory Service. For example, you may wish to exclude Exchange 5.5 mailboxes that are shared between multiple Windows NT4 users and are not associated with any specific Windows NT4 account. In the same way, synchronizing from the Active Directory to the Exchange 5.5 Directory Service, you may wish to select only those mail-enabled user objects associated with people in a particular geographic location, even though the objects may all reside in the same OU in the Active Directory.

In this chapter, we will explore some more sophisticated configuration options that you can modify on the ADC that will greatly increase the flexibility of ADC synchronization. To be specific, we will first look at different mechanisms by which you can control the selection of objects for ADC synchronization: using LDAP search filters on CAs and making modifications to the ADC's object-matching table.

3.2 Default ADC object matching

The default behavior of a CA is restrictive when it comes to the ability to select specific objects that you may want to synchronize from one directory service to another. Figure 3.1 shows a typical set of CA configuration settings that you might use to synchronize the contents of the Exchange 5.5 Directory Service Recipients container to the Active Directory Users OU. As the settings demonstrate, this intraorganizational CA will synchronize mailboxes, custom recipients, and distribution lists from the Exchange 5.5 Directory Service to the Active Directory. In the Active Directory, these synchronized objects will be represented as user objects, contacts, and distribution group, respectively.

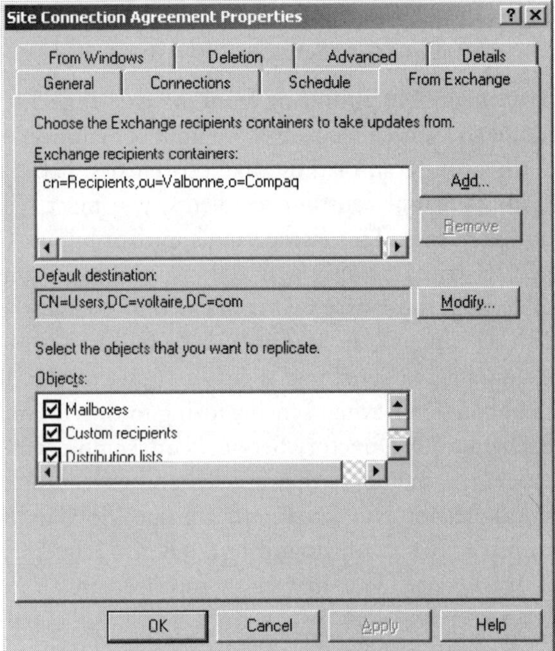

Figure 3.1 *Exchange properties for a site CA.*

You can be more selective with what you'll synchronize between the directories. For example, if you only need to synchronize mailboxes from the Exchange 5.5 Recipients container to the Active Directory, you could uncheck the boxes that dictate that custom recipients and distribution lists should be synchronized. And in the direction from Active Directory to the Exchange 5.5 Directory Service, you can use more or less the same options on the From Windows tab to control whether you'll synchronize users, contacts, or groups to the Exchange 5.5 Directory Service.

3.3 How the ADC uses LDAP

Let's assume that you have mailbox objects existing in the Exchange 5.5 Recipients container, as shown in Figure 3.2. As you can see, there are four mailbox objects represented in the Recipients container. Three of the mailboxes have their Office attribute set to the value Valbonne, while the mailbox for Donald Livengood has its Office attribute set to the value Atlanta.

With the default behavior of the ADC and the CA properties defined in Figure 3.1, the CA would synchronize these four mailbox objects to the Active Directory. There are no configuration options settable on the properties of the CA or the ADC that allow you to specify that only a subset of the mailboxes should be synchronized. The user interface does not allow you to be very specific about objects that you'll process for synchronization. However, let's assume that synchronizing a subset of the mailboxes is exactly what you need to do—that is, force the CA to synchronize only the Valbonne mailbox, and ignore the Atlanta mailbox.

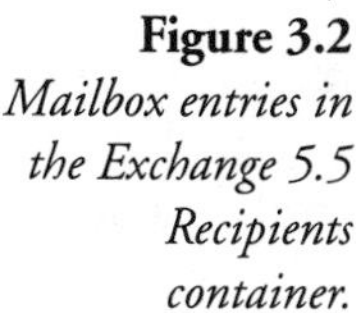

Figure 3.2 *Mailbox entries in the Exchange 5.5 Recipients container.*

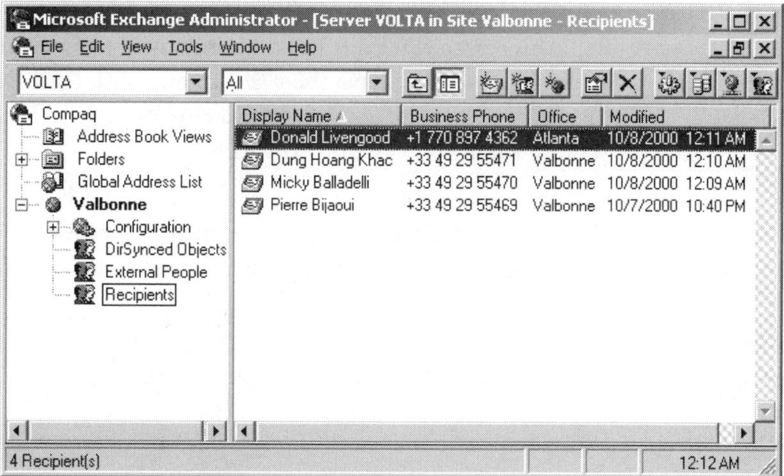

In the direction of Exchange 5.5 Directory Service to Active Directory synchronization, the ADC ordinarily operates by executing an LDAP query on the Exchange 5.5 Directory Service that identifies all mailboxes, custom recipients, or distribution listings, with a search base that specifies the containers that should be used as sources for the CA. This search base is effectively the containers specified in the Exchange Recipients containers box shown in Figure 3.1. By default the LDAP query will select all mailboxes (if you checked the Mailboxes object), but you can customize the LDAP query so that it only selects some mailboxes. Specifically, the following LDAP search filter associated with the query is defined by default for the CA with the settings shown in Figure 3.1:

```
(|(objectclass=organizationalPerson)(objectclass=remote-
address)(objectclass=groupOfNames))
```

This default search filter states that the CA should allow mailboxes (`organizationalPerson`), custom recipients (`remote-address`), or distribution lists (`groupOfNames`) as valid objects to be synchronized.

3.4 Customizing synchronization with LDAP search filters

You can refine the synchronization process so that only Valbonne objects are synchronized by modifying the CA's LDAP search filter so that it reads as follows:

```
(&(|(objectclass=organizationalPerson)
(objectclass=remote-address)(objectclass=groupOfNames))
(physicalDeliveryOfficeName=Valbonne))
```

This search filter dictates that only mailboxes, custom recipients, or distribution lists that have their Office attribute (in LDAP terminology, this attribute is named `physicalDeliveryOfficeName`) set to the value Valbonne will be processed by the ADC.

In fact, you could further refine this search filter to be more exact so that any custom recipient or distribution list, irrespective of location, but only mailboxes in Valbonne, gets synchronized using the following expression:

```
(|(objectclass=remote-address)(objectclass=groupOfNames)
(&(objectclass=organizationalperson)
(physicalDeliveryOfficeName=Valbonne)))
```

3.5 An LDAP search filter primer

LDAP search filters use a variation of what is known as prefix notation in the definition of an expression, unlike everyday mathematical expressions, which use infix notation. In prefix notation, the operator always precedes the operands and the precedence of operators is implicit within the expression. For example, with infix notation, you would represent the expression that adds three to four as: `3 + 4`. With prefix notation, you represent this as: `+ 3 4`. Similarly, the expression that adds three to four and multiplies the result by five is represented in infix notation as: `(3 + 4) * 5`. With prefix notation, you would represent this expression as: `*(+ 3 4) 5`.

The notation used with LDAP search filters uses | (vertical bar) to represent the logical OR operator, & (ampersand) to represent the logical AND operator, and ! (exclamation mark) to represent the logical NOT operator.

The syntax of an LDAP search filter often means that it is difficult to understand just what the filter defines when it is represented as a long string of text. You should find it useful, either when defining your own search filters or analyzing existing search filters, to format the text into separate lines using horizontal tabs. For example, I find the following representation of this search filter:

```
(|
      (objectclass=remote-address)
      (objectclass=groupOfNames)
      (&
            (objectclass=organizationalperson)
            (physicalDeliveryOfficeName=Valbonne)
      )
)
```

easier to parse and understand than this more cumbersome representation:

```
(|(objectclass=remote-address)(objectclass=groupOfNames)
(&(objectclass=organizationalperson)
(physicalDeliveryOfficeName=Valbonne)))
```

The syntax for LDAP search filters is fully defined in RFC 2254, and it is worth taking a look at this RFC if you intend to build complex search filters and use them to achieve sophisticated ADC synchronization. You can find RFC 2254 at http://www.ietf.og/rfc.html.

3.6 Modifying Connection Agreements with LDAP search filters

The ADC Manager snap-in does not offer any interface that allows you to set properties on either an individual CA or the ADC itself to control the LDAP search filter settings for a given CA. To customize the search filter for a particular CA, you must make modifications directly to the CA object that is held in the Active Directory.

As with any kind of object, be it a user mailbox, a contact, or a group represented in the Active Directory, a CA that you may define for a given ADC is similarly represented in the Active Directory. Exchange 2000 stores all configuration information relating to Exchange's operation in the Configuration Naming Context of the Active Directory, and, accordingly, an ADC server stores configuration information for itself and any CAs that may be homed on it in the Configuration Naming Context. If you drill down through the Configuration Naming Context in the Active Directory to the Microsoft Exchange container, as shown in Figure 3.3, you'll find the entries for all CAs defined in the organization. In the example scenario that

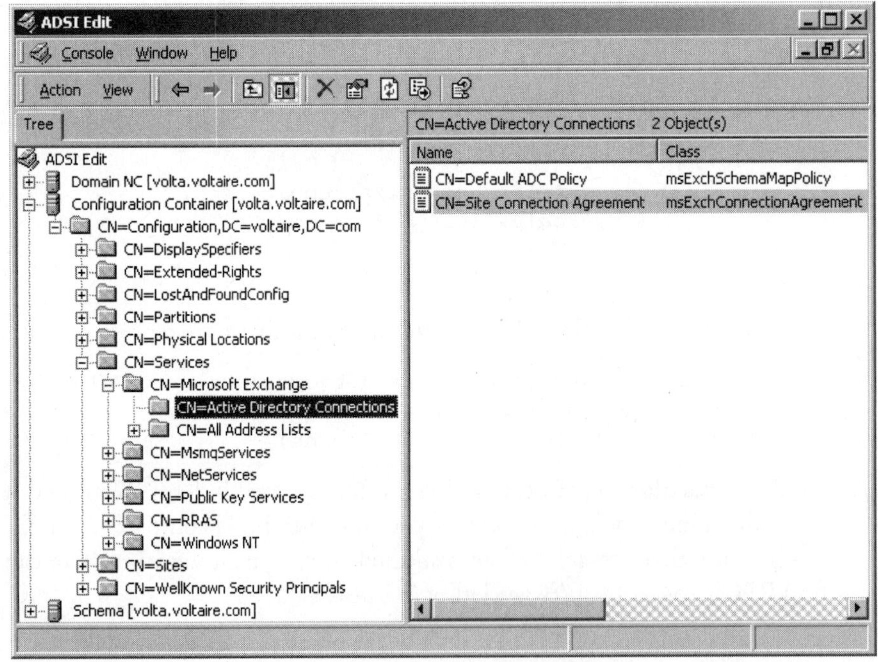

Figure 3.3 *Connection agreements defined in the Active Directory as shown by ADSI Edit.*

I'm describing here, the CA is identified in Figure 3.3 with the name Site Connection Agreement.

While there are many attributes associated with a CA object, we are especially interested in the `msExchServer2SearchFilter` attribute. This attribute defines the search filter that is used when the ADC selects objects for synchronization from the Exchange 5.5 Directory Service to the Active Directory. Correspondingly, and in the opposite direction, the `msExchServer1SearchFilter` defines the search filter that is used when the ADC synchronizes objects from the Active Directory to the Exchange 5.5 Directory Service.

Since there is no user interface that exposes these attributes to an administrator, the only way to modify the value of this attribute is to manipulate the attribute directly in the Active Directory using a tool such as ADSI Edit or LDP.

Using ADSI Edit, as shown in Figure 3.4, you can select the attribute, and then set its value by typing the desired search filter into the Edit Attribute field and clicking on the Set button. The next time you run the synchronization cycle associated with the CA, the new search filter will be active and objects that correspond to its characteristics will be processed accordingly.

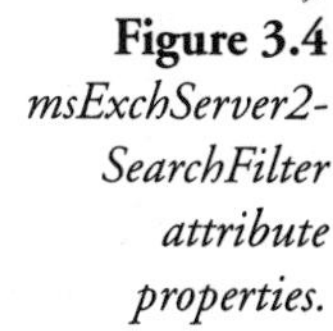

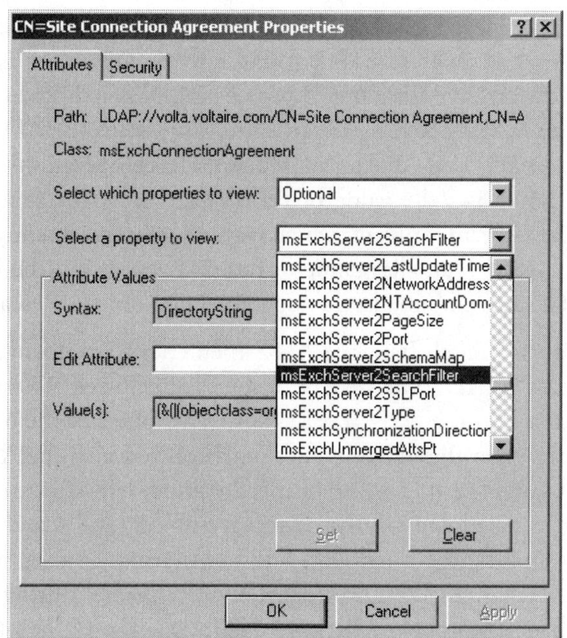

Figure 3.4 *msExchServer2-SearchFilter attribute properties.*

3.7 Default ADC object-matching process

The ADC uses a default set of matching rules that control the actions the ADC takes when it processes an object in the source directory system and attempts to match it with an existing object in the target directory system. Let's take source objects in the Active Directory as an example. As objects are processed, the ADC attempts to match any given Active Directory object with an existing object in the Exchange 5.5 Directory Service by searching on a fixed set of attributes. These matching rules are effective for most environments and especially so for simple synchronization cases where there is little complexity. In the following text, I'll describe the object-matching process.

3.7.1 Matching objects from the Exchange 5.5 Directory Service to the Active Directory

When a CA attempts to synchronize an object from the Exchange 5.5 Directory Service to the Active Directory, it searches the Active Directory to find an existing object with which it can match the source object.

If the source Exchange 5.5 object has previously been synchronized to the Active Directory, the ADC will search for an object that has an `ms-ExchADCGlobalNames` attribute that matches with the DN of the source object in the Exchange 5.5 Directory Service. The ADC populates the `msExchADCGlobalNames` attribute when an object is first synchronized, and the original Exchange 5.5 object's DN is written as the `EX5` value in the `msExchADCGlobalNames` attribute. This helps the ADC keep track of synchronized objects during subsequent search operations. As an example, Figure 3.5 shows the value of the `msExchADCGlobalNames` attribute for an Active Directory object, which is the synchronized copy of an Exchange 5.5 mailbox with an alias name of KarenW located in the Recipients container of the site Valbonne in the organization Compaq Research.

If this match fails, the ADC then tries to perform the match using the object's GUID. The GUID of the synchronized Active Directory object is written into the `ADC-Global-Names` attribute of the original Exchange 5.5 object when the object is first synchronized into the Active Directory. The ADC uses the `NT5` string in this attribute, which is really the GUID of the synchronized copy Active Directory object, and searches the Active Directory looking for a match. (The `ADC-Global-Names` attribute is added to the Exchange 5.5 Directory Service schema during the installation of Exchange 5.5 Service Pack 3.) Figure 3.6 shows the original Exchange 5.5

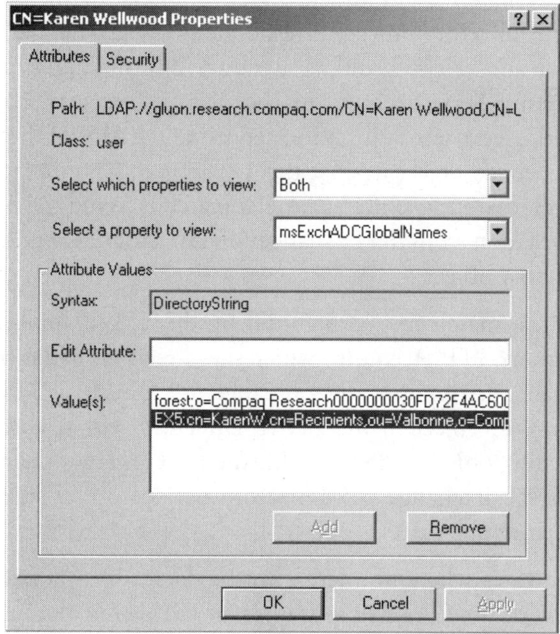

Figure 3.5 *msExchADC-GlobalNames attribute for a synchronized object in the Active Directory.*

object, with its `ADC-Global-Names` attribute updated with the GUID of the synchronized copy Active Directory object due to a previous synchronization.

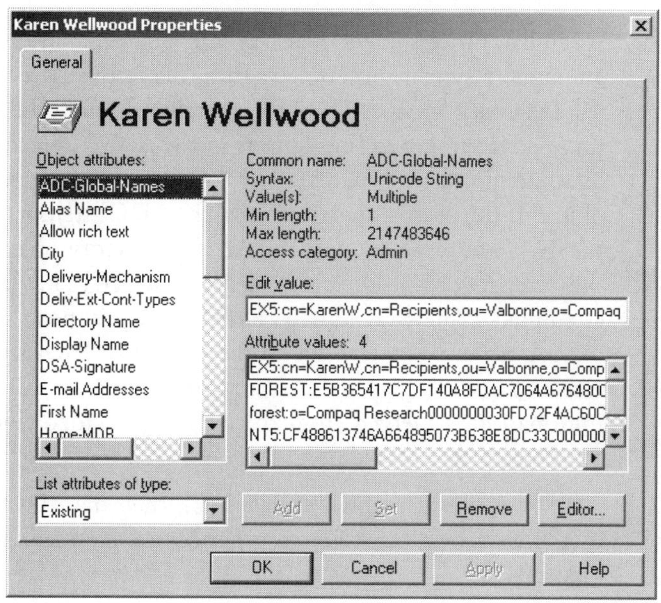

Figure 3.6 *msExchADC-GlobalNames attribute for the original Exchange 5.5 Directory Service object*

If a match is found in the Active Directory, the ADC assumes that the Active Directory object corresponds to the Exchange 5.5 Directory Service object and it synchronizes attribute information from the Exchange 5.5 Directory Service object to the Active Directory object. If no match is found, a new search is performed using the DN of the Exchange 5.5 Directory Service object against the `legacyExchangeDN` attribute of the Active Directory object. Once again, if a match is found the ADC merges attribute information from the Exchange 5.5 Directory Service object with the Active Directory object.

If no match has been found by this stage, the ADC uses the Primary Windows NT Account, which in directory parlance is the `Assoc-NT-Account` attribute of the Exchange 5.5 Directory Service object, to match against an object in the Active Directory with a corresponding SID. If a matching object is determined, the ADC merges the attribute information from the Exchange 5.5 Directory Service object into the existing Active Directory object.

In cases where no match can be determined, a new object is created in line with the CA settings (either an enabled or disabled user, or a contact) and, accordingly, the Exchange 5.5 Directory Service object's attribute information is merged into the newly created Active Directory object.

3.7.2 Matching from the Active Directory to the Exchange 5.5 Directory Service

A similar process takes place in the opposite direction when the ADC attempts to synchronize objects from the Active Directory to the Exchange 5.5 Directory Service. The ADC searches through the Exchange 5.5 Directory Service trying to find objects in the Active Directory with an `Object-GUID` attribute that matches the GUID of the current Active Directory object. If this search operation fails, the ADC attempts another search using the `legacyExchangeDN` of the Active Directory object against the DN of the Exchange 5.5 Directory Service object. The last search operation attempted, if previous searches have failed, uses the SID of the Active Directory object to be matched with the SID of an Exchange 5.5 Directory Service object. If any of these search operations are successful, the attribute information is merged from the Active Directory object to the Exchange 5.5 Directory Service object.

If all of the attempted searches fail, then the ADC creates a new object in the Exchange 5.5 Directory Service to represent the Active Directory object.

3.8 Using custom object-matching rules on the ADC

Using an LDAP search filter allows you to define those objects that you will permit the ADC to process during a synchronization cycle between the Exchange 5.5 Directory Service and the Active Directory or vice versa.

In addition to the use of LDAP search filters, an alternative method exists for controlling the objects that you will allow the ADC to process. LDAP search filters are applied on a per-CA basis, while the alternative, using custom object-matching rules, applies to the ADC itself. Setting a custom object-matching rule means that the rule applies to all CAs that are homed on a particular ADC. These custom object-matching rules can override the default object-matching rules that exist as a basic component of the ADC functionality.

3.8.1 Setting basic custom-matching rules

The ADC offers an interface to allow an administrator to define simple customized object-matching rules. You can access the interface by right-clicking on Active Directory Connector Management from within the ADC Manager snap-in and then selecting Properties. You can set custom-matching rules for synchronization From Exchange or From Windows. Any rules that you set in one direction should be balanced with a corresponding rule in the opposite direction to ensure symmetry of synchronization. For example, if you are synchronizing from the Exchange 5.5 Directory Service to the Active Directory and you are matching all Exchange 5.5 mailboxes in the sales department with potentially matching and existing Active Directory objects using a specific attribute, it's likely that you should define that same matching rule for Active Directory objects synchronizing into the Exchange 5.5 Directory Service. Otherwise, you introduce a potential for object duplication. Having described this scenario, it's important to point out that this is not a hard-and-fast rule. All environments are different and local circumstances may dictate particular policies. For example, Figure 3.7 shows a new custom-matching rule that matches the Primary Windows NT Account of an Exchange 5.5 Directory Service object with the SID History attribute of an Active Directory object.

This is a useful custom object-matching rule to use in an environment where you have migrated accounts from Windows NT4 domains to Windows 2000 domains using the migration tools of the ClonePrincipal API functionality. This preserves the old SID value of the Windows NT4

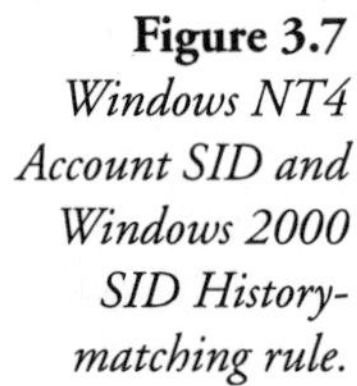

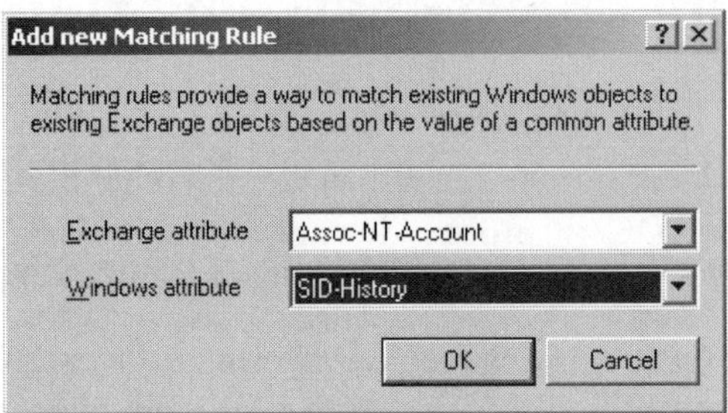

Figure 3.7 *Windows NT4 Account SID and Windows 2000 SID History-matching rule.*

account object in the SID History attribute of the new Windows 2000 user account object. In such an environment, the original Windows NT4 account is likely to have been the Primary Windows NT Account associated with the Exchange 5.5 mailbox. After the Windows NT4 account has been migrated to Windows 2000, the ADC would fail to match an Exchange 5.5 Directory Service mailbox object with the migrated Windows 2000 object (the new Windows 2000 object will have a different SID) unless you used this form of matching rule against the SID History.

It is possible to select a wide range of attributes from an Exchange 5.5 Directory Service object to match against a similar attribute on an Active Directory object to suit your interoperability and migration requirements. For example, you could match the Exchange 5.5 mailbox alias (`Mail-Nickname`) against the Windows 2000 account name (`SAM-Account-Name`), as shown in Figure 3.8, if you know that these attributes are unique and tie together the original Exchange 5.5 mailbox with the new Windows 2000 account.

Similarly, there are many other attributes to match with, including mail address attributes and the complete set of 15 extension attributes from the Exchange 5.5 Directory Service. Such matching opportunities are useful if your particular environment and migration technique rely on the use of custom attributes to store employee ID numbers or Social Security numbers.

Figure 3.8 *Mailbox alias and Windows 2000 account-matching rule.*

3.8.2 Defining custom-matching rules

When you create custom object-matching rules using the interface described previously, the logic associated with the rules is stored in the Active Directory as attributes of the Default ADC Policy object. Figure 3.3 shows where this Active Directory object is located in the Active Directory container hierarchy. In particular, for the custom object-matching rule defined previously that matches the Primary Windows NT Account with the SID History, this rule is stored in the `msExchServer2ObjectMatch` attribute of the Default ADC Policy object. Figure 3.9 shows a view of this attribute from ADSI Edit.

The `msExchServer2ObjectMatch` attribute stores custom-matching rules used when the ADC matches objects from the Exchange 5.5 Directory Service with the Active Directory, while the `msExchServer1ObjectMatch` attribute stores matching rules used from the Active Directory to the Exchange 5.5 Directory Service.

The value of the `msExchServer2ObjectMatch` attribute, which isn't fully displayed in Figure 3.9, specifies the matching rule. The full text of the rule is: `ObjectMatch###Assoc-NT-Account#sIDHistory#sid_match#`.

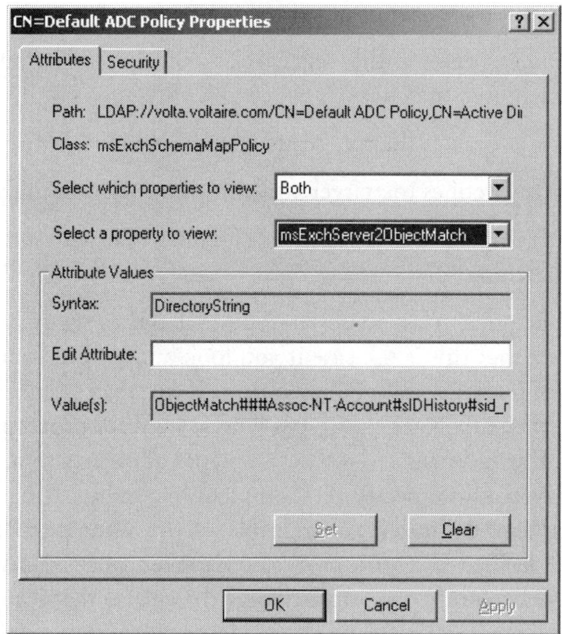

Figure 3.9 *msExchServer2-Objectmatch attribute properties.*

Similarly, if you define multiple custom matching rules using the interface, these rules are all stored in the msExchServer2ObjectMatch attribute. For example, if both matching rules, as shown in Figures 3.7 and 3.8 are defined, the attribute value will appear as follows:

```
ObjectMatch###Assoc-NT-Account#sIDHistory#sid_match#
ObjectMatch###UID#sAMAccountName#sid_match#
```

The examples shown here all rely on creating or modifying the matching rules set on the msExchServer2ObjectMatch attribute. Just as you can use the ADSI Edit tool to view these rules, you also use ADSI Edit to set new values on the attribute.

3.8.3 An overview of object-matching rule syntax

The syntax of the custom object-matching rules is defined as follows: `<name>#<soc>#<toc>#<sa>#<ta>#<flags>#`

With this syntax for a single matching rule, the individual terms are defined as follows:

<name>, defines an arbitrary name for the matching rule

<soc>, defines the object class of the source object used in the attempted match

<toc>, defines the object class of the target object used in the attempted match

<sa>, defines the source attribute/value used in the attempted match

<ta>, defines the target attribute/value used in the attempted match

<flags>, one of a fixed set of values that define the behavior of the matching rule

The object class values are optional and in many cases are omitted. You can see that this is the case if you look at the object-matching rules defined on the Default ADC Policy object. If no object class is entered for a given rule, then all object class types will be valid for processing by that particular rule. If you do wish to restrict the types of objects to which a rule can apply, then you must specify the complete hierarchy of the object class, using a dollar sign delimiter. For example, if you want the SID History matching rule specified in Figure 3.7, to be applied only against user objects in the Active Directory, you must change the rule so that it now reads as follows:

```
ObjectMatch##user$organizationalPerson$person$top#Assoc-
NT-Account#sIDHistory#sid_match#
```

Note that this rule and those that follow it should be specified on single lines.

3.8.4 Matching rule flags

Every matching rule has a flag associated with it that controls the processing that takes place on the rule. In the previous example, the `sid_match` flag allows matching to proceed based on SID comparison. A `guid_match` flag also exists, and its presence assumes that the objects being synchronized have previously been matched (in the Active Directory to Exchange 5.5 Directory Service direction). For example, the default matching rule that controls how Exchange 5.5 Directory Service objects are matched and synchronized to Active Directory objects is as follows:

```
ObjectMatch###Assoc-NT-Account#ObjectSID#
sid_match EscapeBinaryBlob#
```

This matching rule attempts to match the SID of the Windows NT4 account associated with the Exchange 5.5 Directory Service object with the SID of an object in the Active Directory. The `EscapeBinaryBlob` flag is used in conjunction with the `sid_match` or `guid_match` flags when the source attribute is in ASCII format, but the target attribute is in binary (which is the case with the SIDs referenced here; you can see this if you try to look at these attributes on their respective user objects).

If no match is found in the target directory to correspond with the source object, then the ADC will attempt to create a new object in the target directory that will correspond to the source object.

Assume that you want some means to prevent this new object creation from happening should a match not be determined. For example, you may decide that Exchange 5.5 Directory Service objects that have an Office attribute set to Atlanta should not be synchronized. To do this you can change the rule set to the following:

```
ObjectMatch###Assoc-NT-Account#ObjectSID#
sid_match EscapeBinaryBlob#
ObjectMatch###physicalDeliveryOfficeName#"Atlanta"#veto-
previous#
```

The `veto` and `veto-previous` flags indicate that the object that is currently being processed should be not be synchronized if a match is found on the source attribute and the specified attribute value. The `veto` flag (which is not shown here) indicates that the object will not be replicated at all and abandons all subsequent matching for that particular object. The `veto-`

previous flag is somewhat more refined and indicates that if the current match is true—that is, the source attribute value matches the specified value in the rule—then the previous matching rule should be ignored, but match processing should continue with the next matching rule.

With the example rule shown here, this rule structure indicates that if the Office attribute matches with the text string Atlanta, then the previous rule (that defines the matching between SIDs) is ignored. In this case, the Atlanta mailbox will not be synchronized and no corresponding user object will be created in the Active Directory. Similarly, you could add further matching rules to ignore all Exchange 5.5 Directory Service objects that have Custom Attribute 5 set to IgnoreADC, as follows:

```
ObjectMatch###Assoc-NT-Account#ObjectSID#
sid_match EscapeBinaryBlob#
ObjectMatch###Extension-Attribute-5#"IgnoreADC"#veto-
previous#
```

As another example, any Exchange 5.5 Directory Service objects that have any value set in Custom Attribute 6 to be ignored by the ADC, as follows:

```
ObjectMatch###Assoc-NT-Account#ObjectSID#
sid_match EscapeBinaryBlob#
ObjectMatch###Extension-Attribute-6#NotNULL#veto-
previous#
```

The ADC uses default matching rule behavior to deal with objects that have the value NTDSNoMatch in Custom Attribute 10. In such cases, the ADC will not attempt to match Exchange 5.5 mailboxes with existing Active Directory user objects or even to create new user objects in the Active Directory.

3.9 The NTDSNoMatch utility

The NTDSNoMatch utility can be run from a Windows 2000 system using an account that has the correct read permissions for the Exchange 5.5 Directory Service. Executing the command:

```
NTDSNOMATCH <servername>:<optional LDAP port number>
```

causes the NTDSNoMatch utility to scan the complete Exchange 5.5 Directory Service using LDAP and identify those mailboxes that it determines to be resource mailboxes.

The logic for determining if a mailbox is a resource mailbox or not is particularly straightforward. NTDSNoMatch compares the Exchange 5.5 alias name of the mailbox with the SAM Account Name of the mailbox's associated Windows NT4 account. If the values match (e.g., the mailbox alias name is BARRYF and the SAM Account Name is BARRYF), then NTDSNoMatch assumes that this is a mailbox associated with a real person's Windows NT4 user account. If the mailbox alias name and SAM Account Name do not match (e.g., the mailbox alias name is CONFROOM and the SAM Account Name is BARRYF), then NTDSNoMatch assumes that this is a resource mailbox.

When run, the NTDSNoMatch utility produces a series of CSV files, one for each Exchange 5.5 site, that contains the appropriate data so that when you import the CSV file in the Exchange 5.5 Directory Service for each site, resource mailboxes are updated with the value NTDSNoMatch in Custom Attribute 10. (You need one CSV file for each site because Exchange 5.5 Directory Service objects are read-only outside the site.)

For environments where the Exchange 5.5 alias for a user mailbox generally coincides with the SAM Account Name, NTDSNoMatch can be a useful tool for identifying resource mailboxes. However, in those environments where there is no real synergy between mailbox aliases and SAM Account Names, the utility is of little use due to its primitive decision logic. In environments such as these, you'll need to use some other mechanism to identify resource mailboxes. This alternative mechanism might be implemented using a manual process, especially if you have a small and easily managed environment. If your environment is a little more complicated, you'll be left with little alternative but to write your own utility to identify the mailboxes. If you're lucky, there may be some syntax or naming structure that you've implemented for process mailboxes (or even user mailboxes) that makes the resource mailboxes easily identifiable to an algorithm. If not, then you may well have to resort to a long and tedious manual exercise.

Whatever approach you take, you should invest adequate resources to sanitize your Exchange 5.5 Directory Service before you start any ADC synchronization. Using third-party tools to analyze your environment is a good approach to follow, or even writing your own scripts may well be appropriate. This is important for many reasons. If you have not aligned Exchange 5.5 aliases with SAM Account Names, there is the potential for name clashes as you begin ADC synchronization. The Exchange 5.5 Directory Service does not enforce uniqueness checking on aliases outside the boundary of a container. Even if you have aligned alias names with SAM Account

Names, large environments that use multiple domains may incur name clashes, since SAM Account Names are unique only within the domain.

3.10 Active Directory Connector attribute mapping

When the ADC synchronizes an object, let's say from the Exchange 5.5 Directory Service to the Active Directory, the attributes associated with the Exchange 5.5 object are synchronized to their attribute counterparts on the matched or newly created Active Directory object.

While you can exercise a little control over which attributes you select to synchronize from one directory service to the other, and we'll see how to do this later, there's little that you can do to control the mapping of individual attributes with the functionality provided by the ADC Management snap-in. To perform sophisticated attribute manipulation during synchronization you must move beyond the conventional user interface and make modifications directly to the configuration of the ADC and CAs.

3.11 Default attribute mapping behavior

The ADC Manager snap-in provides little capability to control the mapping of attributes for an object in the Exchange 5.5 Directory Service to the Active Directory or vice versa. The ADC Manager offers a predefined list of attributes that you can define either to be included in the synchronization activity or not. It's a simple Yes or No for synchronization.

By using the default ADC configuration most attributes of an Exchange 5.5 mailbox or custom recipient that would be meaningful to be replicated to the Active Directory are synchronized automatically when a CA is activated between the source container and the target OU. Useful attributes that are synchronized by default include those such as naming and addressing information, telephone and location details that can be used in the GAL, and mailbox properties such as the Home MDB (indicating on which server a user mailbox is located), these are necessary for Exchange to deliver mail.

To select whether or not attributes should be synchronized you should make modifications to the Default ADC Policy. You can do this by right-clicking on the Active Directory Connector Management root in the ADC Manager snap-in, and then select Properties and either From Exchange or From Windows depending on the flow direction in which you're interested. Figure 3.10 shows the interface that you'll use: If the box beside an attribute

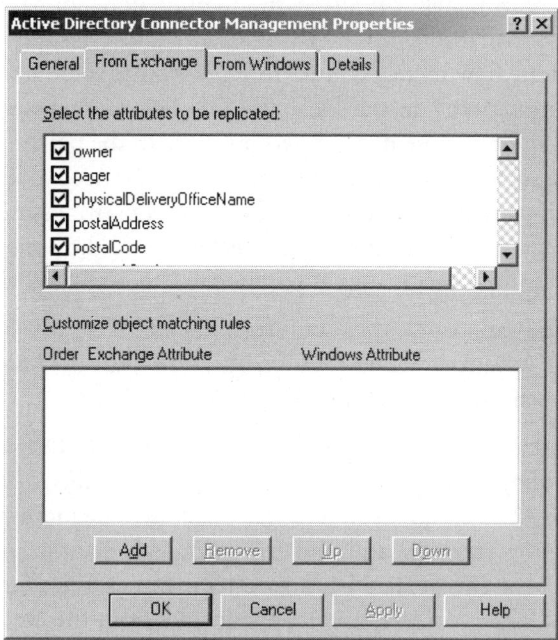

Figure 3.10 *Controlling attribute flow from Exchange on the default ADC policy.*

is checked, then the ADC will synchronize the attribute; no check in the box means the attribute will not be synchronized.

You should not need to spend much time modifying these settings. Microsoft has already decided which attributes are necessary and most useful. Typically, you might only want to suppress the synchronization of an attribute, say a Custom attribute, that holds some legacy information whose value you don't want or need to synchronize to the Active Directory, because the value of the Active Directory attribute is coming from some other directory source, perhaps an HR database.

3.12 The default ADC policy for schema mapping

As you can see in Figure 3.10, there is a limitation in terms of what customizations you can make with the mapping of Exchange 5.5 Directory Service attributes to Active Directory attributes when you use the ADC Manager snap-in. The interface allows you to either map the attributes for synchronization or not. Should you wish to perform more sophisticated attribute synchronizations, such as mapping the value of one attribute in the source directory to a different attribute in the target directory, then the ADC Manager snap-in is not sufficient. You must use an alternative interface for the configuration.

Unfortunately, the alternative method does not have the customary easy-to-use Microsoft GUI. Using the ADC Manager snap-in to control attribute flow merely defines those attributes to be synchronized by manipulating settings on the Default ADC Policy. However, the ADC Manager snap-in only presents a limited interface to the policy. If you need to define more sophisticated mapping operations, you need to bypass the snap-in and manipulate the policy directly by changing settings in the Active Directory. You can use ADSI Edit to get direct access to the policy and manipulate the synchronization settings as required.

You can install ADSI Edit from the SUPPORT directory on the Windows 2000 Advanced Server CD-ROM, and Figure 3.11 shows how ADSI Edit represents the view of the Default ADC Policy.

Attribute mapping rules are defined on the Default ADC Policy, and, accordingly, these rules are enforced for all CAs that are homed on any given ADC server. However, it is possible to be more specific with attribute mapping rules. In addition to setting the mapping rules on the Default ADC Policy, you can set individual mapping rules for each CA homed on an ADC server. Attribute mapping rules from the Default ADC Policy and

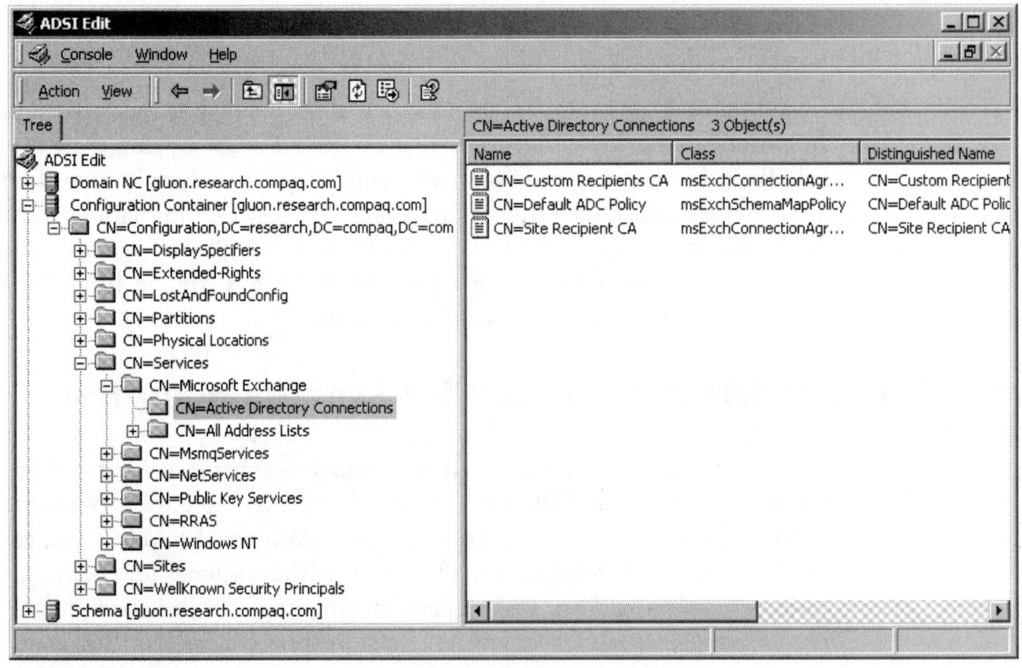

Figure 3.11 *Accessing the Default ADC Policy from ADSI Edit.*

individual CAs are merged during synchronization activity, but where appropriate an attribute mapping rule on a CA will override a corresponding attribute mapping rule on the Default ADC Policy.

3.12.1 Making modifications to the attribute mapping tables

The attribute mapping tables are instantiated by two attributes: either on the Default ADC Policy or on individual CAs. The `msExchServer1-SchemaMap` attribute defines attribute mapping rules from the Active Directory to the Exchange 5.5 Directory Service, while the `msExchServer2SchemaMap` attribute defines attribute mapping rules from the Exchange 5.5 Directory Service to the Active Directory. Figure 3.12 illustrates the properties of the Default ADC Policy object and specifically shows the `msExchServer1SchemaMap` attribute.

The string shown in the `Value(s)` label in Figure 3.12 is actually the first few characters of a rather long string that continues for more than 18,000 characters, or about 269 individual lines. This string is the attribute mapping table from the Active Directory to the Exchange 5.5 Directory Service, and, with some exceptions, each line in the table is a single attribute

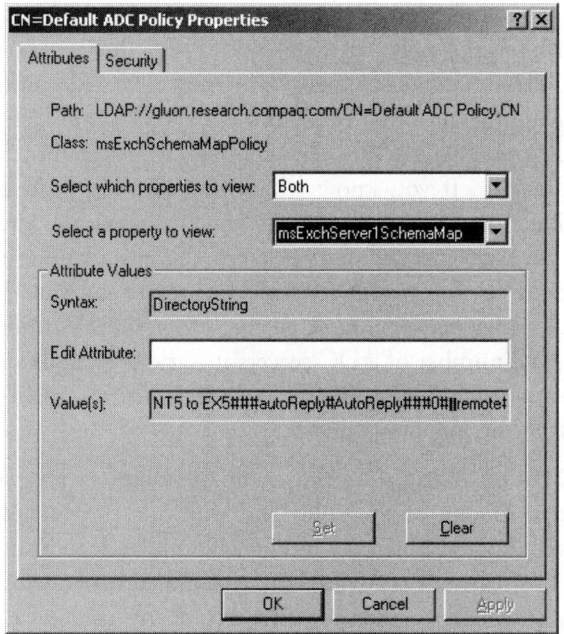

Figure 3.12 *Accessing the value of the msExchServer1-SchemaMap attribute.*

mapping rule. These rules are defined when you install the ADC and reflect the settings that Microsoft believe to be optimal for synchronizing attribute data between the 5.5 Directory Service and the Active Directory.

To make changes to the mapping rules, you need to click on the `Clear` button, and subsequently the mapping rule is displayed in the `Edit Attribute` text box. (You cannot edit the rule when it is displayed in the `Value(s)` text box.) When you've made the required changes to the rule, you can click on the `Set` button and the new rule will be written to the Active Directory and become effective immediately. I find it quite challenging to edit these rules by making changes directly to the text string in the `Edit Attribute` text box. For a simpler editing experience you can copy the text string from the `Value(s)` text box, and then paste it into your favorite editor—Notepad or Wordpad is sufficient for this—where the embedded CR/LFs cause the text to be rendered in a much more readable fashion. Using such an editor, it is much simpler to find the rule that you wish to modify and understand other related rules. However, you cannot make changes directly to the mapping rules displayed using an editor and then paste the new rules back into Active Directory. You must make changes directly to the Active Directory by finding the rule in the long text string and perform the editing there.

When you first install the ADC software, the attribute mapping tables are populated from some predefined text files on the Exchange 2000 CD-ROM. Specifically, in the `ADC\I386` directory there are two files: `LOCAL.MAP` and `REMOTE.MAP`. The `LOCAL.MAP` file contains the complete set of mapping rules that populates the `msExchServer2SchemaMap` attribute, while the `REMOTE.MAP` file defines the rules for the `msExchServer1-SchemaMap`. If you know which modifications you need to make to the attribute mapping files, you can edit these text files and make the appropriate changes (providing you copy the installation kit onto a writeable medium) before you install the ADC server software. Doing so makes for a much easier mapping table editing experience. Furthermore, if you plan to deploy a number of ADC servers in various locations this technique is particularly useful and is an efficient mechanism to make consistent modifications to the mapping tables.

Making changes to the mapping tables is reversible. If you make a change to one of the rules and this rule proves not to perform as you expected, you can simply modify the rule back to its original configuration. For this reason it is advisable to retain a copy of the original mapping table files as well as to monitor and record any changes that you make to the tables. If you fail to control the modifications and you end up with a set of attribute mapping rules whose integrity is questionable, then the only way to restore the mapping tables to their default configurations is to reinstall the ADC server software. Any changes that you make to the attribute mappings only affect the mapping tables in the Active Directory, and an ADC software reinstall normalizes the Active Directory tables by reading the original set of mapping rules from the `LOCAL.MAP` and `REMOTE.MAP` files. Irrespective of the abilities of a reinstall to normalize the tables, you should carefully control and arbitrate any changes you make to the tables after thorough testing in a lab environment.

3.12.2 Changing attribute mappings

Making changes to the schema mapping tables allows you to change how the value of one attribute is mapped to another. For example, you may want to reconfigure the mapping between the City and the Office attributes as you synchronize Exchange 5.5 Directory Service objects to the Active Directory. Figure 3.13 shows the Exchange 5.5 mailbox for Sharon Stafford.

When the ADC synchronizes this mailbox object into the Active Directory, it will map the Exchange 5.5 Office attribute to the Office attribute of the corresponding Active Directory object. In many circumstances this one-to-one mapping consistency is exactly what is required. However, let's

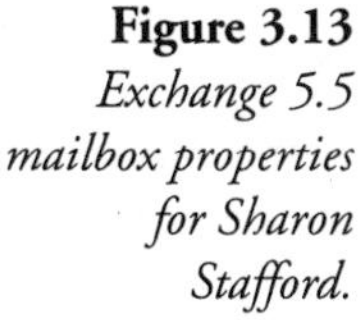

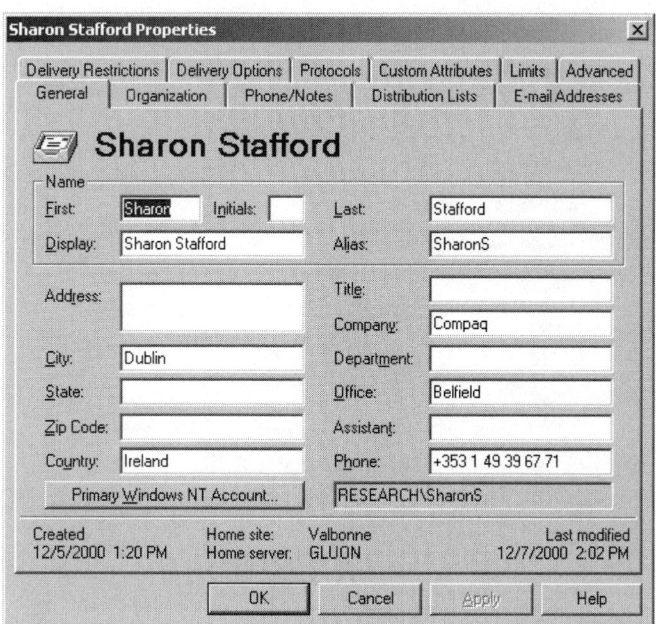

Figure 3.13 *Exchange 5.5 mailbox properties for Sharon Stafford.*

assume that you don't want to have the value Belfield (which is the value of the Office attribute in the Exchange 5.5 Directory Service) written to the Active Directory Office attribute. Instead, let's assume that you would rather have the value of the Exchange 5.5 City attribute written to the Active Directory Office attribute.

Looking at the mapping rules as defined in `msExchServer2SchemaMap` (specifying mappings from the Exchange 5.5 Directory Service to the Active Directory), you'll notice that the value of the Exchange 5.5 Office attribute is defined to map directly to the value of the Active Directory Office attribute; the appropriate rule (we'll call it Rule 1) is as follows:

```
local###physicalDeliveryOfficeName#physicalDeliveryOffic
eName###0#
```

This rule states that for all objects in the Exchange 5.5 Directory Service that will be processed by the ADC, map the Exchange 5.5 Office attribute to the Active Directory Office attribute. (In LDAP terminology, the Office attribute is identified as `physicalDeliveryOfficeName`. See Section 3.14 for more information about LDAP names.) Similarly, you should not be

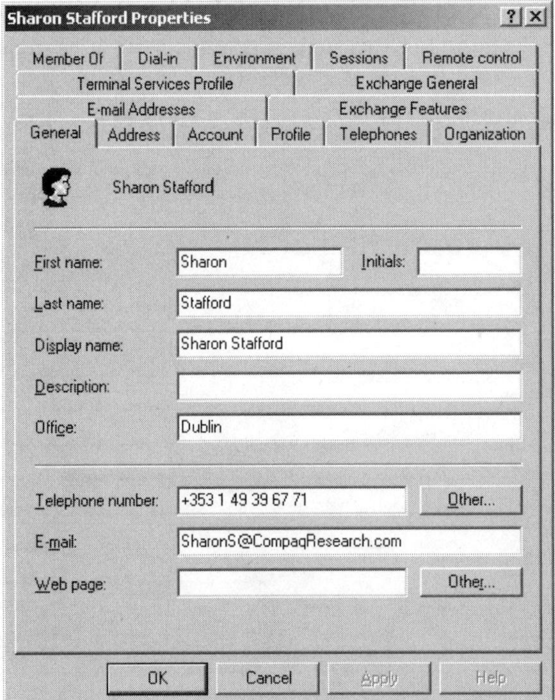

Figure 3.14 *Active Directory user object properties.*

surprised to learn that there is another mapping rule in the mapping table that maps the Exchange 5.5 City attribute value to the Active Directory City attribute. This rule (we'll call it Rule 2) is as follows:

```
local###l#l###0#
```

In this case `l` (the letter ell and an abbreviation for locality) is the LDAP name for the City attribute. (Again, see Section 3.14 for more information about LDAP names.)

For the customized mapping that you require, you want the Active Directory Office attribute to take on the value of the Exchange 5.5 City attribute. This is done by changing Rule 1 so that it now reads as follows:

```
local###l#physicalDeliveryOfficeName###0#
```

There's no need to modify Rule 2, since the ADC can map a single Exchange 5.5 Directory Service source attribute to multiple target attributes in the Active Directory. Thus, when the ADC synchronizes the Exchange 5.5 mailbox shown in Figure 3.13, Sharon Stafford will be represented in the Active Directory with an Office value of Dublin, not Belfield, as shown in Figure 3.14. Furthermore, if you were to look at the Active Directory City attribute for Sharon Stafford, you'd see that the value of that attribute was Dublin. In this situation then, the synchronization has performed a one-to-many mapping of attribute data form the Exchange 5.5 Directory Service to the Active Directory.

3.12.3 Conflicting mapping rules

Within the schema mapping table there is no concept of mapping rule precedence. That is, if you have two rules that define mappings to the same target attribute, the latter rule will not override the former, nor will the former override the latter. In this example, with the `physicalDeliveryOfficeName` target Active Directory attribute, if you have two rules attempting to map to this attribute, the synchronization operation for the entire object being synchronized will fail. Figure 3.15 shows the entry that you'll see in the Event Log if you have two mapping rules directed to the same target attribute.

The Constraint Violation error is returned because `physicalDeliveryOfficeName` is a single-valued attribute and the ADC actually processes both mapping rules and attempts to assign both values to the target attribute. This results in an error and the synchronization operation for this object is aborted. However, for multivalued attributes, having multiple

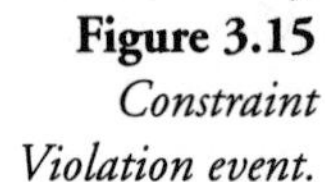

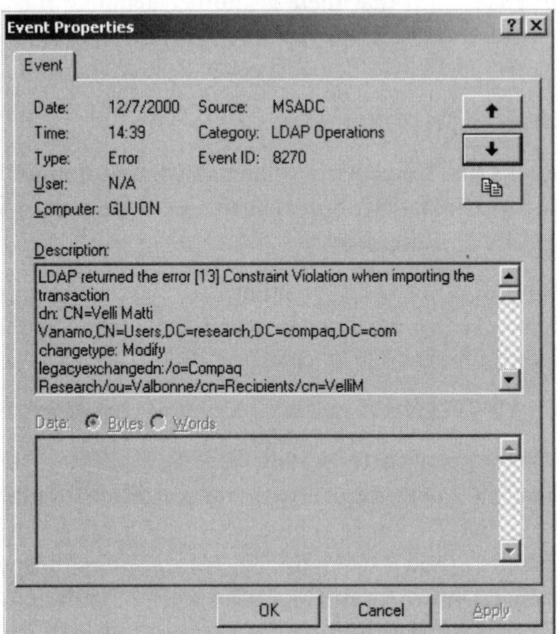

Figure 3.15 *Constraint Violation event.*

mapping rules targeting the same attribute is valid and processing will be carried out as normal.

3.12.4 Attribute mapping rule changes and when they take effect

When you make a modification to the attribute mapping table, the changes in the attribute mapping policy (either on the Default ADC Policy or on individual CAs) take effect the very next time that the ADC initiates a synchronization cycle. If the ADC creates a new object during the subsequent synchronization run, then the new mappings will be applied. However, for existing objects that have already been synchronized either into the Active Directory or into the Exchange 5.5 Directory Service, the mere action of changing the attribute mapping rules is not sufficient to see the target object updated in line with the new mapping rules. In the example used here, if Sharon Stafford's Exchange 5.5 mailbox has already been synchronized into the Active Directory as a user object, and when you make changes to the attribute mapping rules, you will see no changes to the synchronized Active Directory object after you apply the new policy and the ADC initiates its next synchronization cycle.

Updates related to the new attribute mapping rules will only be applied to previously synchronized objects if some change on the source object causes the ADC to process it again for synchronization. Such a change would include updating a telephone number attribute or an address field, for example. In this case, the source object is reselected for synchronization and any attribute mapping that you have specified in the tables will be applied.

In the example cited here, I've described the manipulation of the Office and City attributes more to illustrate the point than anything else, but you can apply these rules to all attributes associated with directory objects. In many cases, "as-is" mapping will be sufficient, but other attributes may deserve some special attention. Custom attributes are the most likely candidates for nonstandard handling, since organizations use them in different ways and often for different reasons. For example, custom attributes might be used to hold cost center information, employee numbers, or Social Security numbers that you don't wish synchronize. Or you may have defined new attributes in the Active Directory Schema specifically for these attributes and you wish to remap custom attributes to these new attributes.

3.13 Active Directory Distinguished Name mapping

Objects created in the Active Directory by the ADC have a Distinguished Name (DN) that is generated from a combination of the Active Directory container in which the object is being created and an Exchange 5.5 attribute associated with the source object. For example, with Sharon Stafford's mailbox, shown in Figure 3.14, the DN that is built in the Active Directory (we'll call it DN 1) is `CN=Sharon Stafford,CN=Users,DC=research, DC=compaq,DC=com`.

Specifically, the least significant Relative Distinguished Name (RDN) part of the DN, in this case `CN=Sharon Stafford`, is determined directly from the Exchange 5.5 mailbox Display Name attribute. In the Exchange 5.5 Directory Service, the LDAP name for the Display Name attribute is `cn`. Accordingly, there is a special rule in the `msExchServer2SchemaMap` table that explicitly defines the RDN for any Active Directory objects that the ADC will create. This rule is the last rule in the mapping table and is defined as `local###cn#Override_RDN_Value###140#`.

The syntax of this rule is different from the other rules in the mapping table. There's no "real" Active Directory attribute that's shown in the rule, but the `Override_RDN_Value` string acts as a directive that instructs the

ADC to modify the RDN of the ADC created object. In this case, the default behavior of the rule is to build the RDN of the Active Directory object based on the `cn` attribute of the source Exchange 5.5 mailbox.

You can modify this rule so that a different source attribute is used for the construction of the RDN. For example, you could replace the source `cn` attribute with the `sn` attribute so that the surname attribute of the Exchange 5.5 mailbox is used, or you could replace it with the `mailNickname` attribute so that the Exchange 5.5 mailbox's alias name is used.

This RDN creation directive, as well as applying to new objects that the ADC creates in the Active Directory, also affects existing objects in the Active Directory with which the ADC successfully carries out a matching operation. For example, let's assume that you had migrated a Windows NT4 user account to a Windows 2000 user object using a tool such as Microsoft's Active Directory Migration Tool (ADMT) before you start synchronizing with the ADC. When ADMT creates the new user object in Windows 2000, it will build the least significant RDN part of the DN using the Windows NT4 SAM account name—let's assume that it is "Stafford" in this case. This will create an object in the Active Directory with a DN (we'll call it DN 2) of `CN=stafford,CN=Users,DC=research,DC=compaq,DC=com`.

When the ADC begins its synchronization activity for the first time, it may well match the Exchange 5.5 mailbox object with this existing account in the Active Directory. (It matches the Exchange 5.5 mailbox `Assoc-NT-Account` attribute with the `sIDHistory` attribute of the Active Directory object.) When the match is made, in addition to synchronizing attributes from the Exchange 5.5 mailbox into the existing Active Directory object, the RDN override rule forces the Active Directory object's DN to be updated from that shown in DN 2 to become one, based on the Exchange 5.5 Display Name attribute, and ultimately it becomes that shown in DN 1—that is, the RDN changes from `Stafford` to `Sharon Stafford`.

While this RDN mapping yields esthetically pleasing, or so-called pretty DNs, as an administrator you may dislike it. The potential reasons for this emotive response are varied, but include the possibility of confusion associated with DNs that change during the course of the migration, the possibility of duplicate Exchange 5.5 Display Names—which results in the appending of `-1` to the DN, and the potential impact to applications or processes that rely on consistent DNs.

In any event, as an administrator you may wish to either disable the RDN mapping rule altogether using the `0x10` flag described in Section

3.15.4, or map it to an attribute consistent with the existing RDN structure—perhaps using the Exchange 5.5 mailbox alias if it corresponds to the Windows NT4 SAM Account Name. In this case, an analysis of your existing Exchange 5.5 environment and possibly a cleanup exercise on the environment before deploying and activating the ADC is crucial.

You can also disable the RDN mapping by setting the `msExch-Server1Flags` attribute on the appropriate CA to the value of 2. (See TechNet article Q269843 for more information.)

3.14 Exchange 5.5 and LDAP names

In the mapping rules discussed previously, `physicalDeliveryOfficeName` in Rule 1 is the LDAP attribute name for the Exchange 5.5 Office attribute. Similarly, `l` (the letter "ell") in Rule 2 is the LDAP attribute name for the Exchange 5.5 City attribute.

You can determine the LDAP name of any Exchange 5.5 attribute by using the Exchange 5.5 Administrator program in raw mode (execute the command `EXCHSRVR/BIN/ADMIN.EXE /R`). While in the Administrator program, drop down from the View menu and select Raw Directory. On the left-hand side of the Administrator window, you'll see the Schema displayed underneath the site, and, upon selecting it, you'll see the entire

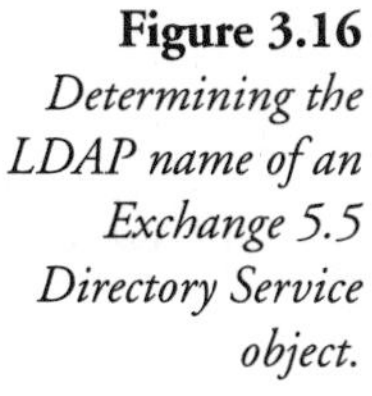

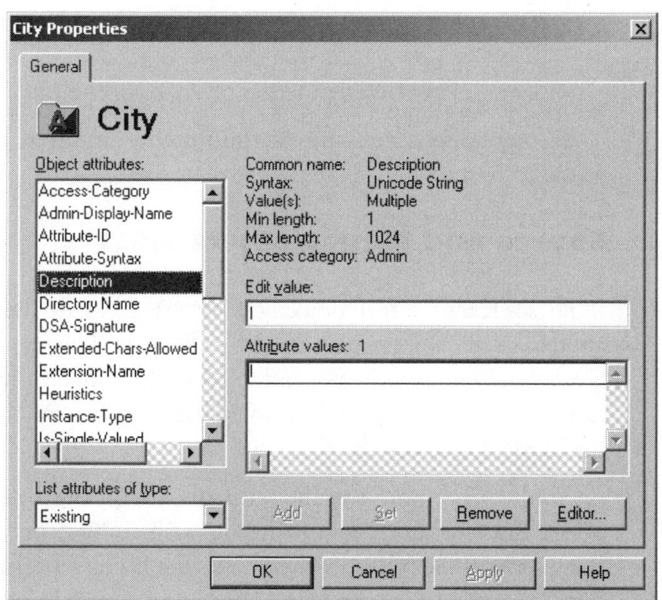

Figure 3.16 *Determining the LDAP name of an Exchange 5.5 Directory Service object.*

Exchange 5.5 Directory Service schema displayed in the right-hand pane of the window. Select an object by Display Name and the LDAP attribute name can be found by looking at the value of the `Description` attribute. Figure 3.16 shows this for the City attribute.

3.15 Attribute mapping rule syntax

The syntax of the attribute mapping rules is defined as follows:

```
<name>#<soc>#<toc>#<sa>#<ta>#<prefix>#<syntax>#<flags>#
```

where,

`<name>`, defines an arbitrary name for the mapping rule

`<soc>`, defines the object class of the source object used in mapping

`<toc>`, defines the object class of the target object used in the mapping

`<sa>`, defines the LDAP name of the source attribute used in the mapping

`<ta>`, defines the LDAP name of the target attribute used in the mapping

`<prefix>`, defines a prefix to the source attribute used in the mapping

`<syntax>`, defines the mapping syntax used in the mapping

`<flags>`, flags that define the behavior of the mapping rule

In most cases, the syntax definitions are intuitive, but let's analyze each of the constructs.

3.15.1 Source and target object classes

If no source or target object classes are defined, then the mapping rule applies to all objects processed by the CA. This typically includes mailboxes, custom recipients, and distribution lists from the Exchange 5.5 Directory Service and mail-enabled user objects, contacts, and groups from the Active Directory.

You can be more specific with mapping rules by specifying the entire object class hierarchy to which you wish to have the mapping rule apply. For example, the following mapping rule is only applied when an Exchange 5.5 distribution list is being mapped to an Active Directory group:

```
local#groupofnames$person$top#group$top#home-
MTA#msExchExpansionServerName###0#
```

3.15.2 Prefix

Using the prefix construct allows you to prepend a fixed text string to the value of the source attribute that will be written to the target attribute. The text string should not be quoted, and all characters in this field will be written directly into the target attribute.

3.15.3 Syntax

In most cases you can leave the syntax construct blank, but if the attribute you are mapping is a DN, then you must specify the value `DN` in this part of the mapping rule. For example, in Rule 1, the attribute being mapped (`physicalDeliveryOfficeName`) is of syntax `DirectoryString`. (You can see this from the Syntax label when using the Exchange 5.5 Administrator in raw mode to look at the source attribute and when using ADSI Edit to look at the target attribute.)

However, the following mapping rule (let's call it Rule 3):

```
local#organizationalPerson$person$top#user$organizationa
lperson$person$top#Manager#Manager##DN#2#
```

defines a mapping for the `Manager` attribute, which is a DN. Accordingly, you must set the syntax to DN on the rule.

3.15.4 Mapping rule flags

A mapping rule flag is a hexadecimal number that refines the specific behavior of the individual mapping. You can aggregate flags together to provide composite functionality. For example, a flag of `0x140` causes the behavior associated with both the `0x100` flag and the `0x40` flag. Table 3.1 provides a summary of the flag mapping behavior.

3.16 Summary

The ADC is very flexible when it comes to controlling those objects that you will synchronize from one directory to another. In this chapter, I've primarily described controlling the flow of objects from the Exchange 5.5 Directory Service to the Active Directory. However, the same sophistication for controlling object flow in the direction of the Active Directory to the

Table 3.1 *Flag Descriptions for the Attribute Mapping Rules*

Flag	Description
0x1	Used when the source attribute is multivalued, but the target attribute is single-valued and causes the first source value to be mapped into the target attribute.
0x2	Used when the source attribute has a DN syntax, but the ADC can't find the DN in the target directory. In such cases the source value is written to the unmerged attributes list for fix-up later when the DN can be resolved.
0x4	Used when the source attribute is single-valued, but the target attribute is multivalued and causes the source value to be written into the first target value.
0x8	Used when the source attribute is multivalued and the target attribute is single-valued and causes all values from the source attribute to be written as a single value in the target attribute as a comma-separated list.
0x10	Disables the mapping rule.
0x20	Used when the source attribute is a custom attribute used for mapping purposes and not exposed in the directory schema. Reserved for internal ADC use.
0x40	Used when the target attribute is a custom attribute used for mapping purposes and not exposed in the directory schema. Reserved for internal ADC use.
0x100	Mapping rule is hidden from the ADC Manager snap-in interface.
0x200	If the CA allows, merge the source value into the target attribute rather than overwriting.
0x400	If the source value is of type DN syntax and the link cannot be resolved, add the value into the Exchange 2000 unmerged attributes list.

Exchange 5.5 Directory Service is available using a similar set of attributes on the Default ADC Policy and on individual CAs.

Using LDAP search filters and/or custom-matching rules offers great flexibility for sequencing object synchronization and controlling the synchronization of resource mailboxes when designing and overseeing migrations from Exchange 5.5 to Exchange 2000.

In many environments there is no need to interfere with ADC attribute mapping. Attributes in the Exchange 5.5 Directory Service have natural counterparts in the Active Directory, and mappings between the two environments are predefined when you install the ADC. Some unique circumstances may require the odd mapping modification here or there, especially if an organization has made heavy use of custom attributes.

While the requirement to change mapping rules is likely to be minimal, what's more likely is the requirement to change the way in which the ADC creates or modifies the DN for objects in the Active Directory. Being able to suppress DN modification or map it using a different source attribute is sure to be a big plus for the integration of the legacy Exchange 5.5 Directory Service with the new Active Directory.

4

The Site Replication Service

4.1 Introduction

The Site Replication Service (SRS) is for the most part a not-so-well-understood component of Exchange 2000. In general, it is believed to be a new component of Exchange that allows an Exchange 2000 server to synchronize directory information with an Exchange 5.5 server. To some extent this is true, but, if anything, the SRS could be said to be old technology. The SRS is a reincarnation of the legacy Exchange 5.5 Directory Service. Its function in life is to allow an Exchange 2000 server to participate in Exchange 5.5–style directory replication. Why might an Exchange 2000 server need to do this? Surely the ADC with its concept of ConfigCAs provides all of the Exchange 5.5/Exchange 2000 interoperability that is required? This chapter sets out to clear up all of that confusion.

4.2 The SRS does not job share with the ADC!

One thing should be borne in mind: Only the ADC provides the mechanism to perform directory synchronization between the Exchange 5.5 Directory Service and the Active Directory. The SRS plays no real direct part with this exchange of information (although it can be involved and we'll discuss this later). But what the SRS does do is present itself as an Exchange 5.5 Directory Service to other Exchange 5.5 servers while running on an Exchange 2000 server. You could say that the SRS fools other Exchange 5.5 servers into thinking that they are communicating (on a directory level at least) with an Exchange 5.5 server, when in reality the server is actually running Exchange 2000. The SRS doesn't run by default on Exchange 2000 servers, only on certain servers, and the SRS is only available if you're running Exchange 2000 in a mixed-mode Exchange organization.

Using the SRS to provide a shadow Exchange 5.5 Directory Service on an Exchange 20000 server allows other Exchange 5.5 servers to continue with Exchange 5.5 directory replication to that server in the same way as before, even after that server has been upgraded to Exchange 2000. Maintaining this kind of functionality is beneficial both to the existing Exchange 5.5 servers and the new Exchange 2000 servers and makes for a simpler coexistence environment.

Bear this in mind: The ADC synchronizes Exchange 5.5 Directory Service information with the Active Directory; the SRS participates only in Exchange 5.5 direct replication and has no connection to the Active Directory.

4.2.1 Exchange 5.5 Directory replication

With the Exchange 5.5 Directory Service, there are the concepts of intrasite replication and intersite replication between servers. Intrasite replication takes place between servers in a site using RPC-based connections, while intersite replication is mail based and takes place over a Directory Replication Connector (DRC) between bridgehead servers in separate sites. The SRS, in its role as a shadow Exchange 5.5 Directory Service, supports both of these forms of Exchange 5.5 directory replication.

4.2.2 When is the SRS activated?

Although the SRS components are installed every time that you install Exchange 2000 or upgrade an Exchange 5.5 server, the SRS service will not always be enabled on each and every Exchange 2000 server. Although the components are installed by default, the SRS service is only configured and enabled under certain circumstances. These circumstances are as follows:

- When you upgrade an Exchange 5.5 server to Exchange 2000 and this Exchange 2000 server is the first in the Exchange 5.5 site
- When you install an Exchange 2000 server into an Exchange 5.5 site and this Exchange 2000 server is the first in the Exchange 5.5 site
- When an Exchange 5.5 bridgehead server is upgraded to Exchange 2000, even if other Exchange 2000 servers exist in the exchange 5.5 site

The SRS works in conjunction with the ADC to make the whole mechanism of Exchange 5.5 Directory Service to Active Directory synchronization simpler and offer reduced burden to system administrators.

Specifically, the SRS makes the management of Connection Agreements (CAs) simpler by providing an alternative and constant source of Exchange 5.5 directory information.

4.3 The components that comprise the SRS

The SRS consists of three major components, as follows:

1. A Directory Service that is based heavily on the Exchange 5.5 Directory Service replete with database and transaction logs along with its own replication engine
2. A Knowledge Consistency Checker (KCC) based heavily on the Exchange 5.5 KCC
3. A Super Knowledge Consistency Checker (SKCC), which is a new piece of code that understands the Active Directory configuration information as well as the Exchange 5.5 site topology and thus has a complete topological view of a mixed-mode Exchange 2000 organization

The SRS functionality is instantiated by a set of files that provides directory replication functionality between the Exchange 5.5 Directory Service and an SRS database on an Exchange 2000 server. You should find the following files on your Exchange 2000 installation:

`SRS.EXE`, which provides the main functionality, similar to the Exchange 5.5 Directory Service

`SRSCHECK.DLL`, which provides directory replication consistency checking

`SRSMAPI.DLL`, which provides directory replication mail services when the SRS is operating in intersite replication mode

`SRSPERF.DLL`, which provides performance information to Perfmon

`SRSMSG.DLL`, which provides event logging functionality

`SRSXDS.DLL`, which provides the API services to access SRS directory using the XDS protocol

`SRS.EDB`, which provides the directory service database file (the file that was formerly known as `DIR.EDB` on Exchange 5.5 servers)

These files all provide the SRS service that runs with the key `MSExchangeSRS`, under the display name of `Microsoft Exchange Site Replication Service`. Additionally, you'll find a set of transaction logs (named similar to EDB00045.LOG), each up to 5 MB in size, that will be removed when the SRS database is backed up.

4.4 SRS operation with intrasite replication

In this section, we'll take a look at some example environments involving the ADC and the SRS and understand how these components operate with each other.

Figure 4.1 shows an Exchange 5.5 site (hosting only Exchange 5.5 servers) with a CA homed against one of the servers, S4. This is a valid configuration and operates well, allowing Exchange 5.5 Directory Service information from server S4 to be synchronized into the Active Directory. Specifically, the CA is well defined, because it has a valid source of Exchange 5.5 directory information—that is, the information from the Exchange 5.5 Directory Service on server S4.

4.4.1 Using the SRS as an Exchange 5.5 server is upgraded

You need to understand what happens when you upgrade the server S4 from an Exchange 5.5 server to an Exchange 2000 server. After the upgrade,

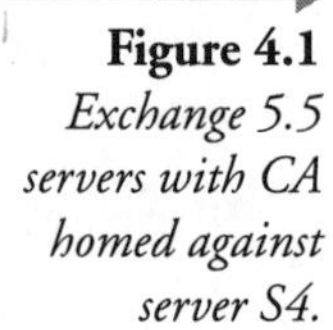

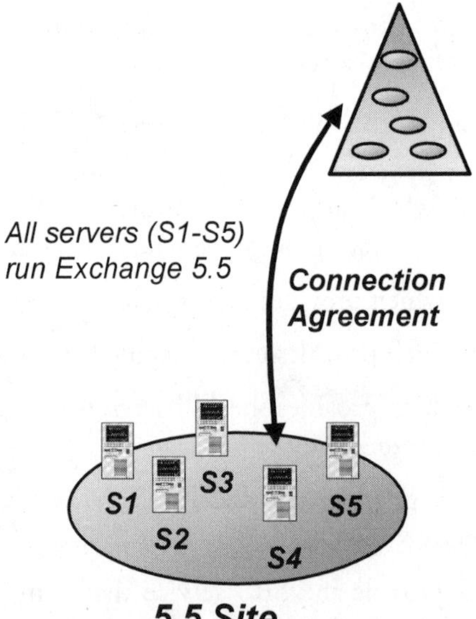

Figure 4.1 *Exchange 5.5 servers with CA homed against server S4.*

and in the absence of the SRS, the integrity of the CA from S4 to the Active Directory is immediately compromised, because if S4 is now an Exchange 2000 server then it will not have an Exchange 5.5 Directory Service that can act as the source end point for the CA. In such a case the CA is unusable. Again, in the absence of the SRS, your only option is to rehome the Exchange 5.5 Directory Service end point of the CA onto another server. Accordingly, you could use server S5 as an alternative Exchange 5.5 Directory Service. This would certainly reestablish the integrity of the CA, but, again, you would similarly have to rehome this CA again to a different Exchange 5.5 server when subsequently you upgrade server S5 to an Exchange 2000 server. This rehoming activity could repeat itself ad infinitum unless you made sure to initially home the CA against an Exchange 5.5 server that you were confident would be the last Exchange 5.5 server in the site to be migrated to Exchange 2000.

The requirement of this form of administrative attention to your CAs and Exchange 5.5 servers isn't altogether unworkable, but it is troublesome, whereas administration effort would be much simpler if you could merely ignore it. That's the primary function of the SRS: to reduce this administrative overhead associated with CA rehoming.

4.4.2 Using the SRS to maintain Connection Agreement integrity

With reference to Figure 4.1, assume that the first Exchange 5.5 server in the site to be upgraded to Exchange 2000 is server S4. This is in line with one of the rules for having the SRS enabled: It is the first Exchange 2000 server to appear in the Exchange 5.5 site. In this circumstance, when the upgrade is performed, the SRS becomes active, and, because it takes part in Exchange 5.5 directory replication, just as any other Exchange 5.5 server, it has a perfectly valid replica of the Exchange 5.5 Directory Service in its SRS database. This scenario is shown in Figure 4.2.

The activated SRS on server S4 means that you have not compromised the integrity of the existing CA that's homed against server S4. Because the SRS is available, the CA has a valid source of Exchange 5.5 directory information and there's no need to manually rehome the CA. This is more straightforward than having to rehome CAs time after time, effectively chasing Exchange 5.5 servers. Having a single server, which you can be confident will always provide a source of Exchange 5.5 directory information, is clearly useful.

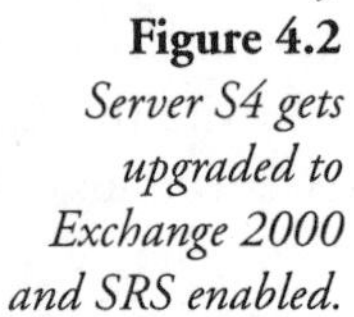

Figure 4.2 *Server S4 gets upgraded to Exchange 2000 and SRS enabled.*

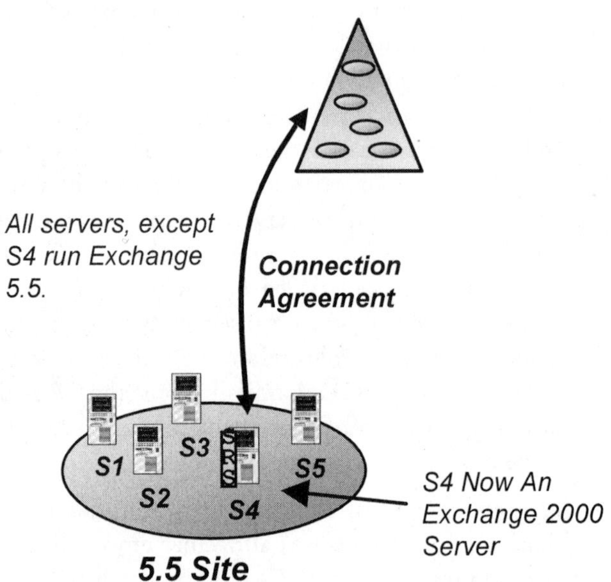

4.4.3 Homing Connection Agreements against the SRS

When you home a CA against a regular Exchange 5.5 server, you must map the Exchange 5.5 end point of the CA to the LDAP protocol of the Exchange 5.5 Directory Service. By default, the Exchange 5.5 LDAP protocol is active on port 389, but you can enable LDAP on any other port number if you wish. Typically, you might only do this for an Exchange 5.5 server if it is running on a Windows 2000 Domain Controller. In such a case, the Active Directory on a Windows 2000 Domain Controller listens on port 389 as well, and, as Windows 2000 is starting up, it will map its own LDAP service to port 389 before the Exchange 5.5 Directory Service and LDAP protocol component can attempt the same operation.

You'll find a similar issue with the SRS. The SRS will only be running on a Windows 2000 system, and it is entirely possible that this system may be a Windows 2000 Domain Controller. CAs always connect to a source of Exchange 5.5 directory information using the LDAP protocol, and, in order to simplify operation, the SRS is designed so that it offers its LDAP service from port 379. This being the case, if you had previously homed your CA against an Exchange 5.5 Directory Service on port 389, you would have to modify the CA configuration so that it now points to port 379 to get to the SRS directory service on an Exchange 2000 server.

There is some system management work associated with the SRS by virtue of the fact that any existing CAs that are homed against a native Exchange 5.5 Directory Service must be reconfigured to be directed to an SRS server. However, a structured approach to your migration strategy, especially in an environment that has many sites and servers, will warrant little reconfiguration work and will reduce constant administrative attention to your coexistence environment.

4.4.4 Modifications to the intrasite replication chain

Within any Exchange 5.5 site, an Exchange 5.5 server communicates with other Exchange 5.5 servers to keep the information in its directory service consistent with the information in the directory services of all the other Exchange 5.5 servers. This is the essence of intrasite directory replication. The component responsible for controlling this process and ensuring that each server has up-to-date directory information is the Knowledge Consistency Checker (KCC). The KCC is found on every Exchange 5.5 server. In order to maintain directory consistency it maintains a memory-resident list of all Exchange 5.5 servers that are to take part in the replication chain. This list is known as the KCC Table.

As most Exchange 5.5 servers in an Exchange 5.5 site are upgraded to Exchange 2000, many will not have the SRS enabled, since only the first Exchange 2000 server in the site and bridgehead servers qualify for the SRS. In these cases, the Exchange 2000 upgrade process removes the entry for the server being upgraded from the KCC Table. For example, for the systems shown in Figure 4.2, presuming that they are not bridgehead servers, servers S1, S2, S3, and S5 will be removed from the KCC Table and accordingly will not participate in the Exchange 5.5 intrasite replication chain. (Actually, it's not the Exchange server that is removed from the KCC Table but the DSA object for that Exchange 5.5 server.) This ensures that they no longer take part in Exchange 5.5 intrasite replication. If this process did not take place, then remaining Exchange 5.5 servers would consistently report errors to the event log, indicating that their intrasite replication partners could not be contacted.

4.5 SRS operation with intersite replication

When an Exchange 5.5 directory replication bridgehead server is upgraded to become an Exchange 2000 server, it must maintain a means by which it

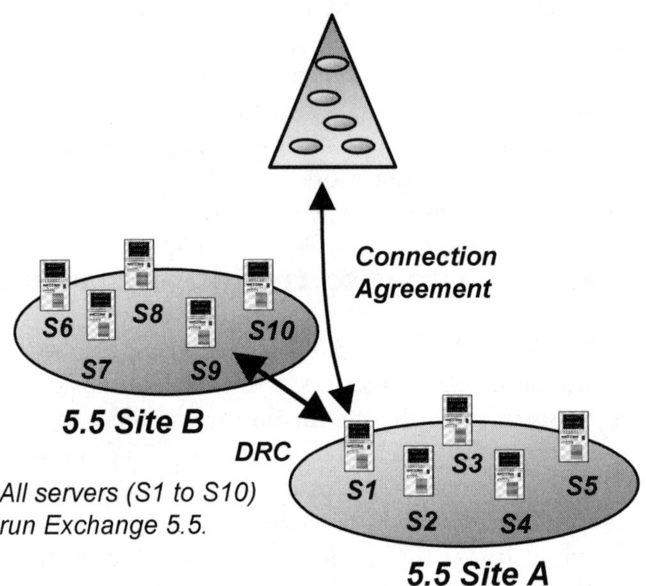

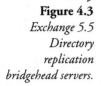

Figure 4.3 *Exchange 5.5 Directory replication bridgehead servers.*

can communicate directory information to its Exchange 5.5 bridgehead replication partner. Remember that upgrading an Exchange 5.5 bridgehead server will always result in the SRS being activated. The SRS allows this replication to take place, since it appears to the directory replication partner that there is still an Exchange 5.5 Directory Service to communicate with, despite the fact that the Exchange 5.5 server has been upgraded to Exchange 2000. This is shown in Figure 4.3, where the figure shows the original situation with two Exchange 5.5 directory replication bridgehead servers, S9 and S1, respectively, communicating across a DRC.

When Exchange 5.5 server S1 is upgraded to an Exchange 2000 server, the scenario that develops is shown in Figure 4.4.

The SRS is clearly indispensable in this circumstance, because, once again, it reduces the administrative effort associated with upgrading servers. Note that there is no CA in the pure Exchange 5.5 site, Site B. This means that all site and topology information for Site B must come from traditional Exchange 5.5 intersite directory replication. In the absence of an SRS service, Exchange 5.5 DRCs must be rehomed to alternative servers as bridgehead servers are upgraded from Exchange 5.5. In this example, upgrading server S1 from Exchange 5.5 to Exchange 2000 would imply rehoming the DRC to an alternative server in the site, say server S2, since this would be a valid source of Exchange 5.5 directory information.

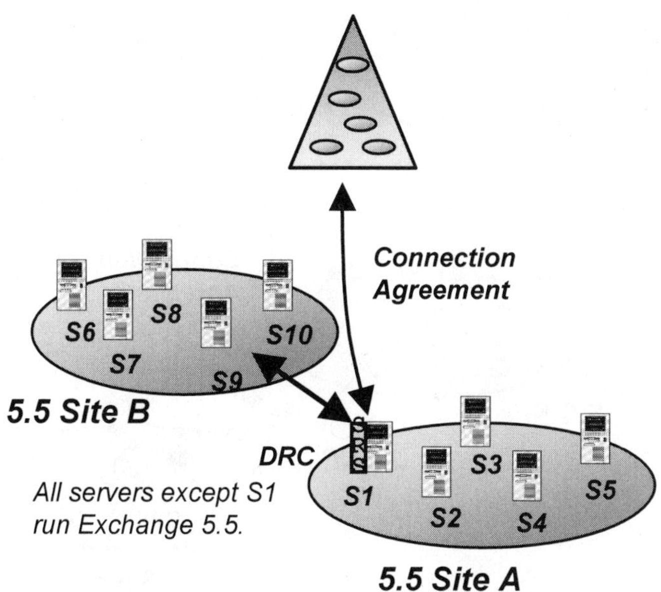

Figure 4.4 *Upgrading an Exchange 5.5 bridgehead server to Exchange 2000.*

By using the scenario I've just described, we can evolve the directory communication by optimizing the relationship between CAs and DRCs. If a CA is configured between the Active Directory and a source of Exchange 5.5 directory information in Site B, then we have two possible means by which recipient directory information can be delivered into that site: across the DRC and via the CAs. Similarly, when an Exchange 2000 server is introduced into Site B for the first time, a ConfigCA will automatically be created to synchronize configuration information to the site. With Exchange 5.5 directory replication, the directory replication model is object based, whereas replication via Active Directory is attribute based. Therefore, it can be more efficient to use the Active Directory to provide directory information rather than the DRCs. This is especially true if the DRC extends across a wide-area network connection. Although, ultimately, the same amount of data needs to be synchronized via a CA from an Exchange 5.5 Directory Service to the Active Directory as might be synchronized across a DRC, if changes are made to objects, only attribute-level replication within the Active Directory will be performed. If the Active Directory extends over a wide area connection, then replicating simply a changed object represents better bandwidth use than replicating the entire object.

In this case, as shown in Figure 4.5, the DRC between the two Exchange 5.5 sites can be disabled, and you can rely on the ADC-based synchroniza-

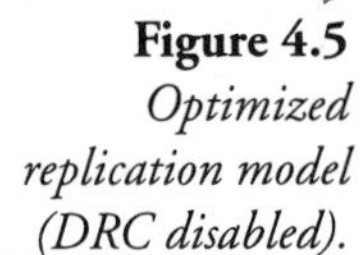

Figure 4.5 *Optimized replication model (DRC disabled).*

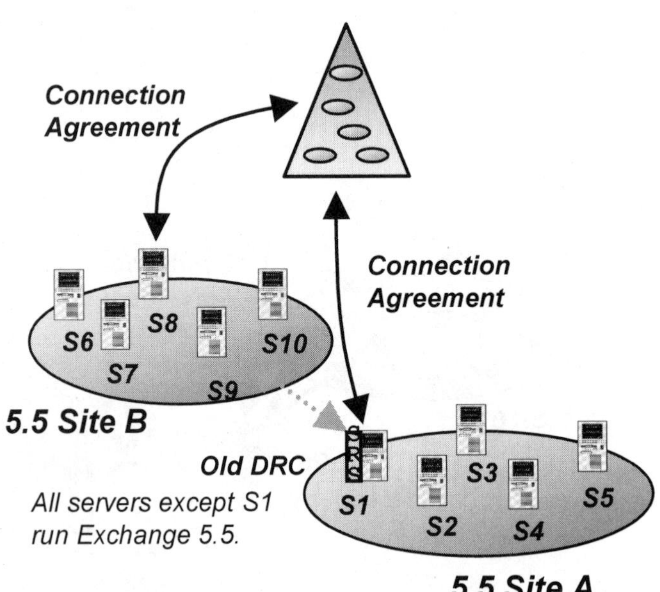

tion and Active Directory replication to communicate user and configuration information between the two Exchange 5.5 sites.

It is obvious with respect to intersite replication that the SRS is absolutely essential. Without it the management of DRCs would become a nuisance and would introduce all forms of administrative overhead. The SRS proves its worth for management of CAs within a site, but, coupled with managing connections between 5.5 bridgehead servers, it's essential.

4.6 What occurs during a bridgehead server upgrade?

In our example scenario, as server S1 gets upgraded to an Exchange 2000 server, the Exchange 2000 Setup program processes the existing local `DIR.EDB` database—the traditional 5.5 Directory Service—readying it for transformation to the SRS database. The upgrade process then copies the new executables for the SRS service from the installation CD-ROM and creates objects in the Configuration Naming Context of the Active Directory.

Specifically, there is an instance of an object of class `ms-Exch-Site-Replication-Service` to represent the SRS created in the Configuration Naming Context. An example of this default SRS object, which is named `Microsoft DSA`, is shown as a screenshot from ADSI Edit in Figure 4.6.

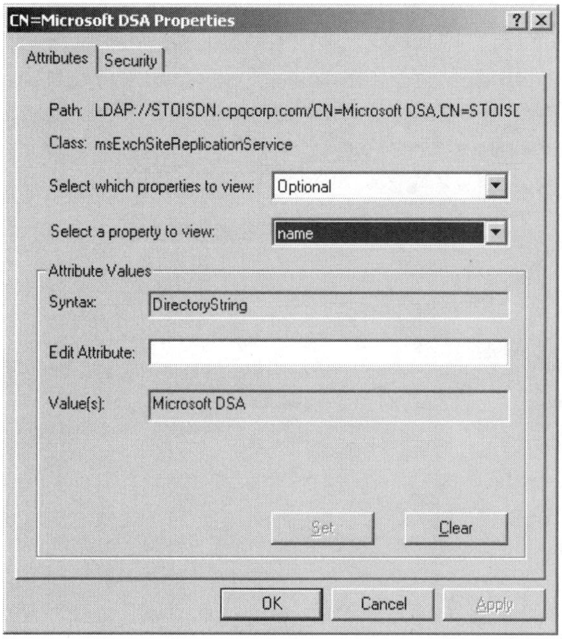

Figure 4.6 *The default Active Directory object for the SRS.*

In this case (when the server is the first Exchange 2000 server in the site), the Setup process also creates a ConfigCA to exchange configuration information for the site between the Active Directory and the new SRS service installed locally. The SRS takes on the ownership of the DRC to server S9 and because the SRS object in the Active Directory has a `legacyExchangeDN` attribute as follows:

```
/o=<OrgName>/ou=<Site>/cn=Configuration - /cn=Servers/
cn=S1/cn=Microsoft DSA
```

and it is a mail-enabled object, it becomes the destination for intersite replication messages from server S9. You should know that you can use any transport to send mail to the DSA and the same is true for the SRS object. Figure 4.7 shows the value of the `mail` attribute of the SRS. As you can see, it has an SMTP address, which means that any other Exchange 5.5 Directory Service can send directory information to it over an SMTP connector.

Reviewing the configuration situation, the SRS is connected via a DRC to the bridgehead server, S9, and via a ConfigCA to the Active Directory. The ConfigCA is two-way, replicating configuration information for the Exchange 5.5 view of Site A from the SRS to the Active Directory and back replicating information for the Administrative Group A (the Exchange 2000 view of the site) from the Active Directory to the SRS.

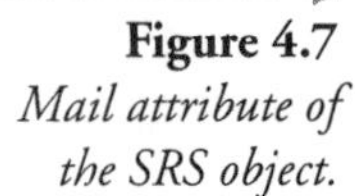

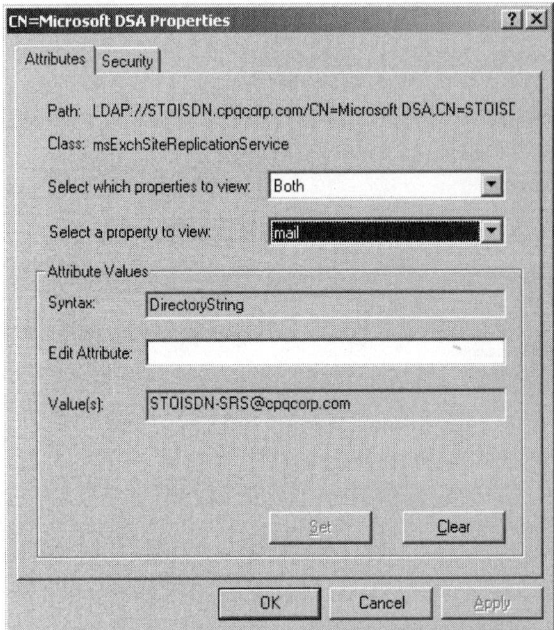

Figure 4.7 *Mail attribute of the SRS object.*

4.7 SRS management requirements

There is little exposed in the Exchange System Manager snap-in to allow control of the SRS. You can navigate to the Tools option, but when you right-click on the SRS object, the lack of any real management functionality is striking. There are few areas of the SRS management that you can control. Basically the service operates with little intervention and you should have no day-to-day management activity.

However, there are some system management operations that are always required. The `SRS.EDB` database is a direct descendant of the `DIR.EDB` database that was part of Exchange 5.5. With Exchange 5.5 servers, it was good system management practice to back up the Exchange 5.5 Directory Service as well as any information stores. While there is no requirement to back up the Active Directory when backing up an Exchange 2000 server, you may wish to consider backing up the SRS database on those servers that have it enabled. This is explicitly catered to from the Windows 2000 Backup Utility, as shown in Figure 4.8, and you should expect to see similar functionality present in your favorite third-party backup product.

Should you elect not to back up the SRS database directly, you can possibly rely on Exchange 5.5-based directory replication to repopulate it. How-

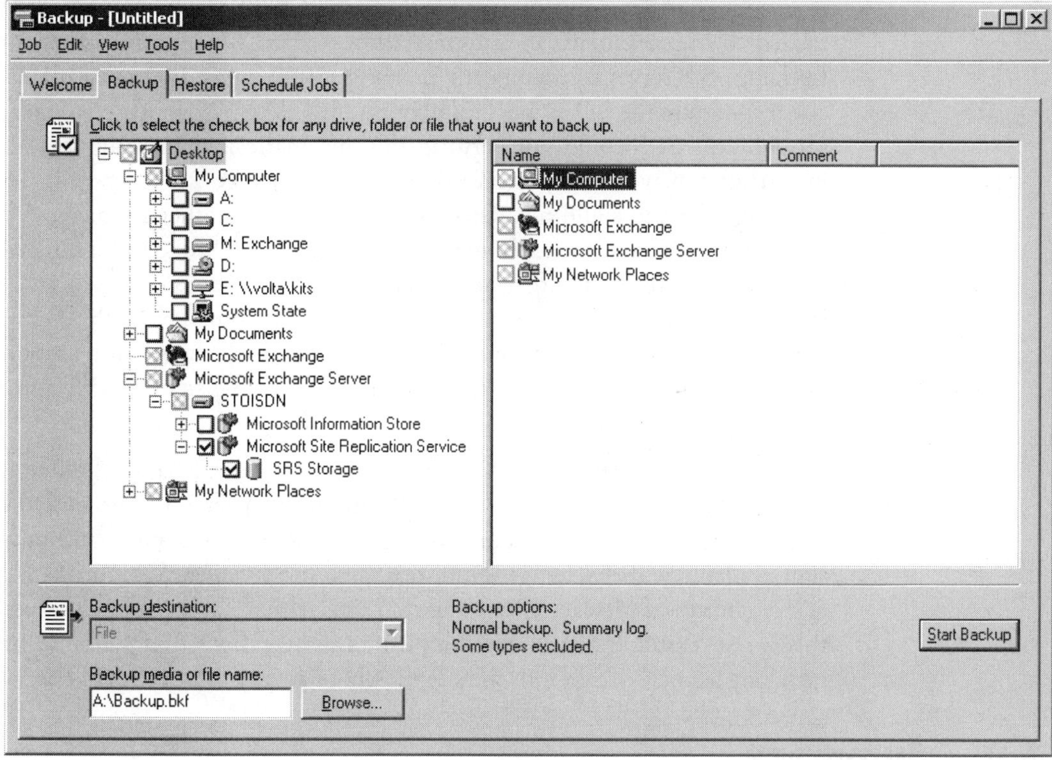

Figure 4.8 *Windows 2000 Backup Utility backing up the SRS database.*

ever, this is not advisable and may well result in significant replication activity on the SRS server and potentially heavy network traffic. On a related note, I'm not suggesting for one second that you do not back up the Active Directory. On the contrary, your Windows 2000 backup procedures should ensure that Active Directory data are suitably backed up and can be made available. However, in many circumstances, the complete loss of a Domain Controller can be more easily rectified by simply reinstalling a member server and promoting that server to become a Domain Controller (thus letting Active Directory replication effectively perform the restore) rather than restoring from backup media. Of course, in remote locations, where bandwidth is at a premium, this may not be the most effective process.

4.8 Other SRS considerations

It should be no surprise to see the functionality of the SRS improve in future releases of Exchange or Exchange Service Packs. This is especially true since the theme of the next few Exchange 2000 Service Packs will be related to improvements in administration. Today, when you upgrade an Exchange 5.5 server to become an Exchange 2000 server, you must manually reconfigure the LDAP port number on the CA to 379. There's little reason why the SRS could not perform this automatically. Similarly, there is little reason why a newly installed and first Exchange 2000 server in an Exchange 5.5 site could not detect a CA homed to another Exchange 5.5 server in the site and then rehome that CA to the local SRS database. All of the requisite information that needs to be modified for both of these scenarios exist in either the Exchange 5.5 Configuration container or the Active Directory Configuration Naming Context. Performing the reconfiguration merely requires analyzing this information and effecting some modification attributes of directory objects.

Currently, the SRS is not supported on clustered Exchange 2000 systems, so the first server that you install into an Exchange 5.5 site must be nonclustered. For organizations wishing to benefit from server consolidation available with Exchange 2000, this is an inconvenience. Similarly, for any organizations that have Exchange 5.5 sites with a single clustered server, this is also a problem. However, the issue can be easily worked around by installing a small system into the site merely to act as a host for the SRS.

4.9 Summary

I'm not for one second suggesting that the SRS was an afterthought in the design of Exchange 2000, but it would have been possible to build a coexisting Exchange 2000 environment without it. While it's a useful component of Exchange 2000, it's notcritical to Exchange 2000's operation or to coexistence with Exchange 5.5 servers. Admittedly, if there were no SRS administration of CAs, sequencing of server upgrades from Exchange 5.5 to Exchange 2000 would be more complicated.

In its present form, SRS augments the functionality of the ADC by guaranteeing a source of Exchange 5.5 directory information. Any migration plans that you draw up to move from Exchange 5.5 to Exchange 2000 will, in all likelihood, involve directory coexistence and use of the ADC. As you plan the sequencing of server upgrades and migrations, bear in mind how you can use SRS to help maintain directory consistency and reduce effort associated with reconfiguration of CAs.

5

Exchange 5.5 and Exchange 2000 Public Folder Interoperability

5.1 Introduction

Understanding and controlling the replication and affinity characteristics of Exchange 5.5 Public Folders has always been considered to be much more art than science. And with the introduction of Exchange 2000, we find ourselves with yet another dimension of Public Folder management with which to be concerned. Mixed mode Exchange 2000 environments must now consider the interoperability requirements of Public Folders that exist in both Exchange 5.5 and Exchange 2000. After a period of coexistence, there comes the inevitable requirement to migrate Exchange 5.5 Public Folders to Exchange 2000 servers.

In this chapter, I'll explore some of the core aspects of Public Folder coexistence in terms of Public Folder Connection Agreements—what they do and why you need them, the replication of Public Folder hierarchy, and the effect of permissions interoperability associated with groups and distribution lists.

5.2 Public Folder Connection Agreements

In addition to the ConfigCAs and Recipient CAs that I've already described, the ADC supports another type of CA for dealing with the replication of address information associated with Public Folders. The Public Folder CA (PFCA) replicates mail addresses assigned to Exchange 5.5 Public Folders into the Active Directory so that Exchange 2000 users have the capability to send mail directly to Public Folders in the same way that they could with Exchange 5.5. A typical application for these mail-enabled Public Folders in Exchange 5.5 environments is to include them as members of Exchange 5.5 DLs so that they offer an archive for all messages sent to the DL.

5.2.1 The need for Public Folder Connection Agreements

A recipient CA synchronizes Exchange 5.5 DLs as a Universal Distribution Group into the Active Directory, but a Public Folder's mail address cannot be included as a member of the Universal Distribution Group unless the Public Folder's mail address is specifically synchronized into the Active Directory too. (This is the same behavior that you expect to see with conventional user mailboxes as members of a Universal Distribution Group; in the Active Directory the user mailbox cannot be included as a member of the group unless it has previously been synchronized into the Active Directory.) You can create a PFCA just like any other CA. From the left Tree pane of the ADC Manager snap-in right-click on the Active Directory Connector Management root and select the option to create a new CA. You'll be prompted to create either a Recipient CA or a Public Folder CA.

By default, all Public Folders in an Exchange 5.5 organization have associated mail addresses. As with any other mail-enabled object in Exchange 5.5, an entry will exist in the Exchange 5.5 Directory Service for this mail-

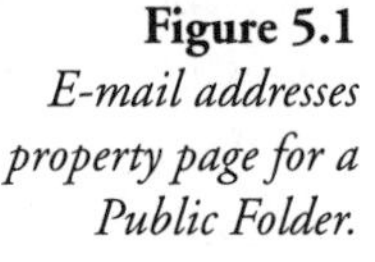

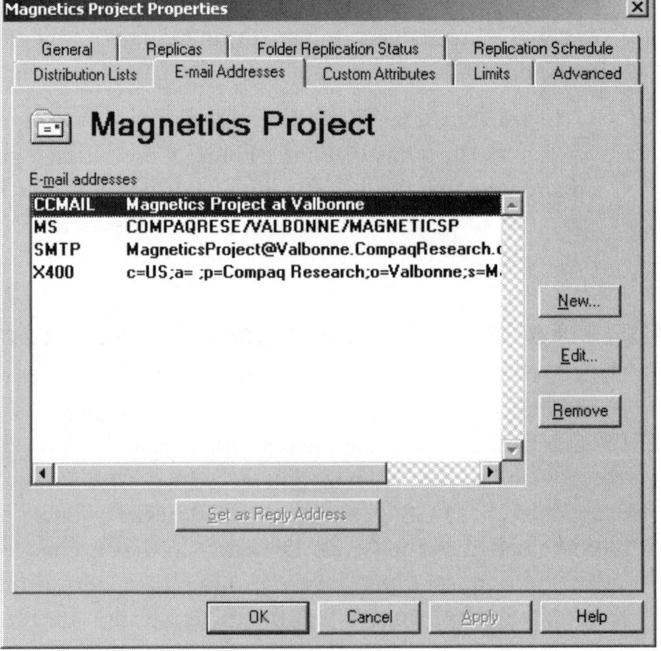

Figure 5.1 *E-mail addresses property page for a Public Folder.*

enabled Public Folder, and by default the entry is created in the Recipients container of the Public Folder's home site. You can change the default location where Public Folder directory entries are created by modifying the Public folder container property on the General property page of the Information Store Site Configuration. Although Public Folders have mail addresses associated with them, the directory entries are by default hidden from the GAL, so you won't normally see them in the Recipients container unless you are explicitly viewing hidden recipients.

Figure 5.1 shows the E-mail Addresses property page of a Public Folder, and, as you can see, it looks like any other mail-enabled object in the Exchange 5.5 Directory Service with addresses associated for the various transports available on the server.

5.2.2 Additional uses of Public Folder Connection Agreements

The basic function of PFCAs is to synchronize the mail addresses of Exchange 5.5 Public Folders into the Active Directory and, conversely, to synchronize the mail addresses of Exchange 2000 Public Folders into the Exchange 5.5 Directory Service. However, there are some other reasons why it is important to use one PFCA for each Exchange 5.5 site. These reasons are as follows:

- If you attempt to administer a Public Folder that is homed on an Exchange 5.5 server, you are using the Exchange System Manager snap-in, and you have not created an entry in the Active Directory for that Public Folder using a PFCA, access errors will be displayed. These errors are generated because the properties of the Exchange 5.5 Public Folder indicate that the Public Folder is mail enabled; however, when the Exchange System Manager snap-in attempts to query the Active Directory to retrieve the address properties, the properties cannot be retrieved. The address properties will only exist if the object has been synchronized to the Active Directory via a PFCA.
- When using the Exchange 5.5 Administrator program to administer Public Folders homed on Exchange 2000 servers, the Exchange 5.5 Administrator program expects that any Public Folders it accesses should have mail address properties associated with them, since this is the default behavior with Exchange 5.5 Public Folders. Accordingly, you must implement a PFCA to synchronize Public Folder mail

addresses from an Exchange 2000 Public Folder into the Exchange 5.5 Directory Service. If not, you cannot administer such Exchange 2000 Public Folders using the Exchange 5.5 Administrator program.

- Since Exchange 5.5 expects to have mail addresses associated with Public Folders, running the DS/IS consistency checker on a server in the Exchange 5.5 environment can cause problems. In a coexisting environment the Exchange 5.5 Public Folder store will have knowledge of Exchange 2000 Public Folders, since the Public Folder hierarchy is replicated by default (see Section 5.5). However, if the consistency checker does not find an associated Exchange 5.5 Directory Service entry for that Public Folder it will generate one. This can ultimately result in two separate and distinct mail addresses existing for the same Public Folder: one held in the Exchange 5.5 Directory Service and another held in the Active Directory. Furthermore, if you introduce a PFCA in the future, this may result in replication errors and mail may not be deliverable to the Public Folder.

5.3 Configuring Public Folder CAs

By using a specific type of CA for Public Folder mail addresses, Microsoft is able to predefine much of the configuration that can often be challenging with Recipient CAs in complex environments. (In prerelease versions of the Exchange 2000 ADC only one type of CA could be created from the ADC Manager snap-in; there was no differentiation between PFCAs and Recipient CAs. The replication of Public Folder mail addresses was included as an option on the single CA configuration.) So why is the configuration of a PFCA simpler? Well, for one thing, there is no option to make PFCAs one-way or two-way; they are two-way by default and you cannot modify this.

5.3.1 Public Folder Connection Agreement default container mapping

Other predefined options that you cannot change include the settings on the From Exchange and the From Windows property pages; you cannot specify the source or destination containers and OUs on either page because they are grayed-out. Nor can you specify the object types that you wish to synchronize, since the only eligible object types available for synchronization with a PFCA are Public Folders. This is shown in Figure 5.2, where the From Exchange properties are defined.

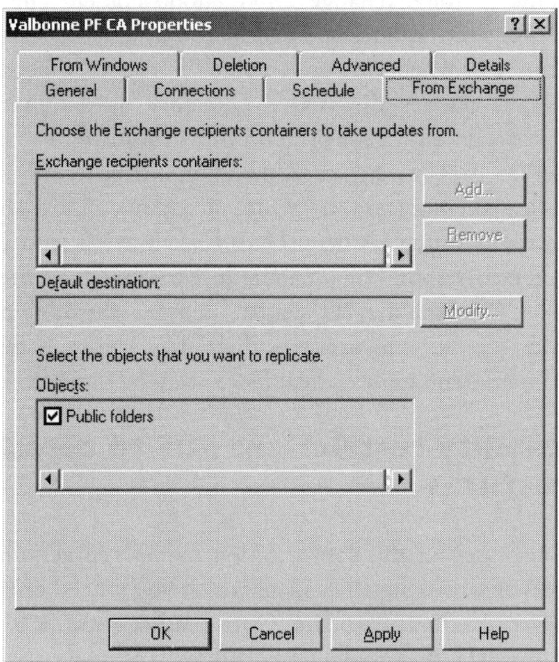

Figure 5.2 *From Exchange property page on a PFCA.*

You do not define the source container for Public Folder directory entries from the Exchange 5.5 Directory Service to the Active Directory, since the ADC searches for Public Folder directory objects in all containers including below the site-level container. However, typically the Public Folder directory objects will have been created in the Recipients container unless you've modified the default setting as described in Section 5.2. Similarly, you do not define a target location for where the synchronized objects will be placed, since these are by default created in the Microsoft Exchange System Objects container in the Active Directory. The Microsoft Exchange System Objects container is not by default part of the Active Directory. This container only gets created in the Active Directory when you run the Exchange 2000 SETUP.EXE program with the /DOMAINPREP option. By implication, you'll also have to run Exchange 2000 SETUP with the /FORESTPREP option to allow /DOMAINPREP to proceed.

In the opposite direction, the ADC only searches for Exchange 2000 Public Folder Active Directory objects in the Microsoft Exchange System Objects container, since all Public Folder directory objects are located here. As the ADC creates directory objects in the Exchange 5.5 Directory Service, it creates them in the container specified by the `legacyExchangeDN` attribute of the Exchange 2000 Public Folder. The legacyExchangeDN attribute is set on an Exchange 2000 Public Folder by the Exchange 2000 Store process when the Public Folder is created. When the Store process initializes, it queries the Active Directory to determine the value of the attribute msExchPfCreation on the Administrative Group object in which the server it is running on resides. This attribute will only be set if you have modified the location in which Exchange 5.5 Public Folder directory objects are created, as described in Section 5.2, and its value is replicated from the corresponding attribute in Exchange 5.5 Directory Service via the ConfigCA for the site. If the attribute is set, the Store process uses this value for the legacyExchangeDN of the Public Folder. If the attribute is not set, the legacyExchangeDN defaults to a value of Recipients.

5.3.2 Flexibility restrictions due to default container structures

Having much of the configuration predefined certainly does simplify the process of setting up PFCAs, of which you'll need one associated with each and every Exchange 5.5 site. On the other hand, it also reduces flexibility. One organization I spoke to recently was using a transition domain to temporarily house ADC-created objects, because it was rolling out Exchange 2000 before completing its Windows 2000 domain rollout. Of course, for this it needed a consistent GAL, so all Exchange 5.5 Directory Service objects, including Public Folders, had to be synchronized somewhere in the Active Directory, even temporarily.

The CA configurations that this organization used to create objects in the transition domain if the final Windows 2000 domain hasn't yet been deployed. When the Windows 2000 domain is finally deployed, the organization uses the MoveTree utility to relocate the ADC-created objects from the transition domain to their rightful home in the final domain. This approach works well for objects created using Recipient CAs, but, unfortunately, MoveTree does not move the Public Folder directory objects created by a PFCA. This means that the organization must maintain the transition domain forever, since it can neither move nor delete the Public Folder directory objects from the Microsoft Exchange System Objects container. Furthermore, PFCAs create Active Directory objects in a flat hierarchy manner in the Microsoft Exchange System Objects container; there is no way to group Public Folder directory objects into separate OUs on a site-by-site basis.

5.4 Public Folder permissions in Exchange 5.5 and Exchange 2000

Permissions on Public Folders are structured differently between Exchange 5.5 and Exchange 2000. In an Exchange 5.5 environment permissions on Public Folders are managed using ACLs on a folder. An ACL defines the access rights (such as the ability to read, create, edit, delete, etc.) that a particular user has on a particular Public Folder. In an Exchange 5.5 environment the ACL is not stored directly as a property of the Public Folder. Each Exchange 5.5 Public Folder has an ACLID property, which points to a single entry in an ACLID table. Each entry in the ACLID table identifies the Public Folder owner and lists the different access rights for the ACL. Each access right has a pointer to entries in an ACL members table that are effectively the DNs of Exchange 5.5 user mailboxes. Figure 5.3 shows the relationship between these tables.

When Public Folder replication takes place from one Exchange 5.5 server to another, the ACL information is packaged up into a property named `ptagACLData`. During replication the receiving Exchange 5.5 server unpacks the `ptagACLData` property and uses the information contained in it to update its own ACL tables.

In Exchange 2000, permissions management is different. The Public Folder Store in Exchange 2000 directly holds the ACL as a property of the

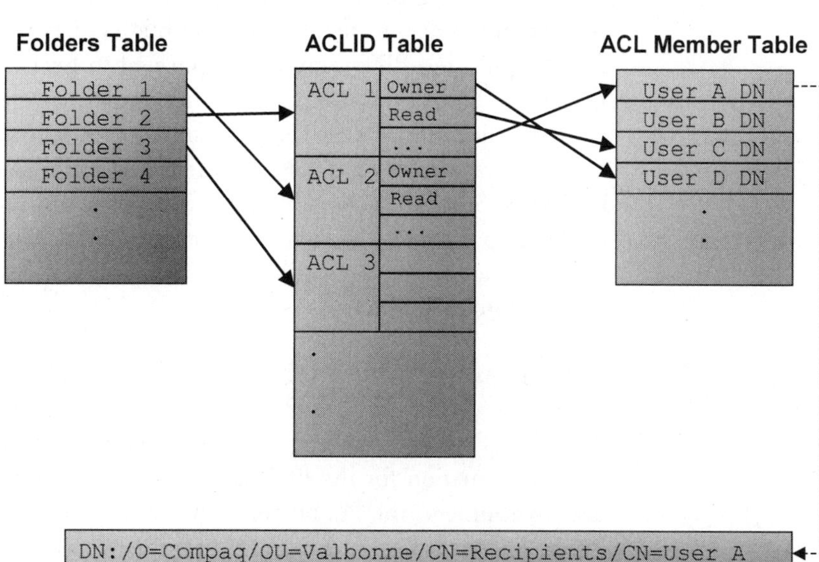

Figure 5.3 *Exchange 5.5 Public Folder ACL management.*

Public Folder. This property, named `ptagNTSD`, contains the Windows 2000 Security Descriptors (SIDs) of the users or groups that are included in the ACLs.

5.5 Exchange 5.5 and Exchange 2000 Public Folder replication

5.5.1 Single and multiple Public Folder hierarchies

Exchange 5.5 uses the concept of a single Public Folder hierarchy, or what is often referred to as a Public Folder Tree (PFT), to host all of its Public Folders. (A PFT is also known as a Top-Level Hierarchy (TLH), but this term is used less often.) Exchange 2000, on the other hand, supports multiple Public Folder hierarchies, and, accordingly, separate PFTs can be associated with separate Exchange 2000 Public Folder Stores. In Exchange 2000 you can use the term MAPI PFT to refer to that PFT, which is common to both Exchange 5.5 and Exchange 2000 servers.

In Exchange 2000 the MAPI PFT is accessible from MAPI clients such as Outlook and IMAP clients such as Outlook Express. Other PFTs, usually referred to as Application PFTs, are accessible only via Web-DAV clients such as Outlook Web Access or from programmatic interfaces. In Exchange 5.5, only the MAPI PFT is available to clients, and when we discuss Public Folder replication between Exchange 5.5 servers and Exchange 2000 servers this typically refers to replication of Public Folders that exist in the MAPI PFT. Application PFTs cannot be replicated to Exchange 5.5 servers, since Exchange 5.5 has no concept of multiple PFTs. However, since Public Folder replication between servers is simply e-mail based, where one Public Folder Store sends Public Folder content in a mail message to another Public Folder Store, it is possible to backbone Application PFT traffic over Exchange 5.5 servers. In such circumstances an Exchange 5.5 MTA will forward Public Folder replication updates from one Exchange 2000 Public Folder Store to another.

5.5.2 Replicating the Public Folder hierarchy

All Public Folder Stores contain a special Public Folder that holds the hierarchy information for the PFT associated with that Store. In an Exchange 5.5 environment, the Public Folder hierarchy is replicated by default to all Public Folder Stores in the organization even if you disable Public Folder replication. The same is true for a PFT in an Exchange 2000 environment;

the hierarchy associated with each PFT is replicated to Public Folder Stores. Similarly, when you install an Exchange 2000 server into an Exchange 5.5 site, the ConfigCA identifies the Exchange 2000 Public Folder Store that will host the MAPI PFT and synchronizes this information to the Exchange 5.5 Configuration container. The Exchange 5.5 Public Folder Store can then replicate the MAPI PFT hierarchy information to the appropriate Exchange 2000 server and Public Folder Store.

Replicating Public Folders from Exchange 5.5 servers to Exchange 2000 servers is really not any more complicated than replicating Public Folders from one Exchange 5.5 Public Folder Store to another. You add the appropriate Exchange 2000 Public Folder Store to the list of replicas for the Exchange 5.5 Public Folder, and the replication process takes care of replicating the Public Folder content as usual. To replicate Public Folders in the opposite direction you use the same technique, adding the Exchange 5.5 Public Folder store to the list of replicas for the Exchange 2000 Public Folder. Public Folder replication takes place by content being bundled up into discrete mail messages, the mail messages are sent to the target Public Folder Store that holds the replica, and the messages are then unbundled and the content applied to the Public Folder store.

The process that is used to replicate the Public Folder hierarchy is really no different from the process used to replicate the content of any Public Folder. With hierarchy replication, the content being replicated describes the hierarchy of the PFT, rather than simply being documents or mail messages.

It's important to understand that you don't need to have any PFCAs in place for Public Folder hierarchy or content replication to take place. A PFCA creates directory entries with mail addresses for Public Folders, while Public Folder replication takes place by one Public Folder Store mailing content to another. Creating a new Public Folder store in Exchange 2000 automatically associates a mail address with it, and it is this address that is used in the replication process.

5.6 Permission handling during mixed version replication

I trust that you might agree that the replication of Public Folder content and hierarchy between Exchange 5.5 servers and Exchange 2000 servers is relatively straightforward. However, mixed version Public Folder replication becomes much more interesting when ACLs are present on the Public Folders being replicated.

With an Exchange 5.5 Public Folder ACL, the DN is used in the ACL to identify a user or a DL with permissions. With an Exchange 2000 Public Folder ACL, it is the SID of a Windows 2000 object that is used to identify a user or a group. Therefore, when a Public Folder on an Exchange 5.5 Public Folder Store is replicated to an Exchange 2000 Public Folder Store, the ACL data must be converted in some manner.

5.6.1 The internals of permissions conversions

In Section 5.4, we saw how Exchange 5.5 Public Folder Stores send ACL information for a Public Folder being replicated in the `ptagACLData` property when it sends an outbound replication message. When an Exchange 2000 Public Folder Store is to host a replica of an Exchange 5.5 Public Folder, it receives this ACL information but must promote the ACL information contained in the `ptagACLData` property into its native ACL storage property, `ptagNTSD`. The receiving Exchange 2000 Store process extracts the `ptagACLData` information into a temporary table, and, for every DN that is specified in the Exchange 5.5 version of the ACL, the Exchange 2000 Store process looks up the Active Directory to convert the DN to a SID.

This conversion process is only possible if a Recipient CA has already synchronized all relevant Exchange 5.5 mailbox information into the Active Directory. As a Recipient CA creates an object in the Active Directory for an Exchange 5.5 mailbox, it writes the DN of the Exchange 5.5 mailbox into the `legacyExchangeDN` attribute of the newly created Windows 2000 object. The Exchange 2000 Store process can therefore build the new ACL by searching the Active Directory for objects with a `legacyExchangeDN`, which matches the DN specified in the Exchange 5.5 ACL, and then using the SID of the matching object in the ACL. When all the DNs associated with a particular ACL have been resolved to SIDs, the Store process removes the temporary tables and the native Exchange 2000 `ptagNTSD` property is associated with the Public Folder. This process is shown in a step-by-step manner in Figure 5.4.

5.6.2 Using disabled Active Directory objects in Public Folder ACLs

If any of the Recipient CAs have been configured to create disabled user objects in the Active Directory rather than enabled user objects, then the SID of the disabled user object is of little use with respect to enforcing permissions. In such an event, no user will ever be logged on to it and therefore

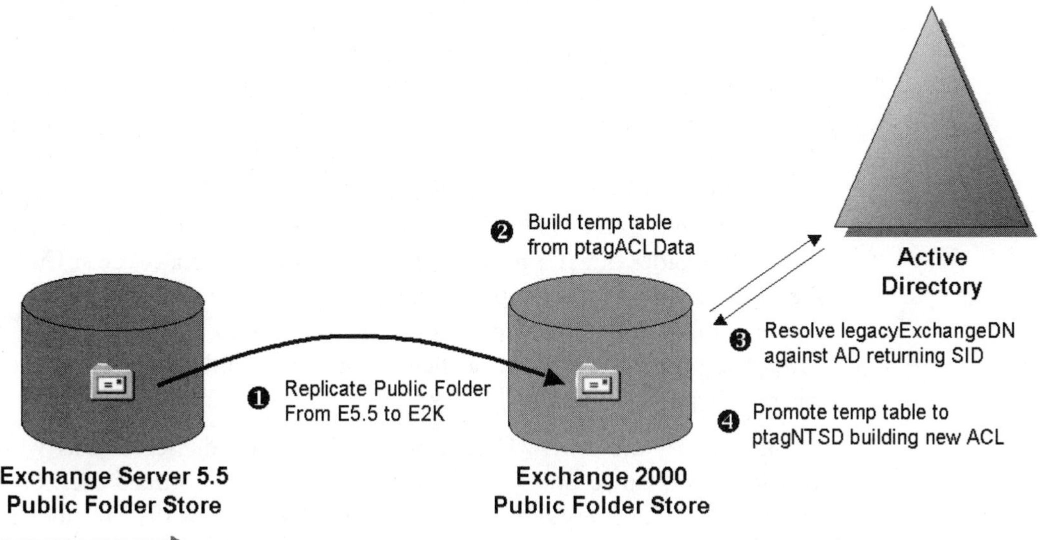

Figure 5.4 *Steps to convert Exchange 5.5 PF ACLs to Exchange 2000 ACLs.*

the permissions model will be useless. In these circumstances, the disabled user object is typically only present to provide a complete GAL.

As the ADC creates a disabled user object in the Active Directory for an Exchange 5.5 mailbox with an associated Windows NT4 account, the `msExchMasterAccountSID` attribute of the newly created Active Directory object is populated with the SID of the Windows NT4 account associated with the Exchange 5.5 mailbox (the `Associated-Nt-Account` attribute from the Exchange 5.5 Directory Service). If a trust relationship exists between the Windows 2000 domain that holds the disabled user object and the Windows NT4 domain that holds the `Associated-Nt-Account`, then the SID of this Windows NT4 account will be used with the `ptagNTSD` property, rather than the SID of the disabled user object in the Active Directory. Using the Windows NT4 account as the so-called associated external account means that Windows 2000 can use pass-through authentication from the Windows NT4 account when access controls are to be enforced.

5.6.3 Dealing with partially complete Public Folder ACLs

If the Active Directory lookup for any one of the DNs specified in the `ptagACLData` can't be resolved, then the entire list of users associated with the

ACL does not get promoted into the ptagNTSD property. Effectively, the ACL does not get applied to the replicated Public Folder and no Exchange 2000 users whatsoever have access rights to the Public Folder. Not surprisingly, anonymous access to the Public Folder is also prevented. Although this action may seem rather draconian, access is blocked for all Exchange 2000 users apart from the Public Folder owners, even if just one DN can't be resolved in the case that a single user has been explicitly denied access to the Public Folder but is a member of a group that has read access. Under such circumstances, the temporary files are retained and the Store process attempts to complete the promotion of ptagACLData permissions to the ptagNTSD property every time a client accesses the Public Folder replica or when replication is attempted.

Similarly, if the Active Directory contains disabled user objects with associated external accounts to represent the Exchange 5.5 mailboxes, then the trust relationship must exist between the domains for the DN to SID conversion to take place. If no trust is in place or there are other problems accessing the associated external account, then the ptagNTSD property is not built and the Public Folder replica will be unavailable to Exchange 2000 users.

You should draw an immediate conclusion from this behavior. Careful implementation of Recipient CAs is positively critical for Exchange 5.5 and Exchange 2000 Public Folder interoperability to be smooth and successful.

5.6.4 Permissions replication from Exchange 2000 to Exchange 5.5

When replicating in the direction of Exchange 2000 to Exchange 5.5, the outgoing replication message from the Exchange 2000 Public Folder Store includes the ptagACLData property so that the Exchange 5.5 server can correctly interpret any ACL information associated with the Public Folder. In addition to providing the properties that the Exchange 5.5 Public Folder Store can understand, the replication message also includes the ptagNTSD property, which Exchange 2000 uses to replicate Public Folder ACL information natively. However, since Exchange 5.5 servers can't understand this property, it is simply ignored by the Exchange 5.5 Public Folder Store. Although the property is ignored by the Exchange 5.5 Public Folder Store, it is present on the Exchange 5.5 replica. Should any modifications be made to the Public Folder replica on the Exchange 5.5 Public Folder Store, the replication messages back to the Exchange 2000 Public Folder Store will include this ptagNTSD property. But since Exchange 5.5 servers cannot enforce any security on this property, an Exchange 2000 Public Folder Store that receives such a replication message ignores the property as well.

5.7 Exchange 5.5 distribution lists and ACLs

Although it is possible to individually permission Exchange 5.5 mailboxes for access to Public Folders, it is more common to associate individual mailboxes with DLs and control access to Public Folders by using the DLs in the ACL. This makes the administrative process simpler, since adding users to a DL with access permissions is much simpler than individually managing hundreds or thousands of users in an ACL.

Windows 2000 supersedes the Exchange 5.5 DL construct with the Active Directory construct of a group. When synchronizing objects from the Exchange 5.5 Directory Service to the Active Directory, the ADC converts DLs to Universal Distribution Groups. Although a Universal Distribution Group offers the same functionality as a DL in terms of mail address expansion, a Universal Distribution Group is not a security principal and therefore cannot be used in an ACL. Hence, there is no one-to-one mapping of an Exchange 5.5 DL used in an ACL to a Universal Distribution Group used in a Windows 2000 ACL on an Exchange 2000 Public Folder. To secure access to PFs using groups, Exchange 2000 must use a Universal Security Group. A Universal Security Group offers the same functionality as a Universal Distribution Group but additionally, and most importantly, can be used in ACLs.

However, Universal Security Groups can only exist in native mode Windows 2000 domains. If you use DLs to control access to Public Folders in an Exchange 5.5 environment and you wish to have a coexisting Exchange 5.5 and Exchange 2000 environment, you must ensure that any Windows 2000 domains that will hold Universal Security Groups are in native mode. In fact, when you configure Recipient CAs to synchronize DLs, the ADC will warn you if the target Windows 2000 domain is not already in native mode. This is a good reason to restructure Windows NT4 domains with new Windows 2000 domains rather than upgrade, although the complexity of your Windows NT4 environment will ultimately dictate the approach that you take.

Since the ADC can only create Universal Distribution Groups for Exchange 5.5 DLs, some process must be employed to convert those Universal Distribution Groups that are associated with Exchange 5.5 DLs used in ACLs. It is the Exchange 2000 Store process that performs this conversion, changing Universal Distribution Groups (including nested Universal Distribution Groups) that the ADC has created into Universal Security Groups under a number of circumstances. This occurs as follows:

- An Exchange 5.5 Public Folder is replicated to an Exchange 2000 server and a Universal Distribution Group is to be used in an ACL associated with it
- An Exchange 5.5 Public Folder Store is upgraded to become an Exchange 2000 Public Folder Store, where a Universal Distribution Group is to be used in an ACL associated with a Public Folder homed on that Public Folder Store
- A Universal Distribution Group is added to an ACL on a Public Folder by an Exchange 2000 client

For the most part these Universal Distribution Group to Universal Security Group conversions take place uneventfully. However, should the conversion process fail for any reason—for example, the Universal Distribution Group is in a mixed mode domain or the membership of a Universal Distribution Group has not been correctly replicated—the Store process will retry the conversion. This conversion retry is attempted the next time the Public Folder is accessed by an Exchange 2000 client or if Public Folder replication occurs again from an Exchange 5.5 server with a modification to the ACL.

Additionally, there are some circumstances where the Store process will not attempt to convert a Universal Distribution Group in an ACL to a Universal Security Group, as follows:

- A Universal Distribution Group was previously converted to a Universal Security Group but was then manually converted back to a Universal Distribution Group. In this case a subsequent access attempt to the ACL from an Exchange 2000 client will not result in a conversion. If, however, the permission associated with the Universal Distribution Group is changed, the conversion will be retried
- A nested Universal Distribution Group has a parent group that is already a Universal Security Group. Therefore, if a system manager manually converts a parent Universal Distribution Group to a Universal Security Group but does not convert the nested members, the Store process will not perform any further conversion. Furthermore, if a Universal Distribution Group is added as a member of a Universal Security Group that has previously been converted, the Store process will ignore this Universal Distribution Group during the conversion process

- The `msExchDisableUDGConversion` attribute (on the Active Directory Organization object) is set to the value `2`.

5.8 Summary

The majority of this chapter describes how ACLs are enforced for both individual users and groups when an Exchange 5.5 Public Folder is replicated to an Exchange 2000 Public Folder Store. Effectively, the same process occurs when an Exchange 5.5 Public Folder Store is upgraded to become an Exchange 2000 Public Folder Store. In this circumstance, the upgrade process analyzes existing Exchange 5.5-style ACLs and converts them to Exchange 2000-style ACLs by resolving the `legacyExchangeDN` against the Active Directory to retrieve a SID in exactly the same manner that the Exchange 2000 Store process operates when dealing with mixed-version replication.

It is, of course, very important to create the appropriate PFCAs for the reasons described earlier in this chapter. But what is also of the utmost importance is the requirement to build a solid coexistence infrastructure to allow this form of interoperability to take place. As I've described in Section 5.6, careful attention to domains, trust relationships, the topology of Recipient CAs and ensuring complete recipient synchronization; and thoughtful account migration are not just important but absolutely indispensable if you wish Public Folders to be accessed seamlessly over mixed environments.

6

Active Directory Connector Deployment

6.1 Introduction

I often describe the Active Directory Connector as the light-saber of Exchange 5.5 migration, because it's extremely powerful and seems straightforward to implement; yet much like its fictional counterpart, the ADC is actually quite a sophisticated tool that requires a good deal of mastery and careful use if it is to ultimately yield success.

As you migrate from Exchange 5.5 to Exchange 2000, it's unlikely that you'll be able migrate all Exchange 5.5 users in one single action. What's more likely, especially when you have thousands of users in your environment and multiple Windows NT4 domains, is a long period of coexistence during which there will be a mixture of both Exchange 5.5 users and Exchange 2000 users. Correct deployment of the ADC and appropriate CA topologies are key to facilitating this coexistence.

Much of the information about the ADC that I've described thus far relates to discrete aspects of ADC functionality. In this chapter, I hope to tie those functionality aspects together and give a complete picture of ADC use in a coexisting Exchange 5.5 and Exchange 2000 environment.

6.2 Why native mode Windows 2000 domains are best

Let's take a step back quickly and review some coexistence fundamentals. A Windows 2000 domain is said to be in native mode if it contains only Windows 2000 Domain Controllers. So long as you meet this requirement, you can have any mix of Windows NT4 and Windows 2000 Member Servers in the domain that you like. A Windows 2000 domain is said to be in mixed mode if it contains any Windows NT4 Domain Controllers.

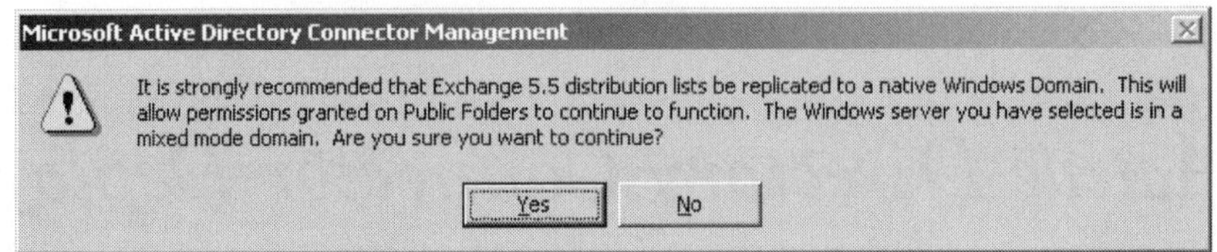

Figure 6.1 *Warning message when you're synchronizing distribution lists.*

In general, it's best for a smooth migration to Exchange 2000 if you can have as much (if not all) of your Windows 2000 infrastructure in place in native mode rather than mixed mode. There are a few reasons for this, but specifically, with respect to the ADC, it's important for the synchronization of certain types of Exchange 5.5 Distribution Lists.

I previously described the situation whereby when the ADC synchronizes an Exchange 5.5 DL into the Active Directory, it always creates a mail-enabled Universal Distribution Group as the synchronized object. Usually this represents no problem, because there are no restrictions on having Universal Distribution Groups in a mixed mode Windows 2000 domain. But how an Exchange 5.5 DL is used is important here. Remember that it is common to find Exchange 5.5 DLs used to enforce access controls on Exchange Public Folders, and, in these cases, the Universal Distribution Groups must be converted to Universal Security Groups. The ADC always creates Universal Distribution Groups (ones that are visible across all domains in the forest and can have membership drawn from any domain in the forest), because these represent the most flexible group objects. After all, the membership of DLs in Exchange 5.5 might be drawn from anywhere in the organization, and in Windows 2000, these user objects might be scattered across many domains. Of course, this conversion process only takes place if the Universal Distribution Group already exists in a native mode domain. If not, then no conversion can take place. So, if you wish to host Universal Security Groups, you must make sure that the CA you use is writing them into a native mode domain. In fact, the ADC MMC snap-in reminds you of this (see Figure 6.1) as you configure the CA.

6.3 Scenarios that require multiple Connection Agreements

In the simplest of environments you can use just one bidirectional CA to replicate one or more Exchange 5.5 Recipient containers to a single Active Directory OU and one or more Active Directory OUs to a single Exchange 5.5 container. Take a look at the example in Figure 6.2.

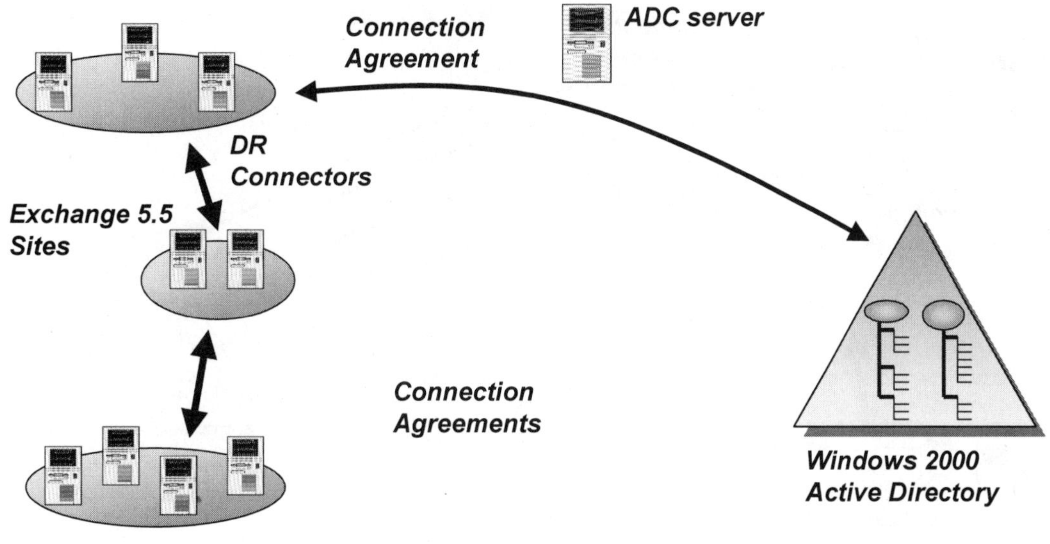

Figure 6.2 *Multiple Exchange 5.5 sites with a single connection agreement.*

The objects contained in the Active Directory OUs are mapped to a single container on the target Exchange 5.5 server, and then the conventional Exchange 5.5 Directory Service replication process allows this container to be seen across all Exchange 5.5 sites. Similarly, any number of Exchange 5.5 containers can be mapped across to single Active Directory OUs replicated across the forest using the conventional Active Directory replication model.

In somewhat more complex scenarios, a single CA is not sufficient. Fundamentally, there are two frameworks where multiple CAs are required.

Since Exchange 5.5 mailboxes can be synchronized into the Active Directory, you can use Active Directory management tools, such as the Active Directory Users and Computers snap-in, to manage Exchange 5.5 mailboxes by modifying their ADC-created synchronized partners and having the modifications synchronized back to the Exchange 5.5 directory. Managing Exchange 5.5 mailboxes from the Active Directory means that you'll need to have a separate CA to each Exchange 5.5 Recipients container for each Exchange 5.5 site in which the mailboxes are homed. In the Exchange 5.5 Directory Service, objects outside the site in which they are homed are read only, so a single CA to an arbitrary Exchange 5.5 site is not sufficient to allow write access to an object if it is homed in another Exchange 5.5 site. You can see an example of such a CA arrangement in Figure 6.3.

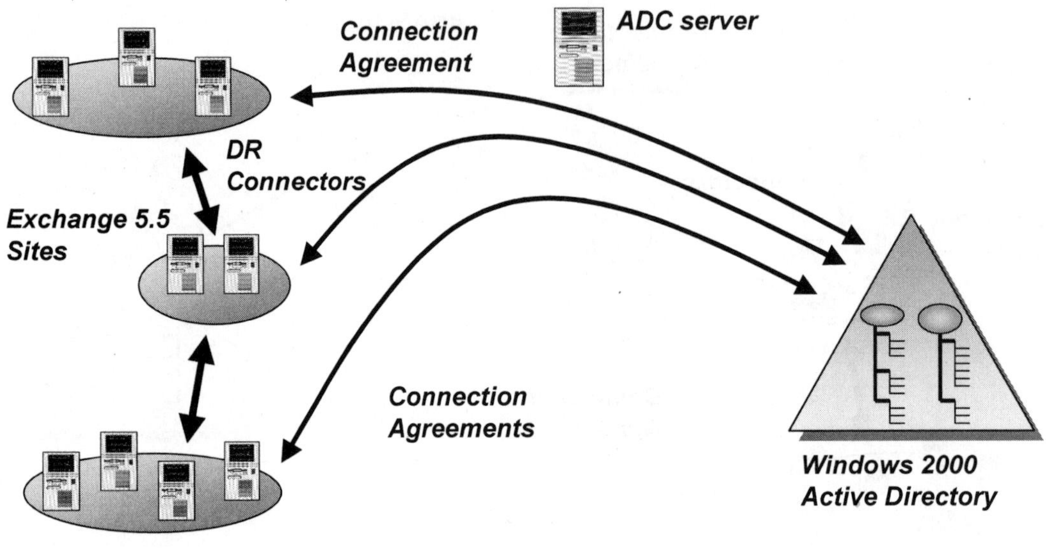

Figure 6.3 *Multiple Exchange 5.5 sites with a per-site connection agreement arrangement.*

In terms of best practice, it makes a good deal of sense to use similar tools to manage similar objects. What I mean by this is that you should, if possible, use the Exchange 5.5 Administrator program to manage Exchange 5.5 objects and the Active Directory Users and Computers snap-in to manage Exchange 2000 objects. In fact, the Exchange 2000 installation menu allows you to install the Exchange 5.5 Administrator expressly for this purpose. Having said that, when you have Exchange 5.5 mailboxes that are replicated to the Active Directory, the Active Directory is now a potential single point of administration for those Exchange 5.5 mailboxes. In this case, using the Active Directory Users and Computers snap-in to manage Exchange 5.5 mailboxes is preferable.

The other framework where multiple CAs are required involves many-to-many mappings of Exchange 5.5 Directory Service containers and Active Directory OUs. In general, a single CA allows one-to-one and many-to-one mappings of Exchange 5.5 Directory Service containers to Active Directory OUs, and vice versa. Many-to-one mappings are realized in two ways: You can select multiple containers from any level in the source directory and container hierarchy is honored from the source. If you need to make many-to-many mappings, then a single CA is not sufficient, since only one container or OU can be specified on the target end point of the CA. In this case, you'll need to use a separate CA for each target container or OU, as shown in Figure 6.4.

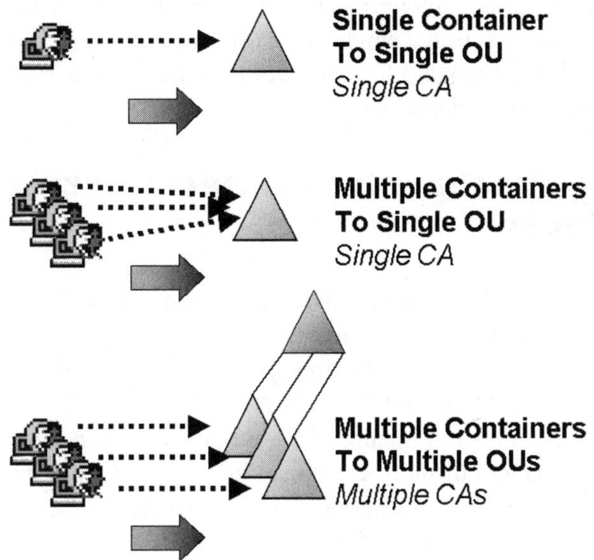

Figure 6.4 *Mapping arrangements for legacy Exchange containers.*

When might you want to do this? Well, let's say you wanted to map users from three different Exchange 5.5 sites—Dublin, Paris, and New York across to three different Active Directory OUs—again called Dublin, Paris, and New York. You would need three separate CAs to perform this type of mapping. However, if you are prepared to bundle all of the replicated objects into a single OU in the Active Directory, then a single CA will be sufficient. Let's describe what happens with container hierarchies.

6.4 Container hierarchy mapping

In general, a specific CA defines a many-to-one mapping of containers between directories. That is, when you define the source locations for a given CA, you can specify multiple containers from which you will synchronize objects. But these objects must all be mapped into a single container in the target directory.

However, this many-to-one mapping doesn't mean that if you have multiple containers in your source directory and you want to retain the same structure, you need to have one CA per source container. Although the mapping function is many-to-one, the ADC does allow container hierarchy to be synchronized across, so it is possible to specify an entire Exchange 5.5 site hierarchy to synchronize to one OU in the Active Directory and have all objects within that site synchronized across with the container hierarchy intact. This is an approach that is typical in many large deployments. It is common to find a single CA with just one source container from each site in the Exchange 5.5 organization mapping to a single OU in the Active Directory, and vice versa.

6.5 Moving synchronized objects between containers

It's interesting to note what happens when a synchronized object is moved between different containers. For example, Figure 6.5 shows a two-way CA in place between the Recipients container of an Exchange 5.5 Site and the Temporary Objects OU in the Active Directory. When an object is synchronized from the Exchange 5.5 Recipients container to the Active Directory, any changes made to the object in either directory will be synchronized to the other. Now, consider that you move the synchronized object to another location in the Active Directory, a container called Final Objects.

Note that no CA maps the Exchange 5.5 Recipients container to the Active Directory Final Objects container. Despite this lack of a CA to the alternative container, if a change is made to the object in the Exchange 5.5 Directory Service, then this change is replicated to the synchronized object in the Active Directory, even though it is now located in a different container. From a visual perspective, it is as if there is an invisible one-way CA from the Recipients container in the Exchange 5.5 Directory Service to the Final Objects container in the Active Directory. In fact, no matter where you relocate such an object in the Active Directory (so long as it remains

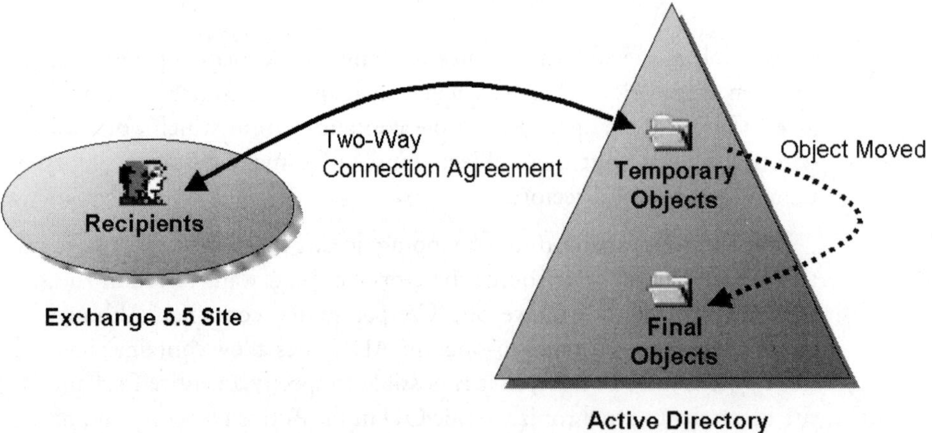

Figure 6.5 *Two-way connection agreement and moved object.*

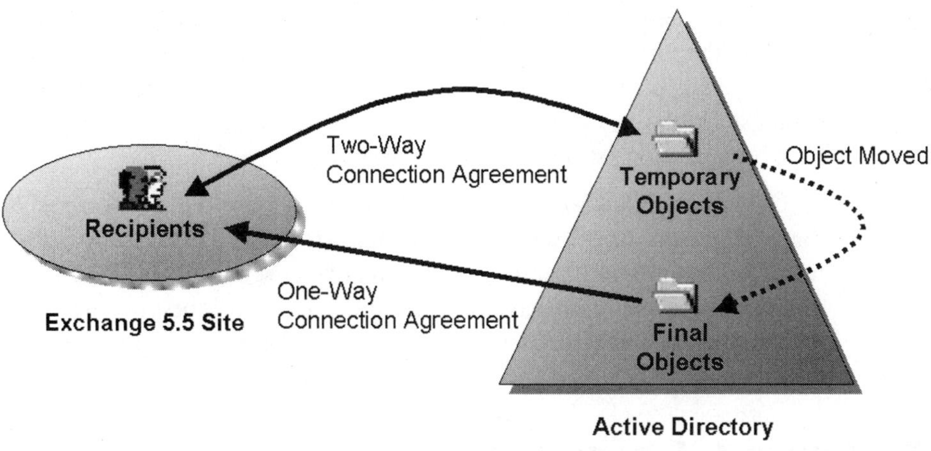

Figure 6.6 *Required connection agreements to ensure complete synchronization.*

within the same domain), the CA linking the Recipients container to the Temporary Objects OU tracks the moved object using the Windows 2000 GUID and will always replicate Exchange 5.5 object changes to the synchronized object in the Active Directory.

The converse, however, is not the case. Any changes made directly to the synchronized object in the Active Directory Final Objects container are not replicated back to the original object in the Exchange 5.5 Directory Service. For these modifications to be replicated, an additional CA is required, one way in this case, mapping the Final Objects OU to the Recipients container in the Exchange 5.5 Directory Service, as shown in Figure 6.6.

In the reverse situation there is no parallel concept of an object moving between Exchange 5.5 containers and retaining the synchronization integrity. Moving an object between containers in the Exchange 5.5 Directory Service implies a change to the object's DN, and this results in a completely different synchronization operation.

6.6 Using multiple ADCs

Depending on the complexity and geographical distribution of your environment, you may decide to use just one ADC hosting multiple CAs, or you may decide to deploy an ADC in major geographical regions around the globe—perhaps one ADC in the Americas, one ADC in Europe, and one ADC in Asia Pacific. From a directory synchronization standpoint, it is easier to conceptualize synchronization if you centralize all synchronization activity to just one location. The downside of this is that intrinsic directory replication latency comes into play, and, as synchronization takes place between the directories in the central location, you must wait for the Exchange 5.5 Directory Service replication and the Active Directory replication schedules to expire before you can be sure that the updated objects have been distributed across your organization.

Distributing ADCs implies that you will use a set of CAs for each ADC that will synchronize Exchange 5.5 containers and Active Directory OUs near it and in a timely manner. While you can have multiple CAs synchronizing the same set of objects (more about this later), it is best if you tolerate or optimize your directory replication settings rather than introducing more complexity into the synchronization environment.

6.7 Exchange 5.5 back replication

Since we're on the subject of what gets synchronized with CAs, it is interesting to discuss some unexpected replication that you might see in your Exchange 5.5 environment when you start to deploy and enable the ADC.

Let's take a straightforward example. Assume that you've got a large Exchange 5.5 environment, distributed globally with multiple sites, hundreds of Exchange 5.5 servers, and tens of thousands of users. Let's say that you decide to implement the ADC without much planning or forethought. Perhaps you plan to install an ADC server and use two-way CAs from the Recipients containers of your Exchange 5.5 sites in your organization to bulk load user objects into the Active Directory. For the purposes of this example, let's assume that the company is based in Chicago and this location has ten Exchange 5.5 servers, each hosting 1,000 users.

You may begin this bulk loading by configuring two-way CAs from the Exchange 5.5 Recipients containers to the Active Directory, configuring the appropriate Recipients containers from each site, enabling the CAs, and then watching the Active Directory become populated with 10,000 user objects as the 10,000 mailboxes in the Exchange 5.5 Directory Service are synchronized over the CAs and into the Active Directory. Network activity is seen from the Exchange 5.5 servers to the Active Directory Global Catalog server, and, moreover, network can also be seen between all Global Catalog servers in the Active Directory as the new objects just created in the Active Directory are replicated across the complete forest.

Although this behavior is indeed what happens, some additional replication activity takes place too. Perhaps unexpectedly, a wave of Exchange 5.5 replication take place across all of the Exchange 5.5 servers that exist in the

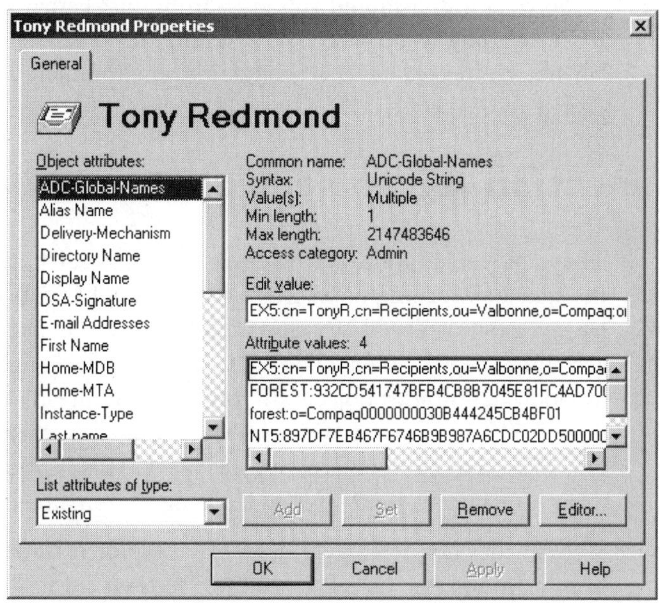

Figure 6.7 *View of the Raw properties from the Exchange 5.5 Administrator.*

Exchange 5.5 organization. Every one of the 10,000 Exchange mailboxes gets rereplicated throughout the Exchange 5.5 Directory Service. What causes this Exchange 5.5 Directory Service replication? It breaks down like this: As the ADC synchronizes each of the 10,000 Exchange 5.5 mailboxes, it modifies an attribute on each mailbox object in the Exchange 5.5 Directory Service. The `ADC-Global-Names` attribute gets updated to reflect the fact that the ADC has synchronized this object. You may ask where this attribute comes from. It gets added to the Exchange 5.5 Directory Schema when you upgrade a single Exchange 5.5 server to SP3 (a mandatory requirement for the ADC in Exchange 2000). You can see the attribute, shown by the Raw Mode Administrator tool, in Figure 6.7.

Of course, when you make any changes to an Exchange 5.5 Directory Service object, the `Object-USN` and `Object-DSN-Signature` attributes get updated, which means that the object will take part in Exchange 5.5 intrasite or intersite directory replication. At a basic level, for each Exchange directory object changed on a server, approximately 5 KB of data is sent to all other servers within the site. For replication between sites, each object compresses to about 1 KB. For more information, see the "Microsoft Exchange 5.5 Advanced Backbone Design and Optimization" white paper on TechNet or on the Web at http://technet.microsoft.com/cdonline/content/complete/srvnetwk/exch/technote/backtraf.htm.

So what lesson should you learn from this? Perhaps the lesson might be: If you're going to do some ADC testing, make sure you use a separate test lab not connected to the production environment to avoid these unexpected anomalies.

6.8 Connection Agreement deployment models

The deployment approach that you take for your CAs is closely related to the state of your migration from Windows NT4 to Windows 2000. If you have already deployed Windows 2000 in the domains that host your user accounts, then the CAs will be able to match Exchange 5.5 mailboxes with Windows 2000 user objects. If you have not already upgraded your Windows NT4 domains to Windows 2000 domains, then the CAs will create new Windows 2000 objects to provide a GAL and allow Exchange 2000 to determine how to route mail to Exchange 5.5 mailboxes.

While it's not possible to describe every potential deployment configuration for your CAs, the following three sections suffice to describe the fundamentals of most approaches.

6.8.1 The simple domain and Connection Agreement model

We begin by looking at a relatively straightforward environment, which comprises a single Windows NT4 domain named HICKORY and two Exchange 5.5 sites named USA and Europe in an organization named DICKORY, as shown in Figure 6.8.

Also shown in Figure 6.8 is the relationship between the Windows NT4 account for the user COPE and his Exchange 5.5 mailbox. These two entities are bound together, because the primary Windows NT Account attribute (known in LDAP as the `Assoc-NT-Account`) of Michael Cope's mailbox references the SID of the Windows NT4 account COPE, 12345 as an example in this case. At this point in time, all that is in place is the normal operating environment of Windows NT4 and Exchange 5.5; there are no ADC servers or Exchange 2000 servers in place.

For this environment, when the HICKORY Windows NT4 domain is upgraded in place to Windows 2000, access to Exchange 5.5 mailboxes is still possible, because, during an in-place domain upgrade, SID values for Windows objects remain unchanged. Having upgraded the domain, the next step in the migration process is to install an ADC server and configure

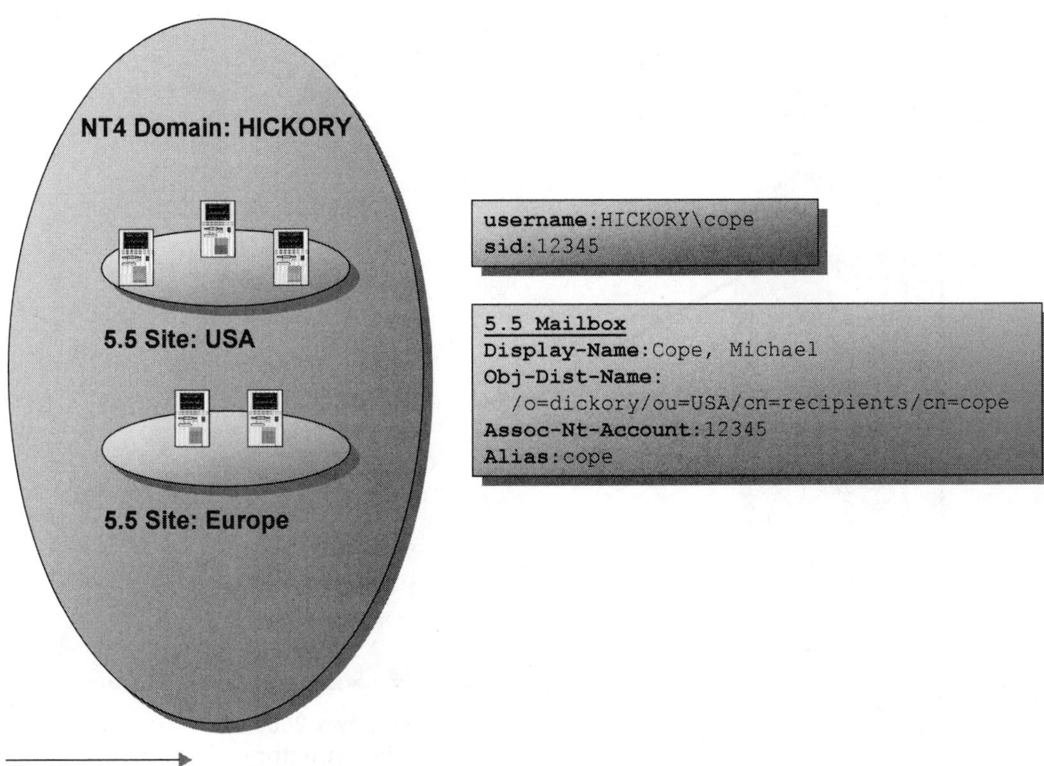

Figure 6.8 *Single Windows NT4 domain and Exchange 5.5 environment.*

some CAs. The CAs should be defined as two-way CAs between each Exchange 5.5 site and the Users OU in the Active Directory, as shown in Figure 6.9. In this example, I've directed the Exchange 5.5 end point of the CA to the Recipients container in the Exchange 5.5 site. It's equally appropriate to direct this end point of the CA to the Site container of the Exchange 5.5 site and thus synchronize objects from all containers within the site to the Active Directory.

When the ADC synchronization cycle begins, it will match the `Assoc-Nt-Account` SID value from each Exchange 5.5 mailbox with the SID of the corresponding user object in the Active Directory. Thus, no new user objects are created in the Active Directory, and the ADC merges mailbox attribute information from the Exchange 5.5 Directory Service into each Active Directory user object.

As you then introduce Exchange 2000 servers into the Exchange 5.5 environment and move user mailboxes from Exchange 5.5 stores to Exchange 2000 stores, the attributes of existing user objects are updated to

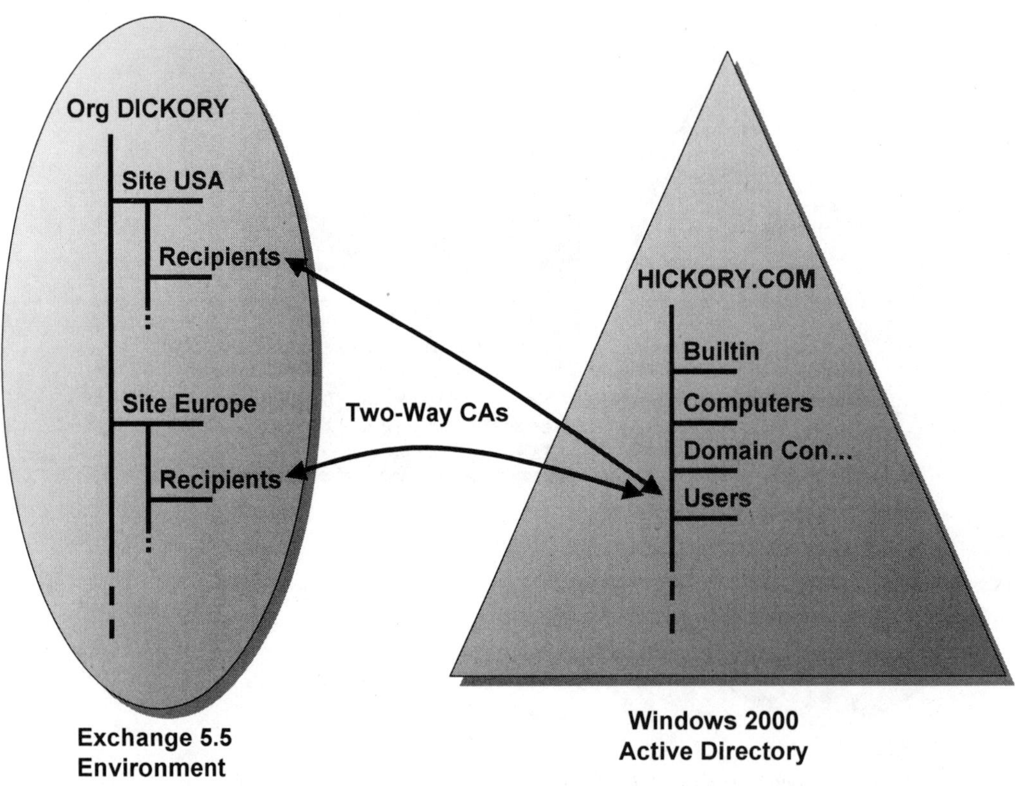

Figure 6.9 *Connection Agreements from Exchange 5.5 sites to users OU.*

reflect the new location of the mailbox: now on an Exchange 2000 server, not an Exchange 5.5 server. No new user objects are created in the Active Directory for the new Exchange 2000 mailboxes.

6.8.2 Connection Agreements to final OU topology

While many smaller organizations may be faced with the migration of a single domain in conjunction with Exchange 5.5, larger organizations typically have more complex environments to deal with.

The domain model shown in Figure 6.10, is typical of that being deployed today by many large organizations. In this environment the bulk of the user accounts, computer accounts, group objects, and so on are found in the child domains of americas.hickory.com, emea.hickory.com, and asiapacific.hickory.com. Little is held in the root domain, hickory.com, and this serves primarily as a placeholder for the domain tree. However, it is

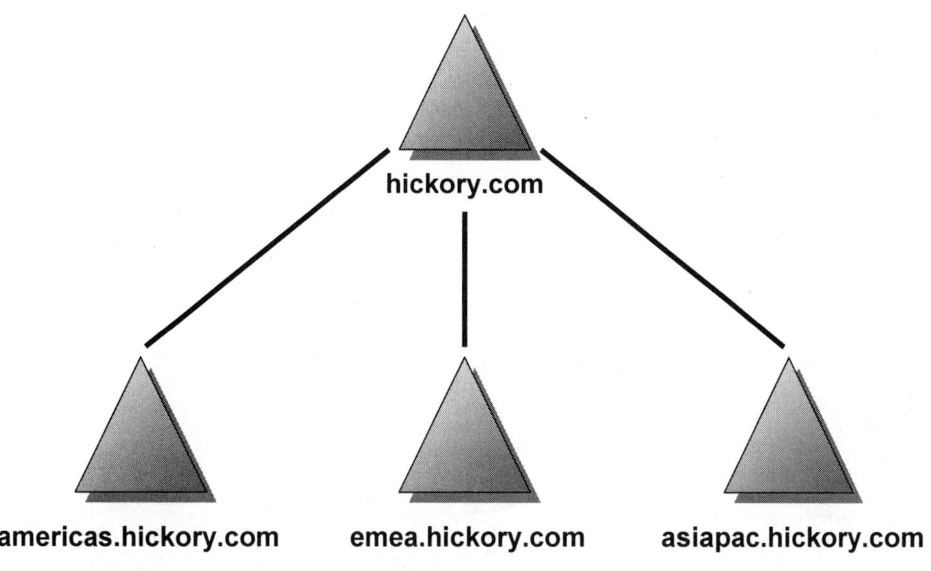

Figure 6.10 *Windows 2000 domain model.*

common to find a small number of administrator accounts or groups held in the root domain.

As far as the deployment of the ADC and the Exchange migration strategy is concerned, it is unimportant how you come to deploy a final Windows 2000 environment. Organizations that have several Windows NT4 domains may choose to perform in-place upgrades of their domains and restructure them into a topology similar to that shown in Figure 6.10. Other organizations, which have many hundreds of Windows NT4 domains, may choose a different approach. For example, in Compaq, there were some 23 account domains and over 1,700 different resource domains. Clearly, performing in-place upgrades of this environment would have posed some significant challenges, and, accordingly, Compaq chose to build a brand new domain structure similar to that in Figure 6.10.

For the following example, let's assume that we have already migrated all Windows NT4 accounts to Windows 2000 accounts and that these accounts are deployed in the domain model shown in Figure 6.10. Using the DICKORY Exchange 5.5 organization as an example, let's assume that this organization consists of 17 Exchange 5.5 sites distributed globally. What combination of CAs can we use to synchronize Exchange 5.5 mailbox information with Active Directory objects? If we can assume that all mailboxes held in an Exchange 5.5 site map directly to user objects in one par-

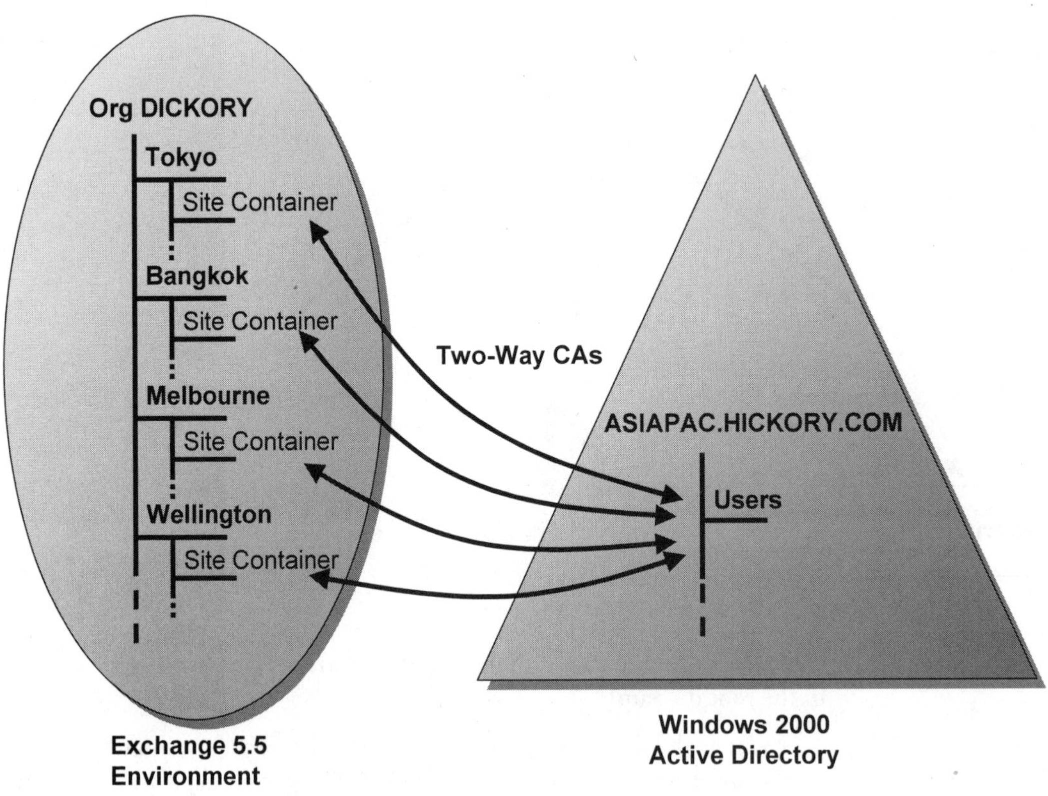

Figure 6.11 *Connection agreements for the ASIAPAC domain.*

ticular domain, then we can use a single CA from each Exchange 5.5 site to an OU in the Active Directory, as shown in Figure 6.11. In our example, we assume that the Tokyo, Bangkok, Melbourne, and Wellington sites all contain user mailboxes that can be mapped into the asiapac.hickory.com domain. With one CA per Exchange 5.5 site, the ADC processes mailboxes from each Exchange 5.5 site and matches them against the user objects in the Windows 2000 domain.

This approach can be used for each of the other Exchange 5.5 sites, since the mailboxes from each site can be synchronized into a particular Windows 2000 domain, as shown in Figure 6.12. You use one CA per site to synchronize objects into an appropriate domain in the Active Directory.

Even if you have not already migrated your Windows NT4 accounts to Windows 2000 accounts, this approach can still work well. Of course, no user objects will be found in the destination domain, so no matching will take place. In this case, the ADC will create new user objects (depending on

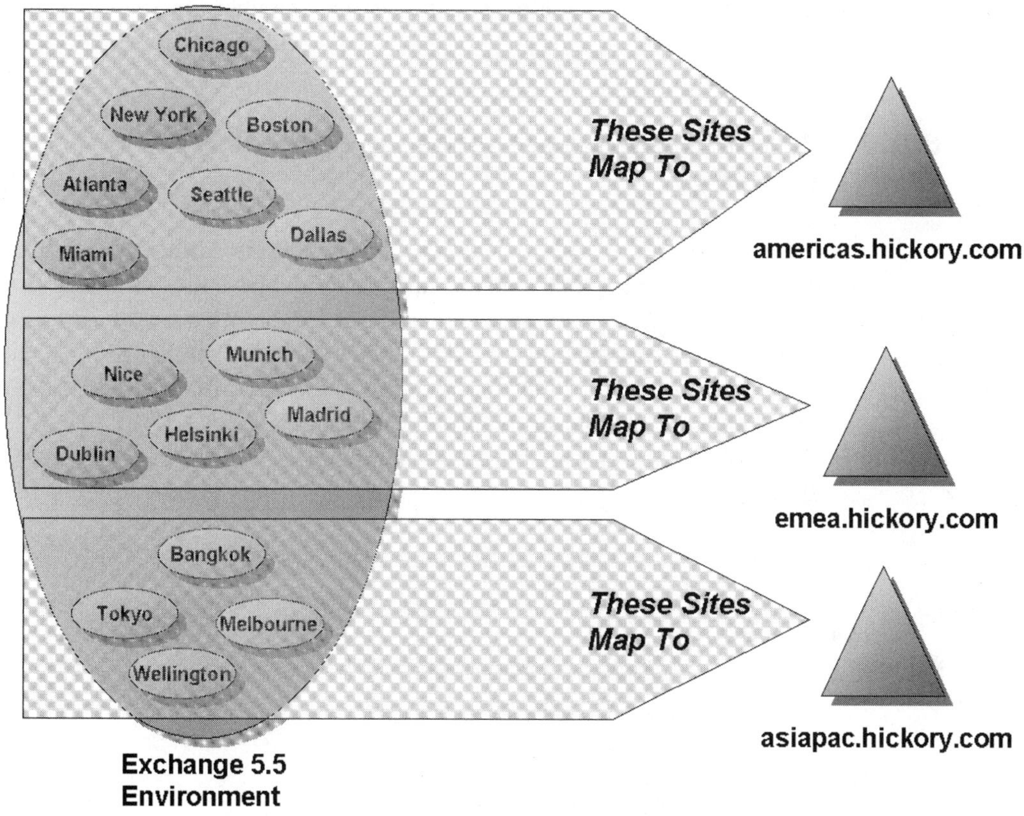

Figure 6.12 *Mapping Exchange 5.5 sites to specific Windows 2000 domains.*

your CA configuration), which can later be matched against Windows NT4 migration tools.

However, using a single CA from each Exchange 5.5 site to an OU in the Active Directory can impose some deployment restrictions. There are three points you should consider, as follows:

1. Mailboxes (or custom recipients or distribution lists) in an Exchange 5.5 site must map to user objects in a single OU in a single domain. If you have Exchange 5.5 directory objects that must map to different OUs in the target domain, then you'll need one CA per target OU.

2. If you have a mix of mailboxes in an Exchange 5.5 container that must be synchronized to different OUs, you'll need to use either an LDAP search filter or a matching rule to select only those objects that you want to synchronize for any given CA.

3. If you do not wish to synchronize the container hierarchy associated with an Exchange 5.5 Site, you will need to use multiple CAs.

6.8.3 Connection Agreements to temporary OU topology

Many organizations wish to deploy Exchange 2000 in advance of migrating their entire Windows NT4 environment to Windows 2000. When all Windows NT4 objects have been either upgraded or migrated to Windows 2000 objects, introducing the ADC merely matches Exchange 5.5 mailboxes with Windows 2000 user accounts. However, if you haven't moved any Windows NT4 objects to Windows 2000, then the Active Directory is effectively empty, at least insofar as its usefulness as a GAL for Exchange 2000.

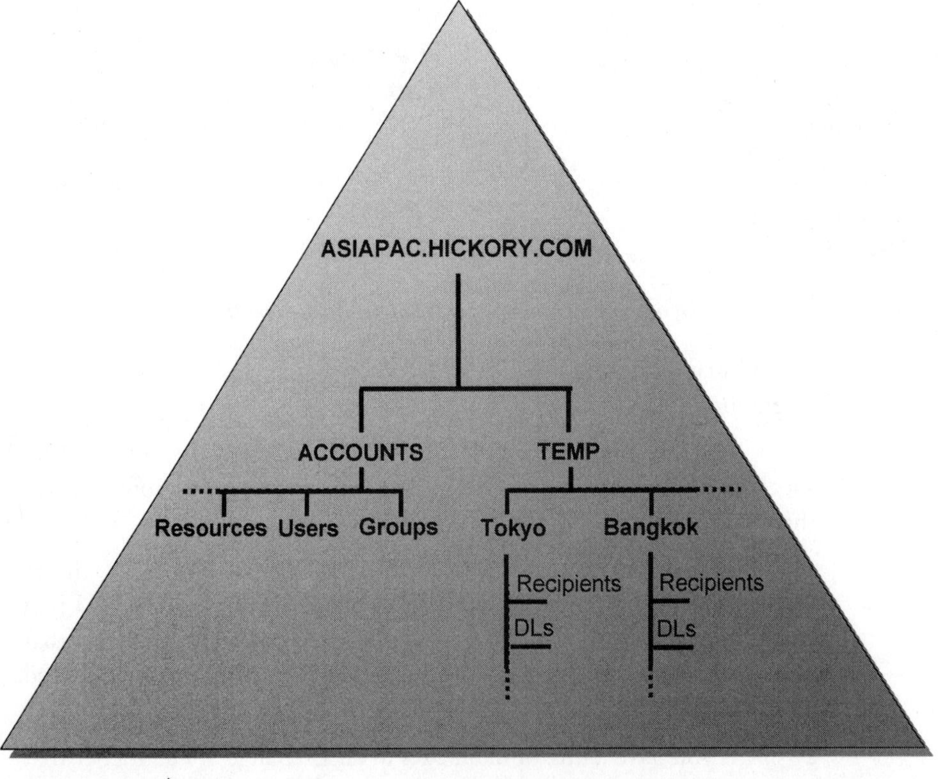

Figure 6.13 *OU hierarchy with temporary migration OU.*

So, in a mixed environment, where you have Exchange 2000 users functioning alongside Exchange 5.5 users, the ADC must create objects in the Active Directory to represent the Exchange 5.5 mailboxes and thus provide a complete and consistent GAL. Many organizations tend to use a temporary OU structure in the Active Directory to hold the ADC-created objects. Separating the ADC-created objects, which are typically disabled user objects, from real Windows 2000 user objects that have been migrated from Windows NT4 has a number of benefits, including the following:

1. The separation allows system managers to easily differentiate between user accounts that have been migrated from Windows NT4 and those that have been created by the ADC, merely because of their difference in location.

2. It is common to find specific access control and Group Policy Object (GPO) settings on the OU structure where the real Windows 2000 user accounts reside, and in general it is not desirable to have these settings apply to ADC-created objects, which are just temporary in nature.

3. From a CA perspective, using the temporary structure allows you to define the minimum number of the CAs (one per site) to represent all Exchange 5.5 mailboxes.

4. Using just one CA per site means that you recreate the container hierarchy from the Exchange 5.5 site only in the temporary OU structure. As you migrate Windows NT4 accounts to Windows 2000 accounts, your migration tools should match against the ADC-created objects, and then you can move the final users' accounts to their desired location in the final OU structure.

Assuming the same domain environment we've already described in Section 6.8.2, you should expect to use an OU hierarchy similar to that shown in Figure 6.13.

The OU hierarchy shown in Figure 6.13 relates to just the asiapac.hickory.com domain, but the same OU hierarchy would exist in the other child domains for this Active Directory forest. Also note the special Accounts OU, which acts as a parent for the Resources, Users, and Groups OU. This allows you to structure the representation of objects in the Active Directory much more flexibly than by using the standard Users and Groups OUs. (Note that the default Users and Groups OUs still exist in the domain but do not contain any objects and, for the sake of clarity, are not shown in Figure 6.13.)

With this model let's step through the migration process for users associated with this domain. Assuming no native Windows 2000 objects exist, effectively we have an empty Active Directory. We then use the ADC to create disabled user objects in the TEMP OU. A two-way CA from each Exchange 5.5 site—in our case, this would be Tokyo, Bangkok, Melbourne (not shown), and Wellington (not shown)—yielding four CAs in total, would create sub-OUs in the TEMP OU reflecting the container hierarchy from the respective Exchange 5.5 sites. The mail-enabled objects created thus provide entries in the GAL for any Exchange 2000 users. As Windows NT4 accounts are migrated to Windows 2000 accounts, the migration tool that you use should detect the matching ADC-created object already present in the TEMP OU and merge the objects together. This results in one object, which can be moved to its final location in the Users sub-OU of the ACCOUNTS OU.

Using this model requires some sophistication with CAs, as shown in Figure 6.14, which represents the CAs required for the Tokyo and Bangkok sites. (Again, Melbourne and Wellington have been omitted from the figure for the sake of clarity.) The two-way CAs between the Exchange 5.5 sites and the Tokyo and Bangkok OUs in the TEMP OU are sufficient to synchronize objects bidirectionally between the Exchange 5.5 Directory Service and the Active Directory for as long as the ADC-created objects exist. As Windows NT4 accounts are migrated to Windows 2000, the migration tool (or the Active Directory Cleanup Wizard, which will be described later in the book merges the ADC-created objects with the migrated objects, and the newly merged objects are moved to the ACCOUNTS OU. Any changes made to the Exchange 5.5 mailboxes will still be replicated to the newly merged objects, because the two-way CAs in place between the Exchange 5.5 sites and the TEMP OU can still access the newly merged object, even though the object is now in a different location in the Active Directory. (The CAs use the `ADCGlobalNames` attribute and the Windows 2000 GUID to track the objects.) However, these two-way CAs are only capable of replicating changes from the Exchange 5.5 Directory Service to the Active Directory for these newly merged and relocated objects; they can't replicate changes from Active Directory to Exchange 5.5. To replicate these changes made directly to the objects in the Active Directory requires additional CAs: one-way CAs from the ACCOUNTS OU back to each Exchange 5.5 site.

This CA topology should be applied to each and every Exchange 5.5 site in the organization. Effectively, every Exchange 5.5 site will require a two-way CA to the TEMP OU and a one-way CA from the ACCOUNTS OU

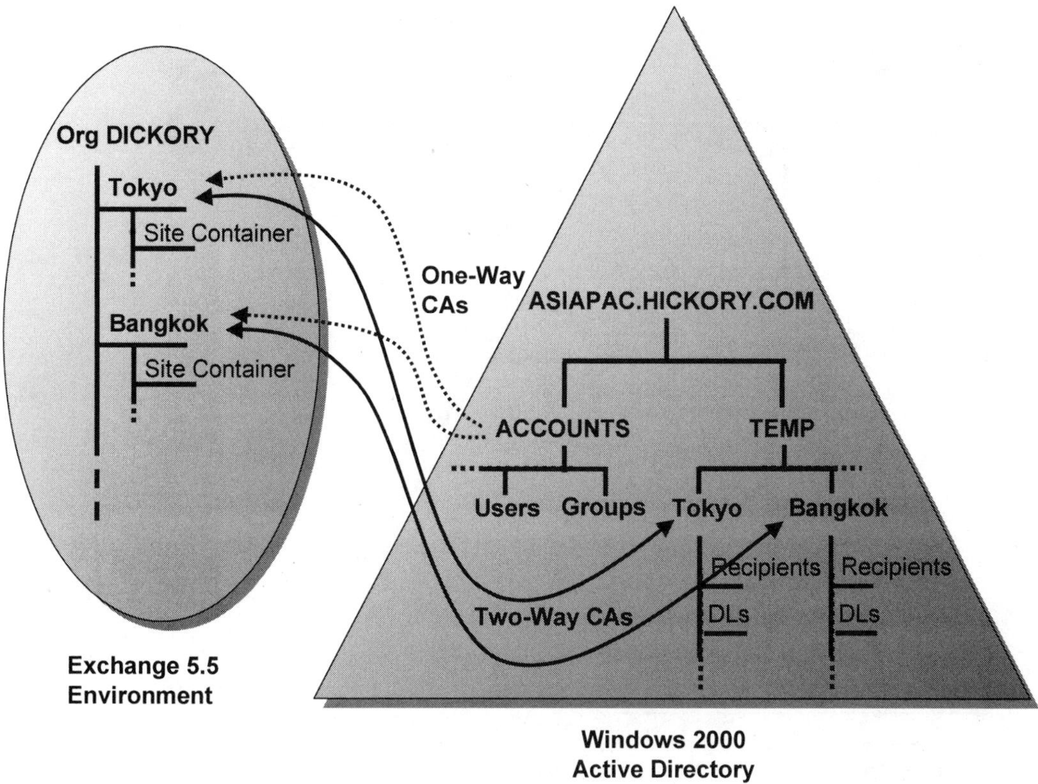

Figure 6.14 *Connection Agreements with temporary OU hierarchy.*

back to the Exchange 5.5 site. For this environment 16 Exchange 5.5 sites require a total of 32 CAs (16 two-way and 16 one-way).

6.9 Deploying ADCs

I've already mentioned that under some circumstances you may find it desirable to deploy multiple ADC servers. In the scenario that I've described in the previous sections, with a globally distributed deployment of Exchange 5.5 sites and domains, it is not surprising that you should use more than one ADC server.

There is little sense in deploying an ADC in Boston that hosts a CA whose end points connect to an Exchange 5.5 server and a Global Catalog server both located in Bangkok. It is more appropriate and more efficient to home the CA on an ADC closer to the end points. This reduces the over-

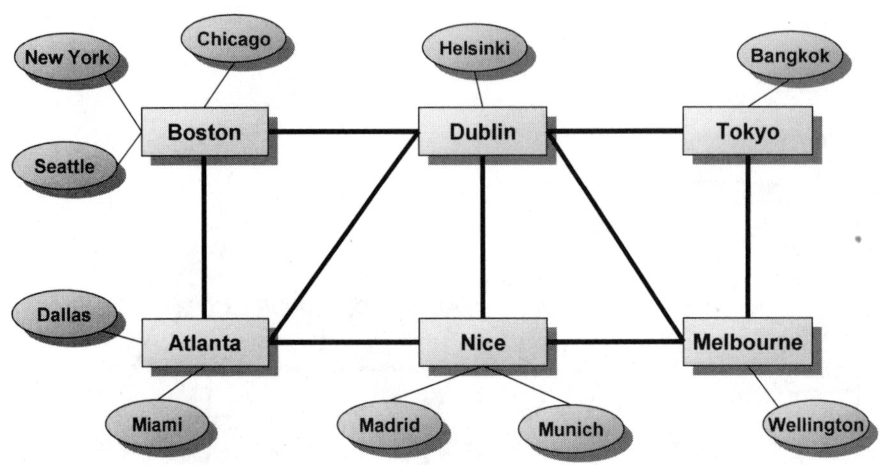

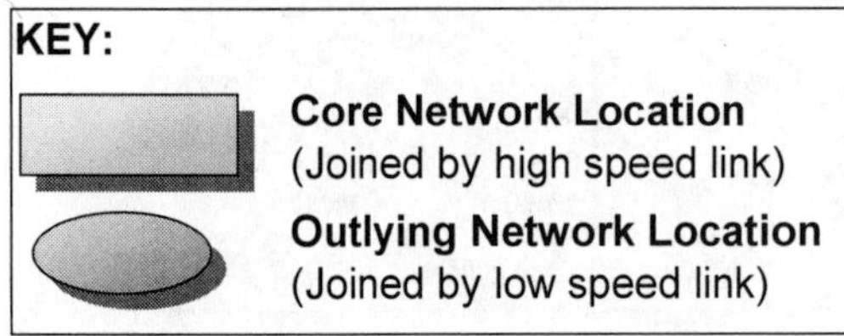

Figure 6.15 *Network topology and Exchange 5.5 environment.*

head of ADC synchronization over wide area connections and relies on the inherent replication mechanisms within the Exchange 5.5 Directory Service and the Active Directory.

Determining the quantity and locations of required ADC servers is largely a matter of understanding the underlying network, Exchange 5.5 topology, and Windows 2000 models. In the example scenario with which we have been working, we'll consider that the environment has a solid hub-based network infrastructure. The network backbone topology is shown in Figure 6.15 and consists of six core network locations joined by high-speed links, which we can assume to be on an ATM or similar backbone. Each core network location acts as a hub for outlying locations, which are connected into the network using lower-speed lines that are typically in the range of 64 Kbps to 512 Kbps. Each network location is also an Exchange 5.5 site.

With such a topology, and bearing in mind the CA deployment requirements that we've already discussed, it makes sense to position ADC servers at each of the core network locations. This results in six ADC servers, each

Table 6.1 *ADC Server Locations and Hosted Connection Agreements*

ADC Location	Connection Agreements
Boston	Boston GC to Boston Exchange 5.5 Server
	New York GC to New York Exchange 5.5 Server
	Chicago GC to Chicago Exchange 5.5 Server
	Seattle GC to Seattle Exchange 5.5 Server
Atlanta	Atlanta GC to Atlanta Exchange 5.5 Server
	Dallas GC to Dallas Exchange 5.5 Server
	Miami GC to Miami Exchange 5.5 Server
Dublin	Dublin GC to Dublin Exchange 5.5 Server
	Helsinki GC to Helsinki Exchange 5.5 Server
Nice	Nice GC to Nice Exchange 5.5 Server
	Madrid GC to Madrid Exchange 5.5 Server
	Munich GC to Munich Exchange 5.5 Server
Tokyo	Tokyo GC to Tokyo Exchange 5.5 Server
	Bangkok GC to Bangkok Exchange 5.5 Server
Melbourne	Melbourne GC to Melbourne Exchange 5.5 Server
	Wellington GC to Wellington Exchange 5.5 Server

hosting a number of CAs: one for each Exchange 5.5 site in close proximity to the network hub.

Table 6.1 shows how each CA is hosted on the various ADC servers.

Using ADC servers at distributed locations mean that you can share the load of synchronization across multiple systems. Furthermore, it means that you can distribute the network traffic associated with ADC synchronization across all of the network, rather than concentrating it at a few locations. As new objects and modifications to existing objects are synchronized into the Active Directory, these changes will be replicated across the network within the Active Directory. Similar replication takes place for those new objects and changed objects in the Exchange 5.5 Directory Service. Since the end points of the CAs are targeted to Exchange 5.5 servers and Global Catalog servers at multiple locations, the replication traffic is balanced. And since synchronization is taking place between systems near the users, there's less impact from replication latency. Users close to the data that are being synchronized are more likely to use it than users located farther afield.

6.10 Network impact from ADC synchronization

Synchronization of data between the Exchange 5.5 Directory Service and the Active Directory takes place over LDAP. Unless you have collocated your Exchange 5.5 Directory Service on the same system as your Global Catalog server, the synchronization process will incur some network overhead merely to move data from one system to another over the CA.

Table 6.2 gives some indication of the network impact associated with ADC synchronization between systems. (I'm indebted to Paul Bowden from the Exchange Product Group at Microsoft for data in this table, based on early testing with the ADC.) For the most part, these figures are based on the synchronization traffic resulting from a change to a single attribute (telephone number) on the directory object.

The following conclusions can be drawn from these data:

- When no modifications are made to either the Exchange 5.5 Directory Service or the Active Directory, there is little network load associated with the ADC. What little traffic is generated results from the ADC querying the directory systems to determine if any objects need to be synchronized.
- Changes made to objects in the Active Directory generate less overall network load than changes made to objects in the Exchange 5.5 Directory Service.
- Network load associated with synchronization from Active Directory to the Exchange 5.5 Directory Service appears to grow linearly with 11 KB overhead for each object that is synchronized.
- Network load associated with synchronization from the Exchange 5.5 Directory Service to the Active Directory appears to grow linearly with 14 KB overhead for each object that is synchronized.

Clearly, the first time you initiate synchronization between the Exchange 5.5 Directory Service and the Active Directory, you can expect to see a significant amount of network traffic generated. This load may be substantial and potentially detrimental to the stability of your network if you immediately attempt to synchronize many tens of thousands of objects at one time. Remember that a lot of other network traffic must be taken into account. Not only is network load associated with synchronization over the ADC

Table 6.2 *Network Load Associated with ADC Synchronization*

Activity	ADC to GC	GC to ADC	ADC to 5.5	5.5 to ADC	Total
No objects to synch	19 KB	14 KB	5 KB	3 KB	41 KB
One change in AD	24 KB	91 KB	9 KB	8 KB	132 KB
Two changes in AD	24 KB	98 KB	11 KB	12 KB	143 KB
Three changes in AD	24 KB	101 KB	14 KB	15 KB	154 KB
One change in 5.5 DS	33 KB	103 KB	10 KB	8 KB	154 KB
Two changes in 5.5 DS	37 KB	111 KB	10 KB	10 KB	168 KB
Three changes in 5.5 DS	43 KB	115 KB	12 KB	12 KB	182 KB

between the Exchange 5.5 Directory Service and the Active Directory but also with the inherent replication mechanisms of these two directory services. As you synchronize new objects into the Active Directory, more network load is generated as the Active Directory itself replicates these data to all of its GCs throughout the forest. Similarly, objects synchronized into the Exchange 5.5 Directory Service are replicated to all Exchange 5.5 servers within the organization. Nor should you neglect the effects of back replication in the Exchange 5.5 Directory Service, since objects are modified in the Exchange 5.5 Directory Service as they are synchronized into the Active Directory. (This also occurs in the Active Directory, but it is less significant since the Active Directory uses attribute-based replication, while the Exchange 5.5 Directory Service uses object-based replication.)

To avoid a potentially crushing tsunami of replication you should phase in the synchronization activity. While you may configure all of the CAs on the various ADCs at the same time, you should only activate them sequentially. With the example environment outlined in the previous sections, you can limit the effects of network overload by activating the CAs on each particular ADC server over a period of days. For example, you could activate all CAs on the Boston ADC on Monday, wait for network traffic to stabilize, then activate all the CAs on the Atlanta ADC on Tuesday, and so on.

Obviously, the approach that you take and the activation interval that you use depends very much on the nature of your own particular environment. Whatever approach you take, you should use a test lab environment to understand and characterize your environment's behavior before you deploy for real in your production environment. Forewarned is forearmed.

6.11 Summary

The expression "one size fits all" is definitely not appropriate when you look at designing a topology of ADC servers and CAs for your organization. Certainly there may well be similarities between many organizations, and in smaller environments these similarities will be more readily identifiable.

However, there is a tendency toward simpler domain models with Windows 2000 and Exchange 2000, and this, coupled with an administrative requirement to use as few CAs as possible, sees the use of the temporary migration OU extend a lead over the other contenders by a short head. This approach facilitates a straightforward migration coexistence model and allows the unwanted hierarchy of the Exchange 5.5 environment to be deleted when migration is complete.

7

Moving to Exchange 2000

7.1 Introduction

Building a solid Windows 2000 infrastructure merely provides a robust platform for a new Exchange 2000 deployment. But what of the work required to evolve your Exchange 5.5 environment to the brave new world that is Exchange 2000? This is not just an upgrade of a few binaries; this is the reengineering of a whole infrastructure. We're presented with almost myriad challenges: providing mail coexistence between Exchange 5.5 and Exchange 2000, providing synchronization services between the Exchange 5.5 Directory Service and the Active Directory, and how to move Exchange 5.5 mailboxes to Exchange 2000 mailboxes. Of course, we haven't even mentioned Public Folder infrastructures, business applications built on top of Exchange 5.5, and potentially other third-party products that have been integrated into your Exchange environment. And, if that wasn't enough, we also need to be concerned with the effort that's required to upgrade the underlying infrastructure that Exchange 2000 will run on. In all likelihood, you'll probably have Windows NT4 deployed for account domains and resource domains for Exchange 5.5 servers; these domains will need to be upgraded to Windows 2000.

As you can see, moving up to Exchange 2000 isn't just about upgrading a single software product: It's about building a new infrastructure and doing so in a smooth and transparent way so that none of your existing users has an interruption in service. It's not impossible to do, and in the remainder of this chapter, we'll explore the different tools and techniques that are critical for your deployment to be successful.

7.2 Migration fundamentals

There are a number of guiding principles we should adhere to with regard to moving from Windows NT4 and Exchange 5.5 to Windows 2000 and Exchange 2000. Any migration activity should be low in risk and easy to recover from should something go wrong. You should impact the users as little as possible (service interruption, rebuilding desktop systems, etc.). Finally, the effort required to complete the migration to Windows 2000 and Exchange 2000 should be as minimal as possible.

You must decide on an approach that can be taken to get you to the end zone of steady-state Windows 2000 and Exchange 2000. Two main approaches exist (although there are variants of each one) when migrating. Either you upgrade existing Exchange 5.5 servers in place, or you establish an integrated coexisting environment by placing new Exchange 2000 servers in the Exchange 5.5 environment and moving users over to the new infrastructure. Irrespective of which approach you take, you still need to provide good interoperability between the Exchange 5.5 and Exchange 2000 infrastructures for the duration of the migration. This coexistence is shown for a single Exchange organization in Figure 7.1.

In Figure 7.1, we've integrated a new Exchange 2000 infrastructure into an existing Exchange 5.5 environment. This is done by creating an Exchange 2000 server (either by upgrade from Exchange 5.5 or fresh Exchange 2000 installation) in an existing Exchange 5.5 site. With this link in place, and the associated ADC connections and mail connections to support it, we can have more or less seamless interoperability between Exchange 5.5 and Exchange 2000. If integration isn't achieved at this level,

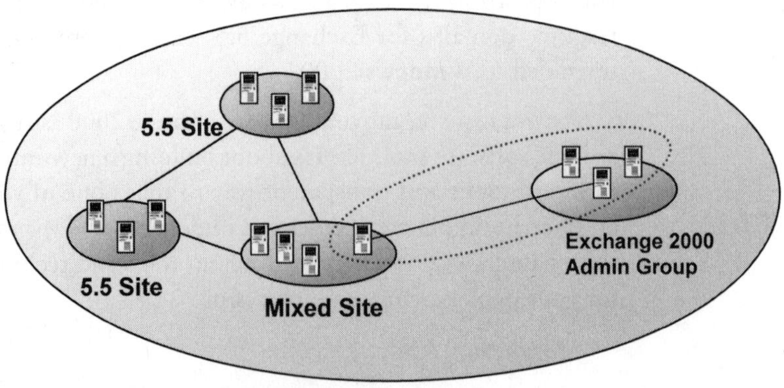

Figure 7.1 *Exchange 5.5 and Exchange 2000 integration.*

then you essentially end up with a separate Exchange 2000 organization (different from the Exchange 5.5 organization). In such a case, you're faced with the age-old problem of interorganization interoperability such as directory synchronization (made easier using the ADC); mail connectivity; and, perhaps most importantly, Public Folder interoperability.

There are pros and cons associated with upgrades or Exchange organizational restructuring using fresh installs. Upgrading existing servers makes use of existing hardware but impacts service levels, since systems are unavailable for the duration of the upgrade. Adding new Exchange 2000 servers to the existing Exchange 5.5 sites results in new hardware being required, but user impact is reduced, since users can be moved from one server to another in a short period of time. Whichever approach you take, the best way to get there is to ensure that you've completed a move to Windows 2000 for account domains. If you haven't fully completed this exercise, then, although you can still migrate to Exchange 2000, it becomes much more complex.

7.3 Making a clean break

Before any migration project is embarked upon, it's important to understand just what level of interoperability and coexistence requirements you will need in your environment. Coexistence and migration means different things to different people, but, basically, you must consider two points: a start point and an end point. The start point represents the Exchange 4.0/5.0/5.5 environment, while the end point represents a pure Exchange 2000 environment. Ideally, if you could move from the start point to the end point in an infinitesimally small period of time, then the problem of coexistence approaches zero. However, the resources required to make such a journey are hard to come by, and, in most cases, some level of sustained coexistence is required in support of a migration project.

An alternative exists, of course. You can still make the move from start point to end point using some quanta of time but ignore the problem of coexistence altogether. In real terms, this means that you begin a deployment of Exchange 2000 alongside an existing or legacy Exchange environment, but we make no effort to perform the following tasks:

- Allow new Exchange 2000 users to communicate with legacy Exchange users
- Move mailbox data from legacy Exchange servers to new Exchange 2000 servers

- Replicate Public Folders from legacy Exchange servers to Exchange 2000 servers
- Maintain group membership, distribution lists, or Public Folder access controls
- Maintain third-party product integration or business applications

This is certainly the easiest migration to make, because we have no coexistence factors to consider. I've heard more and more people suggest the clean break or greenfield migration approach, especially with the sophistication of some of today's third-party migration tools. But I have to say that I don't believe that this is the best way to go forward. Most organizations have too much invested in their existing infrastructures to just let them die gracefully. What's more likely is that some form of coexistence will be required during a period of migration. Typically, this kind of coexistence takes the form of mail and directory interoperability coupled with a plan to migrate data from the legacy Exchange 5.5 environment to the new Exchange 2000 environment.

7.4 Migration terminology refresher

There are a number of key terms that we'll meet over and over again when we discuss migrating from Exchange 5.5 to Exchange 2000. Some of the terms we've met already and explained in passing, but they are critically important to understanding the nature of migration and the behavior that you'll see as users are moved. It's important then that we fully describe them here. They are as follows:

- Distinguished Names (DNs): We'll discuss DNs a lot. There are essentially two types: DNs that we meet in the Exchange 5.5 Directory Service and DNs that we meet in the Active Directory. Objects in the Exchange 5.5 Directory Service are uniquely identified by their DN, while objects in the Active Directory are uniquely identified by their Global Unique ID (GUID).

  An Exchange 5.5 Directory Service example might be:

  ```
  /o=Razorbird/ou=Sales/cn=Recipients/cn=ConorB
  ```

  An Active Directory example might be:

  ```
  cn=ConorB, cn=Users, dc=Razorbird, dc=com
  ```

- legacyExchangeDN: Under certain circumstances—for example, when synchronizing Exchange 5.5 Directory Service objects with

Active Directory objects—it's important that an object that has been migrated from the Exchange 5.5 Directory Service be able to remember how it was uniquely identified in the Exchange Directory Service. The `legacyExchangeDN` attribute of an Active Directory object holds this information and acts as a link back to the Exchange object.

- Security Identifier (SID): SIDs uniquely identify objects in the Windows NT4 SAM account database. So clearly there are two unique representations of objects in Windows NT4 and the Exchange 5.5 Directory Service. The SID is important because it is used as the primary mechanism to enforce security controls in Windows NT4 and for controlling access to resources in Windows 2000.
- sIDHistory: In a manner similar to the `legacyExchangeDN` attribute, it's often important that an object migrated from the Windows NT4 SAM database to an Active Directory object remembers its SID from its Windows NT4 lifetime. The `sIDHistory` attribute performs this function, and the ClonePrincipal API utility, which is used by the Windows 2000 migration scripts and tools, populates this Active Directory attribute when a new security principal is created in Windows 2000. You should note that upgrading a Windows NT4 domain to Windows 2000 does not populate the `sIDHistory` attribute.
- msExchMasterAccountSID: The ADC, when creating security principals in the Active Directory does not populate the `sIDHistory` attribute, but it will inspect it when trying to match objects. Instead, the ADC stores legacy SID information (which links the Exchange 5.5 mailbox object to a Windows NT4 account) in this attribute and, importantly, some migration tools and the Active Directory Cleanup Wizard use this attribute for object-matching purposes.

7.5 The importance of SID History during migration

A SID is a unique value used by both Windows NT4 and Windows 2000 to identify an account or a group. The most important use for SIDs with respect to migration is the construction of ACLs and the protection of Windows resources during a period of migration. The ability to create a new Windows 2000 account from a source Windows NT4 account and placing the source account's SID on the destination account's SID History list (`sIDHistory` is a multivalued attribute) is critical for any Windows 2000 migration.

Many large organizations execute migration projects from Windows NT4 to Windows 2000 that are gradual and take place over time. For those organizations that restructure their Windows NT4 environment to a new Windows 2000 environment, some particular circumstances are applicable. New Windows 2000 user objects are created for existing Windows NT4 users. Since a SID is unique to an account, when a user receives a new Windows 2000 account, he or shewill be using a new SID. Resources are typically migrated over time, too, as existing Windows NT4 resource domains and resources in Windows NT4 account domains are migrated in a structured manner. This means that a user's account may have been moved to Windows 2000 before any of the resources that he or she requires access to have been moved from Windows NT4. Since the original Windows NT4 account's SID exists in the destination account's SID History, this provides the user with the ability to access legacy resources, still present in the Windows NT4 environment, until the migration process moves the resources into the Windows 2000 domains. Typically at that point, the migrated resources are re-ACLed to reflect the new Windows 2000 accounts.

7.6 The ClonePrincipal toolkit

The ClonePrincipal toolkit is a group of VBScript and DLLs that provides the ability to migrate accounts and groups from a Windows NT4 domain to a Windows 2000 domain, adding the SID of the source account or group to the SIDHistory attribute of the destination account or group. This allows the destination account or group to effectively masquerade as the source (or cloned) account. This functionality is implemented via an API that was developed by Microsoft to support the migration of accounts to a Windows 2000 environment.

The ClonePrincipal toolkit is used by a number of other third-party tools to facilitate the migration of Windows NT4 accounts to Windows 2000. Specifically, Microsoft's Active Directory Migration Toolkit (ADMT) uses the ClonePrincipal logic as the basis of its operation. Several third-party tools have also been developed based on this API. While the tools are certainly useful and enhancements to the basic functionality, the ClonePrincipal tool is still useful in its own right. Its operation relies on scripts and DLLs and, subsequently, it's very possible to customize it or write your own migration scripts and procedures.

The ClonePrincipal toolkit is part of the Windows 2000 Support tools, which are installed from the `Support\Tools` folder on the Windows 2000 distribution media. The installation will copy the required files to `\Program Files\Support Tools` and will register the `CLONEPR.DLL`.

The following list, based on Microsoft's *Clone Principal User's Guide*, describes the core components:

- `CLONEPR.DLL`: COM object with methods to support ClonePrincipal operations.
- `SIDHIST.VBS`: Sample script that adds the SID of a source account to the sIDHistory of a destination account in a different forest.
- `CLONEPR.VBS`: Sample script that clones a single security principal.
- `CLONEGG.VBS`: Sample script that clones all the Global Groups in a domain.
- `CLONEGGu.VBS`: Sample script that clones all the Global Groups and Users in a domain.
- `CLONELG.VBS`: Sample script that clones all the Local Groups in a domain.
- `CLONEPR.DOC`: ClonePrincipal documentation.

7.7 Requirements for writeable access to SID history

A number of configuration actions must be taken before you can use the ClonePrincipal tool, or any migration tool based on it, to write to the `sIDHistory` attribute. Specifcally, you must ensure that the following has been performed:

- You must set the `TcpipClientSupport` registry value. On the source primary domain controller, create and set the following registry key:

  ```
  HKEY_LOCAL_MACHINE\System\CurrentControlSet\Control\
  Lsa
  Value name: TcpipClientSupport
  Value type: DWORD
  Value data: 1
  ```

  Then, reboot the source domain controller. This registry value makes the Security Account Manager (SAM) listen on the TCP transport. ClonePrincipal will fail if this registry value isn't set on the source domain controller.

- You must enable auditing in the source and destination domains. In the destination Windows 2000 domain, perform the following tasks:
    1. In the Active Directory Users and Computers MMC snap-in, select the destination domain Domain Controllers container.
    2. Right-click on Domain Controllers and then choose Properties.
    3. Click on the Group Policy tab.
    4. Select the Default Domain Controllers Policy and select Edit.
    5. Under Computer Configuration\Windows Settings\Security Settings\Local Policies\Audit Policy, double-click on Audit Account Management.
    6. In the Audit Account Management window, select both Success and Failure auditing. Wait 15 minutes for the policy auditing change to take effect or reboot.

  In the source Windows NT4 domain, perform the following tasks:
    1. In User Manager for Domains, click the Policies menu and select Audit.
    2. Select Audit These Events.
    3. For User and Group Management, select Success and Failure.
    4. In User Manager for Domains, click the User menu and select New Local Group.
    5. Enter a group name composed of the source domain NetBIOS name appended with three dollar signs, `HICKORY$$$`. Ensure that there are no members for the group.
- Finally, ensure that a trust relationship exists from the source domain to the destination domain.

7.8 Running Exchange 5.5 on Windows 2000 servers

As part of the journey to Exchange 2000, many organizations will first update their complete Windows NT4 infrastructure, both account domains and resource domains, to Windows 2000. Particularly if you intend to do in-place upgrades of Exchange 5.5 servers to Exchange 2000, it is an absolute requirement that at some stage you have Exchange 5.5 running on a Windows 2000 server.

Apart from in-place upgrades there's no requirement that you must have Exchange 5.5 running on Windows 2000. If you don't wish to upgrade servers in place, but instead perform a restructuring migration, then you don't need to upgrade an Exchange 5.5 server from Windows NT4. The restructuring approach allows you to move users from Exchange 5.5 servers running Windows NT4 to Exchange 2000 servers. This is in line with the guiding principle: minimal effort.

If you do wish to upgrade in place, be sure to get existing Exchange 5.5 servers deployed with at least Exchange 5.5 SP3, but preferably SP4, before you start the process of upgrading the OS from Windows NT4 to Windows 2000. This approach provides an opportunity to flatten Windows NT4 domains into a more manageable model and eliminate a potentially wealth of resource domains you may have had. If you had Exchange 5.5 servers running on Windows NT4 Backup Domain Controllers, you now have an opportunity to fold them back into Windows 2000 Master Account Domains as Member Servers. It's important that you do this, since it simplifies topology and administration.

In the Exchange 5.5 and Windows NT4 environment it was a best practice to either have Exchange 5.5 running on a Backup Domain Controller for a resource domain or at least have a Backup Domain Controller logically close by. In moving to Windows 2000, it's desirable to get the domain into native mode as quickly as possible. It's easy to do this with Windows NT4 Member Servers, since they can exist in a Windows 2000 native mode domain. However, Windows NT4 Primary Domain Controllers and Backup Domain Controllers can't exist in a Windows 2000 native mode domain, so it's imperative to have these servers upgraded to Windows 2000 quickly. While there's no great technical challenge associated with this move, it is yet another hurdle that you have to face before you can begin your Exchange 2000 migration in earnest.

In general it's a matter of best practice to eventually have Exchange 2000 running on Member Servers, not Domain Controllers or Global Catalog servers. During this upgrade period, it's best if you can avoid running Exchange 5.5 on Windows 2000 Domain Controllers. However, if you do have Exchange 5.5 running on a Windows 2000 Domain Controller, remember that there will be some contention for access to the LDAP port 389, so you will need to take the appropriate action to reassign Exchange 5.5's LDAP port.

Deploying a Windows 2000 platform for your Exchange 5.5 environment can be done in a number of ways. The most straightforward method is to perform in-place upgrades of the OS itself, but you need to balance this with the complexity of your overall infrastructure. One approach that has proved successful with a number of organizations has been to install a completely new OS platform on brand new hardware. Exchange 5.5 databases can be saved off onto a backup medium, the server reinitialized, Exchange 5.5 reinstalled, and then the databases restored to the new server. This also allows organizations that have invested effort in designing a standard OS platform an opportunity to apply this new platform to existing Exchange 5.5 systems.

7.9 Exchange 2000 migration approaches

There are several approaches that you can take when it comes to moving from an Exchange 5.5 deployment to Exchange 2000. Primarily, we'll look at three different deployment scenarios: upgrading to Exchange 2000, restructuring approach after Windows 2000 deployment, and the accelerated restructuring approach before Windows 2000 deployment.

7.9.1 The upgrade approach

Upgrading from Exchange 5.5 in place to Exchange 2000 is one of the most intuitive means by which to get Exchange 2000 deployed. Let's take a closer look at the process.

Upgrade assumptions

The most important assumption associated with the classic upgrade approach is what needs to be done to the Windows NT4 accounts. You can't have an Exchange 2000 mailbox unless you have a Windows 2000 account. So you must have completed your migration from Windows NT4 account domains to Windows 2000 account domains before you start upgrading an Exchange 5.5 server that hosts mailboxes. You must also have taken the steps to get Exchange 5.5 running on Windows 2000 so that the upgrade can proceed, specifically running Exchange 5.5 SP3 or preferably SP4.

Upgrade process

Before starting the upgrade process, you must have an ADC in place. This is required at the very least for the automatic configuration of a ConfigCA, since a server in an Exchange 5.5 site becomes the first Exchange 2000 server. Furthermore, you need the ADC to host any Recipient CAs that are required to represent Exchange 5.5 mailboxes, custom recipients, and DLs in the Active Directory.

Upon running the SETUP program, you are confronted with the options to upgrade the existing Exchange 5.5 server to Exchange 2000 (as shown in Figure 7.2). Exchange 2000 uses a database structure different from Exchange 5.5, so in addition to the time required just to upgrade the binaries, the total upgrade time is dependent on the size of the Information Store databases. The SETUP process upgrades the Information Store databases at the rather impressive rate of about 25 GB per hour, although this is very much dependent on the configuration of your system and especially the configuration of disk spindles and IO controllers that you use on the server. During setup, the databases are not upgraded completely. Instead, only a minimum part of the Information Store is upgraded, and the remainder of it is upgraded as a background thread that runs as soon as Exchange 2000 starts up. As an interesting historical aside, the original behavior was to perform a minimal upgrade of the database while SETUP was executing, and then only upgrade the parts of the Information Store on demand by the user. However, this plan was short lived, when the first usability tests

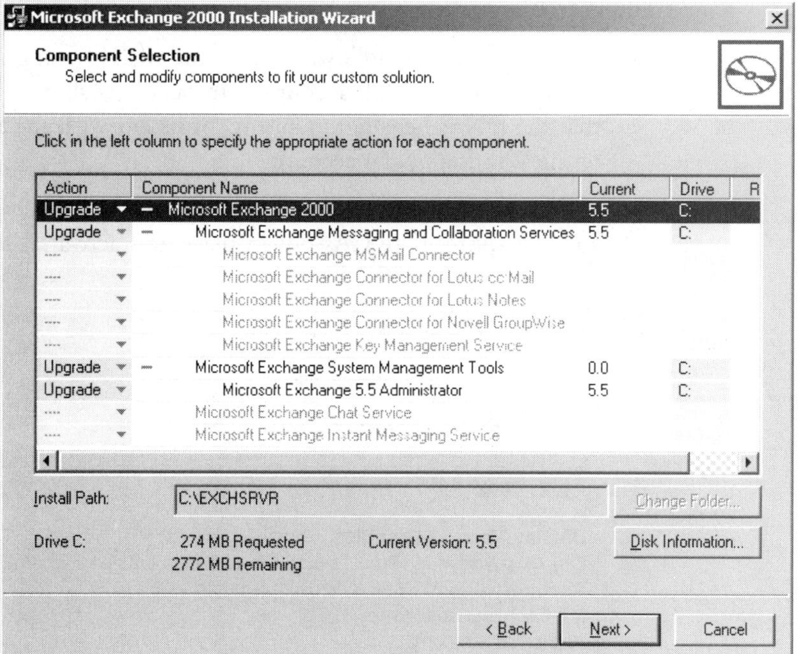

Figure 7.2 *View of the Exchange 2000 upgrade process.*

revealed that the load on the system was somewhat more than expected, to say the least, when newly upgraded users all logged on at the same time!

While this background thread is running, there is a slight performance penalty, a loading on the IO system of around 5 percent. The duration of the background thread operation is similar to the time required by SETUP, again about 25 GB per hour. Rather than suffer this slight penalty during production operation, you can force a total database upgrade to take place. To do this you should dismount the databases once Exchange 2000 starts up and execute the following command from a command window: `ESEUTIL /F <database name>`.

Upgrade Internals

Let's look at the simple case of what happens when a single Windows NT4 and Exchange 5.5 server is upgraded to Windows 2000 and Exchange 2000. We begin with a Windows NT4 SAM entry for the user and an Exchange 5.5 Directory Service entry, shown in Figure 7.3.

After an upgrade from Windows NT4 to Windows 2000, users still get access to their Exchange 5.5 mailboxes, because the access information has been preserved through the in-place Windows NT4 upgrade. That is, the Assoc-NT-Account that points to the Windows NT4 SID is consistent, because the same SID is available after the upgrade. An object's Windows NT4 SID does not change when the domain is upgraded to Windows 2000. Immediately following the Windows NT4 upgrade, we'll be left with a new Windows 2000 account with details as shown in Figure 7.4. Notice that the DN is kensington and is consistent with the SAM Account Name of the Windows NT4 account.

Following the account domain upgrade, the ADC should be installed and the appropriate CAs put in place and activated to map the Exchange

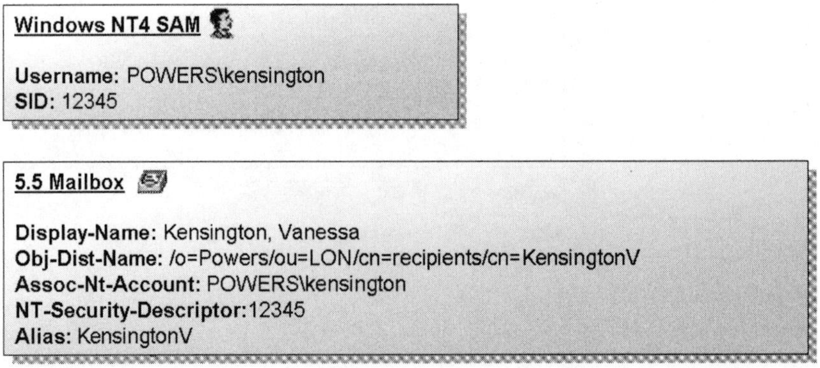

Windows NT4 SAM

Username: POWERS\kensington
SID: 12345

5.5 Mailbox

Display-Name: Kensington, Vanessa
Obj-Dist-Name: /o=Powers/ou=LON/cn=recipients/cn=KensingtonV
Assoc-Nt-Account: POWERS\kensington
NT-Security-Descriptor: 12345
Alias: KensingtonV

Figure 7.3 *Windows NT4 and Exchange 5.5 information before upgrade.*

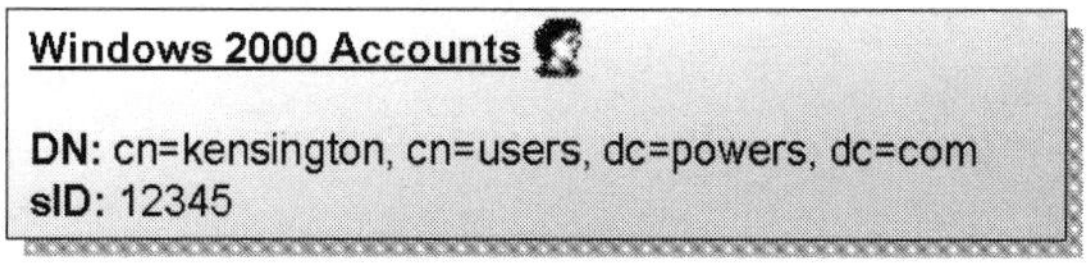

Windows 2000 Accounts

DN: cn=kensington, cn=users, dc=powers, dc=com
sID: 12345

Figure 7.4 *Windows 2000 account details after upgrade.*

5.5 mailbox to the new Windows 2000 account. After running the CA, the Windows 2000 account will be updated to reflect the Exchange 5.5 mailbox, but you should specifically notice that the DN changes after ADC synchronization. This is evidence that the Exchange 5.5 mailbox details have been merged with the Active Directory object, and some of the new values that you should expect to see are shown in Figure 7.5.

The important concern here is access to the Exchange 5.5 mailbox. There is no interruption to access to the mailbox since the down-level account name and SID has remained the same.

Following the ADC synchronization the Exchange 2000 Setup program can be executed and the Exchange 5.5 server is upgraded to Exchange 2000.

Upgrade benefits and drawbacks

Performing in-place upgrades means that you reuse your existing hardware, so these upgrades are attractive from this perspective. Also, if your environment is reasonably straightforward and requires little modification in terms of domain modeling for Windows 2000, this is the natural approach to take, since it requires little in the way of restructuring or external migration tools. Additionally, account passwords remain intact.

On the other hand, the existing hardware on which you are running Windows NT4 and Exchange 5.5 may not be suitable for Windows 2000 or Exchange 2000. If that's the case, and you need to upgrade hardware, then you'll have to cover the extra cost in any event.

But perhaps the biggest drawback is service interruption. Servers must be taken off-line to perform both Windows 2000 and Exchange 2000 upgrades. Even if you do this afterhours, it is a major disruption and can

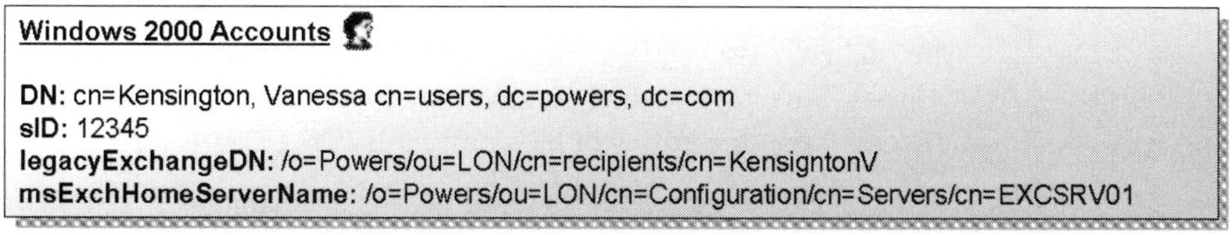

Windows 2000 Accounts

DN: cn=Kensington, Vanessa cn=users, dc=powers, dc=com
sID: 12345
legacyExchangeDN: /o=Powers/ou=LON/cn=recipients/cn=KensigntonV
msExchHomeServerName: /o=Powers/ou=LON/cn=Configuration/cn=Servers/cn=EXCSRV01

Figure 7.5 *Updated Windows 2000 account details following ADC synchronization.*

take a significant period of time. As well as that, because the upgrade process has a server granularity, if something goes wrong, it can take considerable time to recover from it, restore backup tapes, and get your users up and running again.

Upgrading Exchange 5.5 clusters

Upgrading a cluster is not a straightforward task. Upgrading a nonclustered system is more or less a self-contained process after you double-click on SETUP.EXE. However, upgrading a cluster is a less self-contained process. Instead, you must use one of two approaches: a cluster server rebuild process along the same lines as the disaster recovery process for Exchange 5.5 or introduce a new Exchange 2000 cluster into the same site and move users onto it. Let's look at the disaster recovery style option first.

With the disaster recovery mode of upgrade, you essentially save off the existing Exchange 5.5 databases, reinitialize the existing server—that is, reinstall the operating system and Exchange 2000 from scratch—and build a new Exchange 2000 cluster. (A certain Exchange program manager, who shall remain nameless, described this much more eloquently to me some time ago, employing the phrase *torch the existing box* in place of the somewhat more mundane *reinitialize the existing server.*) When you've got the new cluster built using existing hardware, you can restore the old cluster databases onto the new cluster, and after the databases have been upgraded you find yourself with a new Exchange 2000 cluster. This approach is somewhat convoluted, but it is well documented and should be relatively straightforward. As an in-place upgrade, of course, it suffers from the fact that the server is taken out of service for a period of time, probably a few days, while it's backed, rebuilt, and then restored, so this represents a considerable impact to user service levels. The upgrade steps for an Exchange 5.5 cluster are as follows:

1. Back up all user and configuration data on the cluster.
2. In Cluster Administrator, bring the Exchange 5.5 Cluster group off-line.
3. From My Computer, go to `H:\exchsrvr`, where `H` is the letter of the shared cluster drive, and rename the `MDBDATA` directory. (Choose a new name such as `MDBTEMP`.) If you do not rename this directory, the directory will be removed in step 4.
4. Remove Exchange 5.5 Server (and all the Exchange 5.5 system files) from both nodes by running Exchange 5.5 Setup and selecting Remove all on the Installation Options screen.

5. From My Computer, go to `H:\exchsrvr`, where `H` is the letter of the shared cluster drive, and change the directory that you renamed in step 3 back to `MDBDATA`.

6. Install Exchange 2000 on both nodes of the cluster. (Follow the procedure for Exchange 2000 cluster installation outlined in the file `\DOCS\C20_CLUSTERING.RTF` on the Exchange 2000 installation CD.) Do not install both nodes at the same time. After you finish installing the first node, restart that node and then begin the installation on the other node.

7. Create a resource group in the same cluster group that the Exchange 5.5 virtual server was in, but do not bring the group on-line. (See the previously referenced document for information on creating a resource group.)

8. From My Computer, go to `H:\exchsrvr\MDBDATA`, where `H` is the letter of the shared cluster drive.

9. In the `MDBDATA` directory, delete all the files except `PRIV.EDB` and `PUB.EDB`. Rename these files `PRIV1.EDB` and `PUB1.EDB`, respectively.

10. In Cluster Administrator, right-click the resource group, and then click Bring Online. As the databases come on-line for the first time, Exchange 2000 recognizes that they are in Exchange 5.5 format and immediately initiates a process to upgrade them to Exchange 2000 format.

The alternative upgrade approach is along the lines of the general restructuring approach that you can use for any type of Exchange 5.5 server. We'll discuss this approach in more detail later, but essentially it allows you to install a brand new cluster into the same site that the Exchange 5.5 cluster is in and simply move users from the old cluster to the new one. This approach has many attractions, not the least of which is the fact that you get an opportunity to use new hardware, which is particularly important for Exchange 2000 clustering, and also because of the fact that there is significantly less impact on server availability to the users. Bear in mind that this will cause a significant amount of data to be written to the transaction log files.

With either of these approaches, bear in mind that the first Exchange 5.5 server in a site that you upgrade to Exchange 2000 must run the SRS. And since the SRS cannot run on a cluster, if you wish to upgrade an Exchange 5.5 cluster to become an Exchange 2000 cluster, you must previously have installed or upgraded a nonclustered Exchange 2000 system into that site.

7.9.2 The restructuring approach

As an alternative to the upgrade approach, it's possible to build a new Exchange 2000 environment alongside, but integrated with, the existing Exchange 5.5 environment. This approach, similar to the upgrade approach, relies on Exchange 5.5 intraorganizational coexistence with Exchange 2000 servers.

Restructuring assumptions

One of the biggest assumptions that we make with this approach, and, in fact, the most important factor related to its relative ease as a migration mechanism, is that the migration of account domains from Windows NT4 to Windows 2000 is complete. If the migration isn't complete, then the restructuring scenario becomes quite complicated from an Active Directory perspective and essentially turns into the accelerated restructuring approach that I describe in Section 7.9.3.

Of course, with a restructuring approach, as with the approach that you might take for Windows 2000 restructuring, you need to invest in at least some new hardware on which to run the parallel Exchange 2000 environment. This does not mean that you need to replace every single Exchange 5.5 server system with new hardware for Exchange 2000. You may do this, or you may take an opportunity to consolidate server systems and replace several Exchange 5.5 systems with a single Exchange 2000 server, perhaps even a cluster. This *Pacman approach* is appealing because it builds on the strengths of Exchange 2000. Alternatively, you may be able to reuse old Exchange 5.5 hardware with a moving train or leapfrog approach—that is, kick start the restructuring operation by introducing a new Exchange 2000 server on new hardware and move Exchange 5.5 users onto this new server, freeing up the old hardware on which Exchange 5.5 was running for recycling, perhaps for the next Exchange 2000 server.

Restructuring process

In terms of Exchange 2000 restructuring, what you do not want to do is build a new Exchange 2000 organization that is separate from the existing Exchange 5.5 organization. This does not offer a coexistent environment or rich interoperability, especially in terms of restrictions around cross-organizational scheduling and Public Folder interoperability. What you do wish to build is a new Exchange 2000 environment that is integrated into the existing Exchange 5.5 environment. The simplest way to do this is to select an installation option that will join an existing Exchange 5.5 site during the ForestPrep phase of Exchange 2000 installation, as shown in Figure 7.6. Selecting this option prompts you on the next setup screen to specify the name of an Exchange 5.5 server in the site that you wish to join; subsequently, RPC communications take place and configuration information is read from the Exchange 5.5 Directory Service Configuration container and written into the Active Directory Configuration Naming Context. ForestPrep uses a temporary ConfigCA to read the configuration information from the Exchange 5.5 Directory Service to the Active Directory, so you must already have an ADC configured somewhere in your organization.

With the restructuring approach you install the new Exchange 2000 server into an existing Exchange 5.5 site: a site that must have at least one Exchange 5.5 SP3 (or SP4) server. Such a site is often referred to as a mixed vintage site, because it hosts both legacy Exchange 5.5 servers and new Exchange 2000 servers. The site can have previous versions of Exchange in it as well—that is, Exchange 4.0 and Exchange 5.0.

Figure 7.6 *Running Exchange 2000 ForestPrep to join an existing Exchange 5.5 organization.*

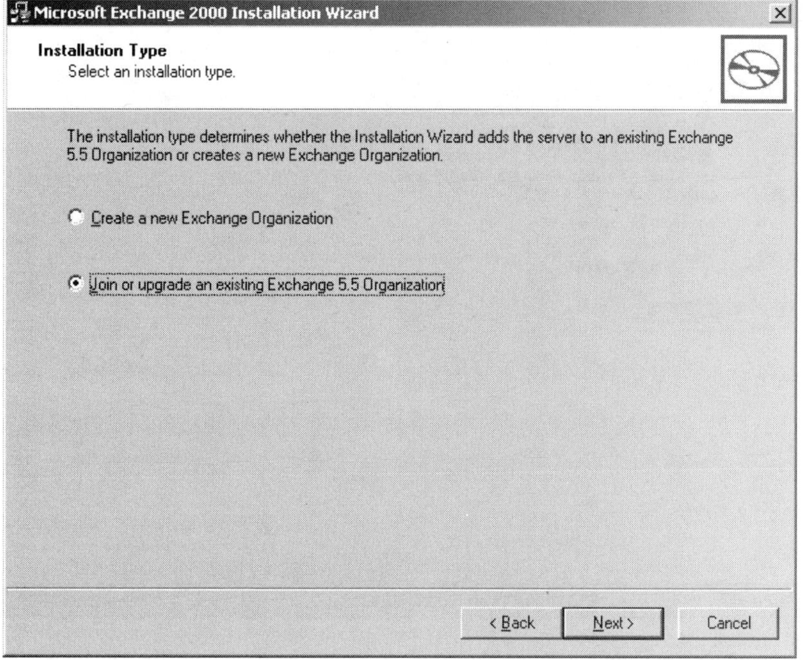

Before an Exchange 2000 server can be installed into an Exchange 5.5 site, you must already have an ADC available. You'll need the ADC there to support CAs for the Recipient containers and OUs that you wish to synchronize, but, just as importantly, the installation process associated with the first Exchange 2000 server also creates a ConfigCA so that configuration information can be synchronized between the Exchange 5.5 and Exchange 2000 environments. During installation, Setup chooses the first ADC returned to it by a Domain Controller in order to home the ConfigCA. If you have multiple ADCs then, say one in each major geographical area, it's possible that you may find an Americas ADC being used to host a ConfigCA for a site in Europe. There's no way to control this during installation, but you should review the placement of ConfigCAs after installation and rehome remote ConfigCAs to local ADCs if they've been homed incorrectly, thus improving configuration information synchronization performance.

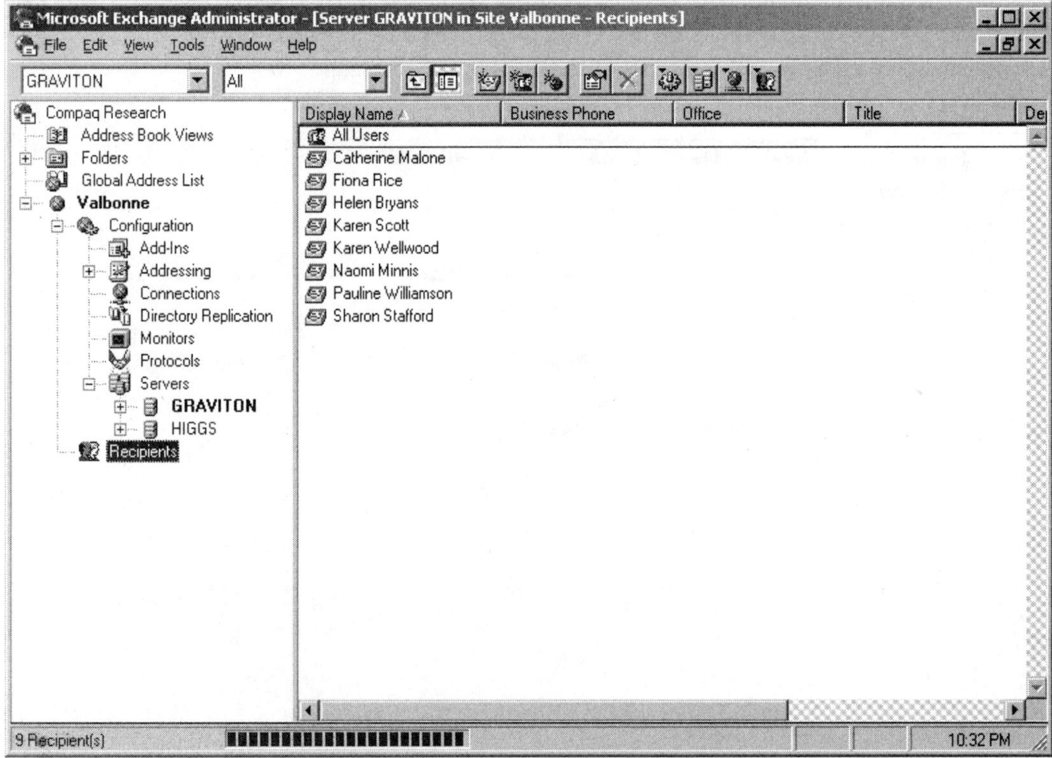

Figure 7.7 *Exchange 5.5 Administrator program showing mixed vintage site (server HIGGS runs Exchange 2000).*

The beauty of the mixed vintage site is that you have Exchange 2000 servers in Exchange 5.5 sites operating seamlessly and transparently to your users. Within the site, the Exchange 2000 server looks much like any other Exchange 5.5 server when viewed from the Exchange 5.5 Administrator program, and, similarly, Exchange 5.5 servers can be viewed from the Windows 2000 Exchange System Manager snap-in and appear, more or less, like any other Exchange 2000 server. (Examples of these views are shown in Figures 7.7 and 7.8.)

Although the servers are visible from both management interfaces, you should not "cross the streams" when it comes to server management—that is, be sure to use the Exchange 5.5 Administrator program to manage Exchange 5.5 servers and use the Exchange System Manager utility to manage Exchange 2000 servers. Hybrid management practices are not recommended. If you need any further encouragement for this, you should take a look at the Exchange 2000 installation process: It explicitly offers an option

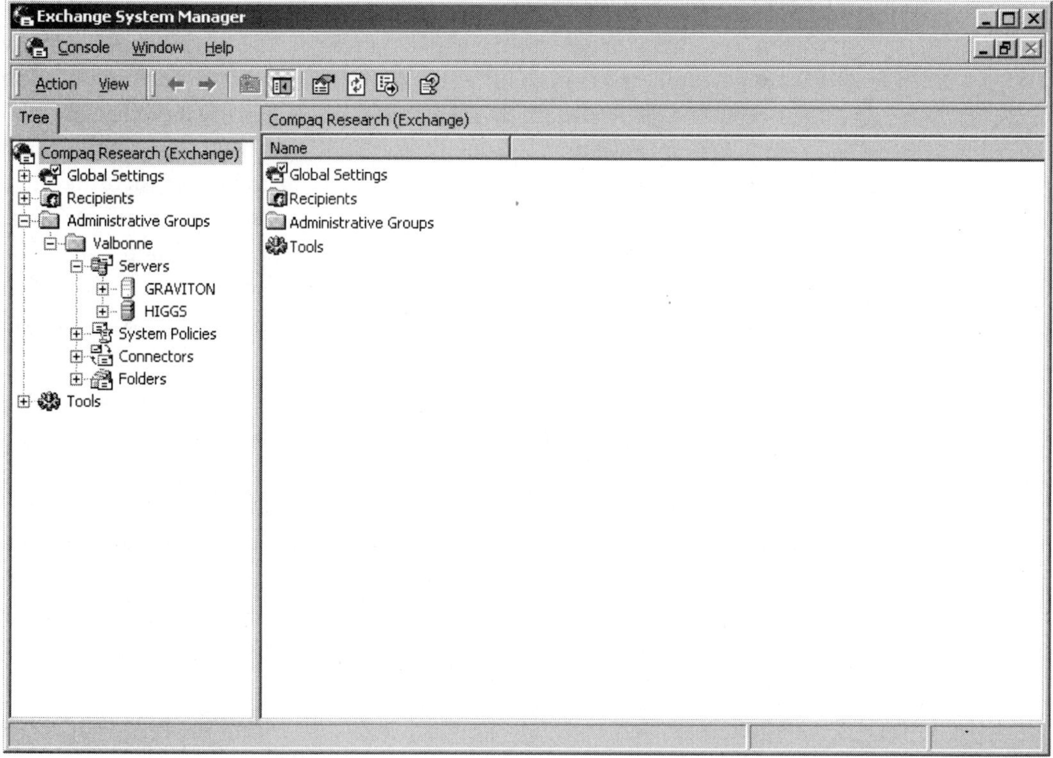

Figure 7.8 *Exchange System Manager showing mixed vintage site (server GRAVITON runs Exchange 5.5).*

to install the Exchange 5.5 Administrator program so that you can manage Exchange 5.5 servers in mixed vintage sites.

Within a mixed vintage site, legacy Exchange servers and Exchange 2000 servers communicate using RPCs for MTA-to-MTA communication, SRS-based intrasite replication, and Exchange 5.5 Administrator communications.

In an Exchange 2000 mixed mode organization, Exchange 5.5 sites map directly to Exchange 2000 Administrative Groups (individual servers can't be moved between Administrative Groups and Routing Groups until the Exchange 2000 organization is running in native mode). Sites are represented as a fixed Administrative Group/Routing Group pair. You can see this mapping of sites and Administrative Group/Routing Group pairs in Figures 7.7 and 7.8. The Valbonne site as viewed from the Exchange 5.5 Administrator program is shown as an Administrative Group from the Exchange System Manager.

Although Exchange 5.5 server to Exchange 2000 server communication within a mixed vintage site takes place using RPCs, if there are multiple Exchange 2000 servers in the site, they communicate with each other using the native SMTP transport, as they would do in a normal Exchange 2000 Routing Group. Additionally, one of the Exchange 2000 servers in a mixed vintage site acts as the Routing Group Master and generates the Link State Table to provide optimized routing information to the other Exchange 2000 servers in the site (Administrative Group/Routing Group pair). The Routing Group Master generates information on how to connect to other Exchange 5.5 servers based on what it receives via the ConfigCA. (This will be discussed at length later in the book.)

Having built a closely integrated mixed vintage site, there's now a straightforward mechanism to move user mailboxes from Exchange 5.5 servers to Exchange 2000 servers. It's called point and click! You can use the Windows 2000 Active Directory Users and Computers snap-in to select the Exchange 5.5 mailbox (which is associated with a Windows 2000 user object), right-click and select Exchange Tasks and then Move Mailbox Wizard, and then select the appropriate database on the new Exchange 2000 server to which the mailbox should be moved. (Figure 7.9 shows a screen capture from part of this process.)

Mailbox move performance, which relies on MAPI for its operation, is affected by the throughput that you can glean from the IO subsystem on both the source and target Exchange servers. As a rough guideline, on my single disk test systems, a 115 MB mailbox took some nine minutes to

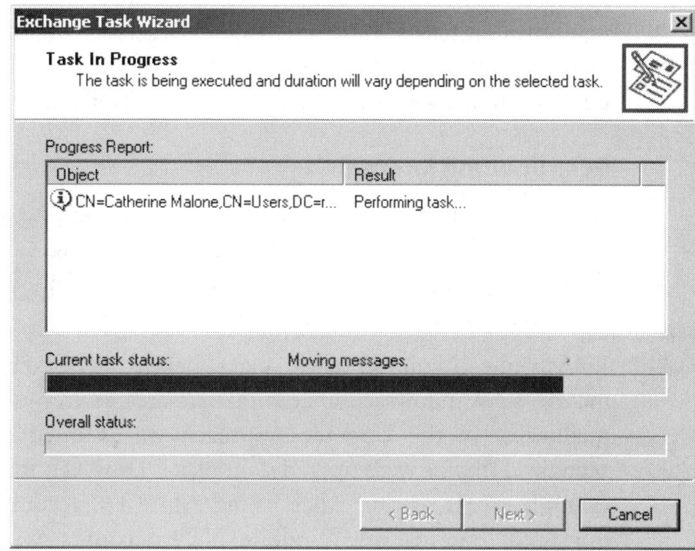

Figure 7.9 *Active Directory Users and Computers Move Mailbox Wizard.*

move. Thus, the effective transfer rate was about 12 MB per minute. Faster disks, controllers, high spindle count, and low workload on the servers and the network should all contribute to speedier migrations. To get a realistic figure for your environment, there's no substitute for testing exhaustively in your testing lab.

Single, instance storage is not preserved across moves, even if the mailboxes are moved from the same source Exchange 5.5 information store. However, this may not be too important to you, since many organizations, especially larger organizations, have observed poor single-instance sharing ratios. Moves between any Exchange 5.5 server to any Exchange 2000 server (and back to the Exchange 5.5 server if required) are supported within a site or Administrative Group/Routing Group pair. However, moving a mailbox from an Exchange 5.5 server in one site to an Exchange 2000 server in another Administrative Group/Routing Group pair is not supported—that is, mailbox moves between mixed vintage sites is not supported in Exchange 2000 mixed mode; you must be in native mode before you can move Exchange 2000 mailboxes between servers in different Administrative Groups or Routing Groups.

Although moving mailboxes from Exchange 5.5 servers to Exchange 2000 servers is a convenient way to migrate data, there are some restrictions on its operation. If the Exchange 5.5 server is running on a Global Catalog server, while Exchange 2000 is running elsewhere in the forest, you cannot move mailboxes from the Exchange 5.5 server. The attempt to do so results in `MAPI error 80040111-0286-00000000`. To allow the migration of mailboxes from such an Exchange 5.5 server, you must reconfigure the server so that it is no longer a Global Catalog server. (But obviously another Global Catalog server in the forest must be available.)

Restructuring internals

Let's take a look at the process of restructuring and what happens when Windows NT4 accounts are migrated to Windows 2000 in advance of an Exchange 5.5 mailbox move. We start with a Windows NT4 account and Exchange 5.5 mailbox, as shown in Figure 7.10.

Account migration takes place before any Exchange mailboxes are moved, so Windows 2000 accounts are created to host the Exchange 2000 mailboxes. In the Upgrade Approach we assumed that Windows NT4 account domains were upgraded in place. However, for the purposes of this example, we'll assume that Windows NT4 account domains are not upgraded, but instead Windows NT4 accounts are migrated using the ClonePrincipal technique into a new Windows 2000 account domain. This account migration process can either disable the existing Windows NT4 accounts or they can remain enabled and in use. However, it makes sense to disable the old accounts and use the new Windows 2000 accounts. Because we're creating new accounts, the new Windows 2000 user objects get a new SID. Using appropriate migration tools, such as Microsoft's ADMT, Bindview's Direct Migrate, FastLane's DM Suite, or NetIQ's One Point Suite means that the `sIDHistory` attribute will be set on the new object to reflect its relationship to the old Windows NT4 account, as shown in Figure 7.11. This yields a new relationship between the Exchange 5.5 mailbox and the account used to access it: now a Windows 2000 account is used.

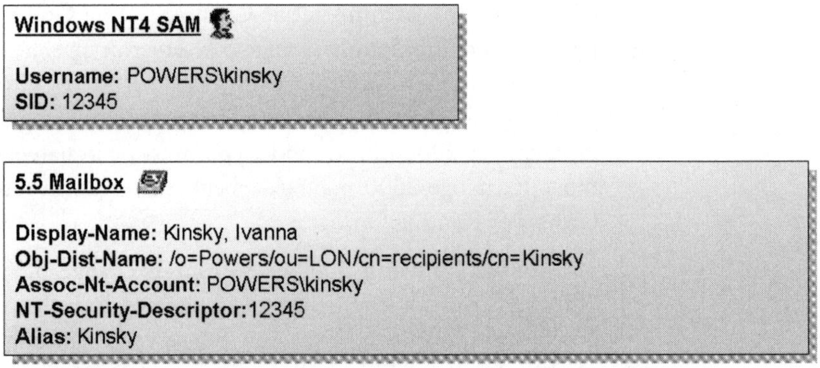

Windows NT4 SAM

Username: POWERS\kinsky
SID: 12345

5.5 Mailbox

Display-Name: Kinsky, Ivanna
Obj-Dist-Name: /o=Powers/ou=LON/cn=recipients/cn=Kinsky
Assoc-Nt-Account: POWERS\kinsky
NT-Security-Descriptor: 12345
Alias: Kinsky

Figure 7.10 *Windows NT4 and Exchange 5.5 mailbox information before account migration.*

Windows 2000 Accounts

DN: cn=kinsky, cn=users, dc=austin, dc=com
sAMAccountName: kinsky
sID: 56789
sIDHistory: 12345

5.5 Mailbox

Display-Name: Kinsky, Ivanna
Obj-Dist-Name: /o=Powers/ou=LON/cn=recipients/cn=Kinsky
Assoc-Nt-Account: POWERS\kinsky
NT-Security-Descriptor:12345
Alias: Kinsky

Figure 7.11 *Restructured Windows 2000 account still with access to Exchange 5.5 mailbox.*

Access to Exchange 5.5 mailboxes is preserved, since down-level account names and the `sIDHistory` attribute are maintained in the new account. When the first ADC synchronization cycle occurs, the Exchange 5.5 mailbox is successfully matched against the Windows 2000 account using the `sIDHistory` attribute. (You must explicitly configure the global ADC policy so that matching occurs based on `sIDHistory` values.) The Windows 2000 account information is merged with information from the Exchange 5.5 mailbox directory entry, resulting in an updated Windows 2000 object, as shown in Figure 7.12.

Following the ADC synchronization, you can install Exchange 2000 servers into Exchange 5.5 sites and subsequently move Exchange 5.5 mailboxes to information stores on Exchange 2000 servers.

Restructuring benefits and drawbacks

The restructuring approach has the lowest impact when it comes to migration to Exchange 2000. In place of the extended time required to upgrade a server to Windows 2000 and then subsequently upgrade to Exchange 2000,

Windows 2000 Accounts

DN: cn=Kinsky, Ivanna cn=users, dc=austin, dc=com
sAMAccountName: kinsky
sID: 56789
sIDHistory: 12345
legacyExchangeDN: /o=Powers/ou=LON/cn=recipients/cn=Kinsky
msExchHomeServerName: /o=Powers/ou=LON/cn=Configuration/cn=Servers/cn=EXCSRV01

Figure 7.12 *Updated Windows 2000 account details following ADC synchronization.*

during which user mailboxes are unavailable, you can build the new Exchange 2000 server alongside the existing Exchange 5.5 service and move users either one at a time or using scripts written with Collaboration Data Objects for Exchange Management (CDOEXM). From a user perspective, there is little interruption to service; only the time required to move users from one server to another is needed.

As well as making migration from Exchange 5.5 servers straightforward, it's also quite possible to move users from Exchange 4.0 and Exchange 5.0 systems without the need to upgrade those servers to Exchange 5.5. Only one server in the mixed vintage site needs to run Exchange 5.5; other servers can run any supported version of Exchange. Since the Move Mailbox functionality takes place over MAPI connections, Exchange 4.0 and 5.0 mailboxes can also be migrated. The migration granularity, this time on a mailbox, as opposed to a server with the upgrade approach, also presents significantly less risk should something go wrong. Furthermore, if your new deployment is leveraging the server consolidation aspect of Exchange 2000, then the restructuring approach offers a simple way to consolidate hardware systems and reuse hardware by virtue of the Pacman and moving train approach described previously.

While the restructuring approach is desirable for many reasons, it can be expensive, since a parallel infrastructure of some description must be in place. However, it's likely that your hardware will need to be improved for Windows 2000 and Exchange 2000 anyhow, so this point may be moot. Similarly, the moving train approach allows existing hardware to be reused, so the costs may not be that prohibitive.

7.9.3 The accelerated restructuring approach

The conventional restructuring approach assumes that Windows NT4 account domains are migrated to Windows 2000 domains before deploying Exchange 2000 and specifically before deploying the ADC. This assumes that some form of CA topology is used to allow the ADC to match Exchange 5.5 mailboxes with Windows 2000 accounts.

However, many organizations strive urgently to deploy Exchange 2000. Exchange 2000 is often described as the killer app for Windows 2000, and in many cases the deployment of Windows 2000 is only in support of Exchange 2000. In such circumstances, it's common to see deployments of the ADC and Exchange 2000 in advance of a complete migration of Windows NT4 account domains to Windows 2000 domains. In support of even a single Exchange 2000 user, an infrastructure must be in place to create a GAL in the Active Directory, and, accordingly, the appropriate CAs must be deployed. If organizations urgently wish to deploy Exchange 2000, but can't wait to complete the migration from Windows NT4 to Windows 2000, then the accelerated restructuring approach is a natural fit.

Accelerated restructuring assumptions

The assumptions associated with the accelerated restructuring approach basically negate the good practice associated with both the upgrade and the restructuring approaches. In both of those approaches, you ensure that all account domain migration from Windows NT4 to Windows 2000 had been completed. If this is done, any form of migration is relatively straightforward.

The basic premise of the accelerated restructuring approach is that this account domain upgrade is either not completed before you start to move to Exchange 2000, or it is started at the same time and runs in parallel to an Exchange 2000 migration. Effectively, it's the sequencing of when ADC synchronization is run in relation to account domain migration that's important. Put the ADC in place any time before you've completed your account domain migration and Exchange 2000 migration becomes more challenging.

Accelerated restructuring process

With the accelerated restructuring approach, during the mid point of the migration we find ourselves with a mix of Windows NT4 and Windows 2000 users, along with a mix of Exchange 5.5 and Exchange 2000 users. Although this kind of migration is the most complex, it's equally likely that it will be the most common for sizeable organizations.

The major complication with the accelerated restructuring approach is the risk of Active Directory object duplication. With the other approaches, the ADC was always able to match an Exchange 5.5 mailbox to an existing Windows 2000 user account, but with the accelerated restructuring approach, an unmigrated Exchange 5.5 user will have two account identities. There'll be a Windows NT4 account associated with the Exchange 5.5 mailbox and there will also be a Windows 2000 user object (or potentially a contact) in the Active Directory. The potential problem occurs when the Windows NT4 account is migrated to Windows 2000. In this circumstance, we rely on intelligence in the account migration tools to recognize that an object already exists in the Active Directory referencing this user. In that case, the migration tools should merge information from the Windows

NT4 user object with the existing Windows 2000 object already created by the ADC.

Simply creating a new account in Windows 2000 may not be appropriate, since this process will not carry across any Windows NT4 account history (so permission structures will be lost). Similarly, just using an object already created by the ADC may not be appropriate, since there is no `sIDHistory` associated with an ADC-created object, so, again, permission structures are lost.

The leading Windows 2000 migration tools seem to be able to deal with the situation relatively well. For example, the tools from Microsoft, Bindview, FastLane, and NetIQ all help with varying degrees of sophistication to merge legacy Windows NT4 accounts with Windows 2000 account objects (probably created by the ADC). At an early stage in your deployment project you should evaluate the characteristics for each of these tools and choose the one that most suits your needs and your environment. Of course, the ADC allows you to create mail-enabled contacts (as well as enabled or disabled user objects) in the Active Directory to represent Exchange 5.5 users, but because these contacts aren't security principals, it's more difficult to merge with them at Windows NT migration time.

If you use migration tools that aren't intelligent enough to detect an existing account and merge with it, or you just create new users, then you may well end up with a live user account as a result of the account domain migration and a user account or contact as a result of previous ADC synchronization. You'll need some way to rationalize the duplicate objects and merge them together. In such cases, you'll need to use the Active Directory Cleanup Wizard, as described in Section 7.10.

Accelerated restructuring internals

Let's take a look at a typical sequence of events that you might expect to see with the accelerated restructuring migration. We do not assume that there is an object in the Active Directory that references the Exchange 5.5 mailbox, but we do assume that the ADC will create a security principal (either an enabled or disabled user object, but not a contact) when synchronization takes place. We begin with a Windows NT4 account and an Exchange 5.5 mailbox, similar to that shown in Figure 7.13.

As a matter of best practice, you should configure the ADC's CAs to create disabled user accounts for an Exchange 5.5 mailbox if it can't match it against an existing Windows 2000 account. The disabled user object gets a

Windows NT4 SAM

Username: POWERS\roseville
SID: 12345

5.5 Mailbox

Display-Name: Roseville, Molly
Obj-Dist-Name: /o=Powers/ou=LON/cn=recipients/cn=Roseville
Assoc-Nt-Account: POWERS\roseville
NT-Security-Descriptor: 12345
Alias: RosevilleM

Figure 7.13 *Windows NT4 and Exchange 5.5 mailbox before account migration.*

new SID in Windows 2000 and, of course, has a new DN. The Active Directory DN is built from the Exchange 5.5 mailbox display name. The primary Windows NT4 account SID is saved in the `msExchMasterAccountSID` attributes. Remember that the `sIDHistory` attribute is not populated by the ADC. The old Exchange 5.5 DN is stored in the `legacyExchangeDN` attribute. Note that the SAM Account name for the Active Directory user account is built from the Exchange 5.5 mailbox alias. This results in an ADC-created Active Directory object similar to that shown in Figure 7.14.

Typically, the next step is to migrate the Windows NT4 account to a Windows 2000 account. Using the proper migration tools, you'll avoid object duplication, but in the worst case, without using the correct tools, you may end up creating another security principal in the Active Directory. For example, using the ClonePrincipal API scripts to migrate the Windows NT4 account will result in a new object being created for this user with a new DN, a new SID, and the old SID being placed in the `sIDHistory` attribute. This results in two objects in the Active Directory now referencing the same person, as shown in Figure 7.15.

Windows 2000 Accounts

DN: cn=Roseville, Molly, cn=users, dc=austin, dc=com
sAMAccountName: RosevilleM
sID: 56789
msExchMasterAccountSID: 12345
legacyExchangeDN: /o=Powers/ou=LON/cn=recipients/cn=Roseville
msExchHomeServerName: /o=Powers/ou=LON/cn=Configuration/cn=Servers/cn=EXCSRV01

Figure 7.14 *ADC-created disabled user object.*

Figure 7.15 *Two user objects in Active Directory referencing the same person.*

Notice the different SID values for these objects and also pay particular attention to the DNs for each one. The DN for the ADC-created object (uppermost in Figure 7.15) has an RDN of Roseville, Molly built from the Exchange 5.5 Display Name, while the migrated Windows NT4 account has an RDN of roseville built from the Windows NT4 account name.

Before you can proceed, it is common practice at this stage to run the Active Directory Cleanup Wizard to merge both the security principals for Molly Roseville together into a single Active Directory object. When the Active Directory Cleanup Wizard operates, the source (disabled) object attribute information is always merged into the target (live) object attribute information, resulting in a single enabled security principal. This results in an enabled user account, similar to that shown in Figure 7.16.

Notice that the DN information for this merged object has reverted back to that for the migrated user account. When the ADC next initiates a

Figure 7.16 *Merged Active Directory user object details.*

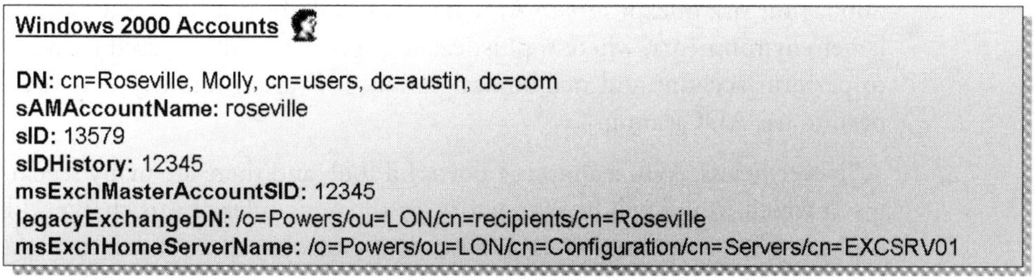

Windows 2000 Accounts

DN: cn=Roseville, Molly, cn=users, dc=austin, dc=com
sAMAccountName: roseville
sID: 13579
sIDHistory: 12345
msExchMasterAccountSID: 12345
legacyExchangeDN: /o=Powers/ou=LON/cn=recipients/cn=Roseville
msExchHomeServerName: /o=Powers/ou=LON/cn=Configuration/cn=Servers/cn=EXCSRV01

Figure 7.17 *ADC-updated merged Active Directory user object details.*

synchronization cycle, it will update the object's DN with the Exchange 5.5 mailbox's Display Name, similar to that shown in Figure 7.17.

The final step in this process is to migrate the Exchange 5.5 mailbox to an Exchange 2000 mailbox. You can do this using the Move Mailbox functionality of the Active Directory Users and Computers tool in the same way as you would for a conventional restructuring operation. Alternatively, you could upgrade existing Exchange 5.5 servers in a more hybrid fashion. Either way, the real complexity in this approach relates to manipulation of data in the Active Directory.

Accelerated restructuring benefits and drawbacks

The only benefit associated with the accelerated restructuring approach is that it facilitates a timely and rapid move to Exchange 2000, because there is no need to wait for the completion of an account domain migration from Windows NT4 to Windows 2000.

This is its greatest strength and its greatest weakness. The synchronization model is more complex and can result in duplicate object creation in the Active Directory unless you use the appropriate migration tools. To avoid any cleanup headaches, using migration tools is a must. Although there may be some cost associated with these tools, it's likely that they will save much effort in the long run.

7.10 Active Directory Account Domain Cleanup wizard

The Active Directory Account Domain Cleanup wizard (hereafter referred to as ADCleanup) is an invaluable tool in any Exchange 2000 migration toolbox. In the simplest of environments, where Windows NT4 account domains associated with Exchange 5.5 mailboxes are upgraded to Windows

2000, your risk of exposure to ADCleanup should be minimal. Similarly, in larger environments, where sophisticated migration tools are used correctly to perform account and mailbox migration, it is again unlikely that you'll need to use ADCleanup.

Nevertheless, ADCleanup is a powerful tool, and there are many scenarios in which its use will be mandatory. In the remainder of this chapter, I'll explain the operation of ADCleanup and how it can be used to make account and mailbox migration as straightforward as possible.

7.10.1 Creating duplicate objects

There are many circumstances that can cause duplicate objects to exist in the Active Directory. Migrating from Exchange 5.5 is typically the most common and the reasons for duplication are more or less obvious. Let's look at an example situation.

In this scenario, you have used the ADC to create disabled user objects in the Active Directory corresponding to Exchange 5.5 mailboxes. The next step in most environments is to migrate Windows NT4 accounts to Windows 2000 accounts. But many migration tools can't match an ADC-

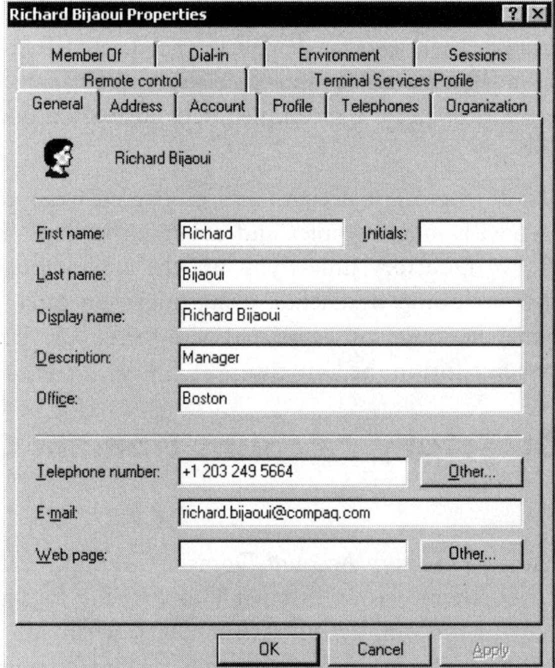

Figure 7.18 *Properties for the disabled user object created by the ADC.*

created disabled user object with the NT4 account that's being migrated. Modern migration tools can perform SID-based checking (using the `msExchMasterAccountSID` attribute), but less advanced tools can only match on account name or alias name attributes, which very often is of little use. Failure to use the appropriate tools means that you end up with two user objects in the Active Directory: a disabled user object created by the ADC and a live user object created by your migration tool.

Simply deleting one or the other of the objects is not an option, since they both hold important information. The ADC-created disabled user object contains information about the user gleaned from the Exchange 5.5 Directory Service, such as job title, office location, telephone number, and e-mail addresses. A relevant example for the user Richard Bijaoui is shown in Figure 7.18. Similarly, the live user object created by the migration tool lacks the above attributes (shown in Figure 7.19) but does contain important information about the user's Windows 2000 group membership (shown in Figure 7.20) and other security attributes, such as the `sIDHistory`. Your mantra for migration should be to merge directory information, but all you've done here is partition the information for a single user into two distinct objects.

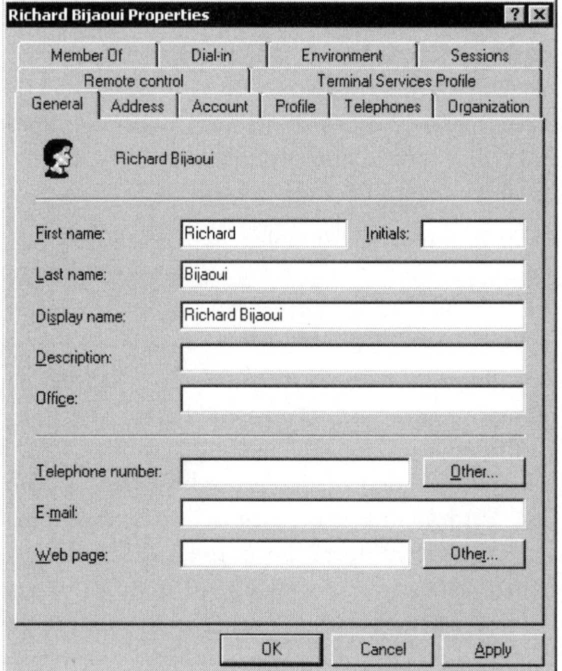

Figure 7.19 *General properties for the enabled user object created by the migration tool.*

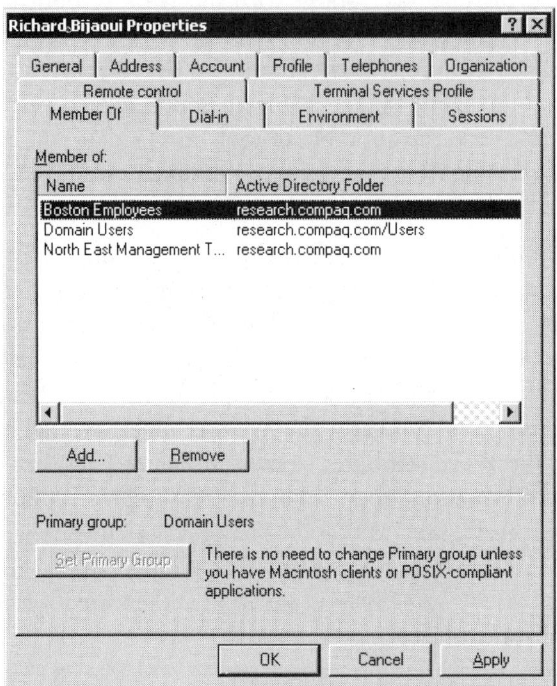

Figure 7.20 *Group membership properties for the enabled user object created by the migration tool.*

7.10.2 Merging duplicate user objects

Since two representations of an individual user are of little use, it makes sense to merge information from both of these objects into a single object. This is where the ADCleanup Wizard comes into play

In our example, the disabled user object has been created in an OU called `Temporary Migrated Users` (Figure 7.21), while the enabled user account has been migrated from Windows NT4 into the `Users` OU in the Active Directory (Figure 7.22). Accordingly, when you use ADCleanup, you should limit the search scope only to a well-defined set of containers—in this case `Temporary Migrated Users` and `Users` containers (Figure 7.23). Although it's not imperative that you do this, it is sensible, since it reduces the likelihood of the Wizard selecting inappropriate accounts for merging. Performance is a factor here too, and limiting the search scope helps execute merge operations more quickly. Rough performance testing shows that it takes approximately 40 minutes to search through a forest with 10,000 user objects, so limiting your search to particular containers in the forest should give more timely results. This phase of ADCleanup only focuses on identifying accounts that the Wizard thinks should be merged; it

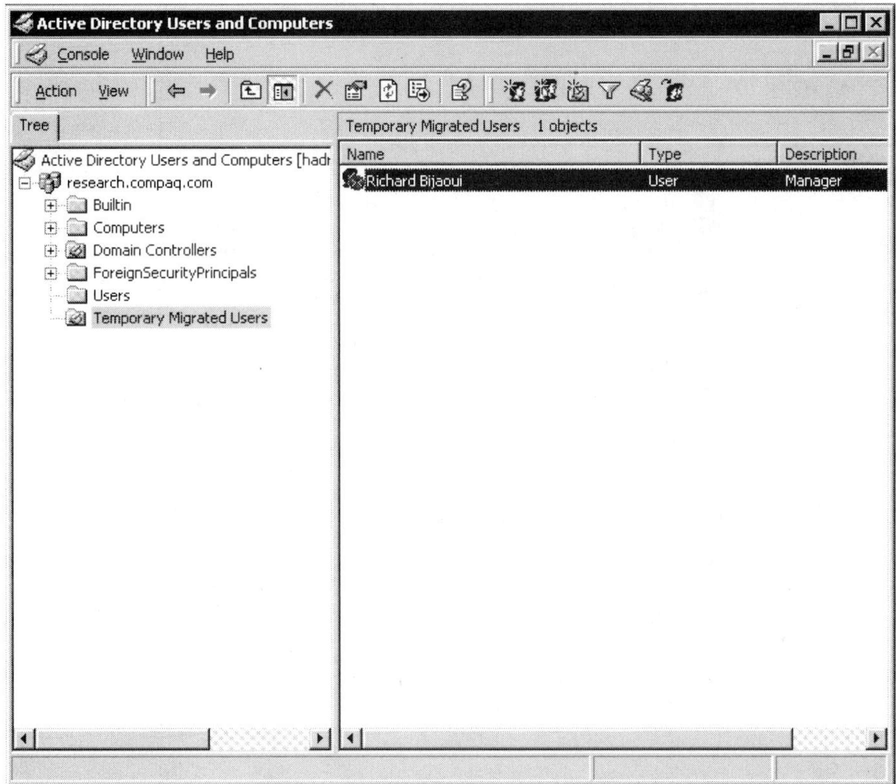

Figure 7.21 *Disabled user object created by the ADC homed into Temporary Migrated Users.*

doesn't actually proceed to merge the account data: This is done during a later operation.

ADCleanup uses different matching rules as it attempts to match different types of objects. When matching a disabled user object against an enabled user object, which is the case here and the most common scenario, ADCleanup matches the `msExchMasterAccountSID` attribute of the disabled user against either the `objectSID` or `sIDHistory` of the enabled user.

You should take a look at Figure 7.24 to understand why this matching attempt is processed in the way that it is. When the ADC creates a disabled user object in the Active Directory, the disabled object is assigned a new SID, because it is a completely new security principal in the Windows 2000 domain. The existing Exchange 5.5 mailbox is associated with a Windows NT4 account (which itself has a SID) and the Windows NT4 account is identified using the Exchange 5.5 Directory Service attribute `Assoc-NT-Account` (the primary Windows NT account). To preserve the linkage back

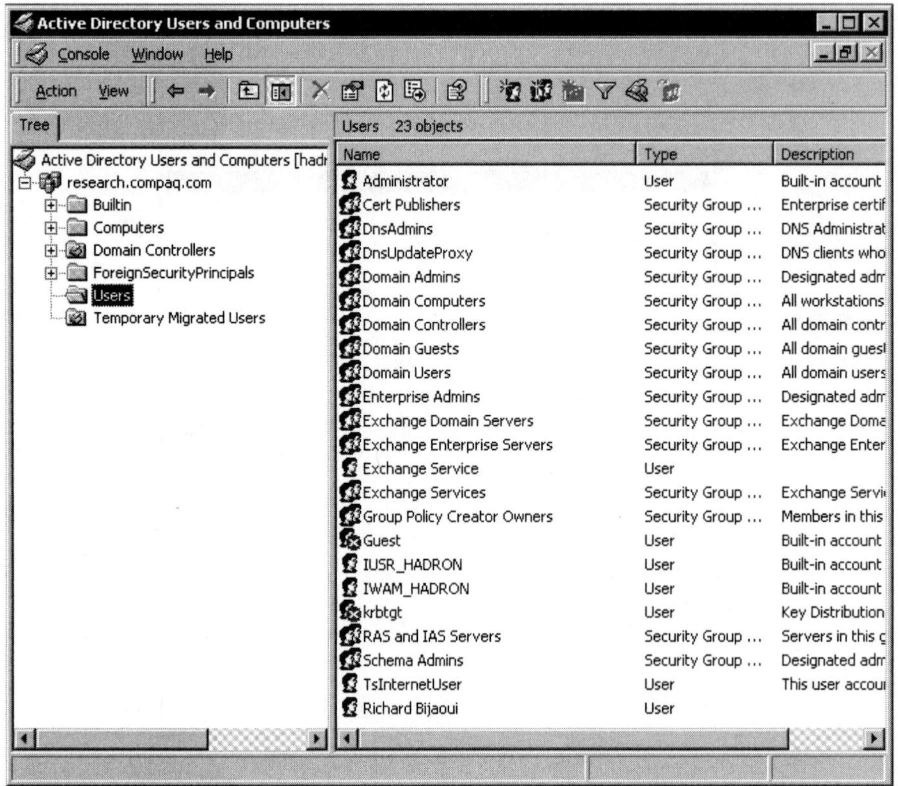

Figure 7.22 *Enabled user object created by migration tools in the Users OU.*

to this Windows NT4 account, the ADC populates the disabled user object's `msExchMasterAccountSID` attribute with the value of the `Assoc-NT-Account` attribute when it creates the new Active Directory object.

Subsequently, when the Windows NT4 account is migrated into Windows 2000, the new enabled user object receives a new SID (since it is a new security principal), but the SID of the Windows NT4 account is placed into the `sIDHistory` attribute (assuming that the domain is being restructured). So now we have a means to link both the disabled and enabled user objects: The `msExchMasterAccountSID` and `sIDHistory` attributes share the same value.

In our example, the ADCleanup selects both Windows 2000 accounts for user Richard Bijaoui and displays the potential merge operation before asking you to confirm—and you need to confirm twice—that you really want to merge them. Merging accounts is a one-way operation. When you've merged objects together, they cannot be unmerged, so you need to be

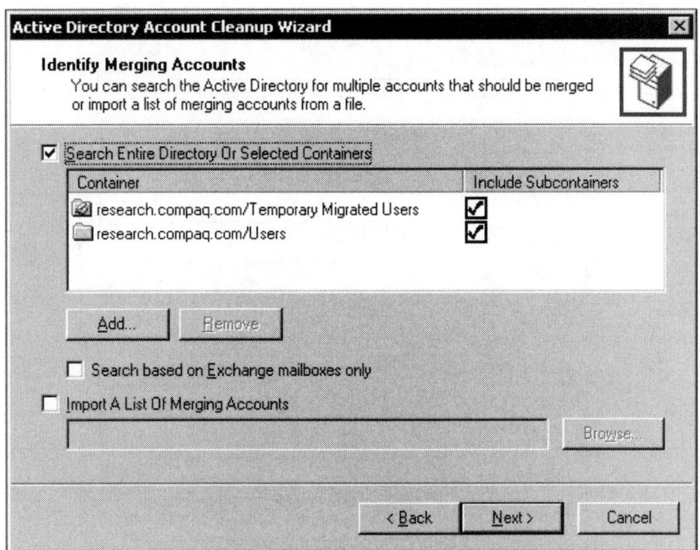

Figure 7.23 *Active Directory Cleanup Wizard search scope.*

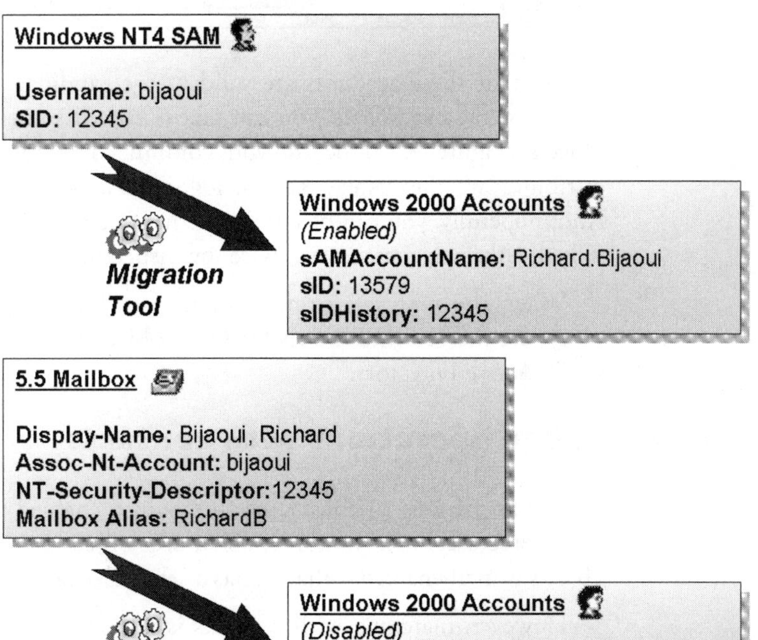

Figure 7.24 *SID relationships between account objects.*

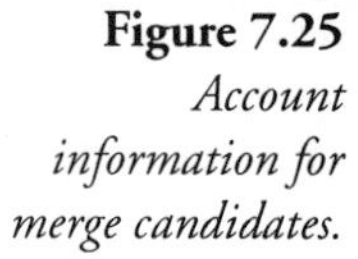

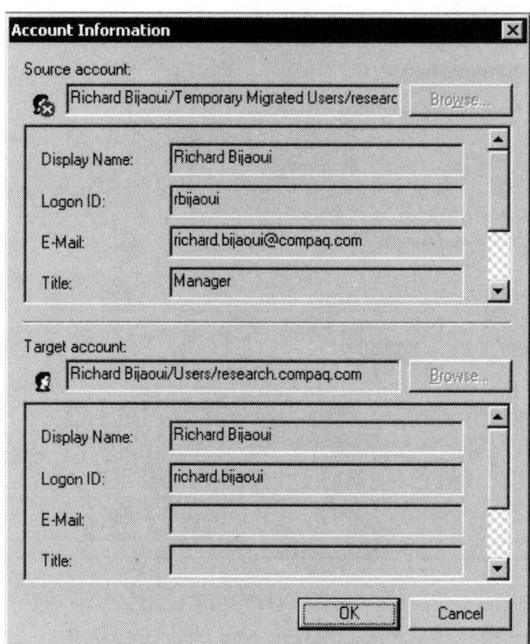

Figure 7.25 *Account information for merge candidates.*

certain that these accounts are valid merge candidates. For any particular pair of merge candidates, you can take a look at some key attributes of the objects (Figure 7.25) before you commit to merging them. These key attributes are the display names, logon IDs, e-mail addresses, and titles. And, hopefully, you can be confident that you're dealing with a single individual, although represented twice, by inspecting these attributes.

When the merge is completed, the attributes from the disabled user object are merged into the enabled user object and only one object remains in the Active Directory.

7.10.3 Merge operations with contacts

As well as merging disabled user objects into enabled user objects, you can also merge a contact into an enabled user object provided only one of the objects is mail enabled—that is, has a set of Exchange mail addresses.

However, matching with contacts is not an exact science and certainly not as accurate as the matching that you get with disabled user objects and enabled user objects where, the matching is based on SIDs. Matching with a contact is based on names (SAM account names, aliases, etc.) and consequently is less precise because inherently there is more scope for ambiguity. When you match on a number (i.e., a SID value), it's simpler and more likely to be accurate because there's no room for ambiguity and subsequently less opportunity for confusion. As you can see in Figure 7.24, the match is clearly defined on the value `12345`.

Contacts don't have SID values, or a `sIDHistory` attribute, because they are not security principals. If you wish to have ADCleanup merge a contact with a user object, searching is performed using the common name (`cn`) and/or display name (`displayName`) attributes of the contact and the user object. If you have maintained good synergy between the Exchange 5.5 mailbox and the Windows NT4 account naming structures, then these merge operations will have a high probability of success. Success is less likely to be guaranteed if significant variation exists between these naming structures in the legacy Windows NT4 and Exchange 5.5 environments. For example, you may have a contact with a display name of Steve Balladelli. This will be matched against an enabled user object and judged to be a merge candidate, if either the display name or common name of the user object matches Steve Balladelli. In addition to matching on names, ADCleanup will also match the Exchange 5.5 mailbox alias (`mailNickname`) against the Windows NT4 login name (`samAccountName`). Again, by way of example, consider an Exchange 5.5 mailbox that has an alias name with a value of SteveB. If the ADC creates a contact in the Active Directory based on the Exchange 5.5 mailbox, the alias value is synchronized into the `mailNickname` attribute of the contact. ADCleanup will match this attribute value against the `samAccountName` (hopefully, SteveB) of the enabled user object.

This flexibility of matching on common name terms, mailbox aliases, and account names is a great benefit for contact-based merge operations. Often, naming information isn't consistent between Exchange 5.5 and Windows NT4, and, in our example, if the Exchange mailbox was named for Steve Balladelli but the Windows NT4 account was named for Steven Balladelli, a match would not exist based on common and display name operations. (The given name is different: Steve versus Steven.) Using a match based on Exchange mailbox alias and Windows NT4 login ID provides a useful alternative mechanism should naming standards be inconsistent. (Of course, many environments don't have synergy between their Exchange 5.5 alias names and login account names, so this too can be problematic.)

7.10.4 Manual merges

Occasionally, you may have a requirement to force a merge operation to take place rather than rely on ADCleanup to select merge candidates. Consider an example where a new account is created in Windows 2000 for the user Fiona Tipping. Since this is a new account and not a migrated one, there's no SID History associated with it. If the ADC then creates a user object for Fiona Tipping's Exchange 5.5 mailbox, no matching can take place on `sIDHistory` by the ADC, and thus a duplicate account is created. Correspondingly, when ADCleanup runs, it won't detect a match, since these are two user objects and user object matching is only performed using SIDs, not names.

Hopefully, scenarios such as this will be rare, but when they do happen you have to manually select the two duplicate objects using the Add button on the Review Merging Accounts window. This is a powerful feature of ADCleanup, but do remember that merging objects is a one-time operation, which can't be undone. Make sure the objects really do represent the same person before you merge them.

7.10.5 Command-line operation

ADCleanup has a useful command-line interface as well as its GUI-based interface. The various options and commands are shown in Table 7.1, and you can get full descriptions of these qualifiers in the on-line help in the Exchange System Manager tool.

Using the command-line version of the tool allows you to script ADCleanup operations so that they can be performed automatically and potentially unattended. For example, you may have a migration process that runs at regular time intervals to migrate Windows NT4 accounts over to Windows 2000. If this were a scripted task, you could execute a script that performs ADCleanup operations immediately after it to ensure Active Directory integrity.

Even if you don't script the migration activity, there is some value in running ADCleanup from a scripted interface. Running the command-line version of ADCleanup explicitly splits a merge operation into two separate phases. The first phase performs a search on the Active Directory for duplicate objects and creates a file that contains the list of merge candidates. You must then explicitly run the ADCleanup command again to process the merge candidate data file and merge the objects. Obviously, this is done for safety, but the ability to generate a report of potential duplicate objects from

Table 7.1 *Active Directory Cleanup Command Line Qualifiers*

Option	Description
/?	Displays a list of available options.
/S	Searches the entire Active Directory forest for ADC-created duplicate objects (i.e., those objects that have the `msExchMasterAccountSID` attribute set) and creates a file called `MergeFileName.CSV` in the working directory.
/C	Used in conjunction with /S to specify a file containing a list of containers in the Active Directory to be searched (e.g., `ADCLEAN /S /C:E:\MyFiles\Containers.CSV`).
/X	Extends the /S operation to include more than just ADC-created duplicate objects.
/M	Performs a merge using the merge candidates listed in `MergeFileName.CSV`.
/O	Specifies an alternative file containing merge candidates (e.g., `ADCLEAN /M /O:E:\MyFiles\Candidates.CSV`).
/L	Specifies the location of the Active Directory Cleanup Log file (e.g., `ADCLEAN /S /L:E:\MyFiles\MyLog.LOG`).

a script is a useful feature that any organization in the midst of a migration project can use. As a good management practice, you should consider running such a script automatically every night and analyzing the results the next morning.

7.10.6 When you do and don't need to use Active Directory Cleanup

I've described some of the rules for automatic detection of Active Directory objects as merge candidates. Under ideal circumstances, these are based on SIDs and naming structures. You can infer two things from this: the importance of using good migration tools and the need for good naming standards.

Migrating all your Windows NT4 accounts to Windows 2000 early in the overall Exchange 2000 migration exercise usually minimizes the requirement for using Active Directory Cleanup. All of the major migration tools (e.g., Active Directory Migration Tool from Microsoft, Direct Migrate from Bindview, DM Suite from FastLane, and One Point Suite from NetIQ) rely on the ClonePrincipal API from Microsoft, which allows the `sIDHistory` to be populated into the migrated account and, subsequently, the ADC will match on it. Thus, there is a significantly reduced potential for duplicate objects.

In many organizations it is unlikely that you'll be able to wait for a complete migration of your Windows NT4 domains before you put the ADC in place, so the likelihood of object duplication is very real. In fact, it's often advisable to use the ADC early and create disabled user objects in the Active Directory in a temporary location, thus using the least number of CAs. Following this approach typically means using one or another of the migration tools I've described in this chapter. These tools are becoming more Exchange 2000 aware and are therefore capable of matching the SID of a Windows NT4 account undergoing migration to Windows 2000 with the `msExchMasterAccountSID` of an existing ADC-created object. Clearly, this reduces the need to run ADCleanup. Similarly, some of the tools are also becoming good at matching on name terms. So the need to have Windows NT4 account naming data in line with naming data from Exchange 5.5 becomes important too. Any effort spent on sanitizing your existing environment (e.g., tying up names such as Rich and Richard, or Steve and Steven) will reduce headaches during migration.

7.11 Summary

However you decide to move to Exchange 2000, I cannot overstate the importance that I place on planning, design, and testing. Whether you perform in-place upgrades, mixed vintage sites, or interorganization migrations, you have a huge responsibility to thoroughly test all relevant migration activities.

Each migration approach that I've described has its own unique set of characteristics, and you'll find one approach more suitable to your environment than another. Or, perhaps, and this appears to be quite common, a mix of different migration techniques might be required.

The possibility of creating duplicate objects in your Active Directory during or after a migration to Exchange 2000 is a very real one. ADCleanup provides an invaluable way to detect and merge such duplicates while preserving attribute and access control information and ensuring the integrity of groups and distribution lists. But ADCleanup has its restrictions too. It can't merge objects between forests. Nor can it merge enabled objects in different domains within the same forest (you must move them into the same domain first). It can't merge two objects that both have Exchange mailboxes associated with them—that's an entirely different problem—nor can it merge two objects that are both mail enabled: Which mail address would it choose as the primary address?

By selecting the right migration approach to get to Exchange 2000, with adequate planning and testing, and carefully choosing the appropriate migration tools for the job, your move to Exchange 2000 should be straightforward, more or less transparent to your users, and uneventful.

8

Messaging Technology Fundamentals

8.1 Introduction

This chapter discusses the basic concepts of a message transfer service and introduces Simple Mail Transfer Protocol (SMTP). In addition, we'll cover the SMTP service offered in Windows 2000 and discuss some of the characteristics available in Windows 2000's SMTP service that differ from those required or needed in the Exchange 2000 transport.

8.2 Transfer protocols

Most readers realize the importance of a message transfer service within a product as it pertains to electronic messaging. In its simplest form, a transfer service allows multiple systems to easily exchange information, typically e-mail. Add to that service a solid routing model and the transfer service can now efficiently transfer information through a network. The architecture used to build a transfer service can also enhance a messaging service by providing the following:

- Basic communications
- Horizontal scalability
- Separation of services

8.2.1 Basic communications

When a messaging system must span more than one physical server, a transfer service enables communication between those servers. Typically, a store-and-forward transfer service is implemented to ensure message delivery. Information communicated is normally in the form of messages, but the

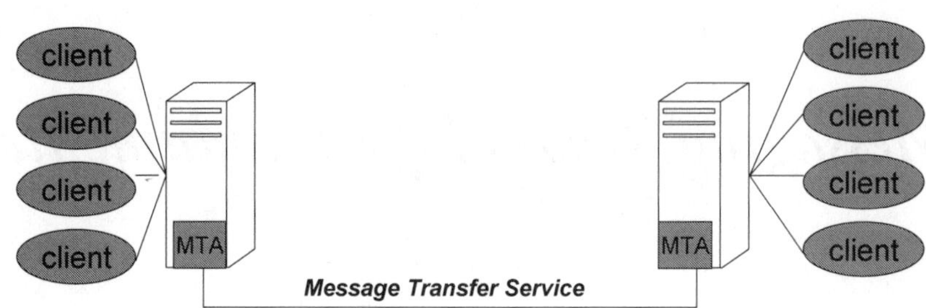

Figure 8.1 *Message transfer service.*

content could be messages, directory information, or application data. Figure 8.1 depicts servers communicating via a transfer service.

It may come as a surprise to many that in the early days of PC-based messaging, Message Transfer Services were not built into the messaging systems. For example, cc:Mail and MS-Mail were designed for LAN use and did not include a store-and-forward transfer service. Instead, they were built on a shared-file model. This model was fine for small groups of users but was viewed by most as not scaling very well. Quite an odd argument when you consider that there were cc:Mail implementations of 15,000 to 20,000 users or more. That seems like pretty good scalability to me! In reality though, those systems could never adequately support enterprises of over 30,000 users nor could they act as an Internet Service Provider (ISP) very well. These systems didn't support Internet protocols natively anyway, so the ISP environment would never have worked well.

This does not mean that transport systems were nonexistent before cc:Mail and MS-Mail—far from it. For example, ALL-IN-1 and PROFS both had transfer services, or distribution services, built into them long before the popularity of the PC LAN–based messaging systems. Even before that, VMSmail provided a pretty darned good mail service for free, with one of the coolest operating systems of all time. As with many things in the computer industry though, the developers of both cc:Mail and MS-Mail forged out on their own without taking into account the lessons learned from the mainframe/minicomputer world. In so doing, they ended up learning those same hard lessons on their own. In this case, the lesson was that a messaging system without a Transfer Service is less than optimal. So, naturally, they built their own Message Transfer Agents (MTAs). In reality, these transfer agents were, in essence, no more than file transfer services; that's right, nothing more than a COPY command equivalent.

This is old news, and we all know that cc:Mail and MS-Mail have had their day in the sun and are limited in terms of their long-term viability. As

I've said, I hesitate to say that they don't scale. I've seen some large implementations of MS-Mail and, especially, cc:Mail. Because of licensing hassles, and other political reasons I'm sure they will both live on for quite some time. Even so, I'd really shy away from implementing them given the choices available today.

8.2.2 Horizontal scalability

As well as enabling base communications between disparate systems, a transfer service also enables horizontal scalability. Horizontal scalability is the ability to increase the capacity of the service offered through the implementation of multiple servers. So, if a service becomes saturated, adding MTAs will increase throughput, as in the case of the three MTAs shown in Figure 8.2. Without a reliable, automatic transfer service, horizontal scalability is somewhat less than seamless. I'm reminded of the days of "sneaker net," when we'd place files on a magnetic medium and hand carry them to their destination. At one site where I worked, we attempted to speed up this process through what we called Frisbee-Net or gnome-net. We'd attach a floppy (an eight-inch floppy in those days) to a Frisbee, using Velcro, and sail it across the data center. Data centers were bigger in those days, since they needed to house monster mainframes and the really cool minis of the day (in our case VAXes, NOVAs, and PRIME systems). So Frisbee-Net seemed like a decent idea. It didn't work, but it was a decent idea and a lot of fun. It brought home the idea of point-to-point networking. Ahh…, the good old days when networking and memory were scarce and code was elegant. Granted, this problem was fixed by FTP, not e-mail, but I hope you get the point: Having a transfer service built into a system natively allows me to send messages directly, point to point, or to pass information through hubs or switches; in this context, defined simply as a set of servers primarily dedicated to message transfer. If the hub is being saturated, I can easily add more servers to the hub and increase the throughput.

8.2.3 Separation of services

A transfer service also allows for deployments that separate specific service functionality. For example, it is very common with contemporary messaging systems to see deployments of hub-and-spoke systems or dedicated messaging servers. The advantage of these types of deployments is that they allow a company to deploy servers that are sized for the specific task at hand—in this case, message transfer. It also allows a company to deploy

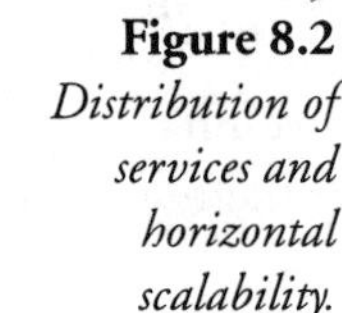

Figure 8.2 *Distribution of services and horizontal scalability.*

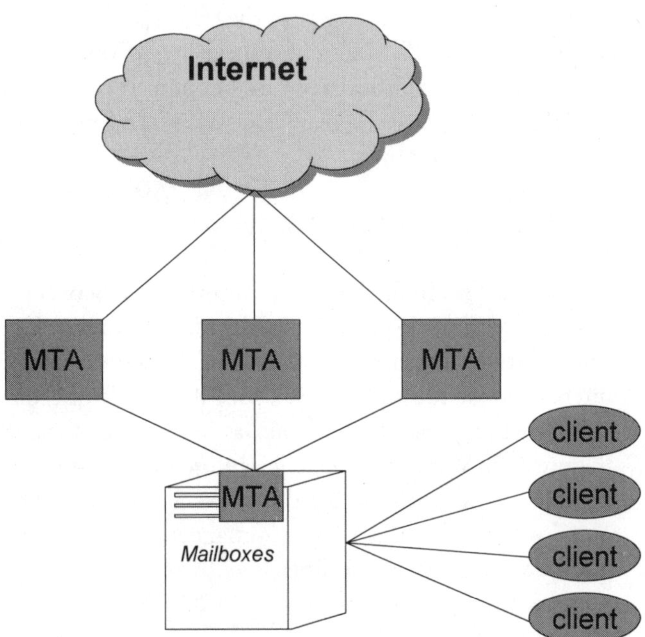

messaging services in such a way as to control the path that messages take within the network. Without a separate transfer service, this capability would not exist, thus limiting the ability to optimally deploy a complete messaging service. In addition to a basic separation of service, an SMTP-based transfer service allows for simple fault tolerance and failover configurations through the use of DNS settings. In Figure 8.2, the three MTAs at the top of the illustration can be deployed on servers sized specifically for messaging, new MTAs can be added, and the servers can be accessed or used in a round-robin manner. This capability is used heavily both within Enterprise deployments (e.g., at the firewall) and deployments within a Service Provider (SP) environment, which will be discussed later in this book.

8.3 Transfer and routing embedded as a core service

To gain the benefits of distribution of services, seamless communications, and horizontal scalability, a transfer service should be a core component of the messaging service as a whole. Better yet, if the transfer service is part of the basic operating system, and is only enhanced with the addition of a messaging application, the seamless nature of the service is only enhanced. At some point a vendor needs to choose the core transfer protocol.

8.3.1 X.400 or SMTP?

As I said, it's pretty clear that having a transfer service is a good thing. Today, it's also clear that there is only one logical choice to base a transfer system upon: SMTP. While that may be clear today, history shows that not only did vendors not use SMTP early on, but that it wasn't a clear-cut choice. The primary protocol choices on which to base a transfer service were X.400 and SMTP. The sad truth is that in many cases, even with those clear choices, the PC messaging vendors chose to write their own transfer services, as I stated earlier. Again, that's history, but before we move onto the de facto choice today, SMTP, let's look at X.400. (For more informtion, see *X.400 and SMTP: The Battle of the E-mail Protocols*, John Rhoton, Digital Press [1997].)

8.3.2 X.400

Oh, I can hear people groaning now over this section! My friends at Software.com/Openwave, Sun, and even Microsoft are saying, "Not X.400!" Well, let me say this, X.400 was and is important. First, there are still places in the world where X.400 makes sense and is the only good option for message transport. Also, and most importantly, X.400 gave us a great glossary.

Think about it. In its initial state, SMTP was fairly..., well, simple. It didn't handle binary types or multipart messages, it had no clue about delivery receipts, and still has no concept of checkpoints, at least from an implementation perspective. Sensitivity flags? Nonrepudiation? No way! All of these features were in X.400 and, be aware, these concepts were, and are, important. Why are they important? Think about it: Most of us rely on many of these concepts and capabilities every day. I know within Compaq I see many messages tagged as "Company Confidential" or "Urgent"; usually they are in reference to some comment I made in a public forum, but you get the point. Granted, the concepts for these features existed before X.400, but X.400 really drove the interoperability of these features between multiple platforms and messaging products.

So, let's explore some of the more important X.400 terms and definitions. In the process we'll also mention the ones that have been incorporated, or are being incorporated, into SMTP.

MTA

X.400 defines an entity in a messaging network known as a Message Transfer Agent or MTA. The function of an MTA is to provide store-and-forward messaging services in a distributed network. It also provides a message submission agent that clients can make use of, meaning that a user agent could connect to an MTA in order to submit a message for delivery to some recipient. (A user agent is the user interface to a messaging system—for instance, Outlook 2000 can be considered the user agent for an Exchange 2000 messaging service.) I have certain quirks about the use of some of these terms. For instance, a certain colleague of mine used to continually ask me questions such as, "… now that Exchange 2000 uses an SMTP service for communication, what does the MTA do?" Trust me, this is a pretty famous person in the Exchange space and even he let standard terms digress into Microsoft specifics. So theoretically, the new SMTP Service is an MTA. I knew what he meant: He was referring to the pre-Exchange 2000 Message Transfer Service that was based on X.400, and, since it has been carried over into Exchange 2000, he wanted to know what specific functions it performed. I'd always give him his answer, but I would continually hound him about the terminology; especially when he'd say things such as "The MTA is no more."

Body part definitions

X.400 provides a standard mechanism for registering body types and it inherently understands multiple body parts. Once registered, messages containing various body types can be exchanged relatively seamlessly between X.400 systems. X.400 also supports the concept of Binary body types, so that any body type can be transferred as an attachment with X.400. Contrast this to the pre-MIME days of SMTP, which had no concept of body parts.

MIME, in my opinion, was the single most important extension to SMTP, especially when you look at the simple elegance of its implementation. This isn't too surprising, since its author, Ned Freed, has probably forgotten more about messaging than any of us will ever know.

Two-Way Alternate

X.400 MTAs support the concept of Two-Way Alternate (TWA). TWA allows an MTA to pick up messages being sent to it when it connects to another MTA to deliver messages. Think of it as picking up your snail mail when you go to the post office. Sure, you could just drop off messages you want to send, but since you're already at the post office, and assuming you have a post office–based mailbox, you might as well see if there is any mail waiting for you in your mailbox. This capability to pick up e-mail messages when a connection to send is made makes for efficient use of network resources.

SMTP introduced a similar capability with TURN/ETRN. When implemented, TURN/ETRN allows for the storage of messages until a connection is initiated by another SMTP MTA. When the remote MTA connects and transfers messages, the sending and receiving MTAs switch roles and the queued messages are delivered to the, once sending, MTA. The important point here is that SMTP is always a push-mode protocol; SMTP never pulls information.

Checkpointing

In low-bandwidth, high-latency environments, X.400 is a very reliable protocol. Part of the reason for its reliability is its support for checkpointing. Essentially, when a connection is broken between two MTAs, checkpointing allows them to pick up their conversation from the point they left off. Simply put, if a 10,000 byte message is being sent between two X.400 MTAs and the connection is broken after 7,000 bytes, checkpointing allows the two MTAs to recover their connection and begin sending at byte 7,0001.

The SMTP specification has no specific standard definition for the support of checkpointing, although an experimental RFC was submitted. Therefore, as a store-and-forward protocol, SMTP must ensure that a message in transit is in the control of another MTA before it relinquishes control of that message. So, in the case of the 10,000 byte message, a failure in the link will lead to the resending of the entire message. Checkpointing is a great feature, so don't be surprised if you see Microsoft come out with a checkpointing feature for their SMTP service. In the meantime, X.400 is still an excellent choice in environments where there is frequent transmittal of large binary files but low bandwidth and high latency.

For you folks who have implemented Exchange 5.5, this feature is one of the reasons that X.400 connectors are a typical best practice when bandwidth won't support site connectors.

Priority

As with traditional postal mail, prioritizing messages allows the sender to expedite the delivery of a message. X.400 defined three priorities: express, first-class, and second-class mail. The specifics of how each priority is handled is specific to a particular vendor's implementation, so there was really no guarantee of how these messages would be handled between vendors. In fact, so many features in X.400 were left as optional that achieving consistent and highly reliable interoperability between vendors was challenging.

Reply requested

Here's a feature that most of us are very familiar with and probably make use of fairly often. Reply requested allows the sender to request that the recipient respond to the message.

Delivery notification

Delivery notifications are used to notify the sender of the message that the message was actually delivered to the recipient. Three different levels of delivery notification are available in X.400: basic, full, and no notification. This feature has been implemented in SMTP by the DSN, Delivery Status Notification, RFCs (RFC 1891, 1892, and 1894).

Receipt notification

Many people confuse receipt notification with delivery notification. The difference is that receipt notification takes place when the recipient manipulates the message in some way. Manipulation can be via the actual reading of the message, deletion of the message, or printing of the message. As with delivery notification, there are three levels of receipt notification: basic, full and none.

Sensitivity or confidentiality

While this is only an informational flag from a strict X.400 perspective, most high-quality messaging systems that support this feature define some sort of restriction for messages tagged with certain sensitivities. For instance, messages flagged as Company Confidential or Personal could be restricted from being delivered outside of the company. Another example of how these flags are implemented is that some messaging systems that support sensitivity and confidentiality tagging treat private messages in a way that restricts the messages from being forwarded. X.400 defined four sensitivity flags: not restricted, personal, private, and company confidential.

These are just a few of the features and capabilities that X.400 defined. Using messaging systems such as Exchange, you are accustomed to seeing and using these features. The point here is that without X.400 and the inclusion of these features, the ability to interoperate among various messaging systems would have been almost impossible. Because of its fully defined, feature-rich capabilities, many vendors chose to base their initial core transports on X.400 rather than SMTP—witness Exchange 4.0 and 5.5 as examples. Over the years many of these features, and even better features, have been implemented in SMTP or can be encapsulated in messages that traverse an SMTP-based backbone. So, instead of looking at X.400 as a "bad thing," just appreciate it as a model and a set of definitions that got the electronic messaging community moving in the right direction ... despite the headache that OSI networking gave to people and vendors.

X.400 addressing

Be aware that X.400 was and is far from perfect. It is so far from perfect in fact that few vendors wanted to implement it. Further, the fact that many people found it hard to implement made it less than a stellar solution. There was also the argument that X.400 was hard to use. Specifically, people complained about the complexity in the X.400 name space, or naming conventions. While this may be true, I never bought the argument that the name space was too complex. If you recall, the name space was typically defined as follows:

C = Country

ADMD = Administrative Domain

PRMD = Private Management Domain

O = Organization

OU = Organizational Unit

S = Surname

G = Given Name

CN = Common Name

While this may be a bit daunting at first, with most Windows-based user interfaces, the address prefixes can be defaulted. For instance, the X.400 prefix of C = US; A = *; could be defaulted in my client/user agent. From there, all I need to do is fill in the fields associated with the recipient, as follows:

P = <companyName> (e.g., Compaq)

S = <Lastname> (e.g., Livengood)

G = <Firstname> (e.g., Donald)

How different is that from typing Donald.Livengood@compaq.com? I never saw the real problem with this, but then I had always used a very nice client. For folks having to type the entire address, including the various codes for country, administrative domain, and so on, the syntax is far too long, clunky, and prone to error. Granted, it's not quite as easy as a standard RFC 822 SMTP address, but it's not that big a deal. So, this inconvenience, combined with the difficulty in getting separate X.400-based products communicating with each other, was the death knell for X.400. There it is ... I admit it.

To be fair, it really wasn't that difficult to implement. Once you set it up initially, setting it up again was pretty much a piece of cake. The fact that X.400 initially relied solely on the full OSI stack did add a lot of complexity. (Fortunately for me, most of the X.400 and X.500 implementations I did were on Digital platforms using their OSI stack (DECnet/OSI), which was fairly straightforward once you got used to it.) Those of us in the consulting business saw this as goodness, though, as we had loads of business setting this stuff up. Call it greed, call it occupation preservation, call it whatever. Either way, things got simpler once RFC 1006 was introduced and implemented. RFC 1006 allowed X.400, actually all OSI applications, to be implemented on top of a TCP/IP transport.

Again, the glossary of terms is important. The so-called protocol war is over and SMTP won. So let's look at SMTP

8.3.3 SMTP basic protocol

At its core, SMTP involves the relay of a message from one Message Transfer Agent (MTA) to another. In doing so, the MTAs communicate via a specific protocol (SMTP) as defined by RFC 821. When communicating, the MTAs use TCP and initiate connections to each other via port 25. The basic SMTP commands are as follows:

- HELO—used by a client to identify itself, usually with a domain name.
- MAIL—normally used in the form `MAIL FROM:` to identify the sender of the message.
- RCPT—used in the form of `RCPT TO:` to identify message recipients.
- DATA—used by a client to begin the transfer of message content.
- RSET—nullifies or voids the entire message transaction.
- VRFY—used to verify that a mailbox is available for delivery; as in `vrfy dlivengood`; this would identify whether a mailbox for dlivengood resided on the local server.
- EXPN—used to return the true recipients of a message. Normally used in association with a distribution list name to expand the distribution list into its individual recipients.
- HELP—returns a list of commands supported by the SMTP service.

- NOOP—used to check that the SMTP service is still operating on commands. When issued, and assuming the service is still running, a `250 "OK"` code is returned.
- QUIT—quits the session.

As these commands are sent by the initiating MTA, a response is made by the receiving MTA acknowledging the command.

MIME

Before the definition of MIME, SMTP was fairly limited in what it could deliver. Because of its popularity and the ease with which it is deployed and enhanced, it was realized that an extension needed to be made to SMTP in order to support complex, multiple body part messages. MIME is the extension by which complex messages are supported over an SMTP transport. Specifically, MIME stands for Multipurpose Internet Mail Extensions, and it defines the structure for Internet message bodies, much in the same way that RFC 822 focuses on the structure of message headers.

The clever thing about MIME is that it was implemented without requiring that changes be made to the underlying SMTP transport. A requirement to modify all of the SMTP services would have made adoption not only unlikely, but nearly impossible. So, instead, the MIME approach to dealing with increasing message requirements is straightforward.

The MIME standards incorporate 8-bit ASCII messages and attachments by encoding them so that they could be represented in a 7-bit format. The encoding algorithm is normally base64 but occasionally uuencode is used. In essence, binary files were encoded so that they appeared to be simple text files. A MIME message reads just like a text message, a very long text message. This method enables the sending of complex messages across an SMTP network easily, because the messages are treated just like any other text message. When the message arrives at its destination, that receiving MTA or client takes on the responsibility of converting the text-based MIME message back into its native parts. Only portions of the message that are not already in text format are converted. As you might expect, the conversion of messages does incur a bit of overhead. On average a MIME message is approximately 33 percent larger than its binary representation.

MIME not only provides encoding of 8-bit information, but it also tags the contents of a message. This tagging allows for features such as the preservation of file names as well as dealing with multiple attachments in a single message. MIME is fully described in RFC 1521.

Figure 8.3 is an example of a simple MIME message and illustrates some of these points. Notice the Content-Type header in the header section of the message. This indicates that the message is composed of multiple parts.

Figure 8.3
A simple MIME message.

```
MIME-Version: 1.0
Content-Type: multipart/mixed;
     boundary="----_=_NextPart_001_01C030DD.C58F9C98"
Subject: FW: winroute file
Date: Sat, 7 Oct 2000 21:11:02 -0700
Message-ID:
DE1B1F489EDD6D4C9A0118DC3F6C3E73C33C56@DINO.platinum.corp.microsof
t.com
X-MS-Has-Attach:
X-MS-TNEF-Correlator:
Thread-Topic: winroute file
Thread-Index: AcAvtfOv7xc35ZHsRreq8rehGHltbwBJ306g
X-Priority: 1
Priority: Urgent
Importance: high
From: "Somebody atMicrosoft" <somebodyat@Exchange.Microsoft.com>
To: <donald.livengood@compaq.com>
X-OriginalArrivalTime: 08 Oct 2000 04:11:03.0183 (UTC)
FILETIME=[C5DC51F0:01C030DD]

This is a multi-part message in MIME format.

------_=_NextPart_001_01C030DD.C58F9C98
Content-Type: multipart/alternative;
     boundary="----_=_NextPart_002_01C030DD.C58F9C98"


------_=_NextPart_002_01C030DD.C58F9C98
Content-Type: text/plain;
     charset="iso-8859-1"
Content-Transfer-Encoding: quoted-printable

------_=_NextPart_002_01C030DD.C58F9C98
Content-Type: text/html;
     charset="iso-8859-1"
Content-Transfer-Encoding: quoted-printable

------_=_NextPart_002_01C030DD.C58F9C98--

------_=_NextPart_001_01C030DD.C58F9C98
Content-Type: application/octet-stream;
     name="red-pt-01.rte"
Content-Transfer-Encoding: base64
Content-Description: red-pt-01.rte
Content-Disposition: attachment;
     file name="red-pt-01.rte"

------_=_NextPart_001_01C030DD.C58F9C98--
```

In order to separate one part of the message from another, a MIME-capable MTA or client will generate a unique string (or boundary), which can be used as the delimiter between attachments in the message. The boundary string is declared in the header of the message. The receiving MTA can then simply parse the whole text body line by line and recognize a different message part whenever it encounters the boundary string.

You can see from the tagging of the message that there are multiple body types with different content: plain text, HTML, and alternative.

Each message part has tagging information associated with it so that the type of the body part can be deduced by the receiving MTA. The tags are produced by the sending MTA performing a lookup against some kind of MIME mapping table. If you look at the last part of the sample message, you'll see that it's tagged as multipart/alternative. This tuple is the MIME type and subtype pair, and, in this case, there was no specific mapping for the file type/extension `rte`. Even so, for this message part, the file name of the original document is maintained in the MIME header (content disposition), and you can see that it's called `red-pt-01.rte`. There is more information in this part of the MIME header that is of interest to us. We're explicitly told that this message part is to be handled as an attachment. Alternatively, you may see a value of in-line from time to time, but this is more common for text-type message parts. For a text message, if it's marked as in-line, then the recipient of the message will see it rolled into the main cover memo part of the message, not explicitly dealt with as a real attachment to the message.

The receiving MTA will be able to use all of this information when it reconstitutes the attachment. If the file name is not passed on (some gateway implementations don't provide it), the MTA should provide a default file name such as att1.doc.

The current list of MIME types and subtypes is maintained by IANA, the Internet Assigned Numbers Authority. If you take a look at the list of types, you'll notice that some major file types aren't registered. For example, there's no registered type for application/msaccess, although you might expect one. Of course, this begs the question: How do you tag an access file? Well, according to the MIME rules, a binary file for which no explicit tag exists should be tagged as application/octet-stream. This is an indication that it's a binary file, but there's little else to tell us just what type of file it is. In most cases, the name of the file should be passed along with the octet-stream subtype, so a smart MIME MTA should be able to work out the file type based on the file name suffix.

RFC 1521 allows other subtypes to be defined provided that they are only used privately between cooperating parties. In such cases, the subtype should start with an X- and under no circumstances should private subtypes be sent to other parties that are not privy to the X- tagging agreement. Thus, a private sub-type for an application that generates files with a suffix of .myt would appear as follows:

```
Content-Type: application/X-mytype;
     name="my_doc.myt"
Content-Transfer-Encoding: base64
```

There is a lot more to the MIME specifications and we can't go into them here. We have covered enough of the basics to allow us to understand how MIME works and how we can use it to connect to other SMTP messaging systems.

In addition to the basic commands mentioned previously, SMTP services may also support the following commands:

- VRFY (RFC 821): verify or ensure that the message can be delivered to a local recipient.
- EXPN (RFC 821): expand a distribution list into individual recipients. The command asks the server whether the recipient is a distribution list, and, if so, to return the membership of the list.
- ETRN (RFC 1985): an extension of the standard TURN command, which reverses sender and receiver roles. The standard TURN command enables clients to download messages for a domain but does not include any validation mechanism. Thus, it is possible that a rogue system could attempt to download messages held on a server

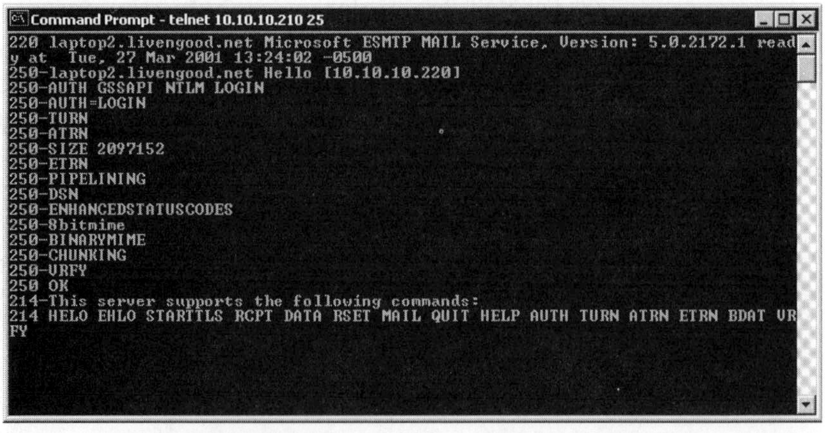

```
Command Prompt - telnet 10.10.10.210 25
220 laptop2.livengood.net Microsoft ESMTP MAIL Service, Version: 5.0.2172.1 read
y at  Tue, 27 Mar 2001 13:24:02 -0500
250-laptop2.livengood.net Hello [10.10.10.220]
250-AUTH GSSAPI NTLM LOGIN
250-AUTH=LOGIN
250-TURN
250-ATRN
250-SIZE 2097152
250-ETRN
250-PIPELINING
250-DSN
250-ENHANCEDSTATUSCODES
250-8bitmime
250-BINARYMIME
250-CHUNKING
250-VRFY
250 OK
214-This server supports the following commands:
214 HELO EHLO STARTTLS RCPT DATA RSET MAIL QUIT HELP AUTH TURN ATRN ETRN BDAT VR
FY
```

Figure 8.4 *SMTP commands advertised by the Exchange 2000 SMTP service.*

(normally managed by an ISP) for a site or domain other than itself. ETRN provides a mechanism for a client SMTP system to request download for a specific queue of messages. The host server can then decide whether or not to honor the request and dequeue the messages.

- SIZE (RFC 1870): provide an indication of how large a message is. SIZE also advertises the maximum message size a server will accept.
- TLS (RFC 2487): a method to use transport-level security to protect the communications between SMTP clients and servers.
- AUTH (RFC 2554): a method to allow an SMTP client to negotiate an agreed authentication mechanism with a server. Exchange 2000 supports GSSAPI, NTLM, and LOGIN as authentication and encryption mechanisms. Exchange 5.5 supports NTLM (NT Challenge/Response) and TLS (Transport Level Security), both of which implement an SSL-secured connection.

The Internet Mail Consortium maintains a chart comparing functionality of different SMTP servers. The chart is available at http://www.imc.org/features-chart.html.

The list of commands may vary in the future with support packs and updates to both Windows 2000 and Exchange 2000. To verify the current list of commands supported by SMTP on your server, Telnet to port 25 on the server and issue an EHLO command. The server returns a list of keywords for the commands supported by the server, as shown in Figure 8.4. As an exercise, you can issue the same command to an Exchange 5.5 server to discover the set of new ESMTP commands supported by Exchange 2000.

8.4 SMTP in Windows 2000

The SMTP service in Windows 2000 came from the Exchange engineering team. (Active Directory also came from the Exchange engineering team.) To be more specific, it came from the SMTP code, which was originally written for the Microsoft Commercial Information Services (MCIS) product. MCIS has been focused on the ISP market and its SMTP service was written to meet the requirements of that marketplace. In short, it is fast and fully functional.

The SMTP service in Windows 2000 runs within the context of inetinfo.exe, basically, the Internet Information Server (IIS). IIS implements all of its services via objects called virtual servers. A virtual server is made up of the binding of a protocol, a port, and an IP address. In the case of SMTP, the protocol is pretty clear: The port is almost always port 25, and the IP address varies depending on the IP addresses supported on the server. There may be cases where you change the port number for some third-party application, such as a virus scanning tool or a firewall, but this is a rare requirement and, even when required, is normally only necessary on a small number of servers.

The Windows 2000 SMTP service is fully functional, as you would expect with any modern operating system. It supports all of the basic SMTP commands as well as most of the Enhanced SMTP commands (ESMTP).

8.4.1 Message flow in Windows 2000 SMTP

The inclusion of SMTP, and other Internet protocols, within the operating system itself is unlike the NT4 world, which did not include SMTP. The SMTP service built into the operating system can be used for Active Directory intersite replication and can also be used as a transfer service for POP3 and IMAP4 clients as well as other applications.

The Windows 2000 SMTP service uses NTFS as its storage mechanism and can use LDAP to expand distribution lists. The Windows 2000 SMTP service is illustrated in Figure 8.5.

Messages enter the service via port 25, their recipient information is expanded via an LDAP query (optional), and the destination is determined via a call to DNS.

The default path for the directories used by SMTP in Windows 2000 is `\inetpub\mailroot\`. There are several subdirectories as follows:

- Badmail—an area to store messages that cannot be delivered or returned. As an example, if a message being sent generates an NDR (Non-Delivery Report) but the NDR cannot be returned to the sender, it is placed in the Badmail directory. This directory should be checked periodically and reconciled, since an inordinate number of messages in this directory could potentially affect system performance.
- Drop—this directory is a collection area for incoming messages. You could conceivably use the Windows 2000 SMTP service to be a mail receiver for other applications. You can also assign a drop directory on a per-domain basis for domain-specific processing.
- Mailbox—not currently used, but could be incorporated into a messaging application.

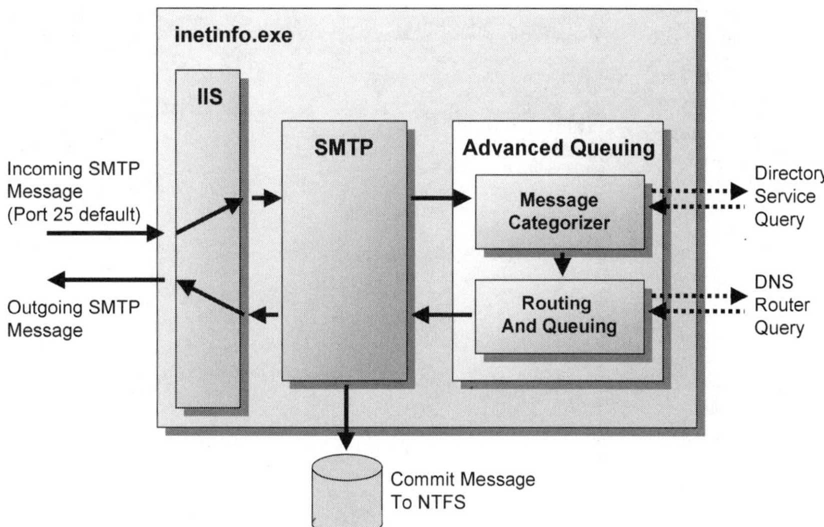

Figure 8.5 *Message flow in Windows SMTP.*

- Pickup—properly formatted messages placed in this directory will be processed for delivery. You can either place messages here from an application or you could use something as simple as Notepad to create a message and save it in this directory for transport processing. The SMTP services picks messages up from this directory and moves them to the queue directory to process them for delivery.
- Queue—contains messages queued for delivery. There are usually .rtr (remote transcript) files in this directory that may give a clue as to why messages aren't being delivered.
- Route—not used at this time.
- SortTemp—not used at this time.

8.4.2 Configuration of Windows 2000 SMTP

It should also be noted that since the Windows 2000 SMTP service is implemented within the context of IIS, its configuration is managed through the IIS Administration utility (see Figure 8.6) and its configuration information is stored in the IIS metabase. As we'll see, the interface to manage Exchange 2000's SMTP service is different and, in fact, Exchange 2000's SMTP service is not exposed via the IIS Administrator interface.

Many more things change with the installation of Exchange 2000, but we'll save that for later. For now though, there are a couple of interesting

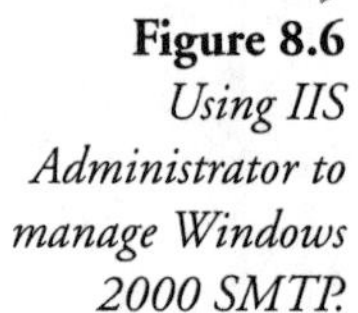

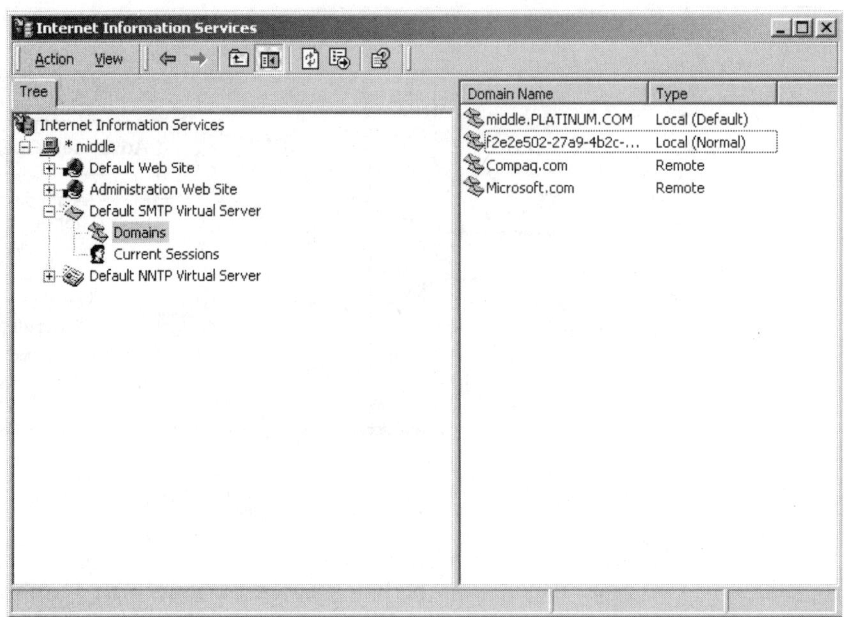

Figure 8.6 *Using IIS Administrator to manage Windows 2000 SMTP.*

things to see using IIS Admin when managing the Windows 2000 SMTP service, so I'll point out a few of those now.

Number of configuration tabs

OK, so this is a bit cheesy, but there are more configuration tabs available when configuring the Windows 2000 SMTP service from IIS Admin. When you open the properties of the default SMTP virtual server, you will see that there are two more tabs than you will see later when we discuss SMTP virtual servers with Exchange 2000. Specifically, the two tabs are for configuring LDAP routing and security.

LDAP routing

The LDAP Routing tab, shown in Figure 8.7, allows you to let the SMTP service use an LDAP directory for name and distribution list resolution. Obviously, you can use Active Directory as the LDAP server, but you can theoretically use any other LDAP directory. Once configured, the SMTP service will use LDAP commands to resolve names.

Server

This field should be self-explanatory; it is the name of the LDAP server.

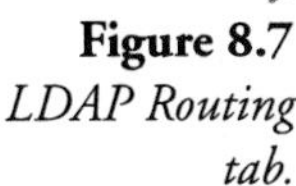

Figure 8.7 *LDAP Routing tab.*

Schema

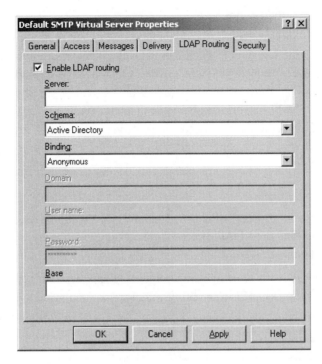

Schema contains the following items:

- Active Directory: Select this if you will be using Active Directory for name resolution. You will still need to use Active Directory Users and Computers to actually create/manage users, groups, and so on.
- Site Server Membership Directory: If you have been using Microsoft Commercial Internet System (MCIS) version 2.0 Mail, you may want to use that directory for your LDAP name resolution.
- Exchange LDAP Service: Select this option to use a Microsoft Site Server 3.0 or later LDAP server to manage mailboxes.

Binding

You can select the type of binding that will be used when the SMTP virtual server authenticates to the LDAP directory. The available types are as follows:

- Anonymous
- Plain text

- Windows SSPI
- Service Accounts—this tells the SMTP service to use the user information under which it is running. That information is controlled by Component Services, under Administrative Tools.

Domain

This is the domain of the account you use to bind to the LDAP directory. This option is only applicable if you use the plain text or Windows SSPI binding types.

User Name

You enter the distinguished name (DN) of the account you want to use to bind to the LDAP directory—for example, cn = Livengood; ou = users; o = Compaq.

As with Domain, this option only applies when you choose plain text or Windows SSPI in the binding type.

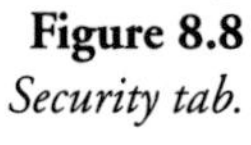

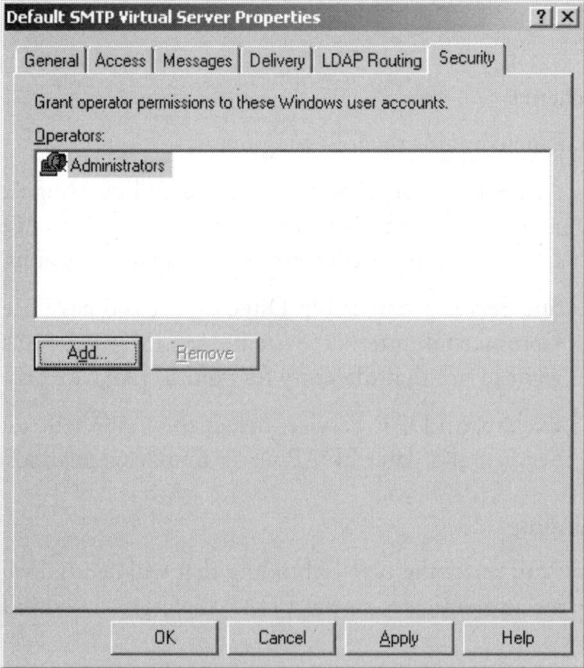

Figure 8.8 *Security tab.*

Password

This field is self-explanatory.

Base

Use this entry to specify where you want the SMTP service to start searching the LDAP directory. To establish the base, you enter the distinguished name of the starting point within the directory from where all searches will begin. The base directory itself will be searched, as well as any subcontainers of the base.

Security

The security tab, shown in Figure 8.8, allows you to add accounts and groups to the list of SMTP virtual server operators. These individuals can change the configuration characteristics of the virtual server.

8.5 Summary

In this section, I've outlined the basics of message transfer services. We'll see how these are used by Exchange 2000 in later chapters.

9

Routing and Connectivity Basics

9.1 Introduction

Before we discuss Exchange 2000 routing and connectivity, let's look at the way routing was handled in the earlier versions of the product. We've mentioned that X.400 was the transport protocol used in earlier versions of Exchange, but how did that transport service determine how to route messages through its network? The algorithm for prior versions of Exchange was based on a distance vector routing algorithm. Specifically, pre-Exchange 2000 systems used the Gateway Address Resolution Table (GWART) to determine routing. This routing approach was flawed at the first release of Exchange 4.0 because of its use of distance vector routing. Distance vector routing is susceptible to routing loops in certain cases and these surfaced for many customers with early versions of Exchange. In fact, customers went through a series of "hacks" from Microsoft to fix various routing problems. The initial patches fixed message looping. Once that was fixed, many customers found out that looping wasn't their only problem. The other major issue was dubbed the "ping-pong" effect. This occurred when a route was tried, failed, another path was tried, failed, and then the message was resubmitted to the original path. So, if you were actually watching the message flow, it was like watching a Ping-Pong or tennis match—back and forth, back and forth between servers. Needless to say, other less than optimal routing issues showed up with Exchange 5.5, and it was time to move forward with a better algorithm. Being the bright guys that they are, Microsoft engineering chose to move forward with a proven, loop-free routing algorithm: link state routing. As a reference, Open Shortest Path First (OSPF) is an implementation of link state routing in networking.

9.2 The Exchange 2000 SMTP service

With the installation of Exchange 2000 the underlying Windows 2000 SMTP service is modified and certain characteristics of the SMTP virtual server are changed. Specifically, Authenticated Relay and Anonymous Access are enabled with Exchange 2000. The combination of these two characteristics combines to form the most requested environment for a transport service. First, the servers can communicate with each other and can route messages appropriately. Second, only servers and users authenticating themselves to the SMTP MTA are allowed to perform a relay. This characteristic ensures that rogue SMTP servers or users cannot use the SMTP service of Exchange 2000 for SPAM relay. (SPAM is messaging vernacular for Unsolicited Bulk E-mail (UBE) and is in no way meant to discredit the meat product from Hormel Foods, Inc., www.spam.com.)

One side effect of this feature, however, is that enterprise users who are accustomed to using POP- or IMAP-based clients may not be accustomed to authenticating themselves to the SMTP service. Allowing anonymous access to the SMTP server, however, opens up the potential for SPAM relay attacks on the server. One workaround to this is to dedicate specific servers, configured for anonymous access, to host SMTP services for POP and IMAP clients. The other obvious, and more secure, solution is to require the clients to authenticate. Even better, customers accessing these servers from the Internet should implement SSL to increase the level of security provided to their clients and their network.

Since we're talking about authentication, it is interesting to note that the authentication used between Exchange 2000 servers is Kerberos. As you remember from your extensive reading on Windows 2000, Kerberos is one of the many features supplied as part of the operating system. (One great source for Windows 2000 Security and Active Directory information is *Mission-Critical Active Directory*, Balladelli and de Clercq, Digital Press [2000].) Microsoft based its Kerberos implementation on the Kerberos V5 (RFC 1510). As such, Kerberos has the capability of providing single sign-on between Windows 2000 and other operating systems whose authentication is based on the same Kerberos implementation. From a messaging standpoint, you should know that Kerberos is used between Exchange 2000 servers when they communicate to each other via SMTP and can be seen in the handshaking process if you have protocol logging turned on. But that's getting way ahead of ourselves for now and will be discussed in later chapters!

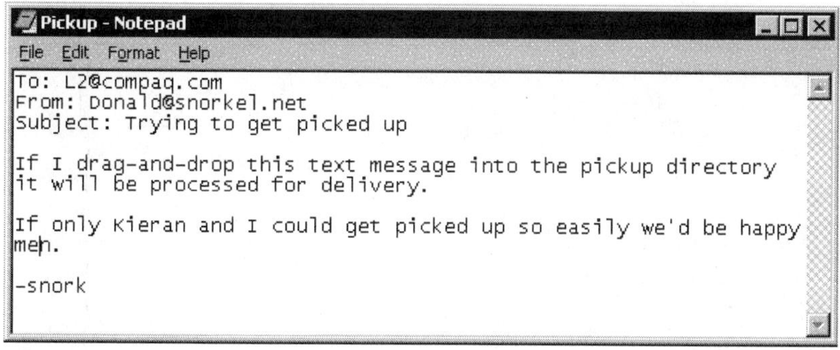

Figure 9.1 *Creating a message using Notepad.*

Messages can be submitted directly to either the Windows 2000 or the Exchange 2000 SMTP service in multiple ways: first, and most obvious, is via the SMTP protocol through port 25. Another method is by using the pickup directory, normally at `\Inetpub\mailroot\pickup` for Windows 2000 and `\exchsrvr\mailroot\vs 1\pickup` for Exchange 2000. By simply placing a properly formatted e-mail message in the pickup directory, that message will be delivered.

Using the example in Figure 9.1, and to prove the point, I've dropped this particular file into an Exchange 2000 pickup directory and, in Figure 9.2, you'll see that it did, in fact, get delivered to user L2. The same concept holds true for the SMTP service in Windows 2000.

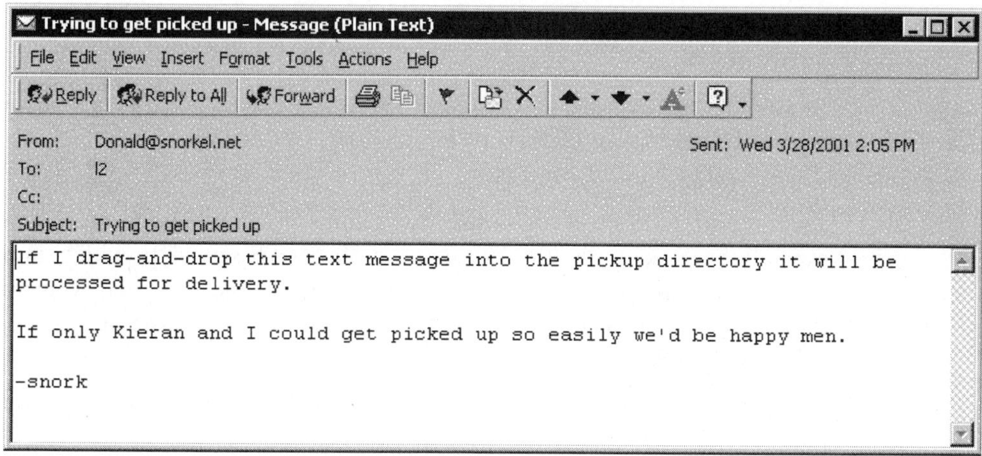

Figure 9.2 *Message delivered via the Pickup directory.*

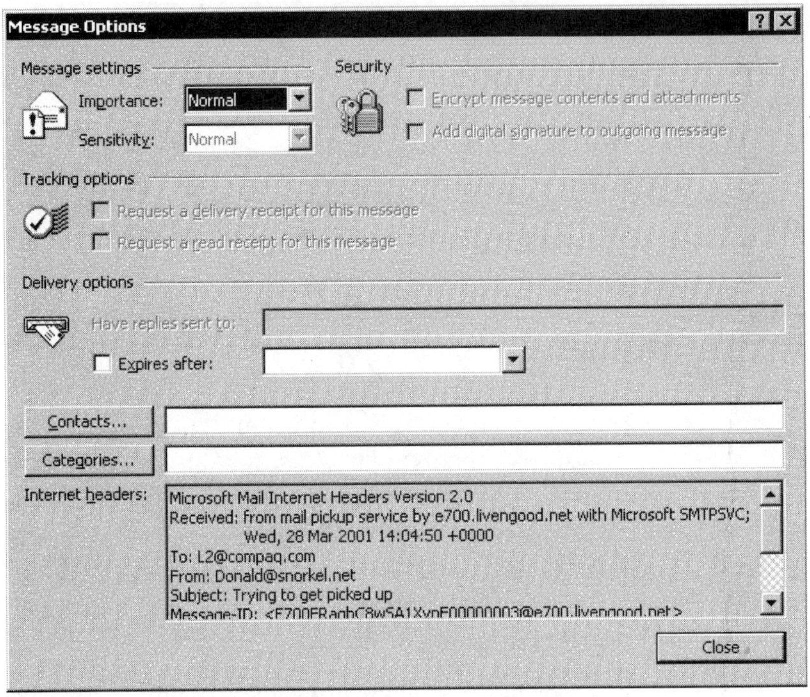

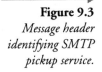

Figure 9.3
Message header identifying SMTP pickup service.

An interesting point regarding this message is that if we examine the headers of the message (see Figure 9.3), it does, in fact, identify that the message was received from the mail pickup service.

The same capability is available in the default Windows 2000 SMTP service as well.

Another method that can be used to submit messages is by using Collaboration Data Objects (CDO).

The Windows 2000 SMTP component, and therefore Exchange 2000, also supports various event sinks, which allow programmers to extend its capabilities. Specifically, the Windows 2000 SMTP service provides sinks for transport and protocol events and, in fact, Exchange 2000 makes use of these sinks to extend the basic SMTP functionality to incorporate its specific functionality.

An Exchange 2000 installation modifies the basic SMTP service as follows:

- An Exchange Installable File System (IFS) store driver is added that allows message pickup and drop-off to the Exchange Storage System (the Information Store). Note that for store-and-forward purposes, messages are still queued to NTFS, but the Exchange IFS is used to write messages destined for the local server to the Web Storage System.

- Advanced queuing is added to manage message queuing.
- Enhanced message categorization is added that examines messages and queues the message for delivery based on certain message attributes. Windows 2000 includes a basic message categorization agent; since Exchange 2000 adds other attributes to a messaging environment, a much more capable categorization engine was needed.
- Support for link state information was added. Link state allows intelligent routing decisions to be made based on the current status of messaging connectivity and cost.
- The SMTP protocol itself is extended to support command verbs (X-LINK2STATE), which are used to communicate link state information between servers.
- Exchange 2000 also changes the location on disk where messages are queued: `\exchsrvr\mailroot\vs 1\pickup`. Note the "vs 1" directory. This represents the first virtual server on this Exchange 2000 server. As you add more virtual servers, which we'll discuss later, each new virtual server will get assigned a new directory: "vs 2," "vs 3," and so on.

Once installed, Exchange 2000 servers will always communicate with each other via SMTP by default. One thing to keep in mind though is that the "old" MTA, the X.400/RPC-based MTA, is still around. It still provides the X.400 service for Exchange 2000 and is used to communicate, via X.400-based RPCs, to down-level (Exchange 5.5) servers in a mixed-mode environment. (A mixed mode Exchange organization is one that contains both 5.5 servers and Exchange 2000 servers. As you know, Exchange 2000 servers can be installed into an existing 5.5 organization/site.) In essence, the old MTA code has been maintained for backward compatibility as well as for any communications to X.400-based systems that may be required.

9.2.1 SMTP extensions

As well as modifying the underlying SMTP service, an Exchange 2000 installation also implements the following, RFC defined, SMTP extensions.

8-bit clean

Exchange 2000 servers, when sending messages between each other, do not convert messages from 8-bit data to 7-bit data for message transmission, as was the case with Exchange 5.5. This means that the messages on the wire are actually smaller than they were with the Internet Mail Service (IMS).

Pipelining

Pipelining is implemented in Exchange 2000 and is always the preferred method of communications. Pipelining, as defined in RFC 2197, allows systems to send multiple SMTP commands without waiting for an acknowledgment for each specific command.

Older implementations of SMTP require that an acknowledgment be received for each command before the next one can be sent. This type of transmission was considered an unfortunate necessity when systems were connected with error-prone, unreliable connections. However, the performance penalty was significant, particularly with high-latency networks.

"Chunking" (BDAT)

"Chunking," or BDAT, is implemented. BDAT is a command from the Extended SMTP specification as defined in RFC 1830. The BDAT command replaces the DATA command found in the standard SMTP specification as defined in RFC 821.

With the older implementation, the DATA command is issued to mark the start of the actual data transmission of the message. With the older implementation of SMTP the end of data is marked by sending a sequence of characters (carriage return, line feed, full stop, carriage return, line feed). This method requires that the receiving system examine all incoming data and determine if this sequence of characters has been sent, thus signifying the end of data.

With implementation of the latest SMTP extensions, specifically the BDAT command, the BDAT command is sent to the receiving system along with a byte count signifying the number of bytes of data that are to be sent. The receiving system only needs to count the incoming bytes to know when all of these data have been received.

Many SMTP servers do not yet use these new features, so Exchange 2000 only uses these features when communicating with other systems that support them. This is automatically negotiated as part of the handshake between systems when communication is established.

9.2.2 Architectural review

There are many changes to the underlying architecture of Exchange 2000 as compared with prior versions of the product. Some of these architectural changes are directly related to the transfer service and others indirectly affect the transfer service. So, as a bit of background, we'll go through a very brief architectural review of Exchange 2000.

Active Directory and the IIS metabase

One of the many interesting things about the Exchange 2000 Architecture (see Figure 9.4) is that it marries the services of the storage engine (STORE.EXE) and IIS (INETINFO.EXE), as well as integrating the management of the services provided by each component.

Exchange 2000 stores all of its configuration information in Active Directory in the Configuration Naming Context tree. One question most people ask is how did Microsoft modify IIS to use Active Directory for its configuration information when we all know it normally uses its own metabase for those data. Well, as it turns out, they didn't change the storage location of IIS's configuration data; it's still in the metabase. How does this work? Configuration of the Internet protocols supported in Exchange 2000 is normally done through the Exchange System Manager console. When information is changed from that GUI interface, it is, in fact, written to Active Directory. What Microsoft did, however, was to enhance the func-

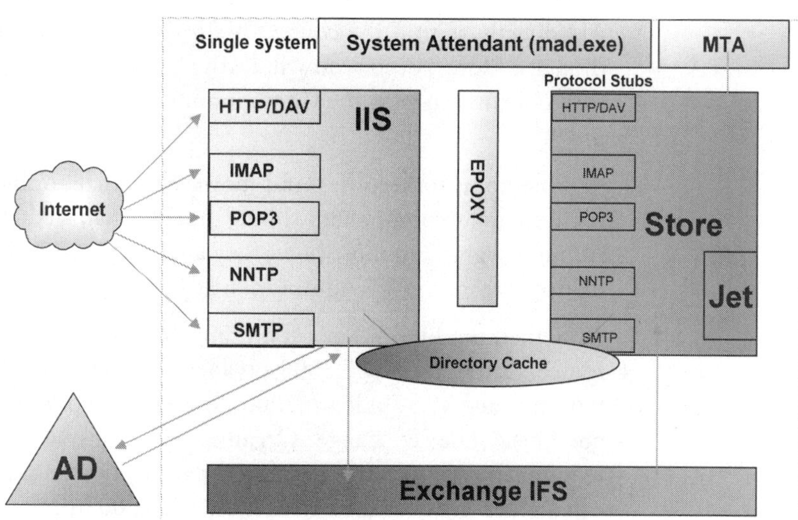

Figure 9.4 *Architectural diagram of Exchange 2000.*

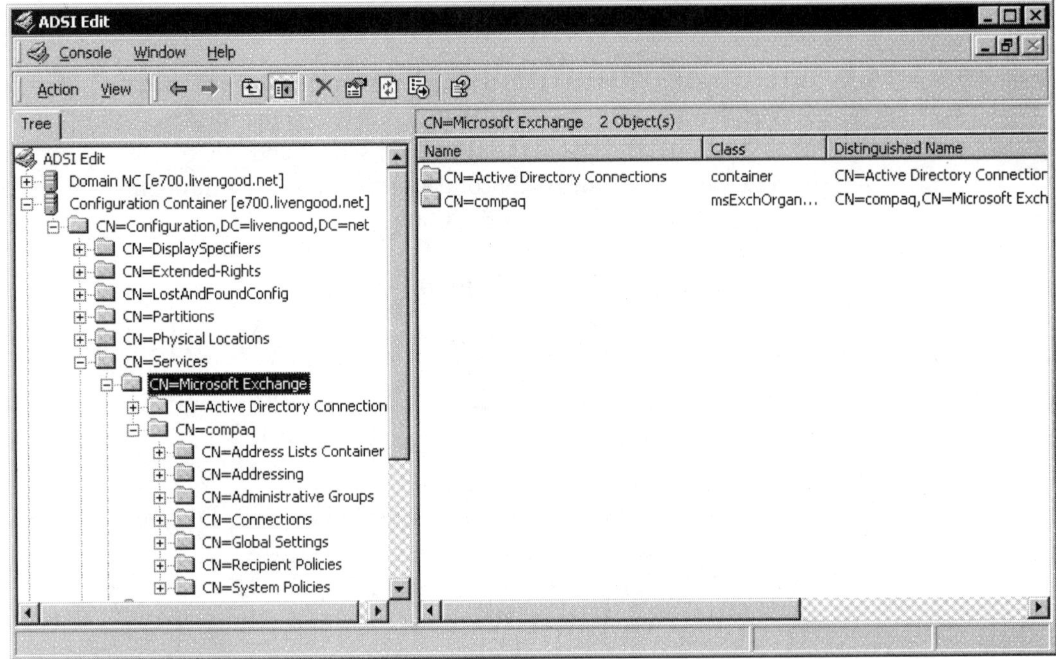

Figure 9.5 *Configuration Naming Context, Exchange 2000 data.*

tionality of the System Attendant so that it would move configuration information about the Internet Services from Active Directory into the IIS metabase. So, while IIS does not yet write its configuration information to AD directly, within the context of an Exchange 2000 installation it acts as though it does. A tool you will learn to know and love is ADSI Edit; using this tool you can view the Configuration Naming Context, as shown in Figure 9.5.

One point to keep in mind, however, is that configuration information for Exchange components should not be managed directly from the IIS Admin program; in most cases, they aren't exposed in a way that they can be managed from the IIS Admin tool, as you can see from Figure 9.6.

Something I tend to point out quite often is the significance, or insignificance, of the Exchange 2000 organization name. As you can see in Figure 9.6, the actual Windows 2000 forest I'm working in is called Livengood.net. The Exchange Organization name is Compaq. There's no requirement that these two entities have to be the same, obviously. So you can, in fact, easily create a new Windows 2000 infrastructure and still maintain your old Exchange organization name. The most significant character-

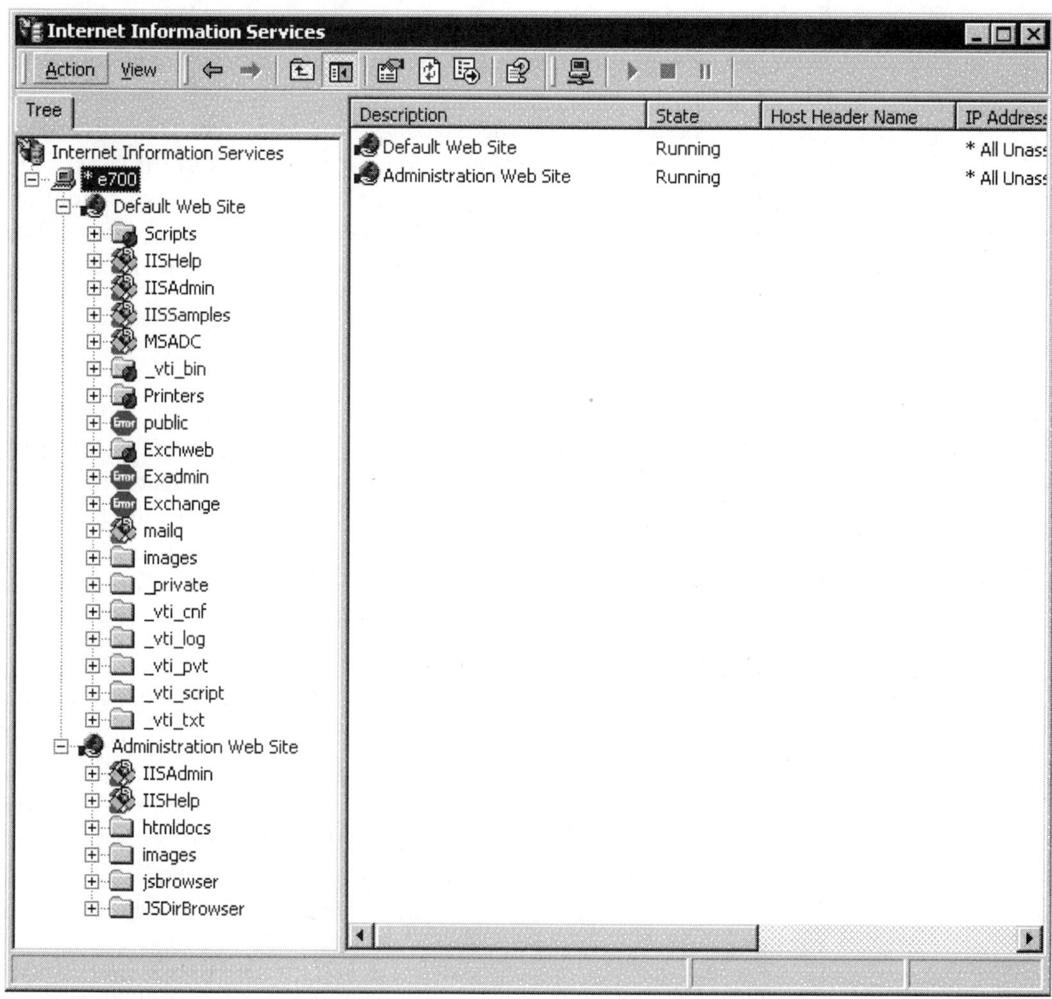

Figure 9.6 *IIS Administrator with Exchange 2000 installed.*

istic of the Organization name is that it is the entry point in the directory under which all configuration information is stored.

You can see in Figure 9.6 that no SMTP virtual server is exposed. This server, E700, has Exchange 2000 installed on it, and, as such, its Internet protocols will be managed, with few exceptions, from the Exchange System Manager MMC. This is in stark contrast to the figures in Chapter 8, which showed that the Windows 2000 SMTP virtual server is, in fact, managed from IIS Admin.

Exchange Storage System

Before we get to the ins and outs of the transfer service itself, and since we're talking about the architecture of the product anyway, I'd like to quickly cover some basics regarding the Exchange Storage System. This discussion will become more applicable as we begin discussing some of the clever tools and interfaces you can build into Exchange 2000 for managing or monitoring the environment. It's also important to cover the Exchange Storage System since it is an integral part of the architectural changes that have taken place with Exchange 2000.

Multiple interfaces

Exchange 2000 exposes all of its data through MAPI, HTTP, and WIN32 layers. This means that an object stored in a Public Folder can be retrieved and manipulated through a Web browser or a standard client with a network redirector. The Exchange 2000 store exposes itself to the operating system as an installable filing system (exIFS), which means that underlying data can be accessed through a drive letter, and, in turn, this drive and its folders can be shared to allow other clients to connect to these data.

The IFS allows access to items within Exchange folders via standard WIN32 file system API calls in the same way as accessing files stored on NTFS. This means that items in Exchange 2000 folders can be accessed just like any other file—directly from the Explorer or from the open dialogs of third-party applications. Be aware, however, that you run the risk of losing properties of items if you manipulate them through this route, since property propagation will not occur. For example, if you extract a mail item from the IFS (an .EML file) and simply put it back, it will not retain attributes such as the TO addresses.

Each store (private or public) exists as a folder mounted under the M: drive of the local machine. The IFS hierarchy, therefore, starts with two folders: MBX and PUBLIC FOLDERS, as seen in Figure 9.7, plus an additional folder for each top-level hierarchy (multiple Public Folder support).

Public Folder items can be enumerated with the standard DIR command and manipulated with other file system operations such as COPY and DELETE. All standard message items are represented with .eml extensions, and the message stream itself can be seen through the TYPE command.

The MBX folder is the root for all mailboxes on the Exchange server. Mailbox folder names are invisible, but if you have access permissions, you can access them by explicitly specifying their names.

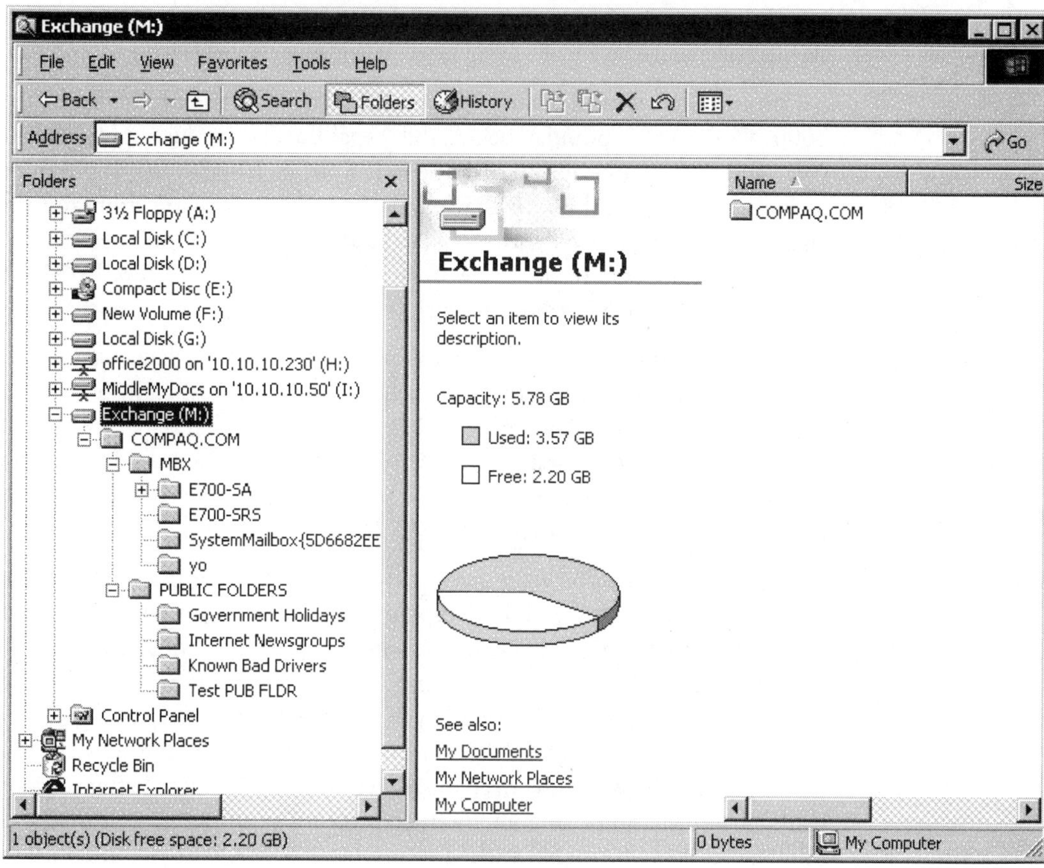

Figure 9.7 *The Exchange 2000 M: drive.*

With Windows 2000, file share users gain the benefit of being able to synchronize file shares for use when disconnected from their network—this is called Offline Folders. Given that Exchange 2000 folders can be accessed just like a file share, Windows 2000 users will be able to synchronize certain Exchange 2000 folders without having any specific client installed on their machine.

Streaming store

With Exchange 2000, Microsoft has introduced a new database to the mix, the streaming store. Now, instead of having just PRIV.EDB and PUB.EDB files, we also have corresponding streaming files for each .EDB file—namely, PRIV.STM and PUB.STM. The streaming store, which shows up as an .STM file, brings some interesting changes to Exchange 2000's storage architecture and also brings some new capabilities to the product.

Streaming capabilities are often mentioned with regards to Exchange 2000. Contrary to popular belief, this capability is not just applicable to voice and video, although they do benefit from it. Instead, the importance of the streaming capability is that data, of any kind, arriving from any IIS virtual server get moved into the database, via IFS, without conversion. Therefore, a message retrieved by an Internet client (e.g., POP3, IMAP) is streamed to the client without requiring a conversion.

This is an important distinction compared with MAPI clients. MAPI clients will download an entire item before allowing access to it. Streaming is suitable for multimedia content, with the condition that data can be processed rapidly and consistently (more or less at the same speed). This is why Exchange 2000 has new storage access patterns, and these should be taken into consideration when configuring Exchange 2000 servers.

Use of the streaming store may, in fact, alter the way that you publish information in Exchange 2000. Keeping in mind that information is stored in the streaming store (.stm) database when it arrives via an Internet protocol client, and that all information in Exchange 2000 is accessible via HTTP (and other access methods), you may decide to use Exchange 2000 as a Web publishing server. If you do plan to publish information via HTTP, for instance, or any mechanism that uses the IFS, it is better to publish this information using an Internet protocol client (e.g., a browser) as opposed to using Outlook. Indeed, Outlook uses MAPI as the interface to Exchange 2000 and will create MAPI objects (stored solely in the .edb database) as opposed to native content in the streaming store.

To be sure, items stored exclusively in the .edb store will not require conversion when fetched by MAPI clients but will require on-the-fly conversion for Internet clients. Items stored in the streaming store (with properties held in the .EDB) will require on-the-fly conversion for MAPI clients and no conversion for Internet clients.

Microsoft has implemented a last writer wins process for storing data in the Web Storage System. This means that if a client modifies data associated with an item, that item is converted and stored in the format appropriate for the client performing the change. So, for a MAPI client that changes information, the item will be written to the .edb file exclusively. If an Internet client changes an item, that item will be written to the streaming store (.STM) file with property promotion to the .EDB happening, as stated earlier.

OK, so we've covered a bit more of the architecture of Exchange 2000; now let's step back into the specifics associated with the new transfer system.

9.2.3 Grouping servers with routing groups

From a transport perspective, Exchange 2000 servers are grouped by a newly introduced concept called a routing group. A routing group can be defined as a collection of well-connected servers that communicate, via SMTP, in a point-to-point manner. Again, from a transport perspective, routing groups are similar to Exchange 5.5 sites. The major difference, and it is major, is that sites in 5.5 defined a common boundary for name space, directory replication, administration, and transport. With Exchange 2000, those elements are separate. Name space is defined in Active Directory by elements for domains and organizational units. Directory replication is another service that is handled by Active Directory. Administration and permissions associated with Exchange 2000 are handled via a combination of new concepts called administration groups and Access Controls in Active Directory. (Directory-based access controls have been around for a long time in a variety of products and were somewhat available in previous versions of Exchange. The point is that access controls are now part of the operating system, since they are part of Active Directory and thus span the forest.) Administration groups are created to manage Exchange 2000 objects. These objects are typically stored in various containers within an administrative group. For instance, there are containers for Servers, Public Folders, Policies, and routing groups. Permissions to access administrative groups are associated with security permissions assigned in Active Directory. administrative groups are also the entity of delegation within Exchange 2000. Delegation allows an IT organization to have tight control over what a person can do and delegate what administrative tasks a person can do. This is an important concept in Exchange 2000, especially as compared with what was, or wasn't, possible with Exchange 5.5 and prior versions of the product.

Moving back to the specifics associated with topology, message transport is now managed and defined by routing groups. In essence, with Exchange 2000 you have the freedom to assign server management permissions to a specific IT support group and assign management and configuration of transport topology to a more messaging- and network-aware organization in the enterprise. This flexibility alone is a huge advantage over the Exchange 5.5 realm in terms of administration.

As an illustration, in Exchange 5.5 deployments it was very likely that administrative control was handed out on a per-site basis. In some cases, message transport was negatively affected by the careless or unknowing creation of extraneous connectors or Internet Mail Services (IMS) at a poorly managed site. How did this happen? Administrators with site permissions in Exchange 5.5 normally had complete access to all configuration information within their site. Creating a rogue IMS was a simple matter of running a wizard. I've run into this exact scenario on multiple occasions and it can be very frustrating to deal with in an Exchange 5.5 deployment. Because of the separation of server administrative from routing topology management (realized in Routing Groups) in Exchange 2000, tighter control can be maintained with regard to available connectors, and the management of transport-specific tasks can be allocated to a focused group—ideally one that has a solid understanding of messaging and the underlying network.

To make things simple during installation, Exchange 2000 servers are automatically created as members of a routing group. By default, for a green-field installation, the first routing group created is called First Routing Group. ("Green-field" is used to describe a brand new environment, which has not been altered in any way and contains no legacy systems.) Interestingly, that routing group container exists within the First Administrative Group container. If other routing groups are present in the Exchange 2000 organization, the installation procedure will prompt the installer for the particular routing group to join. The ability to select routing groups is only available if multiple routing groups have been created.

It should also be noted that in a green-field Exchange 2000 deployment, the Exchange System Manager interface will not show administrative groups and routing groups when it is first launched. Administrative groups and routing groups, other than those created by default, are probably not going to be implemented by small Exchange organizations, or even in ASPs, so displaying that information only makes sense in larger deployments. To display administrative groups and routing groups you must open ESM, right-click on the organization name, select properties, and check the boxes for administrative group and routing group display, as shown in Figure 9.8.

Mixed mode versus native mode: a routing perspective

If you are in a mixed mode environment consisting of Exchange 5.5 and Exchange 2000, you will also notice that Exchange 5.5 sites are represented in Exchange 2000 by a tuple consisting of an administrative group and a routing group, as shown in Figure 9.9.

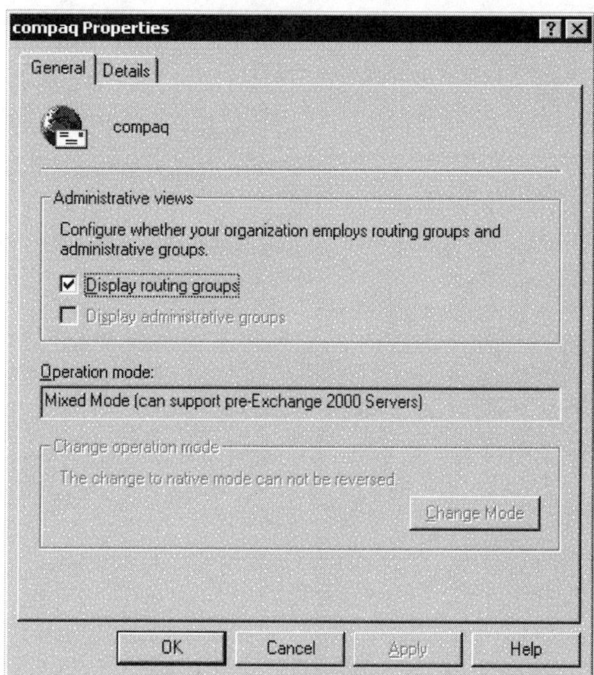

Figure 9.8 *Setting the display of Routing Groups.*

Notice on the left-hand side of the display (the container side) the folders that appear with no coloring. This environment is a mixed mode Exchange organization and these folders are Exchange 5.5 sites. Since the Exchange System Manager interface is viewing information in Active Directory, how does information about Exchange 5.5 sites become available? Well, hopefully, you've read the previous chapters of this book and know that this all happened via the ADC.

One negative side-effect of mixed mode is the lack of flexibility available. For instance, in Figure 9.9, I have an administrative group called Adming for Routing. I had originally created this administrative group to home all of my routing groups. By doing this I would later be able to delegate management of routing information to a specific set of users. Unfortunately, when I created this administrative group, I made a typing error. Now, if I were in native mode I would be able to right-click on this administrative group, perform a rename, and remove the extraneous "g" in the display. Unfortunately, in mixed mode you don't have that capability. The reasoning behind this is that my Exchange 5.5 world would not act kindly to me renaming what it believes to be sites. This awareness of Exchange 5.5 structures while in mixed mode also prevents me from doing really nice

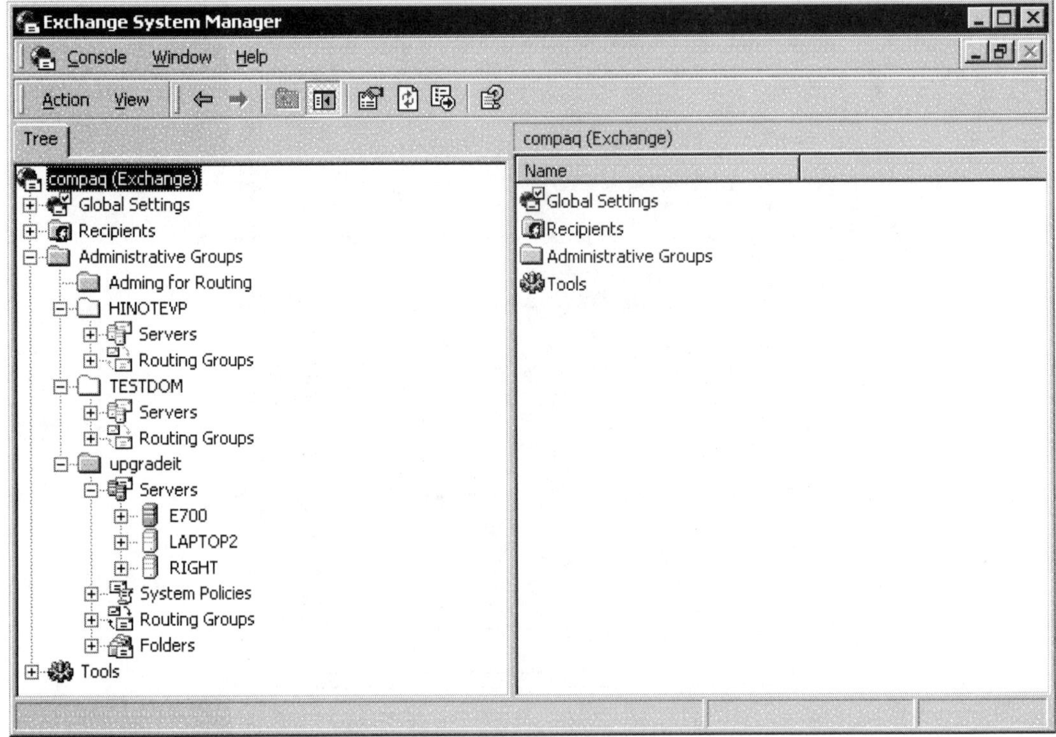

Figure 9.9 *Mixed mode: Exchange 2000 Administrative Groups/Exchange 5.5 sites.*

things like dragging and dropping routing groups from one administrative group to another and/or dragging and dropping server members from one routing group to another. We'll look at a native mode environment a little later and show how this functionality works. Again, though, it makes sense to limit some of this functionality while in mixed mode. Imagine how a 5.5 environment would react if you tried to change its membership from one site to another with a drag and drop. It just wouldn't work!

Just for fun, I thought I'd let you see what this mixed mode world looks like from an Exchange 5.5 perspective. In Figure 9.10, note that my Adming for Routing administrative group appears as a site within the Exchange 5.5 Admin.exe program, and it only contains a Configuration container. Also note that from the Exchange 5.5 administrator's perspective the site called upgradeit contains three servers: E700, LAPTOP2, and RIGHT. Only one of these servers, E700, is running Exchange 2000. If, however, I connect to an Exchange 5.5 server in the upgradeit site via the 5.5 Exchange Administrator, I can see the server recipients associated with

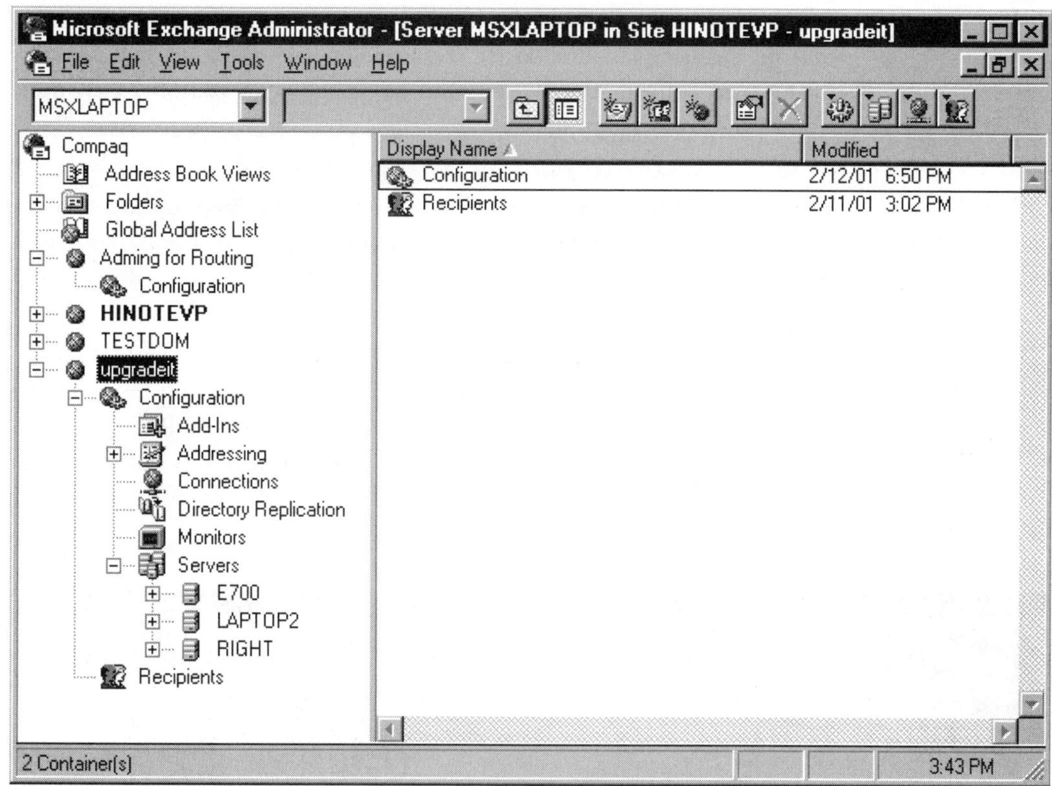

Figure 9.10 *Exchange 5.5 Administrator view of mixed-mode organization.*

the E700 server and make changes to them. This is quite interesting when you consider that those users are actually stored in Active Directory. The changes, of course, are really made within the Exchange 5.5 world's directory service and replicated back to Active Directory via the ADC. As pointed out earlier, however, the best practice is to always manage Exchange 5.5 servers with Exchange 5.5 tools and Exchange 2000 information with Windows 2000 and Exchange 2000 tools.

9.3 Routing groups

As stated, a routing group is merely a collection of well-connected servers that communicate in a point-to-point manner over SMTP. In the context of a routing group, "well connected" can be defined as a persistent, point-to-point connection between servers and, most importantly, a persistent connection to the Routing Group Master server.

Although we'll discuss it in detail in the next chapter, for now be aware that the Routing Group Master is the server responsible for broadcasting connectivity information within the Exchange organization to all other servers in its routing group.

So, as a member of a routing group, any server has immediate network access to other members of the routing group. Routing group membership is maintained in the Configuration Naming Context of the Active Directory and is displayed through the Exchange 2000 System Manager Console, as shown in Figure 9.11.

Note that the server E700, in Figure 9.11, is designated as the "master" for this routing group. It is also possible to see routing group membership through ADSI Edit (see Figure 9.12) as well as LDP. (LDP is an LDAP-based Active Directory management tool and will be described in Chapter 12.) You can also view routing group membership via the WinRoute tool, which we will discuss in Chapter 12.

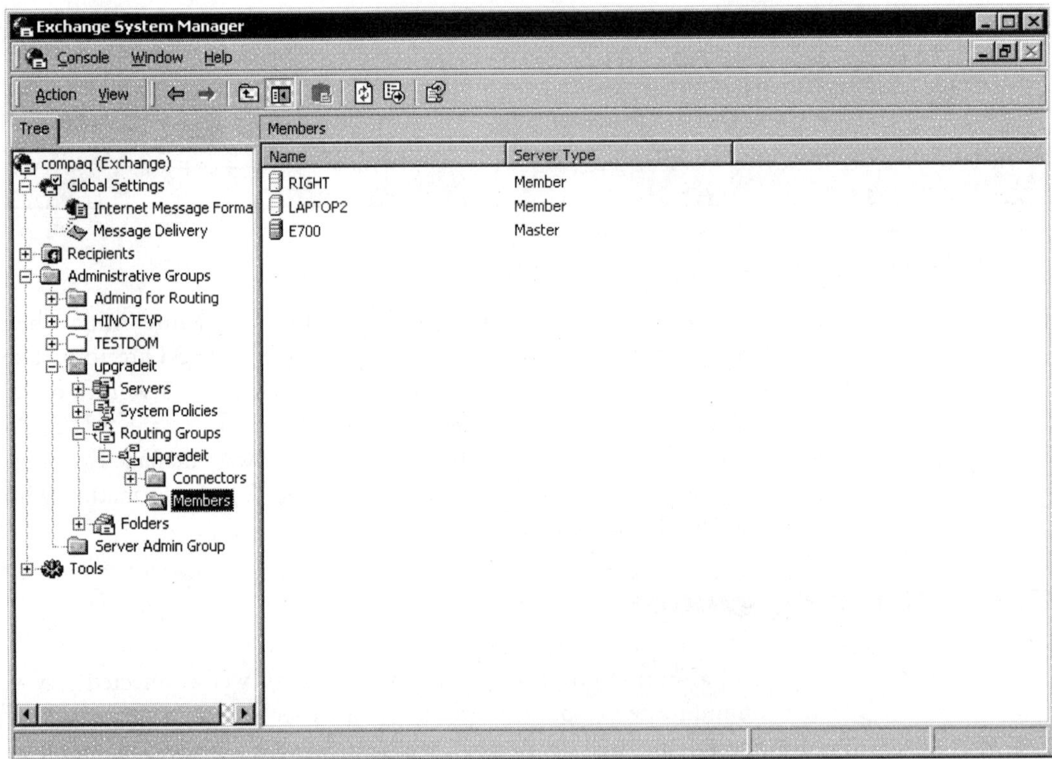

Figure 9.11 *Routing group members.*

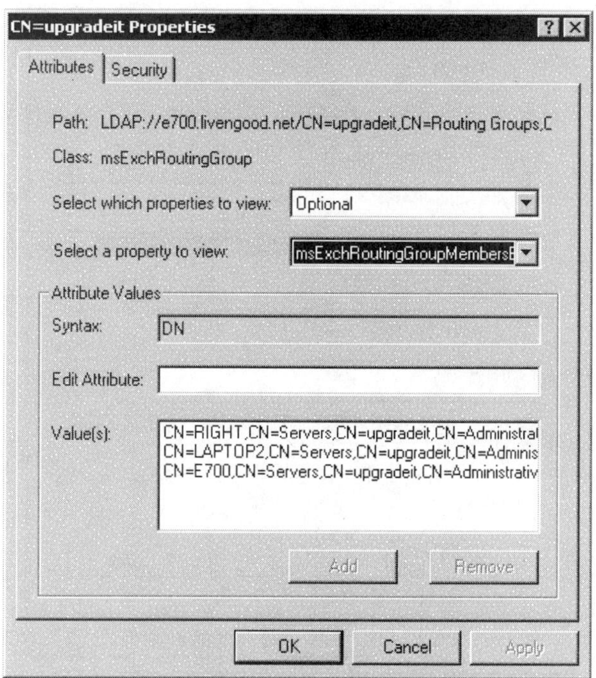

Figure 9.12 *Viewing routing group membership using ADSI Edit.*

We've mentioned ADSI Edit quite a bit, but keep in mind that the Exchange 2000 System Manager Console is the primary management interface for Exchange 2000. ESM is an Exchange 2000–specific collection of MMC snap-ins and is the supplied and preferred interface for managing and viewing Exchange 2000 configuration information, which is stored in Active Directory. Remember that the Active Directory Configuration Naming Context is replicated throughout the Active Directory forest. Therefore, the Configuration Naming Context is accessible by all Exchange servers in the same Exchange 2000 organization. This is a key concept to keep in mind when we begin to explain how messages actually get routed through the environment in Chapter 10.

When the first server is added to a routing group, it is assigned the role of Routing Group Master. The role of the master is to inform all other servers in the routing group about changes that have occurred in the routing topology. You can almost think of the master as the air traffic controller of the routing group. The master knows which connections out of the routing group are up or down, and it passes this information to every server in its routing group as the information changes. Referring to Figure 9.12, you can see that the server E700 is designated as the master for the upgradeit rout-

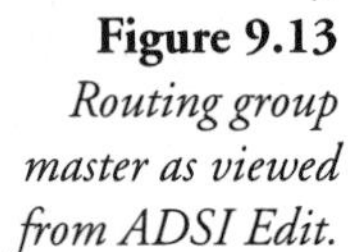

Figure 9.13 *Routing group master as viewed from ADSI Edit.*

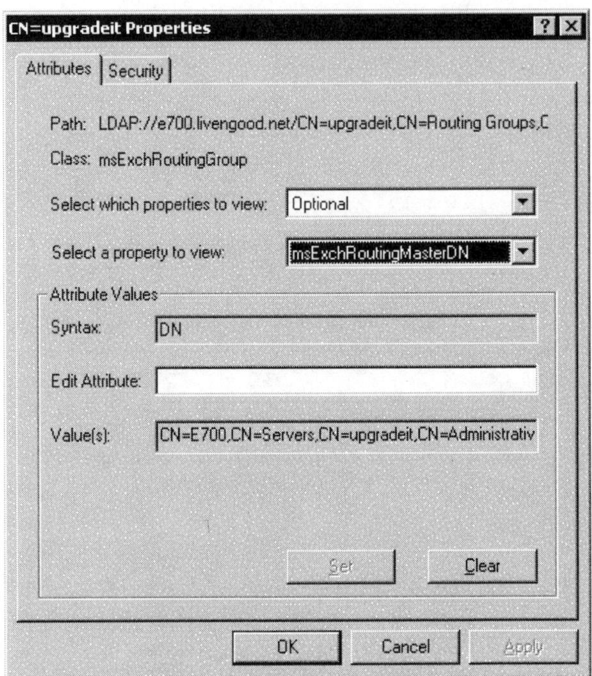

ing group. As with everything else associated with an Exchange 2000 configuration, the routing master information can be seen (see Figure 9.13), and changed, through ADSI Edit. Only with the guidance of an experienced professional (or Microsoft PSS), should you change information in your production environment via ADSI Edit. Play all you want in your test environment, but stomping around the directory and making changes with ADSI Edit can be dangerous. On several occasions, while learning the product, I modified or removed information via ADSI Edit and subsequently gave myself the opportunity to perform a reinstall. With that, you have been warned!

9.4 Multiple routing groups

Since the message transport in Exchange 2000 is SMTP-based, and since SMTP works well over low bandwidths, there is a real possibility of building a single, large routing group to service an entire company. Remember, we no longer have minimum bandwidths as we had with Exchange 5.5, because we are no longer using RPC for communication. This being the case, we must now ask the question of when, or why, an enterprise would create multiple routing groups. The first obvious reason for having multiple routing groups is that the minimum requirements for membership to a routing group have not been met. A specific example is the requirement for a persistent (not necessarily high speed) connection to the Routing Group Master. Another might be the need for a scheduled connection. Still another is the desire to control the path that a message takes through the network. Remember, within a routing group, all servers communicate in a point-to-point manner.

9.4.1 Nonpersistent or scheduled connections

In an environment where a server is only connected to the rest of the environment on a temporary basis, you may want to split that server, or set of servers, off into a separate routing group. There is no technical reason or restriction in the interface to prevent you from keeping these servers as members of one huge routing group. However, in order for servers to make optimal use of the routing information distributed by the Routing Group Master, these servers should be continuously connected to the network. Otherwise, as link information changes in the environment, these servers will not receive updates and will thus operate on noncurrent information. Again, there's no danger of message looping in this scenario; it will just result in inefficient routing of messages.

9.4.2 Controlling the path of messages

In a huge routing group, servers communicate point to point. Should you have the need to control the path that messages take through the network, this behavior is not desirable. Another possibility is that you need to perform billing, or traffic analysis, in a simple, manageable fashion. Having to monitor message traffic on every single server is quite a task! Splitting servers up into a few or several routing groups, applying BridgeHead connectors (BH) between them, and monitoring message flow across BH connectors may prove to be much more manageable.

9.4.3 Politics

Politics may still play a role in routing group creation, but in the case of Exchange 2000, the underlying technology doesn't force multiple routing groups. Some organizations wish to separate management of certain functions to various organizations. Some may choose to create multiple administrative groups based on organizational function and may divide the management and organization of their routing topology along those same lines. Unfortunately, this approach will not lend itself to the full flexibility delivered in Exchange 2000. I suppose, however, one of the advantages of the flexibility of Exchange 2000 is that it does allow an IT organization to create the administrative model any way it likes, even if that model is one dictated by politics. So, if your Exchange 5.5 design was dictated by politics, your Exchange 2000 design can be dictated by politics as well, including the routing design.

9.4.4 Public Folders

As you may recall, there are several ways of giving people physical access to Public Folders in Exchange 5.5. One method is to replicate the Public Folder to various servers spread throughout the organization. The other method is via Public Folder affinity. Affinity allows the administrator to create a special table to determine which servers a local user should go to in order to access a Public Folder that doesn't exist within that user's site. Well, while that method works pretty well, it is a bit unwieldy to manage, since the table exists on a per-server/site basis. And besides, if you think about it, what is a manager usually trying to accomplish with this table anyway? Basically the

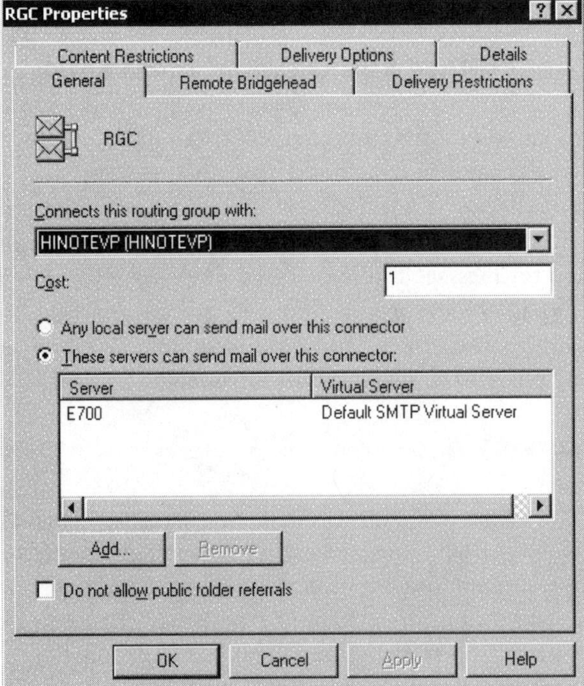

Figure 9.14 *Public Folder referral checkbox on the routing group connector.*

manager is trying to direct the client to a nearby copy of the Public Folder, right? Public Folder affinity was established in Exchange 5.5 via an affinity table. From there, Public Folder referral occurred using the following algorithm:

1. Check for a server in the same subsite.
2. Check for a server in the same site.
3. Check for a server in sites that have Public Folder affinity configured to this site.

Now, think about what we have with routing groups and the various connectors. For each connector we assign a cost. That cost identifies how close, network-wise, one group of servers is to another group of servers. So, what Microsoft has done with Exchange 2000 is allow Public Folder affinity to be determined by costs associated with connectors that link the organization.

For each connector there is a checkbox (see Figure 9.14), which, when checked, excludes the connector and the cost of the connector in determining Public Folder affinity. More simply put, Public Folder affinity in Exchange 2000 is determined by the following set of rules:

1. Server within the same routing group
2. Closest server, sorted by connector cost over connectors, allowing affinity

This method really does make sense when you think about it from a connectivity point of view. If I don't have the required connectivity for a single routing group, I create another one. To connect the two, I configure a connector and assign a cost. If I continue down this path and define lots of routing groups, because of the costs I've assigned, I can determine which set of servers is closest to me (or the cheapest to connect to). Remember, I'm a messaging- and network-aware professional, so my design will have some rhyme and reason to it. By using the connectors themselves to determine Public Folder affinity, I am managing two pieces of information at once. Figure 9.14 shows the checkbox on a routing group connector, but the checkbox is available on other connectors as well (SMTP, X.400).

Well, there are some potential problems with this plan. The most obvious relates to the rule of thumb that applies to nearly all technology: the olde KISS principle—Keep It Simple Stupid. With routing groups the KISS principle would stipulate that it's easiest to use one routing group (assuming I'm in native mode). Here's the rub: Many of the larger enterprise customers I've worked with have really beefed up their connectivity. Some, in fact, have done this because of the overhead associated with Exchange 5.5: RPCs, Exchange replication, and so on. Now, with Exchange 2000, we have a transfer protocol (SMTP) that works really well over lower bandwidth and isn't nearly as sensitive to timeouts as RPCs. So, from a routing topology perspective, one routing group will work pretty well for many large organizations.

On the other hand, these customers would like their employees in New York to connect to Public Folder servers in New York, or at least to servers in the Northeast United States, not to some server in Singapore. The way affinity currently works with Exchange 2000, there's no easy way to do this without creating a new routing group. This may be one feature that you'll see Microsoft change, or allow administrators to change, as Exchange 2000 evolves.

9.4.5 Connecting remote locations

Finally, any organization that wishes to use either the Internet or an X.400 service provider to connect servers within its organization will likely need to implement multiple routing groups. Both the SMTP connector and the X.400 connector have a Connected Routing Groups tab to assist with handling this type of remote, public network connectivity.

Regardless of the reasons, there are three choices to connect routing groups, as follows:

1. Routing group connector (RGC)
2. SMTP connector
3. X.400 connector

9.4.6 Routing Group Connector

The Routing Group Connector (RGC) should be the first, and most common, choice for connecting routing groups. Unlike RPC-based site connectors in previous versions of Exchange, in a pure Exchange 2000 environment routing group connectors use SMTP as their base transport protocol and, therefore, are much more tolerant of high-latency and low-bandwidth connections than site connectors. RGCs are actually protocol independent, since they will use the RPC LAN-MTA protocol when communicating to Exchange 5.5 site connectors. RGCs can also be scheduled, unlike site connectors. However, as with the site connectors of Exchange 5.5 and earlier versions, routing group connectors are very easy to configure and allow for automatic generation of the remote end (remote bridgehead) of the connection. One thing to note is that to create the remote end of the RGC, the account you are using must have permissions in the administrative group homing the particular routing group to which you are connecting.

9.4.7 SMTP Connector

The SMTP Connector can be thought of as the Exchange 2000 version of the IMS. Its primary function is to connect Exchange 2000 environments to the Internet or to non-Exchange 2000 SMTP-capable systems (e.g., Process Software's PMDF or Sendmail). This connector can also be used to connect routing groups, but when you consider that the protocol used for RGCs and SMTP connectors is the same in a pure Exchange 2000 environment, it is unlikely that it will be used to connect routing groups. It should be noted that since every Exchange 2000 system is capable of communicating via SMTP, there is no hard requirement that an SMTP connector be implemented to communicate with the Internet. While allowing every server to have direct access to and from the Internet is not a wise configuration guideline, it is possible. From a practical perspective, however, it makes much more sense to configure an SMTP connector to serve as the interface between the internal Exchange 2000 world and the external world, as we will see later.

9.4.8 X.400 connector

The X.400 connector is virtually identical in Exchange 2000 as it is in previous versions of Exchange; the user interface for the connector is almost identical to that in previous versions. The X.400 connector can be used in the same scenarios for Exchange 2000 as it was for prior versions of Exchange—namely, low-bandwidth scenarios, connectivity to X.400 providers, or to connect Exchange 2000 routing groups (but again, RGCs should be the first choice). The X.400 connector can also be used to connect to Exchange 5.5 systems that are not connected by other means.

9.4.9 Encryption with connectors

It should be noted that one feature that RPC communications brought us, both in an Exchange 5.5 site and through the use of site connectors, was encrypted communications. By default, this is not the case in an Exchange 2000 routing group or through any of the connectors. Encryption can be handled at the TCP/IP level through the implementation of IPSEC. With IPSEC, all TCP/IP communication will be encrypted.

9.5 Planning routing groups

OK, so here we are, we've got the concept of a routing group under our belts. We understand the basic requirements for a routing group. We also understand that there may be certain times where multiple routing groups make sense. So, now the obvious question is how do we design the routing environment for Exchange 2000? Do we perform a deep network analysis and combine that with a strategy for server consolidation and employee dispersement? What happens if our network is in a state of change, either reducing links or increasing network bandwidth? Just what is the future impact of our initial design?

Well, here's the true beauty of Exchange 2000's transport: Your design can evolve with your needs and with your knowledge of the underlying net-

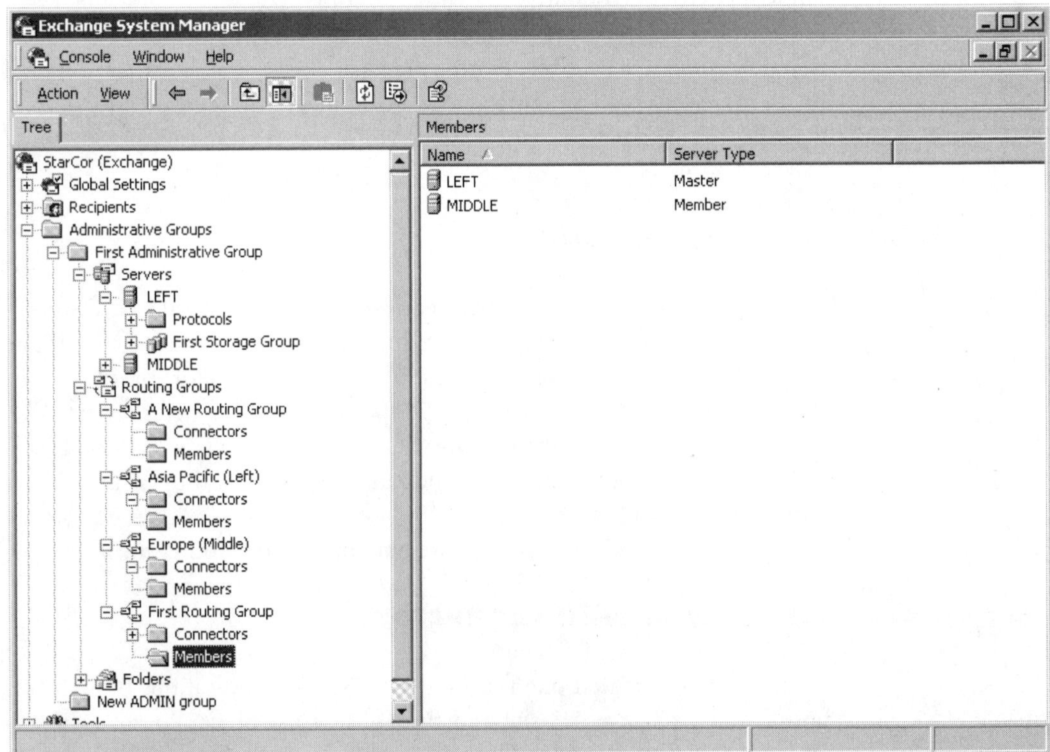

Figure 9.15 *Multiple routing groups in a native-mode Exchange 2000 environment.*

work. Basically what I'm saying here is, "Don't sweat it!" If you do a poor job, no problem, you can always go back and change it—provided you're in native mode.

Now you might be thinking: Well, sure ... I could change my topology with Exchange 5.5 too, but it was a lot of work. Do you want to know how difficult it is in a pure Exchange 2000 world? How does "drag and drop" sound? It really is that easy.

Check out the example shown in Figure 9.15 of a native mode Exchange 2000 organization. I've got several routing groups created. From Figure 9.15 you can see that I have two servers that are members of the routing group called First Routing Group. Remember, this is the default routing you get when you first install Exchange 2000. Since the initial installation, I've created other routing groups, two of which represent geographic regions: Asia Pacific and Europe. So, let's say that the servers LEFT and MIDDLE actually reside in the Asia Pacific region. To change these servers' memberships, all I need to do is select them (via CTRL-SHIFT) and drag them into the Asia Pacific Routing Group. Figures 9.16 and 9.17 show the process and the result.

As it turns out, when I attempted to move these servers, I got an error stating that they were bridgeheads for some connectors I had previously set up. The error screen in Figure 9.16 reminds you to move the connectors to other servers before attempting to proceed. What I did was just remove the connectors completely, since I'm in a test environment. In a production environment I would definitely want to rehome the connectors if I wish to

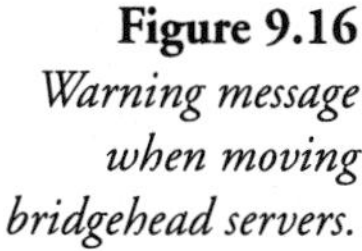

Figure 9.16
Warning message when moving bridgehead servers.

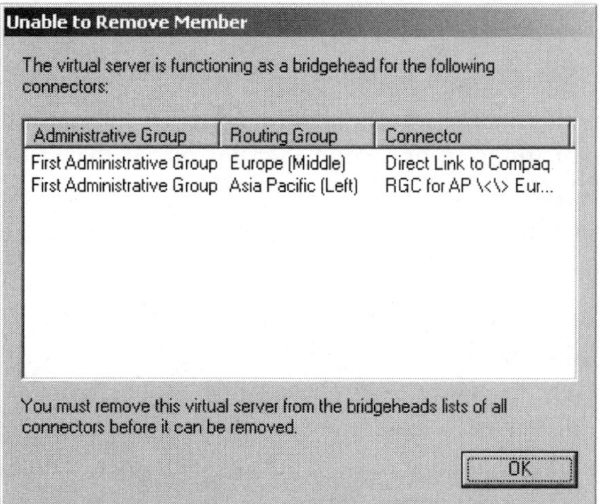
Unable to Remove Member
The virtual server is functioning as a bridgehead for the following connectors:
Administrative Group
Routing Group
Connector
First Administrative Group Europe (Middle) Direct Link to Compaq
First Administrative Group Asia Pacific (Left) RGC for AP \<\> Eur...
You must remove this virtual server from the bridgeheads lists of all connectors before it can be removed.
OK

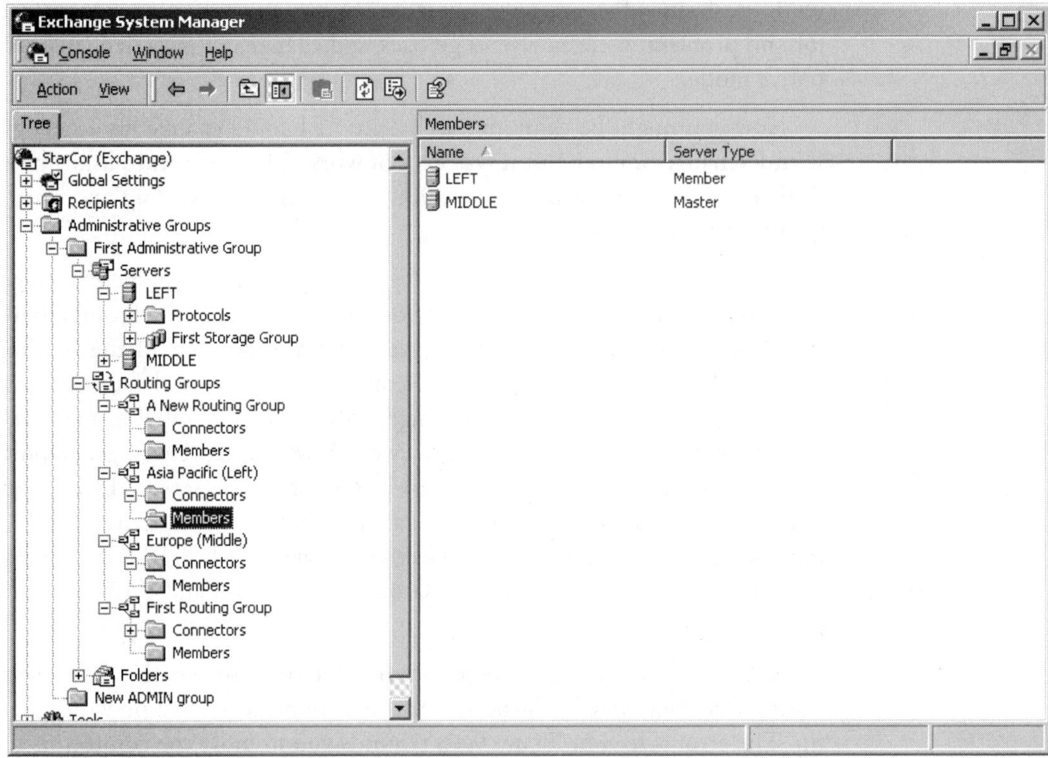

Figure 9.17 *Successful drag and drop between routing groups.*

maintain connectivity to this routing group. Rehoming can be done easily by just recreating the connector on another server. Once I've either removed the connectors or rehomed them, the operation completes, as you can see in Figure 9.17.

Note that the server called MIDDLE is the routing group master for the Asia Pacific Routing Group. The reason for that is that I moved the server MIDDLE first, and therefore it became the master. If I want to change server LEFT to be the routing group master, then all that is required is to right-click on server LEFT and make it the master. Very simple, eh?

So, since it is so easy to change the topology, does that mean there is no planning involved at all with Exchange 2000? Of course not! As you recall, and saw from the example, routing groups exist as containers inside of administrative groups. Another very important container that exists within an administrative group is a servers container. Unlike the objects within a routing group, which can be moved via drag and drop, objects within server containers cannot be moved so easily. Also, remember that delegation of administrative control is realized through the use of administrative groups. Hopefully, you are starting to get the picture. Your administrative model should be carefully planned and well thought out.

9.5.1 Planning rules of thumb

Even with routing groups there is still some planning necessary. Here are some basic rules of thumb to keep in mind for planning routing groups.

- Start with one routing group (the KISS principle).
- If servers are connected to the master via high-latency lines, create a routing group for those servers.
- If a server, or servers, requires scheduled access to the network, and thus the master, create a routing group for those servers.
- If you need to control the specific path messages take through your network, you will need multiple routing groups and you will use connectors to define the path(s).
- If Public Folder affinity is important for your environment, you may need multiple routing groups to control the efficiency of Public Folder access.
- If you need to use the Internet or an X.400 VAN to connect your environment, place those servers in their own routing group.

Before we get carried away though, remember that while you are migrating your Exchange 5.5 environment to Exchange 2000 you will not be in native mode. This means your routing group structure will map one-to-one with your Exchange 5.5 site structure and cannot be changed until you move to native mode.

9.6 Connecting to non-Exchange 2000 environments

Although the enterprise messaging world seems as if it has been consolidated into three major commercial players—Microsoft Exchange, Lotus Notes, and Novell's GroupWise—there still are many folks out there running with products such as cc:Mail, MSMail, ALL-IN-1, and PROFs. More importantly, there are a huge number of people using native, or pure-play, Internet messaging systems today. In Exchange 5.5, communicating to these various systems was accomplished using connectors. Connector is really a nice word for gateway. The function of a connector is to map addresses from one format to another, provide a communications path between systems, format messages according to whatever the transport requires, and optionally synchronize directories.

Microsoft did an excellent job of supplying connectors and migration tools for pre-Exchange 2000 versions of the product. Their apparent strategy was to make it very simple and attractive for customers to move to their platform. A pretty good idea, you must admit. However, since there are fewer dominant messaging systems today than there were three years ago, Exchange 2000 will include fewer connectors than were available with Exchange 5.5.

The connectors that ship with Exchange 2000 are as follows:

- MS-MAIL
- cc:Mail
- Lotus Notes
- GroupWise
- SMTP
- X.400

That's it. The SNADs and PROFs connectors, the ones that were made available as part of Microsoft's acquisition of Linkage, are not included in Exchange 2000. So, if you still have PROFs or SNADs in your environment and are using an Exchange 5.5 connector, what do you do since they're not part of Exchange 2000? Well, you could potentially look for or wait for a third-party tool, or you could rely on the Exchange 5.5-based connector. Since a coexistence environment of Exchange 2000 and Exchange 5.5 servers is possible, it is completely feasible to use 5.5-based connectors in a mixed Exchange 2000/Exchange 5.5 organization. The unfortunate side effect of taking this approach is that the Exchange environment must stay in mixed mode as long as 5.5 servers are part of the environment. This limits the flexibility and use of Exchange 2000 features, such as dragging and dropping servers between routing groups and defining a perhaps more optimal routing topology than the one created based on limitations of previous versions of Exchange.

If the flexibility is absolutely required in your environment, there still is hope. In many cases companies are looking to restructure their Exchange environment. There is the potential to split the servers running the Exchange 5.5-based connectors off onto a new Exchange organization that only hosts those connectors. Of course, you'll need to do some clever directory work so that the Exchange 5.5 server can pass information off to the legacy system in one direction and then back off to the production Exchange organization via SMTP or X.400. Another option is to enable SMTP on the mainframe and connect it directly to Exchange 2000.

On a positive note, systems such as SNADs and PROFs are a dying breed, and it's unlikely that too many companies will require these connectors at all; and, if they do, it should only be for a short period of time. Those customers should definitely consider a migration from those environments ... especially now that Exchange 2000 can take advantage of clusters and Storage Area Network technologies. An Exchange 2000 N+1 cluster should be able to support the needs of an environment consisting of 20,000 mailboxes in a highly reliable and quickly recoverable manner.

What about other connectors such as those from third parties for fax capabilities? Well, you'll need to retest and reevaluate those gateways and ensure that your vendor has a version that works with Exchange 2000. For now, let's quickly cover some of the connectors that do ship with Exchange 2000. However, going into the details of configuring each of these gateways for your particular environment is beyond the scope of this book.

9.6.1 MS-MAIL

The Microsoft Mail connector transfers messages between Exchange 2000 and Microsoft Mail. Also included with the connector is a directory synchronization capability. With Exchange 2000, the connector is now configured through the MMC and this configuration information is stored in Active Directory. As before, directory synchronization is accomplished through a Local DXA (Microsoft Exchange Directory Synchronization) and is configured in either server or requester mode.

Architecturally the Microsoft Mail connector acts as a shadow Microsoft Mail post office. During message transfer, once the message is in the shadow post office, a configured message transfer agent (MTA) moves it to the destination Microsoft Mail post office. The Microsoft Mail Connector can be configured to connect to many Microsoft Mail post offices, as opposed to just one, as is the case with the cc:Mail connector.

9.6.2 cc:Mail

Exchange 2000 Server includes a native Exchange Server connector for Lotus cc:Mail in both the standard and enterprise editions of the product. Exchange 2000 Connector for Lotus cc:Mail is functionally similar to the version included with Exchange 5.5, but it now includes integration with Active Directory and supports the latest versions of cc:Mail.

The connector essentially uses two programs supplied by Lotus: the import and export utilities. It's important to note that these utilities vary in version number with different versions of cc:Mail, and you will need the correct version of each to use the connector effectively. Directory information can also be parsed using the same two utilities, so, in essence, the connector provides two-way message and directory exchange. (See the "Lotus cc:Mail and Exchange 2000 Server Coexistence and Migration Version 3.0 Configuration and Implementation" white paper on the Microsoft Web site for details of configuration.)

9.6.3 Lotus Notes

The Exchange Lotus Notes connector can connect Exchange 2000 with Notes servers. The connector has built-in messaging, directory synchronization, and meeting request capabilities.

From a messaging standpoint, the connector supports the following features:

- Delivery status
- Read receipts
- Delivery receipts
- Delivery notification status
- Options
- Importance (high, normal, low)
- Type (private, confidential)
- Formatting
- Rich text
- Doc-links (RTF, URL, OLE)

From a directory perspective, the connector allows synchronization between Active Directory and Notes address books. Configuration is via the MMC, and there are mapping tables that allow you to appropriately map Active Directory attributes to/from Notes address book attributes. The mapping files (tables) are in the following locations: `\exchsrvr\conndata\dxamex` and `\exchsrvr\conndata\dxanotes`.

9.6.4 GroupWise

The Exchange Connector for Novell GroupWise allows mail and directory synchronization between Novell GroupWise and Exchange 2000. With the connector installed and configured, a GroupWise user in Active Directory will have an address that points to the GroupWise connector. The connector formats the messages coming from Exchange 2000 into a format that can be handled by the GroupWise API Gateway; once in the appropriate format the messages are delivered to the intended recipient using the GroupWise environment's transfer mechanisms.

Messages traveling from GroupWise to Exchange take the opposite route. To start with, sending to an Exchange user incurs a query against a configuration table. From there, the message is passed to the GroupWise API gateway, which, in turn, hands the message to the Exchange connector for GroupWise. Once in the Exchange 2000 realm, the message is delivered as normal.

The connector also handles meeting requests from Exchange and moves them into calendar information in GroupWise. The connector handles GroupWise phone messages and passes them to Exchange in the form of a standard e-mail message.

The Exchange Connector for Novell GroupWise also handles directory synchronization. There is a configuration file associated with directory synchronization, and it is found at `\exchsrvr\conndata\dxagwise`.

9.7 Summary

In this chapter, I've outlined the basics of message routing functionality using the Exchange 2000 SMTP engine. The fundamental routing components and how they operate were also discussed. In the next chapter, I'll describe the details of the Exchange 2000 message transfer service.

10

Transfer Service Details

10.1 Introduction

The new routing architecture in Exchange 2000 is based on SMTP and makes use of a proven routing algorithm. In this chapter, we will discuss how all of this magic works. For starters, let's look at a simplified view of the architecture (see Figure 10.1).

10.2 SMTP Core Transport

Simple Mail Transfer Protocol (SMTP) is the default protocol used for the transmission of messages between Exchange 2000 servers. The protocol is well established and was first defined in RFC 821in 1982. (One of the better sources for messaging related RFCs is the Internet Message Consortium at http://www.imc.org/.) The Exchange 2000 and Windows 2000 SMTP service were also developed using the Internet draft that eventually became RFC 2821, which was actually released after the Windows 2000 SMTP shipped.

As mentioned previously, until Exchange 2000 the message transfer agent, or MTA, in Exchange was based upon X.400 and RPCs. This technology served its purpose well and produced a very functional transport core for companies implementing Exchange 4.0 through 5.5. An obvious question is why would Microsoft change something that is working very well? The answer can be found in the underlying operating system, Windows 2000.

With Windows 2000, Microsoft has exposed and relies heavily upon the Active Directory. Directory services, and especially the Active Directory, bring many benefits to an enterprise. One technical benefit and capability of the Active Directory is the integration of DNS. The other obvious bene-

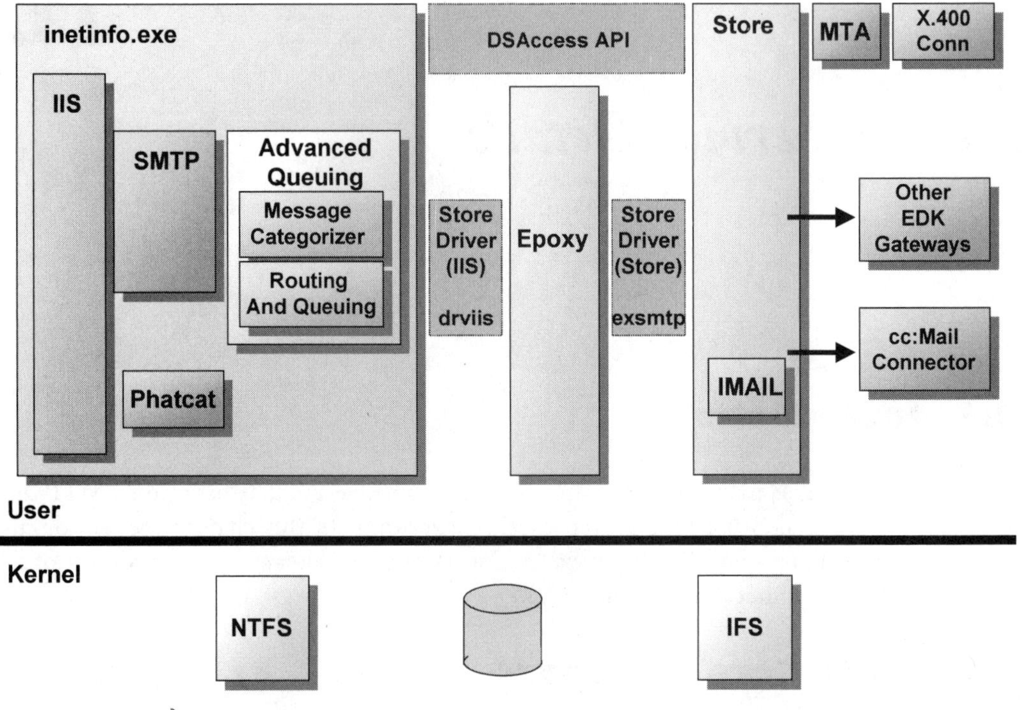

Figure 10.1 *Exchange 2000 messaging architecture.*

fits the Active Directory brings are a single point of authentication, access controls, and the central storage of configuration information. There are myriad other benefits. Microsoft had a specific goal to leverage the capabilities of Active Directory within the transport of Exchange 2000. To do this, it had two choices: modify the current MTA or create a new, more powerful transport core. Microsoft chose the latter.

Creating a new transport core may seem like a lot of work, and no doubt it was. However, this recreation was the only logical step for the following three reasons:

1. The Exchange 5.5 MTA is based on an X.400 MTA purchased from another vendor. X.400, in general, isn't as easy to enhance as SMTP. Modifying the X.400-based MTA is even more difficult when you consider that the code itself was written with different goals in mind from those required for Exchange 2000.
2. Microsoft has proven, via the Internet Mail Service (IMS) in Exchange 5.5, and via its MCIS product, that it can deliver a very fast SMTP-based MTA. As it turns out, the IMS is the fastest

connector (overall, inbound and outbound) in an Exchange 5.5 implementation.

3. The world is Internet protocol based, and this point alone justifies SMTP.

In addition to the features and functions required by Exchange 2000, Microsoft also decided that an SMTP service should be included as part of the operating system. This, too, makes sense when you consider that every UNIX platform includes a basic SMTP service, and Microsoft fully intends to compete head to head with UNIX platforms. As it turns out, the Exchange 2000 engineering team wrote the SMTP service included in Windows 2000.

10.2.1 SMTP virtual servers

It is important to realize that SMTP, along with other Internet protocols, is supplied by IIS version 5.0. Each service supplied by IIS, including SMTP, is implemented as a virtual server. A virtual server is the binding of a protocol, a port, and an IP address. For example, a server with the IP address 10.10.10.250 would have a virtual server consisting of the following:

- Service: SMTP
- Port: 25
- IP Address: 10.10.10.250

The advantage of virtual servers is that they allow you to have multiple instances of the same service (e.g., SMTP) on a single server. More interestingly, each virtual server can be configured with different characteristics. This becomes clear, and important, when you consider that a single NIC can be assigned multiple IP addresses, and, in the case of an ISP, each SMTP virtual server could be dedicated to a particular customer. In short, virtual servers allow a customer to implement an SMTP service on a per-IP address basis or, less likely, a per-port basis. This was not possible with Exchange 5.5, as only a single IMS could be implemented per server. While it is perfectly legitimate to assign a port number other than 25 to SMTP, it is usually only done in special circumstances. One such circumstance might be redirection of messages to a special processing engine. In the past this method was used to incorporate virus-checking services into a backbone.

We discussed in Chapter 8 the specific settings for virtual servers in both Windows 2000 and Exchange 2000. The property pages for virtual servers, however, aren't the only settings that affect the operation of the virtual servers.

Virtual servers and the effect of recipient policies and message filters

As was outlined in Chapters 8 and 9, the services supplied by IIS store their configuration information in the IIS metabase. Most of the configuration associated with virtual servers takes place on the properties page of the virtual server through the ESM interface. There are, however, a few configuration points that do affect the operation of virtual servers that aren't located directly on the virtual server properties page: recipient policies and message filters.

Recipient policies

Policies, in general, allow you to apply certain settings to large number of objects in an easy way. Recipient policies in Exchange 2000 provide the same type of functionality for e-mail addresses. For each Exchange 2000 organization, a default policy is generated automatically that establishes the default SMTP and X.400 addresses for all Exchange 2000–based mailbox-enabled objects. In a mixed mode organization, as can be seen in Figure 10.2, there is a recipient policy created for each site, as defined by Exchange 5.5. This is because in 5.5, the recipient policy functionality was configured to affect all users in one site. In Exchange 2000, you can consolidate this configuration and create only one per organization, or be more flexible than 5.5 and set the policy to affect users based on a particular LDAP attribute, such as department.

The default recipient policy sets the mail domain for which the virtual server accepts e-mail. For my environment that is Compaq.com. But what if I wanted to accept mail for other domains? There are two methods I could choose. First, I could allow relay on my virtual servers. This is not a good plan, since it opens up my system to spam relay to the entire Internet. So, third parties could send spam out making recipients think that it came from my environment and, even worse, make my server do the work! The other, and usually better, choice is to create a new recipient policy, or policies, that define which other domains to accept mail for.

Reasons to accept mail for domains other than your primary domain might include the following:

1. Maintaining legacy addresses. Your company name may have changed through merger or acquisition.
2. You are an ISP or ASP and are supporting multiple domains within the context of a single Exchange 2000 organization. This

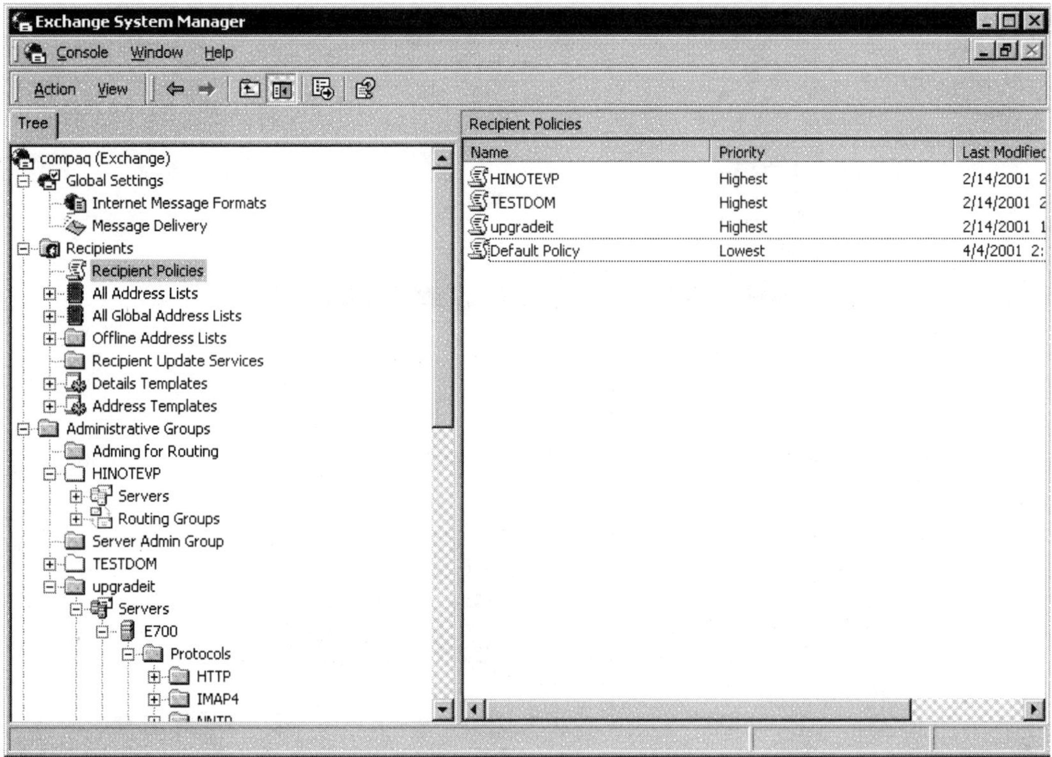

Figure 10.2 *Default recipient policies (mixed mode).*

is perfectly legitimate and quite common. Remember that an Exchange 2000 organization name really just defines the entry point in Active Directory under which all of the Exchange configuration information is stored. It doesn't mean that you can only support one company in your configuration.

3. You are an ISP or ASP and you will, in fact, relay mail for specific domains.

So, if I wanted to accept mail for some new domain, I can create a new recipient policy. For this example, let's assume that I will be accepting mail for the domains mooner.net and fivestar.com. To enable the virtual server to handle this, I create a new recipient policy, as shown in Figure 10.3.

Now that I've created the recipient policy, I can check to see if Exchange 2000 will accept messages for these domains by using telnet and the SMTP VRFY command, as shown in Figure 10.4.

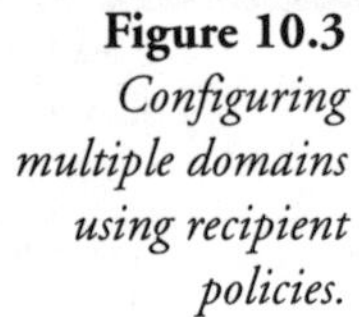

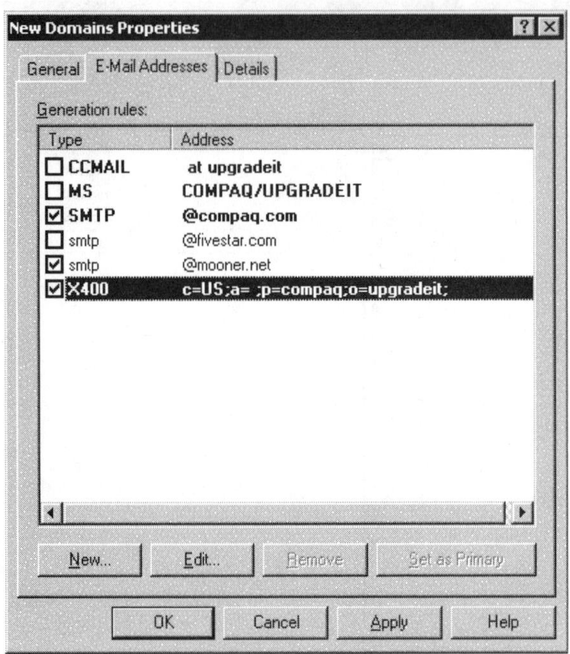

Figure 10.3 *Configuring multiple domains using recipient policies.*

You can see from Figure 10.4 that my SMTP virtual server now accepts mail for mooner.net and fivestar.com but still refuses mail to any other domains, in this case music.net. The setting on the virtual server is still set

```
Command Prompt - telnet e700 25
220 e700.livengood.net Microsoft ESMTP MAIL Service, Version: 5.0.2195.1600 read
y at  Wed, 4 Apr 2001 15:48:10 +0000
250-e700.livengood.net Hello [10.10.10.220]
250-TURN
250-ATRN
250-SIZE
250-ETRN
250-PIPELINING
250-DSN
250-ENHANCEDSTATUSCODES
250-8bitmime
250-BINARYMIME
250-CHUNKING
250-VRFY
250-X-EXPS GSSAPI NTLM LOGIN
250-X-EXPS=LOGIN
250-AUTH GSSAPI NTLM LOGIN
250-AUTH=LOGIN
250-XEXCH50
250-X-LINK2STATE
250 OK
252 2.1.5 Cannot VRFY user, but will take message for <sing@mooner.net>
252 2.1.5 Cannot VRFY user, but will take message for <money@fivestar.com>
550 5.7.1 Cannot relay to <joe@music.net>
```

Figure 10.4 *Verifying acceptable domains using telnet and VRFY.*

not to allow relay. So, as you can see, recipient policies do, in fact, affect the operation of virtual servers.

Relaying mail when relay is disabled on the virtual server

So, if relay is disabled on the VS, but I'm accepting messages for another domain for which I will perform relay, how does Exchange 2000 figure out that it can, in fact, relay messages for this domain? The most effective way to control outbound mail from Exchange 2000 is to use a connector. And, since routing is called for every message that passes through Exchange 2000, any address spaces associated with a connector are, in fact, used to determine a message's path. So, Microsoft has enabled an "allow messages to be relayed to these domains" checkbox on SMTP connectors, as shown in Figure 10.5.

Let me simplify this a bit by explaining it this way:

1. If you want to accept mail for a domain for which you have users in your exchange org with these addresses, add the domain to a recipient policy. If you also want to fall back to another system, don't make it authoritative, and make sure there is an SMTP connector for the domain that points to the authoritative system.
2. If you want to accept mail for a domain for which none of these users is in your exchange org, then the easiest thing to do is to create an SMTP connector with the domain on the address space, check the allow relay box, and set the smart host to the system that houses these users.

Combining recipient policies, disabling VS relay, and enabling relay on a connector allows you to protect your SMTP service from spam relay while still enabling relay for a specific set of domains.

Message filters

Message filters are another way to affect the operation of virtual servers without touching the actual property pages of the virtual server itself.

Creating a message filter in Exchange 2000 is easy enough. You simply open ESM, move to Global Settings and to Message Delivery and then right-click Properties. From there, move to the tab called Filtering, shown in Figure 10.6, and create a filter for a specific user or domain. Piece of cake, right? However, making the filter actually work takes a bit more effort.

Filters are created at a global level but can be applied on a specific level: meaning the virtual server level. So what you can do is create a filter once

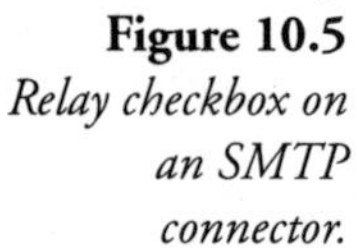

Figure 10.5
Relay checkbox on an SMTP connector.

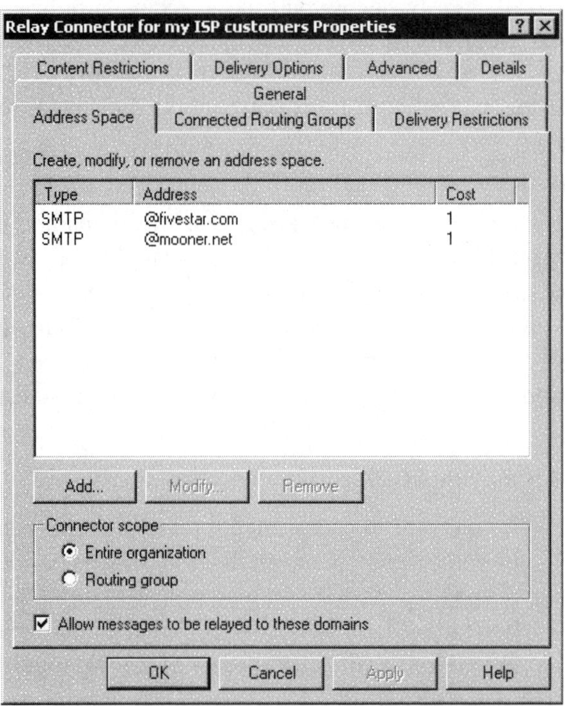

Figure 10.6
Binding a filter to a virtual server.

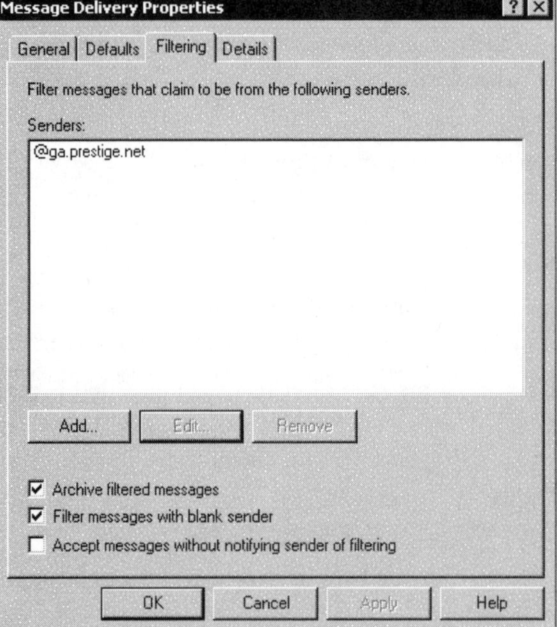

and then apply it to as many virtual servers as you'd like. Now that I've created a filter, I need to figure out which virtual server I want it to be bound to. To do this, I must go modify the virtual server. A bit nonintuitive if you ask me, but we're stuck with it for now. Microsoft has acknowledged that this is not as intuitive as it would like and will probably make it a bit more obvious in a future release.

Enough said ... let's look at how to apply the filter.

First, choose the virtual server to which you want the filter applied and open its property page. Next to the IP ADDRESS field on the General tab there is an Advanced... button. Click it and you'll see a screen similar to that shown in Figure 10.7. If you then edit the IP address to which you want the filter applied, you will see an Apply Filter checkbox. Once the Apply Filter box is checked, your filter will be applied to all messages processed by this particular virtual server.

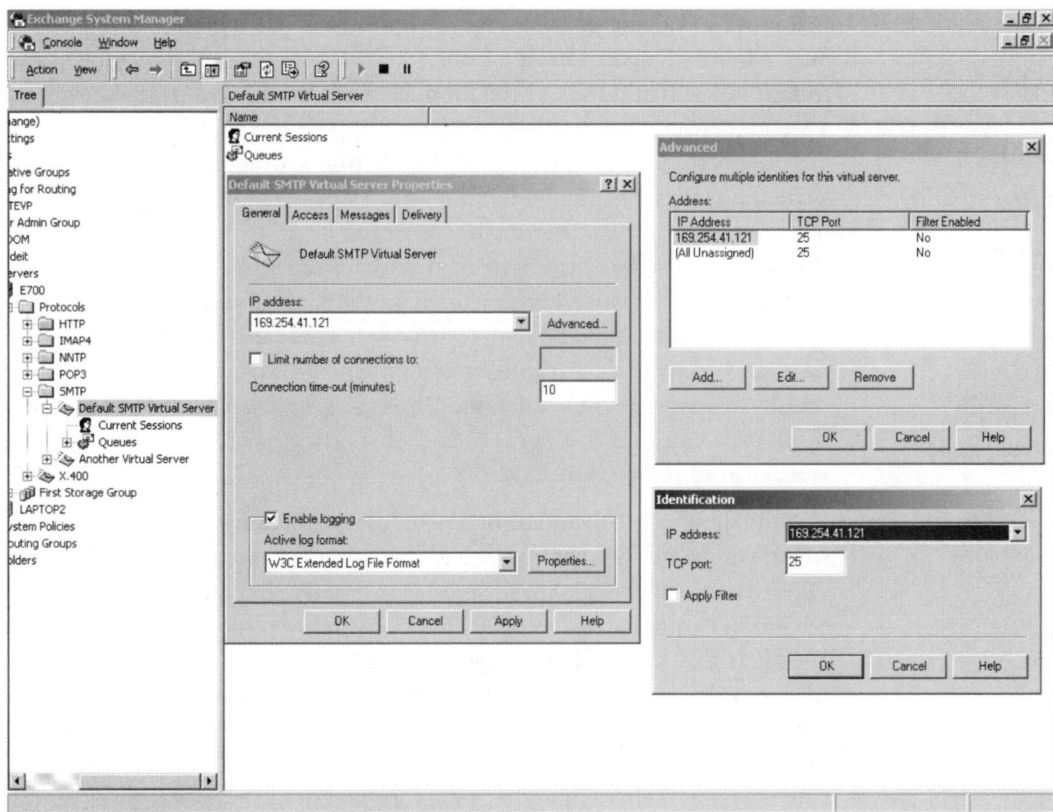

Figure 10.7 *Message filtering*

Again, the way you bind a filter to a virtual server isn't, as they say, intuitively obvious to the casual observer. Expect to see Microsoft improve the mechanism for configuring filters in the future.

Active Directory

A transport system alone does not make for a very interesting messaging system. Having SMTP in the underlying operating system is great, but where are the messages going to be delivered? At a minimum you need a message store. More importantly, even if there is a message store to deliver a message to, how do you determine which one to use? Directory services are key to this location brokering function.

The Exchange 2000 transport must determine the final destination of a message. That destination will either be another transport system or, more likely, a mailbox. In an enterprise environment, mailboxes can be spread over any number of servers and with Exchange 2000, the mailboxes can be present in a wide range of storage groups on a single server. Exchange 2000 Server was designed to handle from one to 15 storage groups but is limited to four in the first release of the product. Each storage group is managed by a separate instance of Extensible Storage Engine (ESE). Each ESE instance can support five databases, or MDBs. Within a storage group, the MDBs share the same set of transaction log files. Because all of this information—users, message store, server name—is stored in Active Directory, the transport system uses the Active Directory to determine the final destination of a message. The transport service will query the Active Directory to determine where a message should be sent or delivered. This capability is called categorization, and there is a categorizer component within Exchange 2000 (phatcat.dll) that supplies this function. Obviously, the Exchange 2000 engineers think their categorizer is "phat." And obviously, they stay in tune with the vernacular of today's youth.

One significant advantage of having user and configuration information stored within Active Directory, combined with the fact that every Exchange 2000 server can accept SMTP messages, is that there is no need for MX records in a pure Exchange 2000 environment, even though the transport is SMTP. Is this kosher? Think about it, what is an MX record for, anyway? MX records just identify which servers (server names actually) can handle the exchange of messages. If every server accepts SMTP messages, then MX records are a bit moot. More directly, because a user's object contains exactly which server their mailbox is on, every server has that information (via Active Directory) and can route to that server as efficiently as possible. MX records can be thought of as a more rudimentary, static, version of this. In Exchange 2000, it happens automatically.

Advanced queuing

Although part of the Windows 2000 SMTP service, advanced queuing is an important component of the Exchange 2000 core transport. Advance queuing builds and manages queues based on domains and links. Domain queues exist for messages grouped by their final destination, and link queues are messages grouped by their next hop. Domain queues are created just as you would expect, for domains such as Compaq.com, Digital.com, and Tandem.com. Link queues represent the next hop messages take. For example, if all messages to an Internet domain must traverse an ISP via a smart host, the link queue would show messages queued for the connector associated with the ISP and the domain queue would be organized by domain name.

As an example, let's assume I have a single connection to the Internet represented by a single SMTP connector. Let's see what happens when I send the message in Figure 10.8, a single message destined for multiple domains.

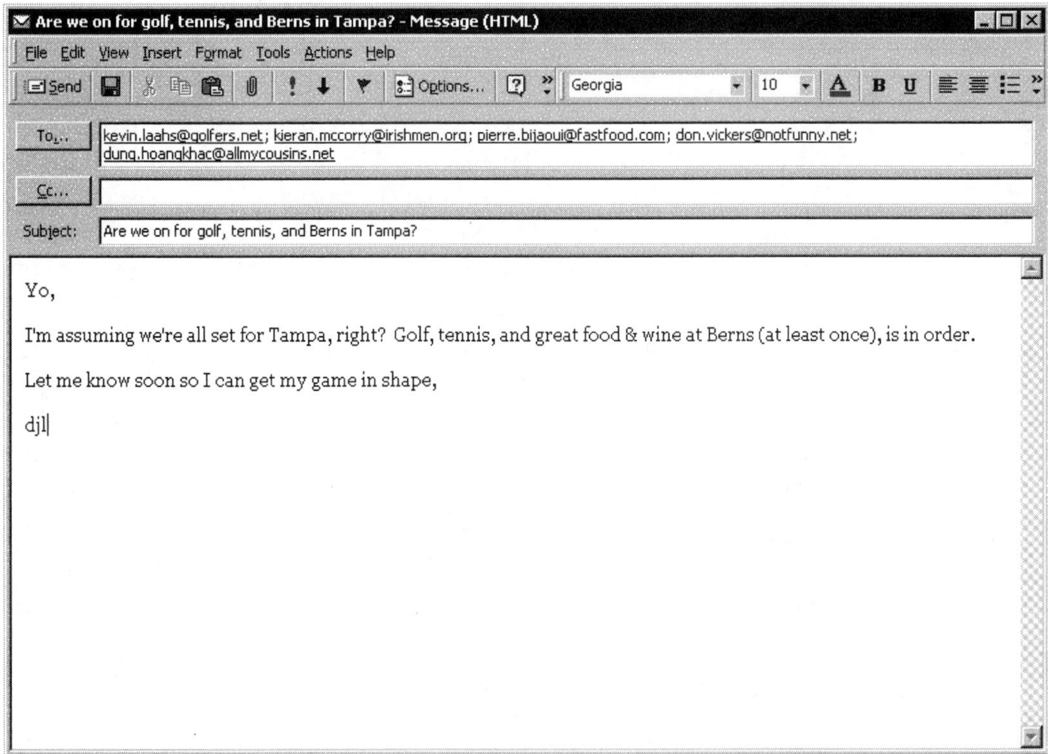

Figure 10.8 *A message sent to multiple domains.*

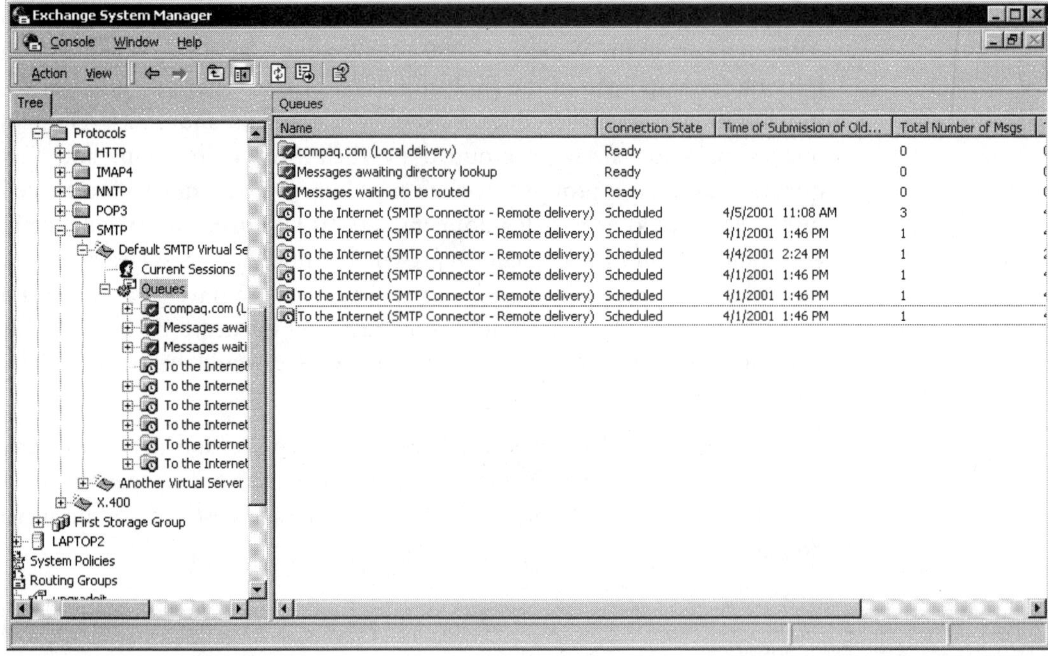

Figure 10.9 *Link queues.*

From the queue viewer interface (see Figure 10.9) in ESM, I will see that there are multiple messages queued for the same link queue: The link queue is represented by the SMTP connector name To the Internet. The reason multiple instances of To the Internet appear is that each instance represents a single domain queue.

So, if I enumerate the first instance of the To the Internet queue and either double-click or right-click and select Properties for each message, I can see (in Figure 10.10) that there are, in fact, three messages queued for the domain irishmen.org. Therefore, the first instance of To the Internet represents the domain queue for irishmen.org.

While Advanced Queuing (AQ) is present with the Windows 2000 SMTP service, it is more heavily used with Exchange 2000. Exchange 2000 introduces the Queue Viewer tool that we've been using, which isn't present in the base, Windows 2000 SMTP service.

SMTP system queues

Along with the domain and link queues, Advanced Queuing maintains special system queues, three of which can be seen in Figure 10.11.

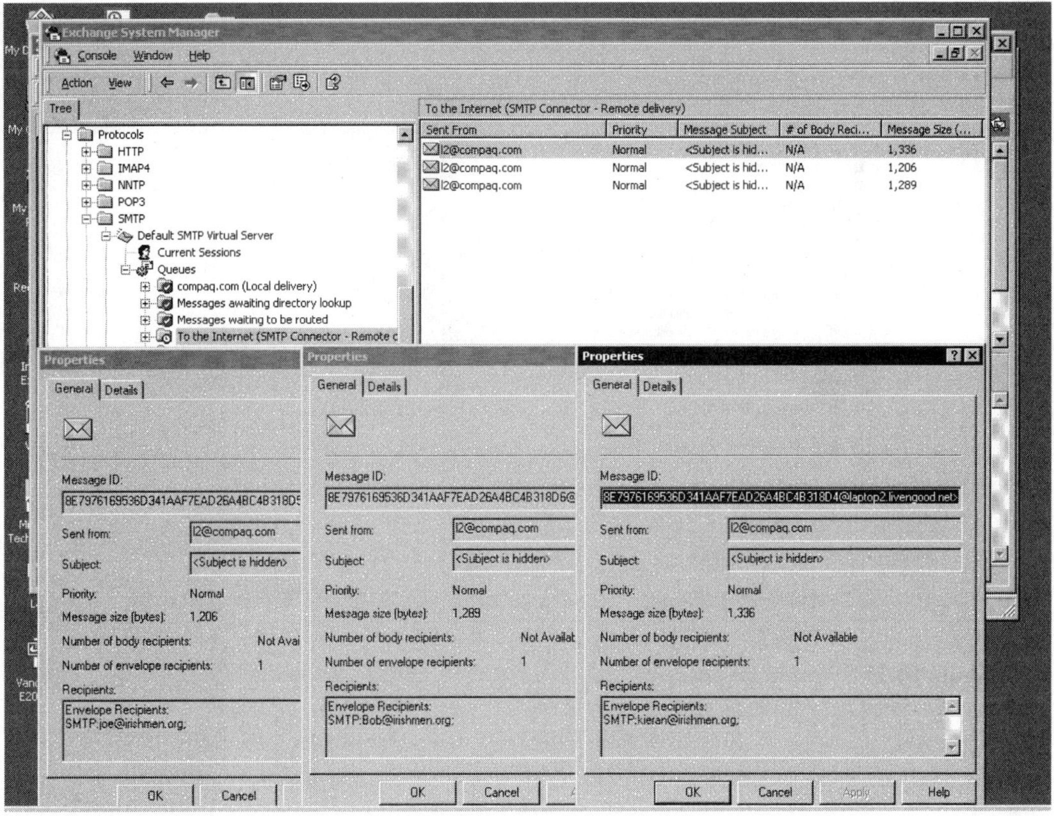

Figure 10.10 *Determining the domain queue.*

The SMTP system queues are as follows:

1. Local delivery—messages bound for local delivery; in Figure 10.11, this is Compaq.com.

2. Messages awaiting directory lookup (precategorizer) queue—messages are in this queue if an AD Global Catalog Server is down or lookups are slow.

3. Messages waiting to be routed queue (preroute queue)—messages that have not been analyzed for next hop. If you see messages in this queue, look in the Event Viewer for routing errors.

4. Final destination currently unreachable—a server that is in DNS but is unreachable (connector to xyz.com or to the smart host is bad). The queue for that scenario will be set to retry because it is unavailable. Messages that are in the currently unreachable link

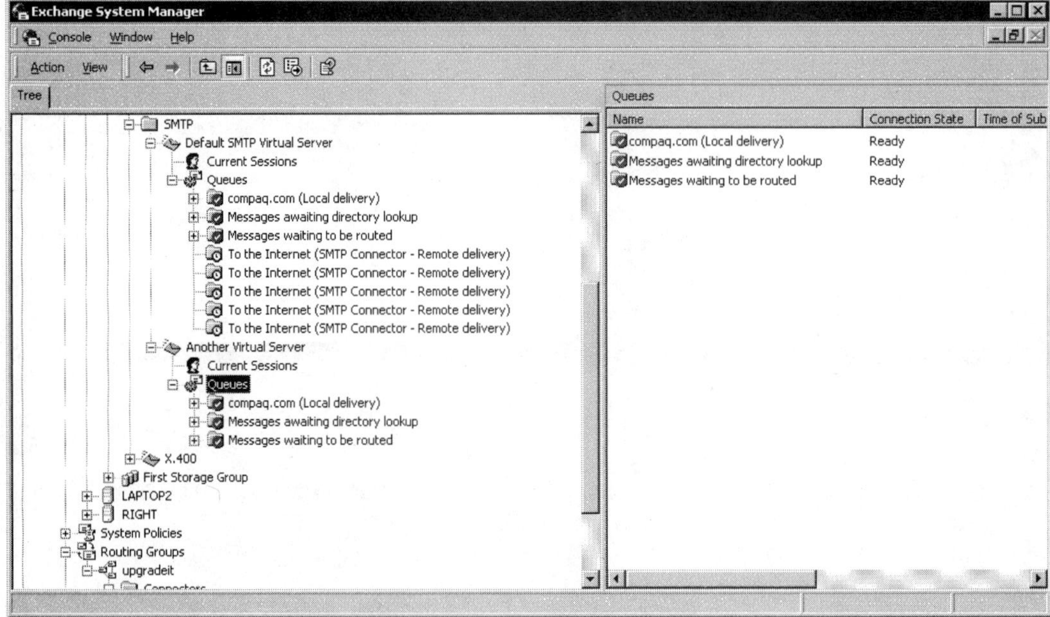

Figure 10.11 *System queues.*

queue are suffering from this sort of problem. Unreachable link queues appear when there is no route to the destination because connectors are down. Note that if there were no connectors at all, the sender would immediately receive NDR.

X.400 system queues

There are two main X.400 system queues, as follows:

1. PendingRerouteQ—this queue is always visible and will remain empty unless there are messages waiting to be rerouted because of a temporary link failure.
2. Server-specific queues—servers in the organization that Exchange 2000 communicates with via X.400 or LAN-MTA (RPC) communications.

MAPI system queues

The following queues are not normally visible within the Exchange System Manager Queue Viewer tool:

- MTS-IN
- READY-IN

- MTS-OUT
- READY-OUT
- Badmail directory (used to store nondelivery reports or other messages that the transfer service may not know how to handle)

For all of these queues, Microsoft provides a management API. This API is realized within the Exchange 2000 management interface via the Queue View tool, which has the capability of stopping, starting, pausing, or freezing a queue.

In addition to managing queue information, advanced queuing is also the component that generates delivery status notifications and events.

It is worth mentioning at this point that the transport system operates on top of an event model. Events are spread throughout Exchange 2000 and are used by various components in normal Exchange 2000 operations. There are several places where events are exposed in the product and this is particularly true for the transfer system, as seen in Figure 10.12.

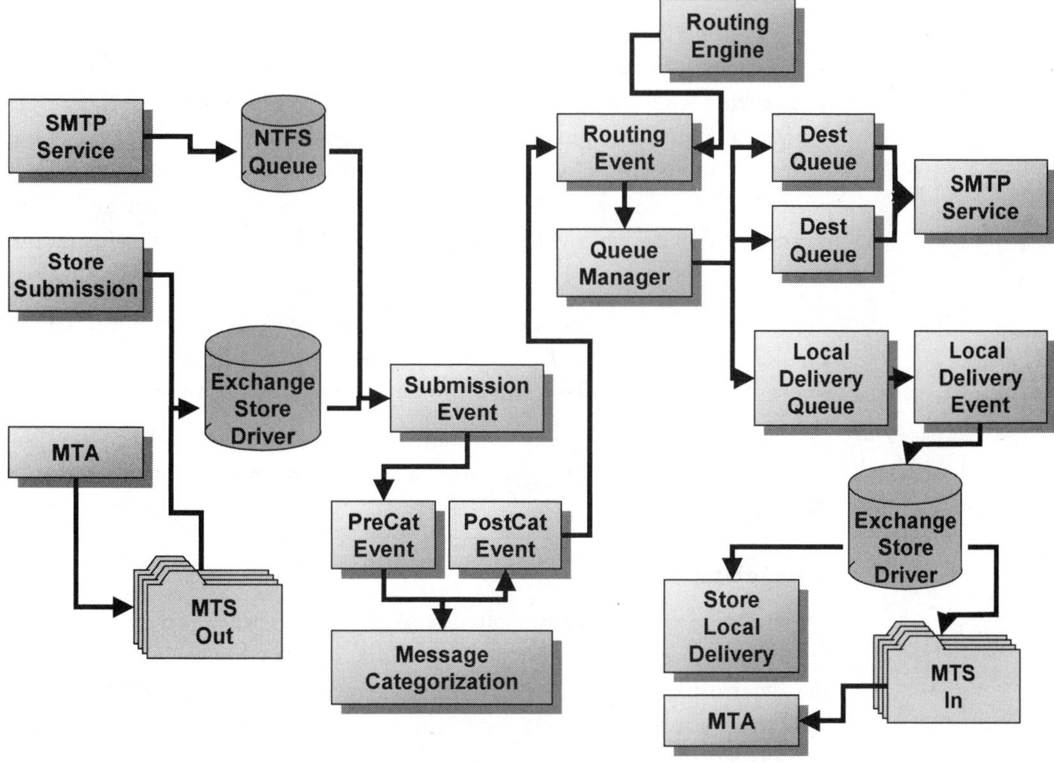

Figure 10.12 *Routing architecture: the ugly version.*

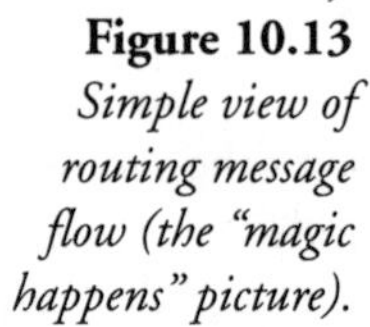

Figure 10.13 *Simple view of routing message flow (the "magic happens" picture).*

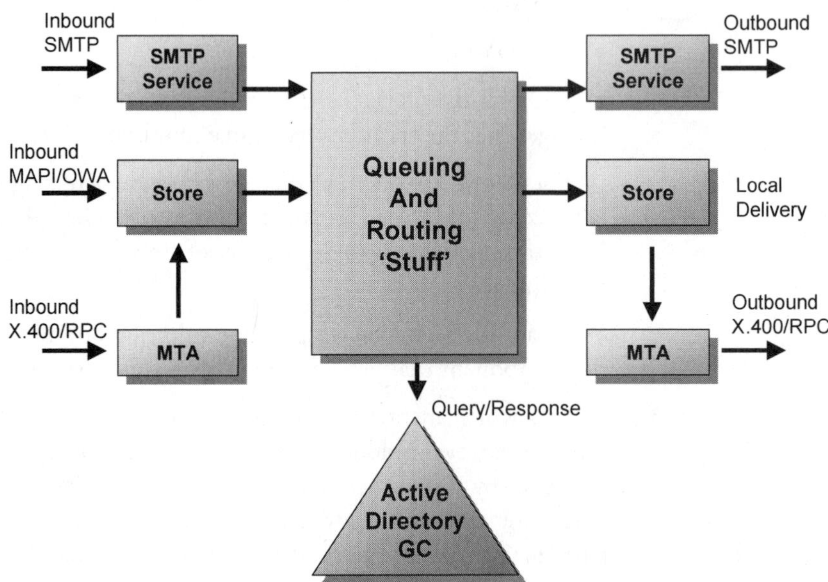

As Figure 10.12 shows, there are several places within the transfer service where events can be triggered. Several third-party vendors have made use of these events within their products. For instance, in Exchange 2000, Sybari's Antigen product not only interfaces with the Information Store, as it did with 5.5, but it also acts upon messages within the transport service via a postcategorization event. This allows Sybari's product to scan and clean messages arriving via SMTP before they are delivered to the information store.

A simpler way to view the routing architecture is shown in Figure 10.13. The key here is that all of this routing stuff happens for you automatically. There's very little you need to do to make it work.

When comparing Figure 10.12 and 10.13, you can see that much of the information we'll be talking about is buried in the Routing Stuff square in the middle of Figure 10.13.

Categorizer

The message categorizer is a plug-in to the AQ engine, and it's high-level function is to examine messages that come into an Exchange 2000 server and determine what to do with them. The messages may be destined for the local store, a remote host via the MTA, a store-based connector, or a remote host via SMTP. The categorizer also handles DL expansion.

The categorizer handles every message going into or coming out of the Exchange 2000 transfer service. It provides quite a lot of functionality, including the following:

- Determination of limits associated with the sender of a message
- Expansion of distribution lists
- Resolution of recipient addresses and applying limits for those users

For these three services the categorizer relies heavily on Active Directory. So, in essence, whenever you see a reference to the categorizer in Exchange 2000, you know that queries to Active Directory are involved.

Additional functionality provided by the categorizer includes the following:

- Create multiple copies of a message if the message requires different formatting for different recipients, as is the case when a single message originating from a MAPI user is destined for another, local MAPI user and also for an Internet recipient. Another reason a message might be split into multiple copies is the case where a message is being sent to BCC recipients.
- The categorizer returns the destination of all message recipients, either local or remote.

Once the categorizer has resolved the names and destinations for the message recipients, it hands the message back to AQ. Advanced Queuing then hands the information to the routing engine to determine the next hop for the message.

DSAccess

To obtain information about recipients and mailboxes, the transfer service, specifically the categorizer, makes calls to Active Directory: specifically, a Global Catalog server. To make efficient use of its directory queries and to reduce the load on the Global Catalog server, each Exchange 2000 server has a directory access cache (DSAccess). This cache enables the components of Exchange 2000 to perform directory lookups and then cache those results for a period of time. Subsequent queries for the same object will be fetched from the cache instead of sending the query to the Global Catalog server.

Four megabytes of directory entries are cached for a period of ten minutes by default. The size of the cache (MaxEntries) and duration of the cache entries (CacheTTL) can be changed via modifications to the registry values mentioned. Navigate to HKEY_LOCAL_MACHINE\System\CurrentControlSet\Services\MSExchangeDSAccess\Instance0 and modify the entries MaxEntries and CacheTTL, or create them if they don't exist.

You can also monitor the effectiveness of the cache through the Windows 2000 Performance Monitor.

It is imperative that you efficiently and affectively deploy Active Directory in your organization. As you have garnered from this book, Active Directory is really hammered by Exchange 2000. When you think about it, Active Directory will be used, at a minimum, in the following cases:

- User authentication
- User queries for resources, such as printers
- User directory lookups from e-mail clients
- Exchange 2000's transport service

A less than optimal directory deployment, either through incorrect hardware configuration or Domain Controller/Global Catalog server placement, will negatively impact your entire infrastructure.

Routing engine

The routing engine is the component that makes use of the link state information, which we'll discuss in detail later in this chapter. Functionally though, the routing engine's job is to determine the next hop of the message. Information used to determine the next hop includes the following:

- Address space
- Cost
- Current state of links that are available
- Restrictions associated with each connector—for instance, scheduled delivery or priority restrictions

Every Exchange 2000 server has its own copy of the link state table, which is held in memory, and takes action based on the information contained in it. How the server obtains its routing information will be discussed later in this chapter.

Once the next hop is determined, the message is placed in the appropriate queue.

Access to the Information Store

The basic transport system must provide store-and-forward capability. For store and forward, the transport service uses NTFS. Eventually though, the transport core must be able to deliver the message to the Information Store. With Exchange 2000, an Exchange store driver is installed that understands the Exchange Installable File System. This driver allows the transfer system to deposit messages directly into the information store. It will be interesting to see if Microsoft actually uses the Web storage system directly for store-and-forward purposes in the future, instead of NTFS. In an enterprise setting it is likely that a vast majority of messages received by an Exchange 2000 server will not be routed elsewhere but delivered to the store. Stay tuned.

For messages arriving into an Exchange 2000 organization via SMTP and the Internet, the message will actually be stored in the new Streaming file (.STM), with certain message attributes (TO:, CC:, SUBJECT:, etc.) being promoted to MAPI properties in the .EDB file. The Exchange store driver enables this capability. When messages are being sent outbound, the store driver is used to pull the message from the Exchange Storage System so that they can be formatted for delivery.

Component location

The objects that make up the transport system, and their location on disk, shown in Table 10.1.

Table 10.1 *Transfer Service Components and Their Location*

Description	Program	Default Location
IIS main process	Inetinfo.exe	\winnt\system32\inetsrv
IIS-based store driver	Drviis.dll	\exchsrvr\bin
Exchange SMTP	Exsmtp.dll	\exchsrvr\bin
Store process	Store.exe	\exchsrvr\bin
Epoxy—used for interprocess communication between IIS and the store	Epoxy.dll	\exchsrvr\bin
Emsmta.exe	X.400 MTA	\exchsrvr\bin
NTFS store driver	Ntfsdrv.dll	\winnt\system32\inetsrv
Exchange installable file system	Exifs.dll	\winnt\system32\drivers
Advanced queuing	Aqueue.dll	\winnt\system32\inetsrv
Exchange categorizer	Phatcat.dll	\exchsrvr\bin
Directory service access cache	Dsaccess.dll	\exchsrvr\bin

Management

It would be cumbersome to manage the environment if each of the components (AQ, categorizer, routing, or Web storage system/StoreDriver/IFS) had their own management tool, so they don't. Instead, each is managed by default via ESM. From a message transfer standpoint, Exchange 2000 enhances the management capabilities of the underlying Windows 2000 SMTP service. The Exchange 2000 System Manager Console includes a common interface to manage not only Exchange 2000–specific information associated with servers, but it also has the ability to manage the protocols that are hosted in IIS. In other words, instead of having to use the IIS management interface to manipulate the SMTP virtual server(s), you can manipulate it via Exchange 2000.

Message flow

Since it is easier to explain the following text by using a scenario, let's put some details around an example environment.

First, assume all of the servers we will discuss are members of an Exchange 2000 organization called Platinum. We'll define a few users and servers, as follows:

- Users: Noelle and Lexie
  - Exchange 2000 home server: Atlanta
  - Routing group: Americas
- User: Rob
  - Exchange 2000 home server: Tampa
  - Routing group: Americas
- User: Pierre
  - Exchange 2000 home server: Valbonne
  - Routing group: Europe
- User: Pat
  - Exchange 2000 home server: Sydney
  - Routing group: Asia Pacific

Now we'll discuss message flow using the following scenario.

10.2.2 Local delivery

Local delivery (see Figure 10.14), in our example, would be Noelle sending a message to Lexie. When a message is sent from one user to another on the

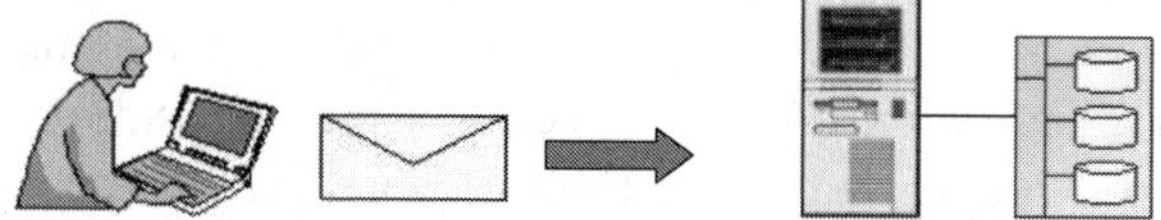

Figure 10.14
Local delivery.

same Exchange server using a MAPI-based client (such as Outlook 98 or Outlook 2000), the message transfer works in much the same way as it did with previous versions of Exchange. Specifically, the message is submitted to the information store and a pointer to the message is passed to the recipient via the transport service. The benefit here is that transport events are fired, even for local deliveries, since we now know that all messages, even those being delivered locally, are processed by advanced queuing and its components.

How did the server determine that the user was local? The user was determined to be local when the categorizer made its query to the Active Directory. When the categorizer queried the Active Directory for the recipient's information, the Active Directory returned a value for `homeMDB`—Atlanta in this case, which is identical to the name of the local server.

10.2.3 Intrarouting group delivery

Intrarouting group delivery (see Figure 10.15), in our example, would be Noelle sending a message to Rob. When a message is sent from one user to another within the same routing group, the scenario changes slightly. When Noelle submits the message, just as before, the message is submitted to the transfer service, and the categorizer performs a lookup in Active Directory for the recipient.

If the recipient's server is an Exchange 2000 server in the same routing group, the message is routed via SMTP to the recipient's server. How would the local server know that the destination server is in the same routing

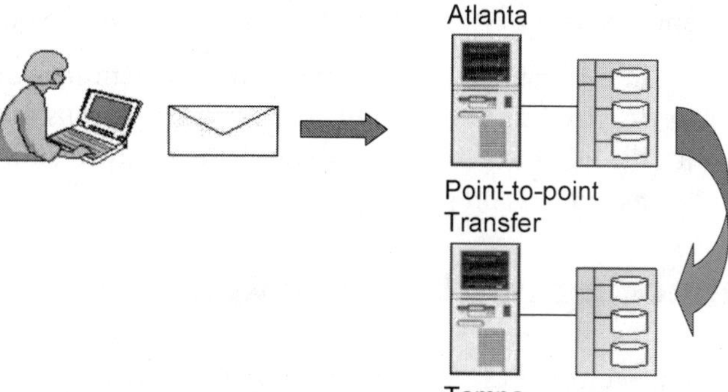

Figure 10.15
Intrarouting group delivery.

group? The routing table holds not only information about links, but also information about routing groups and their membership. Configuration information from Active Directory associated with routing group membership is propagated to the routing table. Message transfer within a routing group is point to point, meaning that the originating server communicates directly with the target server.

What would happen if the recipient server were running Exchange 5.5? In that case Exchange 2000 would transfer the message, in a point to point manner, using the RPC-based LAN-MTA (X.400) protocol, just as in the case of intrasite messaging in a pure Exchange 5.5 environment. The classic MTA is included on every Exchange 2000 server for backward compatibility and to provide an X.400 transport.

When the recipient's server receives the message, it locates the recipient in the Active Directory and transfers the message to the recipient's mailbox.

So, back to the case of two Exchange 2000 servers: How do these two servers actually communicate? Do they use DNS or are MX records required? The servers do, in fact, use DNS but they do not use MX records. Remember that MX records in DNS identify those servers that can handle Mail Exchange (MX). Since every Exchange 2000 server can accept SMTP connections, there's no need for MX records, and, by default, every server automatically gets a DNS "A" record when it is a member of a Windows 2000 domain (assuming you're using dynamic DNS). So, within a routing group, all that is required is the conversion of a host name to an IP address. This is exactly what DNS is used for in a pure Exchange 2000 configuration. The server names themselves are stored in the Active Directory and propagated into the link state or routing table, so DNS is only required to obtain the actual IP address. Once that is obtained, the two servers communicate through port 25 using SMTP. In fact, the Exchange 2000 server connects to the host name as stored in the `ncacn_ip_tcp` attribute in the `networkAddress` attribute of the destination server. This value is created and updated to Active Directory by the system attendant on the server.

In our example, once server Atlanta determines that mail for Rob must be delivered to server Tampa (determined via calls to the Active Directory), it calls DNS to resolve the server name to an IP address and then connects to that address on port 25.

10.3 Connecting routing groups

As you would expect, large organizations are likely to have multiple routing groups. As we've stated, servers within a routing group have direct, point-to-point connections between them. If an environment has multiple routing groups, then the routing groups must be connected somehow. With Exchange 2000, just as with sites in previous versions of Exchange, routing groups are connected via bridgehead servers.

Bridgehead servers are established to define communication paths between routing groups. Single or multiple bridgehead servers can be used between routing groups. The actual mechanism used to join bridgehead servers in separate routing groups is a connector (just as in previous versions of Exchange).

With Exchange 2000 there are three choices when connecting routing groups, as follows:

1. Routing group connector (a transport-independent transport)
2. SMTP connector (SMTP-based transport)
3. X.400 connector (X.400-based transport)

For many environments there may be a certain comfort level associated with X.400 connectors. It has worked well for years and has provided a very reliable service, even over low bandwidth. Because of this, and the fact that X.400 connectors can be scheduled, many Exchange 5.5 environments have used this connector to connect sites. It's important to note that if an Exchange 5.5 server is upgraded to Exchange 2000, any X.400 connectors in place will be maintained after the upgrade.

With the capabilities of the RGC, though, it is expected that most Exchange environments will phase out the use of X.400 to connect routing groups. The most likely scenario is that the X.400 connectors will remain in place and RGCs will be brought on-line in parallel. The RGCs can then be set to a lower cost, validated for their operation and performance, and promoted to being the primary connector. Over time, the X.400 connectors can be removed.

10.4 Interrouting group delivery

The scenario now changes to that of a message that needs to be delivered to another Exchange 2000 server in a different routing group (see Figure 10.16). Let's assume Noelle is sending a message to Pierre in Valbonne. Since we didn't establish the connection method between the Americas and Europe routing groups, just assume that a routing group connector has been configured, with the Atlanta server being the bridgehead for the Americas routing group.

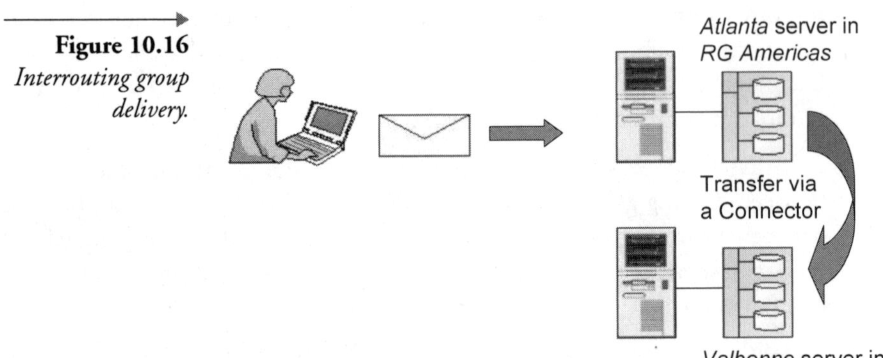

Figure 10.16 *Interrouting group delivery.*

The Atlanta server (specifically, the categorizer on that server) looks up the recipient, Pierre, in the Active Directory and determines that the recipient system is in a different routing group—specifically, Europe. Again, routing group membership is contained in the link state table.

When the recipient's mailbox is on a server in a different routing group, the message must be transferred over a connector. In this case, when the server determines the recipient is on a server in a different routing group, it identifies a route for the message to take and routes the message to the appropriate connector—in our case, an RGC. If the originating server is a bridgehead server, as in our case, it can open a connection and transfer the message directly to a bridgehead server (Valbonne) in the recipient's routing group.

All of the servers in a routing group maintain a table of link state information, which the servers use to determine whether connectors and connections are up or down. The status of the connectors enables servers to determine the optimal route from one routing group to another or, potentially, to reroute messages if a connector or network connection is down.

When a remote bridgehead server receives the message, the delivery process is repeated until the message is delivered to the recipient's mailbox. Depending on the path a message must take to arrive at the recipient's mailbox, the message may travel through multiple servers and routing groups.

This section describes how messages are delivered in an Exchange 2000 environment: point to point (via SMTP) within a routing group and via bridgehead servers and connectors between routing groups. The following sections describe how the link state information is used.

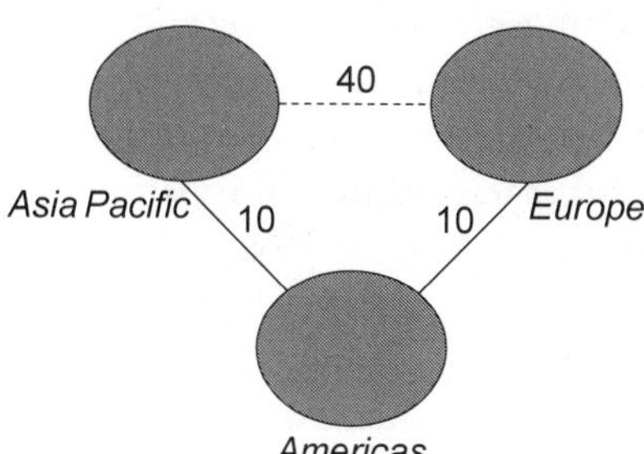

Figure 10.17 *Routing group connector costs.*

10.4.1 Routing within the enterprise

In the previous examples, we described how messages are routed within a routing group and between routing groups. The scenario remains the same when the routing environment is broadened to encompass an entire enterprise (see Figure 10.17). Going back to our previous example, assume that we've built a routing architecture with the Americas routing group as the hub. Furthermore, only one server in the Americas routing group, the Atlanta server, is the bridgehead for connections to both Asia Pacific and Europe.

As you expect, messages sent between Asia Pacific and Europe, in our case Pat sending to Pierre, would traverse the Americas routing group. The direct connection between Asia Pacific and Europe would only be used if the link between the Americas routing group and either of the other routing groups failed. Again, this is exactly what you would expect with a transfer system that has the capability of assigning costs. The interesting point is how this happens in Exchange 2000 and, more impressively, how quickly the routing and rerouting decisions are made. The key to all of this is link state routing.

10.4.2 Link state routing

Link state routing is the method by which Exchange 2000 servers determine the most efficient and cost-effective path for message transport. In effect, link state routing allows a server to determine the best way to get something from point A to point B.

In order for this effective routing to take place, information must be communicated to all servers in an Exchange 2000 environment—specifically, to all servers within an Exchange 2000 organization. Communications within routing groups is handled differently than communications between different routing groups. Routing information needs to be managed somehow, and a routing master server is assigned this task. In Exchange 2000 the first server to join a routing group is assigned as the routing master and manages routing information within a routing group. This is a low-overhead task and can be easily reassigned from server to server within a routing group, as we've already discussed. As a best practice, however, it is probably best not to have a bridgehead server take on this role, since the bridgehead will likely have a lot of transport responsibility and, should the need for troubleshooting the environment occur, it is probably cleaner to separate these functions. It is not necessary, however.

Routing master and link state updates

As stated, the first server in a routing group is automatically designated as the routing master by default. If multiple servers are added to a routing group, they are designated as member servers. The master role can be transferred to another server via a single right-button mouse click.

The job of the routing master is twofold, as follows:

1. The master is the only entity that is allowed to change the state of links belonging to its routing group and increment the version number associated with its view. The importance of this will surface in a moment.

2. The master updates all members in the routing group with link state information associated with its routing group and link information it holds, and has learned, about other routing groups. Link state information about other routing groups is fed to the routing master from bridgehead servers connected to other routing groups.

To communicate routing information to routing group member servers, the master connects via TCP/IP to port 691 on each member server. If you telnet to port 691 (see Figure 10.18) on any Exchange 2000 server, you will see that the Microsoft Routing Service responds. This service is supplied as part of the Exchange 2000 installation and runs within the context of inetinfo.exe.

The protocol used to transmit the link state information is a Microsoft-invented protocol called Link State Update Protocol. The information communicated gives each member server a view or a graph of the entire Exchange 2000 routing environment, as well as a version number associated with that particular information update. Specifically, there is a version number for every routing group in the Exchange 2000 organization, and the ver-

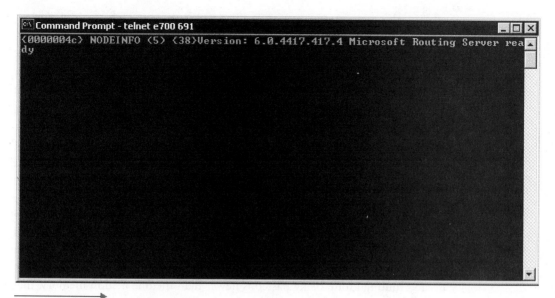

Figure 10.18 *Microsoft Routing Service listening to port 691.*

sion number can only be incremented by the master server of each routing group. Conceptually, each member server has a view of how all routing groups are connected and the state of those connections (up, down, or delayed), as well as the version associated with each view of each routing group.

Link information is sent from the master to each member as the information changes. The master is made aware of changes to the topology via connector servers. So, what happens if a connection is going up and down every few seconds? Does the connector continually flood the master with changes? Actually, the answer is no. Microsoft gets around this problem by making use of a special delay timer called StateChangeDelay. This registry setting defines, at most, how frequently information is updated to the master. You can change this value by making a change to

```
HKEY_LOCAL_MACHINE\SYSTEM\SEVICES\RESvc x
```

and adding keys/values for StateChangeDelay (=600 for example) and/or SuppressStateChanges (=0 for example).

The algorithm used to create the view, or graph, of the environment is based on Dijkstra's algorithm. Dijkstra's algorithm is a well-known, well-accepted method for determining the least cost between nodes in a network. Many network router vendors (e.g., Cisco) use the algorithm in their products, though it is probably more widely called Open Shortest Path First.

The algorithm itself prevents looping and incorporates dynamic rerouting, which fits perfectly with Exchange 2000's transport needs. Using this information, each server within a routing group can make an intelligent decision about which path, defined by connectors, to use when transferring a message. Again, the routing information is updated as it changes.

Along with receiving updates from the master, link state information is passed as part of normal message transfer between servers in the same routing group. So, in the case of a server being rebooted, that server will learn of the link state information as it exchanges messages with any server within its routing group. The point is that the link state information, which is only held in memory, is passed through the routing group not only by direct updates from the master but also as part of normal message flow. During either method the version number associated with each routing group held in the server's memory is compared against the version number for each routing group that is being passed. If the version number associated with any routing group being passed is newer than the one held in memory, that routing group's information is updated.

Updating the master

As stated, the routing master within a routing group receives link updates from the bridgehead servers in the routing group. Each bridgehead server can easily determine the state of its connection to other bridgehead servers; they are either up or down. Determining the link status occurs in two ways: either by sending a message or through periodic polling. In either case, if a bridgehead server cannot communicate with the remote bridgehead, a link status change is sent from the local bridgehead to its routing master. This communication also takes place via TCP/IP to port 691 on the master. This action, in turn, results in the master updating the view of the routing environment and increments the version of the view for the routing group. Also, the master watches for configuration changes to the routing needed on configuration changes. The result: No rebooting is needed on configuration changes, since they are picked up dynamically.

10.4.3 Link state updates between routing groups

In a large environment, it is likely that scenarios will exist where routing groups do not have direct connections to each other—for example, in a case where intermediate routing groups need to be traversed. To obtain updates in this type of environment, the link state information needs to be passed between routing groups. In a pure, or native, Exchange 2000 environment,

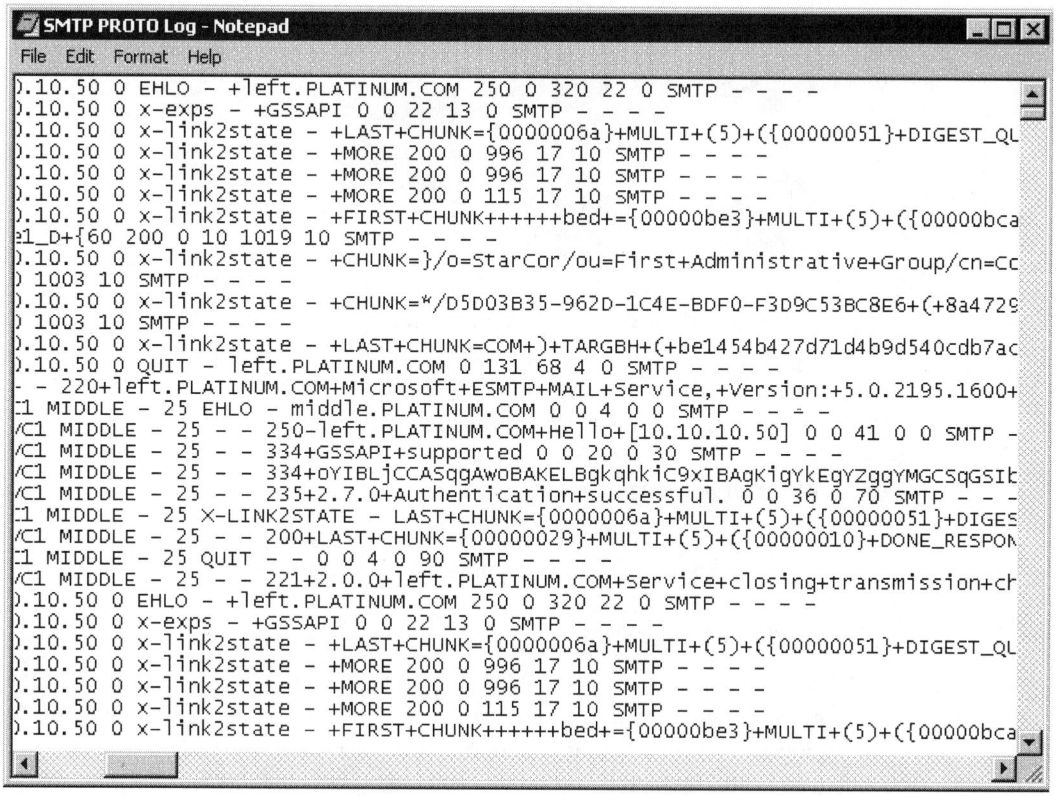

SMTP PROTO Log - Notepad

File Edit Format Help

```
).10.50 0 EHLO - +left.PLATINUM.COM 250 0 320 22 0 SMTP - - - -
).10.50 0 x-exps - +GSSAPI 0 0 22 13 0 SMTP - - - -
).10.50 0 x-link2state - +LAST+CHUNK={0000006a}+MULTI+(5)+({00000051}+DIGEST_QL
).10.50 0 x-link2state - +MORE 200 0 996 17 10 SMTP - - - -
).10.50 0 x-link2state - +MORE 200 0 996 17 10 SMTP - - - -
).10.50 0 x-link2state - +MORE 200 0 115 17 10 SMTP - - - -
).10.50 0 x-link2state - +FIRST+CHUNK++++++bed+={00000be3}+MULTI+(5)+({00000bca
21_D+{60 200 0 10 1019 10 SMTP - - - -
).10.50 0 x-link2state - +CHUNK=}/o=StarCor/ou=First+Administrative+Group/cn=Cc
) 1003 10 SMTP - - - -
).10.50 0 x-link2state - +CHUNK=*/D5D03B35-962D-1C4E-BDF0-F3D9C53BC8E6+(+8a4729
) 1003 10 SMTP - - - -
).10.50 0 x-link2state - +LAST+CHUNK=COM+)+TARGBH+(+be1454b427d71d4b9d540cdb7ac
).10.50 0 QUIT - left.PLATINUM.COM 0 131 68 4 0 SMTP - - - -
- - 220+left.PLATINUM.COM+Microsoft+ESMTP+MAIL+Service,+Version:+5.0.2195.1600+
C1 MIDDLE - 25 EHLO - middle.PLATINUM.COM 0 0 4 0 0 SMTP - - - -
/C1 MIDDLE - 25 - - 250-left.PLATINUM.COM+Hello+[10.10.10.50] 0 0 41 0 0 SMTP -
/C1 MIDDLE - 25 - - 334+GSSAPI+supported 0 0 20 0 30 SMTP - - - -
/C1 MIDDLE - 25 - - 334+oYIBLjCCASqgAwoBAKELBgkqhkiC9xIBAgKigYkEgYZggYMGCSqGSIb
/C1 MIDDLE - 25 - - 235+2.7.0+Authentication+successful. 0 0 36 0 70 SMTP - - -
C1 MIDDLE - 25 X-LINK2STATE - LAST+CHUNK={0000006a}+MULTI+(5)+({00000051}+DIGES
/C1 MIDDLE - 25 - - 200+LAST+CHUNK={00000029}+MULTI+(5)+({00000010}+DONE_RESPON
C1 MIDDLE - 25 QUIT - - 0 0 4 0 90 SMTP - - - -
/C1 MIDDLE - 25 - - 221+2.0.0+left.PLATINUM.COM+Service+closing+transmission+ch
).10.50 0 EHLO - +left.PLATINUM.COM 250 0 320 22 0 SMTP - - - -
).10.50 0 x-exps - +GSSAPI 0 0 22 13 0 SMTP - - - -
).10.50 0 x-link2state - +LAST+CHUNK={0000006a}+MULTI+(5)+({00000051}+DIGEST_QL
).10.50 0 x-link2state - +MORE 200 0 996 17 10 SMTP - - - -
).10.50 0 x-link2state - +MORE 200 0 996 17 10 SMTP - - - -
).10.50 0 x-link2state - +MORE 200 0 115 17 10 SMTP - - - -
).10.50 0 x-link2state - +FIRST+CHUNK++++++bed+={00000be3}+MULTI+(5)+({00000bca
```

Figure 10.19 *Link state updates with SMTP x-link2state command.*

routing groups are either connected via an SMTP-based connector (an RGC or SMTP connector) or an X.400 connector. Microsoft has implemented extensions to both SMTP and X.400 to carry this link state information. For SMTP, the extended command implemented to handle link state information is X-LINK2STATE. So, in the case of SMTP connectivity between routing groups, when one routing group needs to pass link information to another, it first uses the EHLO command, authenticates, and then sends the X-LINK2STATE command followed by the routing information update. This can be seen in Figure 10.19, which is a screen capture from an SMTP protocol logging file.

For X.400 the link information is passed as part of an X.400 message.

The routing information is passed in a binary format. The update operation happens as soon as a connection is made between routing groups and, therefore, before any actual message processing takes place.

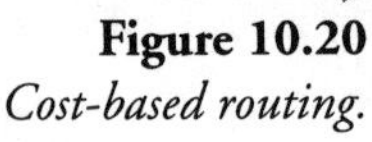

Figure 10.20
Cost-based routing.

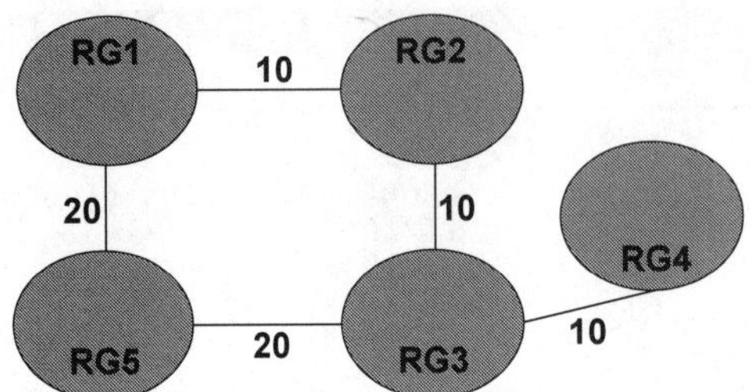

Perhaps the best way of understanding how link state works and what happens to messages in the event of failures is to give an example. Assume we have five routing groups—RG1, RG2, RG3, RG4, and RG5—connected with routing group connectors and costs.

Normal message flow

As you can see from the cost of the connections (see Figure 10.20), a message sent from RG1 to RG4 will hop via RG2 and RG3.

Single in-line failure

Assume that the network fails between RG2 and RG3. Unless there are messages waiting to be transferred over this link, the failure will not be picked up immediately. Therefore, if a user in RG1 sends a message to a user in RG4, the routing process will take place as follows:

1. The bridgehead in RG1 sends the message to a target bridgehead in RG2.

2. Through a call to its routing engine, RG2 attempts to open an SMTP connection to a target bridgehead in RG3.

3. If there are multiple target bridgeheads specified on the connector to RG3, the local bridgehead in RG2 attempts to open a connection in sequential order in case a single bridgehead has failed.

4. If none of the bridgeheads in RG3 can be contacted, the connection goes into a GLITCH-RETRY state. Essentially, the connection backs off three times at 60-second intervals before it goes into the retry interval set on the virtual server.

5. If, after a reconnection attempt, the link is still not operational, the connection is marked as DOWN. This is not communicated, however, until the StateChangeDelay time is met.

6. The bridgehead in RG2 connects to port 691 of the RG master (in RG2) and sends a link DOWN notification. (It is important to note that steps 6 and 7 happen asynchronously.)
7. The RG master (in RG2) updates the routing information for RG2 and sends an updated view of routing to all nodes in RG2, including the bridgehead.
8. The bridgehead in RG2 calculates that an alternate route is available to RG4 via RG1, RG5, and RG3. Remember, all servers in an Exchange 2000 organization contain a routing view of the entire organization and can make routing decisions directly. (This step occurs at the same time as step 6.)
9. Before the messages are routed back through RG1, the link DOWN information (for RG3) is sent to the bridgehead in RG1. The communication takes place using the X-LINK2STATE ESMTP command verb after issuing an EHLO. In essence, the version numbers for each routing group's view are compared. In this case, the version number associated with RG2's view has changed, and RG1 (and the other routing groups in the organization) need to be updated with the new view for RG2.
10. The bridgehead in RG1 updates its copy of RG2's view and the associated version number and immediately connects to the RG master in RG1 through port 691. It then transfers the link DOWN information contained in the new version RG2's view.
11. The RG master in RG1 immediately floods these data to all other Exchange 2000 servers in the routing group. So, all servers in RG1 now contain the latest version of RG2's view of connectivity.
12. Using the new link information, the bridgehead in RG1 calculates that the best route to RG4 is via RG5.
13. Before messages are routed to the bridgehead in RG5, the link state information is propagated to the bridgehead in RG5, as described previously, and the version associated with RG2 is compared and updated. There is a possibility that RG5 already knows that the link is down if messages were trying to route from RG3 to RG2.
14. RG5 continues the process and routes the messages via RG3 and onward to the destination, RG4.

A point to note is that although messages are now flowing through the alternative route, it is likely to be more costly, and we need to know when the original link is available. After a link has been tagged as DOWN, the original bridgehead will continue to retry the connection based on the interval set on the SMTP virtual server. By default, this is 15 minutes. Although there are no actual messages waiting to transfer, the retry is simply an attempt to open port 25 on the destination server. Once a connection has been reestablished, the bridgehead notifies the local routing group master that the connection is available, and link information is again propagated to all member servers. Likewise, the information is transferred throughout the organization.

Multiple in-line failures

An interesting scenario takes place when multiple link failures occur. With previous versions of Exchange, the message would potentially bounce between the links in a frenzied attempt to find an open connection. However, because of link state routing, the Exchange 2000 transport environment is more intelligent. Take the single in-line failure scenario and assume that the network link between RG5 and RG3 also fails. In this case, the following would occur:

1. The bridgehead in RG5 attempts to open the connection to the target bridgehead in RG3 and fails.
2. The connection goes into the GLITCH-RETRY state and retries after 60 seconds.
3. If a connection cannot be established, the link is tagged as DOWN and the routing group master is informed (which, in turn, floods the state to the other servers within the routing group).
4. A call is made to the routing group on the bridgehead server and it calculates that all available routes to RG4 are DOWN. The cost of the connection is therefore INFINITE.
5. The messages wait in the queue and every 15 minutes (by default) another connection is made to the routing group to see if any links are available.
6. If a link becomes available, the messages are rerouted as appropriate. If, after 48 hours (or the configured expiry time, 48 is the default value), the messages are still in the queue, they are returned as NDRs back to the sender in RG1.

This is great stuff and it happens very quickly! So, now you might ask if this will work between different Exchange 2000 organizations? After all, between routing groups we're just using extensions to SMTP and X.400 to update the routing information. What happens if we connect two Exchange 2000 organizations with either an SMTP or X.400 connector? Remember that all routing information, including configured routing groups, is kept within the Configuration Naming Context in the Active Directory (within the context of an Exchange 2000 organization). As such, a server from one Exchange 2000 organization has no knowledge about routing groups contained within another Exchange 2000 organization. Additionally, when link state information is passed between routing groups, a Globally Unique Identifier (GUID) is included in the link information. This GUID identifies the Exchange 2000 organization to which the bridgehead server belongs. If the GUIDs of two bridgehead servers that are communicating don't match, the link information is ignored.

It is clear that link state information between routing groups is very beneficial, but what happens with connections to external environments, such as the Internet? In the case of the Internet, one or more SMTP connectors would be configured to enable the transport of messages. In the case of multiple Internet access points, link information regarding the state of these connections is updated through the environment. If one of the external connections becomes unavailable, messages are no longer routed to that downed link and any messages queued at that SMTP connector will be rerouted. Obviously, considerations such as address space associated with a connector come into play, but the point is that routing is inclusive of external SMTP connections, provided that you are using smart hosts for connectivity. If you are using DNS, as is the norm, links to external SMTP environments are never marked down, since the MX record returned by DNS could, in fact, be a round-robin entry representing multiple servers.

In the case of Exchange Developer Kit (EDK), or store-based gateways, routing information is only available up to the point of submission of messages to the information store. Link information about the remote messaging network—for example, cc:Mail is not propagated via link state updates. In essence, EDK gateways are no different from how they are in Exchange 5.5, with the possible exception of modified management interfaces. From a routing perspective, nothing has changed with regard to EDK gateways.

As you can see, link state routing and the management of routing information are completely different from Exchange 5.5. In Exchange 5.5, routing information was maintained in the GWART. While Exchange 2000 performs dynamic routing updates, the GWART is not updated dynamically. The algorithms used are different, too. Exchange 2000 uses the Dijkstra/OSPF algorithm, where every routing group is treated as a node in a network. If connectivity is lost within the network, the information is immediately propagated throughout the environment. More importantly, messages in transit are dynamically rerouted and new messages are not submitted along paths with broken links.

Exchange 5.5's algorithm is much less dynamic and learns nothing about down links in the network.

10.4.4 Link state table facts

As we've seen, this link state table is pretty cool, but there are some things you may be wondering about. These could include the following:

- Where is the link table stored? It is in memory only. It is not persisted to disk.
- What is contained in the link state table? The GUIDs associated with every routing group, connector, bridgehead, and server are in this table. Address spaces, link status (up or down), and restrictions associated with the connectors are also stored in the table.
- Where does the information in the link state table originate? Information in the link state table originates in Active Directory, since that is where all configuration information is held. Status of links is updated based on information passed between bridgeheads and the master server.
- How big is this database? It is approximately 32 bytes for every server, connector, and routing group in the organization. As an example:
  - 250 Routing Groups = 8 KB
  - 150 Exchange Servers = 4.8 KB
  - 800 Connectors = 25.6 KB
  - TOTAL: 38.4 KB (This information was pulled from an excellent routing presentation given by Paul Bowden of Microsoft.)
- How do you look at the routing table? Well, you'll need to wait until the next chapter! To whet your appetite, the tool is called WinRoute.

10.4.5 Coexistence with Exchange 5.5

As indicated earlier, it is possible to install an Exchange 2000 server as a member of an Exchange 5.5 site. For this to work properly, the Active

Directory connector must be installed in advance in order to populate the Active Directory with Exchange 5.5 directory service information. The installation of the ADC instantiates a Configuration Connection Agreement (ConfigCA), which is the entity that transfers configuration information between Exchange 2000 and Exchange 5.5, as you've learned from earlier chapters. During the installation of the ADC, you will be prompted as to whether the Exchange 2000 server will join an existing Exchange 5.5 site.

Once established as a member of an Exchange 5.5 site, message communication between Exchange 5.5 servers and Exchange 2000 servers takes place via RPCs and the LAN-MTA protocol (basically, X.400). This may seem odd considering that the default method of communication between Exchange 2000 servers is SMTP. However, if you think about it, the only protocol guaranteed to be available on an Exchange 5.5 (or prior) server is RPC. With this in mind, it makes sense for the Exchange 2000 server to use RPCs to communicate with down-level Exchange servers.

The same X.400/RPC-based MTA used in Exchange 5.5 servers is included in Exchange 2000 and is specifically used when communicating with Exchange 5.5 servers. In environments such as this, it's important to keep in mind all of the best practices established for membership within a Exchange 5.5 site, even when the member is an Exchange 2000 server.

Since we're now talking about coexistence, let's paint a quick scenario. Assume we have an Exchange 5.5 server in site Belfast with a site connector configured on it that is communicating with a separate Exchange 5.5 site called Dublin. If we upgrade this server to Exchange 2000, the site connector becomes a routing group connector. In this scenario, the routing group connector will use RPCs when communicating to the Dublin Exchange 5.5 site. The routing group connector is said to be protocol independent due to its ability to use either RPCs or SMTP.

Obviously, SMTP connectors and X.400 connectors could also be used to communicate between Exchange 2000 and Exchange 5.5. Note that when upgrading an Exchange 5.5 system that has SMTP or X.400 connectors to Exchange 2000, those connectors are maintained and available in Exchange 2000 after the upgrade. You will definitely need to verify their configuration settings, especially those for the IMS, to ensure that they will operate and are configured as you intended.

The ability of Exchange 2000 to detect an Exchange 5.5 system and communicate with it using RPCs is just one example of the coexistence capabilities available between Exchange 2000 and Exchange 5.5. One of the larger issues is the coexistence of the Exchange 5.5 directory service and Active Directory. That topic, which I hope you've already read, makes up the first seven chapters of this book.

10.5 Summary

In this chapter, I've outlined the fundamentals and components that comprise those services that allow message transfer in Exchange 2000. In the next chapter, we'll see how these transfer services can be implemented.

11

SMTP Deployment Scenarios

11.1 Introduction

When describing the key features of Exchange 2000, and Windows 2000 for that matter, Microsoft said that they had focused on the "abilities." Examples given were scalability, reliability, manageability, and flexibility. One of the key "abilities" of Exchange 2000 is the ability to scale the product not only vertically (bigger boxes with more users), but also the ability to scale the product horizontally through the incorporation of functional partitioning. In short, this means that specific functions, such as message transport or HTTP access, can be deployed on servers dedicated to a specific task or function. A common term for this is separation of services, and it is usually realized in the form of front- and back-end servers. Basically, a front-end server accepts requests from clients and proxies those requests to the appropriate back-end server. In the case of SMTP, the front-end SMTP server would deliver a message to the appropriate back-end server that hosts the recipient's mailbox. This delivery is accomplished through normal SMTP transport and not via the type of proxying that takes place with the other Internet protocols. With SMTP, both the front- and back-end servers would provide full SMTP services, including store and forward.

While various services can be hosted on a front-end server with Exchange 2000—namely, HTTP, NNTP, POP3, IMAP4, and SMTP—the sections in this chapter focus on SMTP.

11.2 Front- and back-end servers

The architecture for Exchange 2000 allows for the implementation and configuration of front- and back-end servers. The specific architectural change that enables such a configuration is the movement of all Internet

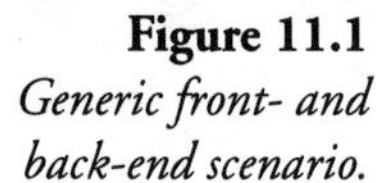

Figure 11.1
Generic front- and back-end scenario.

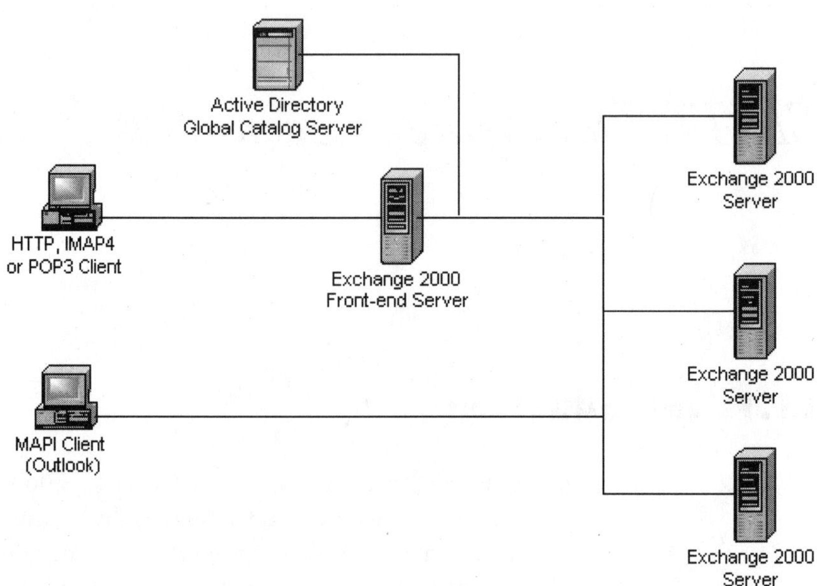

access protocols into the realm of the inetinfo.exe process: IIS. Front- and back-end server topologies are very common in ISP and hosted environments. Products from Openwave, Mirapoint, and others have been capable of being deployed in front- and back-end servers for years. Microsoft's own product, Microsoft Commercial Internet Server (MCIS), also has this ability. All of these products were focused on ISP environments. However, with the growing popularity of Internet messaging and directory protocols at the desktop—specifically, POP3, IMAP4, LDAP, and SMTP—you will probably see more enterprise front- and back-end deployments. (See Figure 11.1.)

Enterprises that have multiserver organizations that use Outlook Web Access (HTTP), SMTP, POP3, or IMAP4 and organizations that want to provide HTTP, SMTP, POP3, or IMAP4 are likely candidates for front- and back-end server deployments. One of the more common reasons for using these protocols is to allow employees to access Exchange 2000 services over the Internet. Once implemented, and upon receiving a request, the front-end server uses Lightweight Directory Access Protocol (LDAP) to query the Active Directory service and determine which back-end server holds the requested resource. Specifically for SMTP, the LDAP request returns the back-end server to which the message will be delivered.

To be sure, a front-end server is a specially configured Exchange 2000 server, as can be seen in Figure 11.2. Back-end servers, on the other hand,

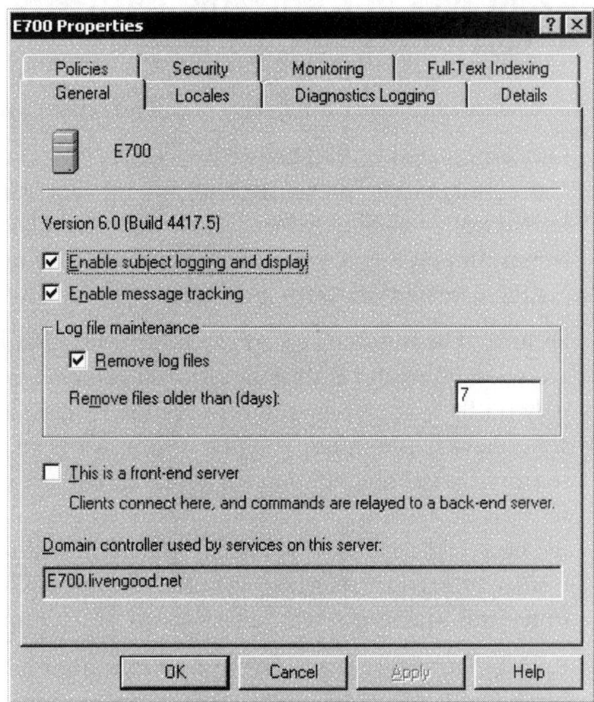

Figure 11.2 *Setting a server as a front-end server.*

are just normal Exchange 2000 servers. No configuration option exists to designate a server as a back-end server. In fact, Microsoft uses the term back-end server to refer to all servers in an organization that are not front-end servers. Back-end servers only make sense when front-end servers are present; otherwise, all servers are just Exchange 2000 servers.

A front- and back-end deployment has certain advantages, most of which are realized through client-access services such as HTTP, POP3, or IMAP4. Detailed discussion of those protocols and the advantage front- and back-end deployments bring to them is beyond the scope of this section. Instead, we will focus on SMTP in front- and back-end deployments.

Strictly speaking, SMTP is not implemented in a front- and back-end service such as HTTP, POP3, or IMAP4. So, when I refer to an SMTP front-end server, I'm really just referring to the ability to split off Exchange 2000's SMTP service to a box dedicated for message transport. That system will perform store and forward, and potentially relay, just as you would expect any transfer service to do. With the client access protocols, the front-end server actually proxies requests to the back-end server (using its native protocol, I might add: either POP3, IMAP4, or HTTP).

11.2.1 Advantages of front- and back-end configurations

The advantages of using front- and back-end servers are as follows:

- Offload processing. Deploying Exchange 2000 in a front- and back-end configuration allows the bulk of message transport to be offloaded from a mailbox server. This is important, because performance is most important to end users and end users are mostly interested in getting e-mail off the back-end server.
- Security. The front-end server can be positioned as the single point of access on or behind an Internet firewall, which is configured to allow only traffic to the front end from the Internet. Because the front-end server has no user information on it, it provides an additional layer of security for the organization. In addition, because only the front-end server is exposed to the external network (when configured properly), the back-end servers are protected from denial-of-service attacks. For further protection, it is even possible to place a firewall between the front- and back-end server to lock down the environment even more.
- Failover/fault tolerance. Having multiple front-end, SMTP servers, combined with round-robin DNS or some other load-balancing service, allows enterprises and service providers to provide a level of fault tolerance for their message transfer system.

It's important to note that MAPI (typically used by Microsoft Outlook 98/2000/XP in an enterprise deployment with Exchange servers) is not supported by the front- and back-end architecture. Front- and back-end topology is not useful to MAPI clients for two reasons. First, MAPI clients have built-in support for handling cases in which users are moved from one server to another, something POP3 and most IMAP4 clients can't handle. IMAP actually does support referral to handle this situation but most clients don't implement it. The Exchange IMAP service has supported it for quite some time, however. Second, MAPI is not an Internet protocol and is not hosted by IIS. Instead, as with previous versions of Exchange, MAPI is hosted out of the store process (store.exe). If you think about it, though, every MAPI operation must be run on the back-end server anyway, and since there is no name space gained with MAPI and a front-end server, there's not much point in implementing front-end servers for MAPI.

11.3 How front- and back-end topology works

Although the general functionality of the front-end server is to proxy requests to the correct back-end servers on behalf of the clients, the exact functionality of the front-end server depends on the protocol. This section focuses only on SMTP. Unlike the other Internet protocols in a front-end configuration, SMTP is fully functional on a front-end server and does not proxy protocol commands to the back-end server.

11.3.1 SMTP in a front-end configuration

SMTP requests are typically sent to the front-end server by an SMTP message transfer agent hosted by an ISP for inbound traffic or, in the case of Exchange 2000 organizations, from another Exchange 2000 server for outbound traffic. The front-end SMTP server receives the message and places it on disk in an NTFS subdirectory to comply with the store-and-forward requirements of being an SMTP MTA. Once stored on disk, the SMTP front-end server will send an acknowledgment to the sending SMTP service indicating that it has taken full receipt of the message. At this point, the SMTP server performs its normal processing involving the categorizer and queries Active Directory to determine the back-end server to which the SMTP message should be delivered.

As in normal processing, discussed in previous chapters, the front-end SMTP server maintains a directory cache that can substantially reduce the number of queries sent to Active Directory global catalog servers. Cache information (provided by DSAccess) expires after a period of time and is also reset when changes in server configuration are detected. The key here is that front-end servers, even in the case of SMTP, need access to a Global Catalog server.

One thing to note about SMTP on a front-end server is that if a back-end server is down for maintenance or is otherwise inaccessible over SMTP, the front-end server will store the message. The front-end server marks that server as down and honors its retry intervals for reestablishing the connection.

11.3.2 Common naming

When you use front-end servers for SMTP, the names of the actual servers that are providing SMTP service are not apparent to the users. For instance, it might make sense to create a DNS entry for a battery of front-end servers called smtp.company.com. Typically this is done as an MX record that resolves to multiple names; for example, consider the following DNS entries:

```
Smtp.company.com    IN    MX    10    mail1.company.com
                                10    mail2.company.com
                                10    mail3.company.com
```

This practice, which should be applied to POP3 and IMAP4 services as well, simplifies the client configuration and allows for easy standardization, since every user's (Internet-based) client is configured to connect to the one host name shared by the front-end servers. Adding or removing SMTP front-end servers is transparent to the user and requires no client reconfiguration.

11.4 Deployment considerations

11.4.1 Recommended server configurations and ratios

Server configuration is dependent on many factors, including the number of users for each back-end server, the protocols used, and the expected use. The configuration of particular models should be done in consultation with a hardware vendor or consultant. Compaq offers storage and server sizing tools for Exchange 2000 on the ActiveAnswers Web site: http://www.compaq.com/activeanswers/.

At initial release of Exchange 2000, Microsoft recommended that one front-end server was reasonable for every four back-end servers. Their caveat was that this number was only being provided to give some idea of the suggested ratio, not as a rule. In practice, I doubt whether an ISP, for instance, would ever implement such a ratio. In fact, it's more likely that you'll see multiple front-end servers for every back-end server. Why do I say this? If you think about it, one of the nice features of having a front- and back-end architecture is that you can focus on building high availability into the back-end servers via high quality and usually fairly expensive hardware.

Front-end servers, on the other hand, can be made up of smaller, less-expensive hardware. However, it's likely that these front-end server configurations will be less reliable than the back-end server. For instance, front-end servers will normally not require external disks, but it is more likely that these disks will fail. If they do fail, how do you continue to provide service to your end users? The obvious choice is to implement multiple front-end servers. On top of that, during normal production you will probably want to spread the load of the service being offered by the front-end server. So, in production environments it's likely that an ISP that plans to host 1 million users will deploy a total of four or five back-end servers and will require multiple servers for each front-end service. For instance, POP3 is a pretty light protocol, so a few front-end servers may be able to handle the POP3 load. For failover, though, it is likely that three or four front-end servers, just for POP3, will be used. In addition, if we assume that we need to support 10,000 simultaneous Outlook Web Access (OWA) clients, it is very probable that we will need three front-end servers to handle that load. Testing has shown that a single OWA front-end server can handle in the neighborhood of 4,000 simultaneous connections. So, in reality, we'll probably need at least four OWA servers just to ensure everything will continue to operate should we lose one of the servers. So, let's examine what we have here: We are already up to seven front-end servers and we haven't even configured our environment for IMAP4 or SMTP. Again, use this information only as a starting point. Front-end servers normally do not need large or particularly fast disk storage but should have fast CPUs and a large amount of memory.

11.5 Scenarios

This section discusses some of the common scenarios where Exchange 2000 SMTP will be deployed. They will incorporate both Enterprise- and ASP-style deployments. Specifically we will cover the following scenarios:

- Typical enterprise
- ISP/ASP with relay
- Coexistence of Exchange 2000 and Exchange 5.5 connectors
- Morphing the best practices

11.5.1 Typical enterprise

Scenario

A typical enterprise has a centralized entry point into its network from the Internet. Alternatively, some companies have a central entry point for their common name space (e.g., company.com) and an entry point for geography-specific name spaces (e.g., us.company.com, emea.company.com, jp.company.com, etc.). The advantage of having the geography-specific name space is that it does allow a fast track into the environment from locations that are distant from the central entry point. So, for instance, a U.S.-based company with offices in Japan might have a name space for jp.company.com for its partners and customers in Japan to use. When using the geography-specific name space, messages enter the network much nearer their final destination.

Setup instructions

Configuring SMTP for the enterprise is straight forward.

SMTP virtual server(s) configuration:

- Create at least two VSs to handle inbound mail. One will work, of course, but I like having at least two for failover. These VSs should have relay disabled, which is the default.
- Create at least one VS to handle outbound mail. An SMTP connector will be configured to use this VS as its source. This VS will also be configured to use an external DNS in order to resolve external domain names, assuming you have separate DNS structures: an internal structure that knows nothing of the Internet and an Internet DNS infrastructure. This VS should not be advertised to the external Internet if possible.

Connectors:

- SMTP connector(s) will be configured and will be assigned an address space of "*" or, alternatively, address spaces that reflect specific connections to another company.

Extras:

- Consider adding an SMTP-based virus scanner to the inbound messages. This will give you a bit of a buffer against virus attacks and will enhance the store-based virus scanning tools you should already be implementing.

Discussion

The outbound VS should be hidden from the Internet to enable your users to still send outbound mail even if inbound mail is undergoing a denial-of-service attack.

Issues

Consider implementing fast-track name spaces if you wish to have multiple entry points into your network. Spinning off the management of the routing topology to a focused group will assist you in avoiding issues of rogue connectors being deployed.

11.5.2 ISP/ASP with relay

Scenario

Your company is an ISP or ASP and must handle inbound e-mail to your users and serve as the primary mail handler for domains that you are hosting.

Setup instructions

Let's start with an initial configuration, albeit misguided, that I've seen repeated in two different implementations involving SMTP connectivity to the Internet. The naming conventions used were nearly identical at both locations, so I'm using ones similar to those that were being used when I arrived on site.

Company A uses Exchange 2000 for all of its e-mail services, including using it to connect to the Internet. For reasons of separation of services and future flexibility, it has decided to create three separate SMTP services: one for inbound, one for outbound, and one for relay. It arrived at this decision because it saw these three functions as being separate and, attempting to simplify their environment, the company wanted to configure each as its own entity. To do this, it created three SMTP virtual servers (VS) and three SMTP connectors on a single system. The VS configurations were as shown in the following chart:

VS Name	*IP Address*	*Relay Setting*
SMTP Outbound	10.10.10.60	Relay enabled for authenticated connections
SMTP Inbound	10.10.10.61	No relay
SMTP Relay	10.10.10.62	Relay enabled for authenticated connections

Company A also created three SMTP connectors and configured them as shown in the following chart:

Connector Name	*Connector VS*	*Address Space*
Outbound Connector	SMTP Outbound	*
Inbound Connector	SMTP Inbound	CompanyA.com
Relay Connector	SMTP Relay	*

A message was then submitted by one of its POP3 clients to the SMTP relay virtual server. Since the SMTP relay VS is configured for relay, the company believed it simply performed a DNS lookup for the MX record associated with the destination domain and retransmitted the message accordingly. Company A believed that tracing would show that the IP address for the system that relayed the message would always be the IP address of the SMTP relay VS (10.10.10.62). But it never did! Why?

Discussion

There is some misconception as to how relay works when you have both virtual servers and connectors configured for Exchange 2000. The following sections will detail how and when each is used.

Relay and SMTP connectors

SMTP relay is just the retransmission of a message over the SMTP protocol. In a relay situation virtual servers handle the initial inbound mail and, since virtual servers are where relay is set, many people mistakenly believe that the SMTP virtual server will merely perform a DNS MX record lookup and then pass the message off to the destination server. It would seem to make sense, actually! Think about it: If the recipient policies are set to only handle mail for companyA.com and a message is received for Compaq.com, it would make sense that the same virtual server would perform a DNS MX record lookup and relay the message off to Compaq.com.

What actually happens is as follows:

1. When a message is received by any Exchange 2000 SMTP virtual server, it is always processed by the Exchange 2000 routing service and its components.
2. Once the routing service determines the appropriate destination of the message, it must hand the message off to an SMTP connector in order to deliver the message outbound.

So, in fact, the virtual server that will be used will be the one associated with the appropriate SMTP connector selected for outbound communication—not necessarily the one listening for inbound connections. There's more to it, though, as we'll see in a moment.

SMTP virtual servers and connectors

As you may recall, attributes associated with an SMTP virtual server are predominantly applied to inbound messages. Most important to our topic is that the IP address assigned to the VS is for listening, not sending. The SMTP virtual server is also the component where SMTP relay is set. So, if you do want to configure relay, you'll need to set that up on your SMTP virtual server(s). In short, the SMTP protocol is provided by SMTP virtual servers.

You may remember that SMTP connectors, from an Internet connectivity standpoint, are used when SMTP messages are sent out of the Exchange 2000 environment. SMTP connectors are selected based on the destination address of the message and the address space associated with a connector. Once the appropriate SMTP connector is determined, an SMTP virtual server is used to actually send the message using the SMTP protocol. You associate virtual servers with SMTP connectors during the configuration of the connector.

So, what happens if you have multiple SMTP virtual servers associated with a single SMTP connector? This is a perfectly legitimate and common configuration. That being the case, for an outbound message, how does Exchange 2000 determine which virtual server to use and what IP address to use as the originating address? For outbound connections, a VS can use any interface available on the box. If you have multiple interfaces, how is one selected? Well, basically it boils down to the IP address associated with the next hop of the message. The destination address, the one returned by a DNS MX record lookup, is used to determine the interface that will be used by the virtual server. This may seem strange, but the the SMTP service can use any interface on the machine for sending outbound mail. The SMTP service will pick the one that is the lowest cost and most appropriate for the destination IP address. The message will be routed to the right VS, based on its association with an SMTP connector, but that VS may use any IP address available to it. Moreover, the way it works is deterministic; all VSs will use the same IP address, if they are all on the same subnet.

Not surprisingly, some folks have asked Microsoft to change this behavior. That may happen in the future, but for the short term it will stay this way because it "always just works." There are times, however, when people want to control the originating IP address, and there is a nice workaround that will usually satisfy them. How? They can control the IP address with the connector by binding it to a VS on a server with a single interface.

Back to the scenario

So, in our scenario, we had several bits of configuration data that were superfluous. For example:

1. Inbound connector—connectors aren't required for inbound SMTP connections in Exchange 2000, only virtual servers.
2. Relay connector—unless this connector handles a completely different address space than the outbound connector, it is not required.
3. SMTP relay VS and SMTP outbound VS—basically, these are configured exactly the same and, from an outbound sending viewpoint, they are redundant. More to the point, they would both use the same interface when sending a message.

So, would you need both? Well, if you are in a classic enterprise environment, the answer is no, since you would probably not be relaying mail for external companies, only for your own users. You could conceivably have one SMTP VS listening for connections and that same VS could be used for outbound connections. In this case you would turn on relay only for those connections that authenticate to your SMTP service. By doing this,

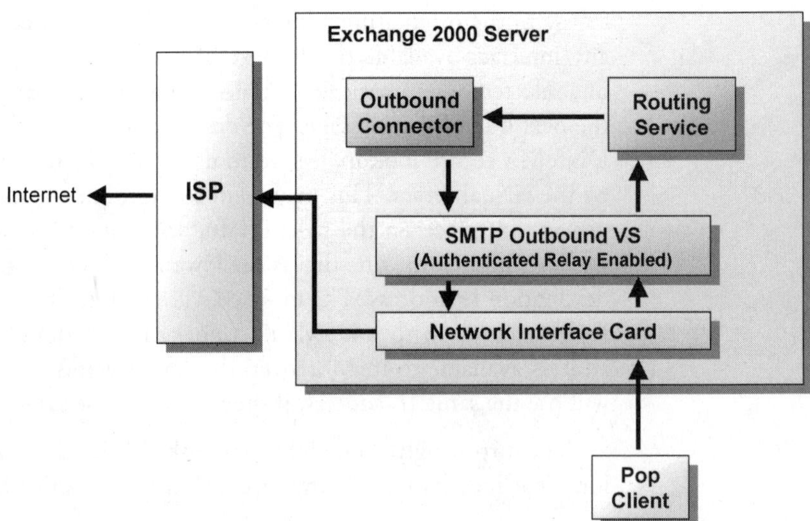

Figure 11.3 *Outbound SMTP VS configuration.*

inbound connections coming from an external source, which will not authenticate, can send messages inbound but will not be able to use your systems for relay. Your internal users, on the other hand, will authenticate and be allowed to relay messages out to the Internet. Figure 11.3 represents the message flow for this type of configuration.

Note that your Exchange 2000 system might relay mail to a wide variety of mail systems within your environment (Notes, cc:Mail, other SMTP systems, etc.) and that can be handled by connectors and address spaces, just as in 5.5.

If you are an ISP, however, the answer is probably yes, you do need multiple VSs. For ISPs, not only do they need to relay mail for their internal users/subscribers, but they would also need to relay mail for companies that use their services to access the Internet. In that situation, using our scenario for reference, the ISP would potentially expose the SMTP inbound/relay VS to the Internet and keep the SMTP outbound VS inside of its own firewall: the former being used for companies it might be hosting and the latter being used for its direct subscribers. Figure 11.4 shows what the message flow for such a configuration might look like.

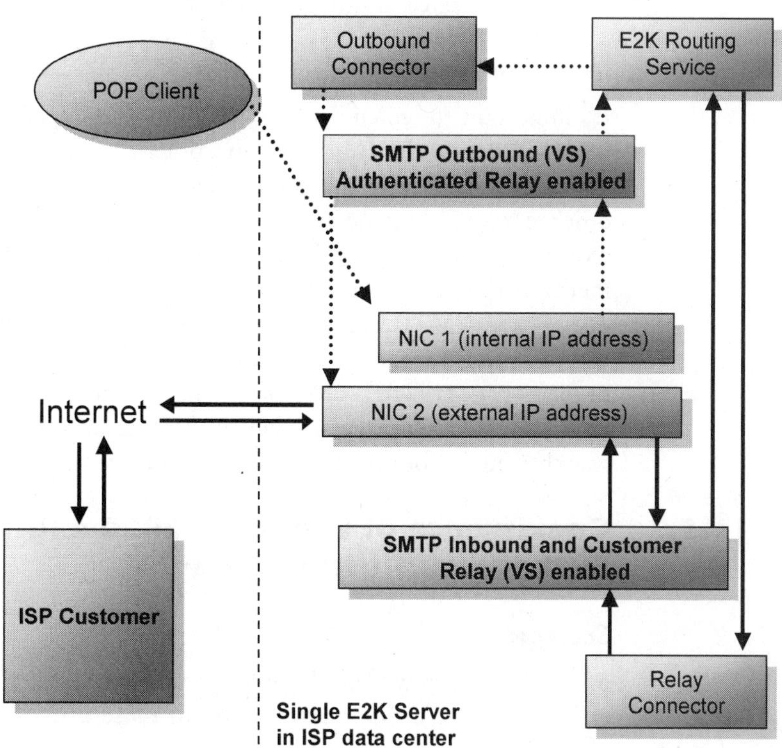

Figure 11.4 *Relay SMTP VS configuration.*

Note that there are two virtual servers. One virtual server is listening for inbound SMTP traffic on an internal IP address (SMTP Outbound). The other is listening for inbound SMTP traffic from the Internet (SMTP Inbound and Customer Relay). There is an SMTP connector (Outbound Connector) configured with an address space of *. Therefore, any messages bound for the Internet will be passed to this connector. The VS associated with this connector will use the external interface to actually send messages out to the Internet and, therefore, would need to be configured to use External DNS. (Configure this on the SMTP VS Properties page/"Delivery" Tab/"Advanced" button/Configure DNS Severs "Configure" button.)

For messages coming in from a company that is obtaining Internet access from the ISP, messages will be received by the external interface and will be handled by the SMTP Inbound and Customer Relay VS. This VS will have relay enabled for a select list of computers. An SMTP connector (Relay Connector) is also configured to use the SMTP Inbound and Customer Relay VS and would have address spaces configured that map to each customer. Messages destined for a paying customer would pass through the Relay connector, messages bound for the general Internet would pass through the Outbound connector. In each case, however, the interface used would be the external interface (NIC 2).

Issues/summary

It's important to remember how SMTP services operate in Exchange 2000 versus Windows 2000 or even any other SMTP service. Exchange 2000 always calls its routing services to determine the path a message will take. In order to have SMTP messages enter Exchange 2000 environments, the only requirement is an SMTP VS. For a message to exit Exchange 2000 environments in the most controlled manner, an SMTP Connector associated to one or more SMTP VSs is required. For outbound mail, the SMTP VS can use any interface available on the system, not just the one shown on its property page (which is used for listening). Understanding the intricacies of how the SMTP service works will enable you to control message traffic in a way that meets your requirements and/or those of your customer.

11.5.3 Coexistence of Exchange 2000 and Exchange 5.5 connectors

Scenario

Many customers will be deploying Exchange 2000 in parallel with their existing Exchange 5.5 infrastructure. In those cases there is the possibility that an SMTP connector homed on Exchange 2000 will have the same address space as that of an IMS on an Exchange 5.5 server.

Setup instructions

The setup is straightforward: You merely create an address and an identical address space (e.g., *, or company.com) on an Exchange 2000 SMTP connector and an Exchange 5.5 IMS server. (See Figure 11.5.)

Discussion

There are a few things to keep in mind with regard to how the connectors will be used. They include the following:

- Status updates—Exchange 5.5 servers will never send state change out to the rest of the environment, so these connectors will not be updated in the Exchange 2000 link state table.
- Scope and address resolution—setting the scope in Exchange 2000 is a bit different from Exchange 5.5, as is the fit of the name space. With Exchange 2000, the directory service is Active Directory and groups can take on various scopes. Since Exchange 2000 relies on Global Catalog servers to resolve distribution list (DL) addresses, the DLs must be scoped in such a way that they are available within a Global Catalog server or they must exist within the domain in which the Global Catalog server is homed.

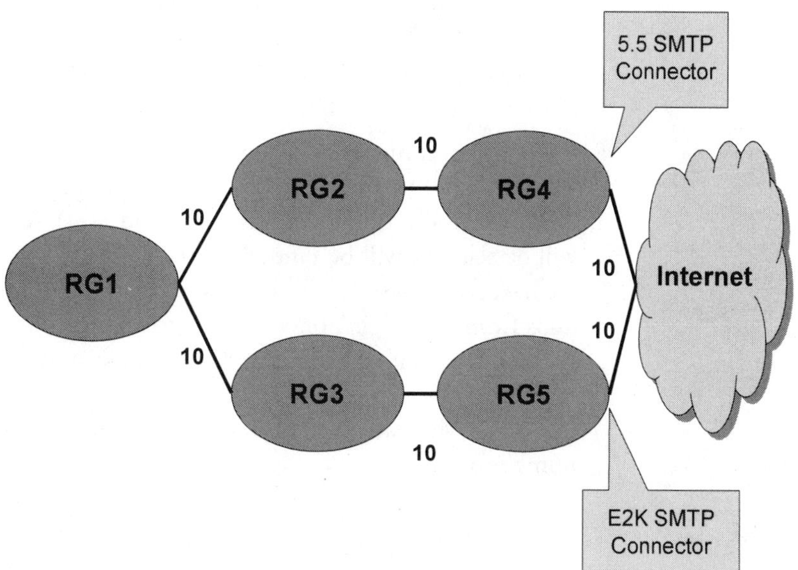

Figure 11.5 *Coexisting Exchange 5.5 and Exchange 2000 connectors.*

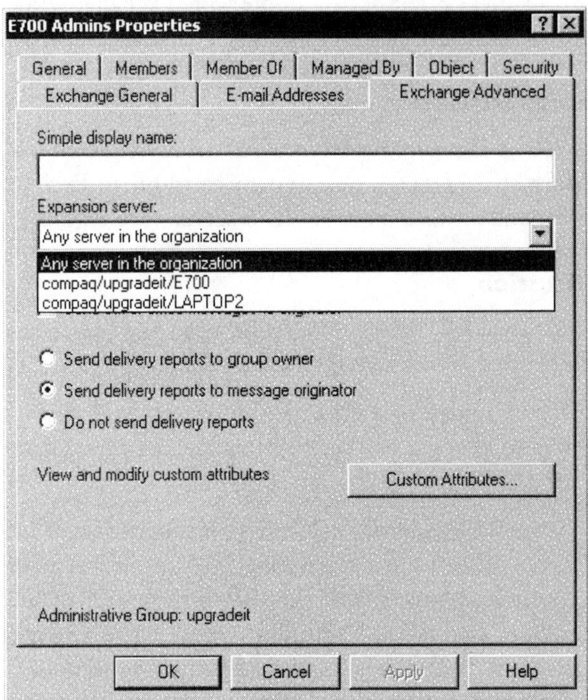

Figure 11.6 *Selecting an expansion server for a specific group.*

- Expansion server—you can choose to have groups expanded by a specific server. To do this you must use Active Directory Users and Computers and select the Advanced Features view. From there you can select a particular group and, using the Exchange Advanced tab, select the server that will be responsible for group expansion. By default this is set to Any server in the organization, as you can see in Figure 11.6.
- Selecting a connector—assume that two connectors, one on an Exchange 2000 server and one on an Exchange 5.5 server, are configured identically (same address space and cost). The connector that will be selected will be random initially. Again, this assumes that the connectors are identically configured and are the same number of hops from the originator. Once a particular connector has been connected though, it will continue to be used in subsequent message submission. In an environment consisting of several nodes, balancing will occur with each connector being selected approximately the same number of times.

Of course, if the connectors have similar, but different, address spaces ("*" versus "*.com"), the address that most closely matches the recipient address will be selected.

Issues

Moving to an Exchange 2000–based connector environment quickly will enable you to take advantage of link state information and get your environment working consistently throughout.

We mentioned previously that when an Exchange 5.5 server with a site connector is upgraded to Exchange 2000 that site connector becomes a routing group connector. One difference that you may have taken advantage of with a site connector is the ability to assign address spaces to it. Routing group connectors do not contain an address space tab. Normally, routing groups don't need an address space, since they are established automatically for the connector. In fact, Microsoft will probably say that an RGC should never have an address space manually assigned to it. Looking back to Exchange 5.5, site connectors potentially needed address spaces assigned to them because they sometimes connected to other sites where no directory replication was taking place. So they needed an address space, since you may not have known which address spaces were supported on the other end of the connector. This just isn't true with Exchange 2000. Since Exchange 2000 uses Active Directory, you always have full directory replication, so there is no need for any address spaces to be added to the RGC.

Theoretically, though, RGCs can have address spaces added to them by populating the `routingList` attribute of the connector via a tool such as ADSI Edit … as shown in Figure 11.7. You will definitely need to test any address space entries you add to the connector before placing the change into your production environment. And, more to the point, Microsoft probably doesn't support doing this, so it may not be worth doing in the first place. It is interesting to view some of these attributes as though, as it gives you an understanding of how the system works.

11.5.4 Morphing topology best practices

In larger enterprises one of the best practices for Exchange 5.5 was to create hubs to connect the various sites. Hub-and-spoke designs have been quite common, as well as the concept of a strong hub.

Figure 11.8 shows the typical hub site design, where the servers that make up the hub are brought together in a central location. The servers in this hub site do not host mailboxes, only connectors. In this example, the location of the hub site might be Atlanta and the connections to each of the sites would be via site connectors or X.400 connectors, depending upon the bandwidth. This is a tried and true design and has been implemented in many enterprises.

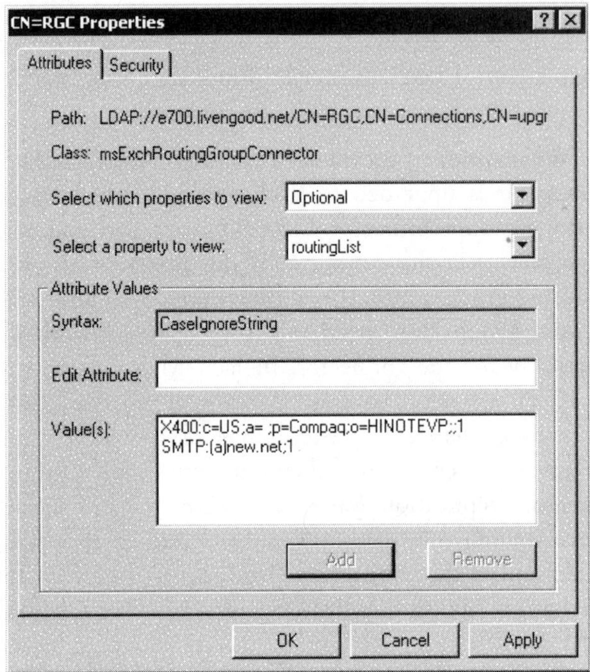

Figure 11.7 *routingList attribute on a routing group connector.*

The only issue with this design is if connections to the hub become unavailable. In that case, message buildup can occur quite rapidly without some sort of manual intervention. The positive aspect of this design is that it works well even in low-bandwidth environments using X.400 connectors as the transport mechanism. Interestingly though, many enterprises have beefed up their networks and have implemented the strong-hub design, as shown in Figure 11.9.

With the strong-hub design servers that belong to the hub are distributed directly into the geographies. These servers are still only used for hosting connectors and do not contain any user mailboxes but, from a network perspective, are collocated with the mailbox servers within each site. The idea here is that since the connector servers are on the same LAN as the mailbox servers, messages will move into the hub site quickly and without risk of network outage. Once within the hub site the messages are routed between the servers in the hub site quickly, since they share a high-speed WAN connection. Further, in the event that a connection between any two servers in the hub is lost, the messages can be rerouted via another server located in the strong-hub site. The strong hub, just as with the hub-and-spoke model, will also home connectors to the external world (e.g., the Internet).

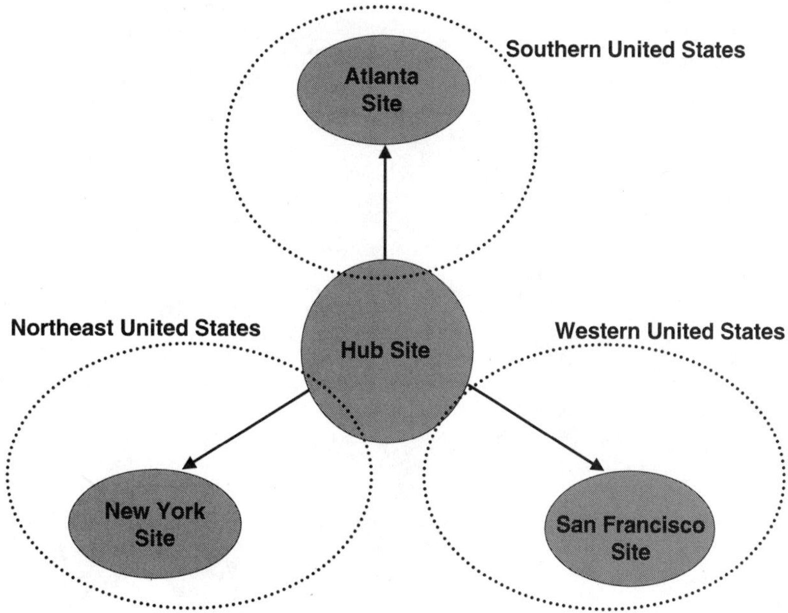

Figure 11.8 *Typical hub-and-spoke site design.*

Not all enterprises have the luxury to implement a strong hub and have relied on the hub-and-spoke model. And, in many environments in which I have worked, politics has dictated the number of sites that were implemented.

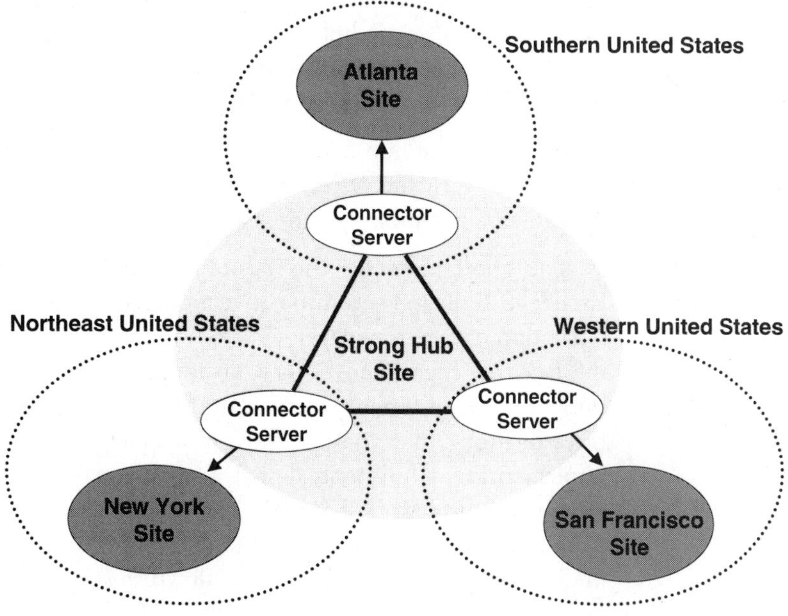

Figure 11.9 *Strong-hub site design.*

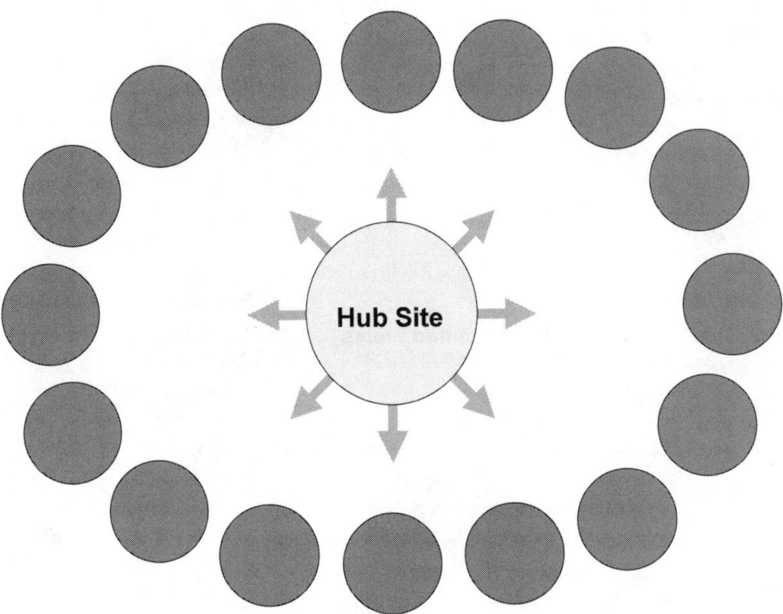

Figure 11.10 *Hub-and-spoke with many sites.*

For example, I worked with one company that had 26 sites strictly due to politics. The issue really boiled down to server administration. This company had personnel in each location who wanted privileges to manage users and servers and didn't want administrators from other locations to be able to alter the environment. In fact, based on bandwidth, we could have implemented a strong hub, but that would have required too many servers so it didn't make sense. Instead, we implemented a hub-and-spoke model similar to that shown in Figure 11.10.

Even with the hub-and-spoke model, we had to implement 26 connectors, one to each site. While not completely ridiculous, as would have been the case in a full-mesh design, it was bordering on being unwieldy.

The good news for this customer, however, is that as it moves to Exchange 2000 and gets into native mode, it will be able to benefit from the separation of server management from topology management. Additionally, the fact that high bandwidth is no longer a requirement for membership into a routing group may allow it to shrink its design from 26 sites down to three or four. Once you get down to a smaller number of routing groups, implementing a full-mesh design starts to make sense. With 26 routing groups, a full-mesh design would require 325 connectors ($n \times (n - 1)/2$). Even at ten routing groups the number of connectors to manage in a fully meshed design is 45. Once you get down to seven or eight routing groups,

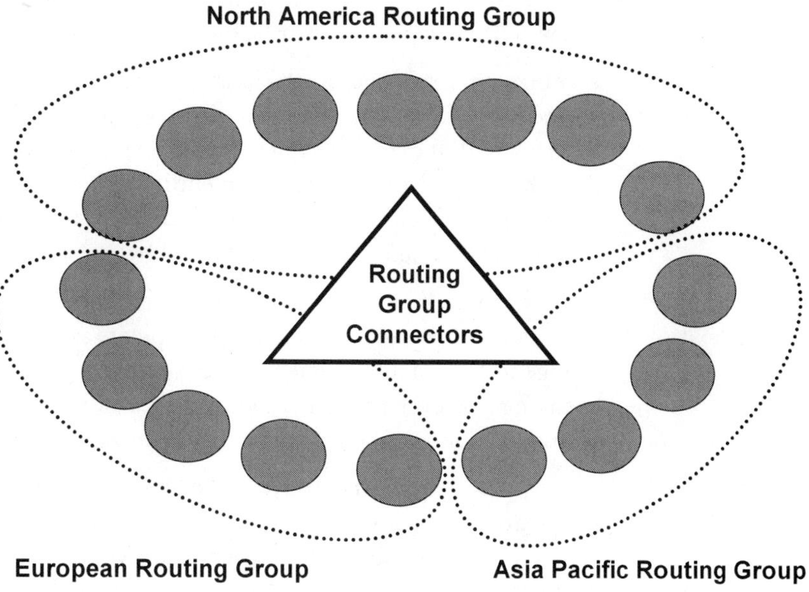

Figure 11.11 *Moving to fewer routing groups.*

though, fully meshed designs, as shown in Figure 11.11, start to make sense.

The obvious limitations associated with any fully meshed design, other than the number of connectors to manage, have to do with the underlying network architecture and your desire to control the exact path that messages take through the network. Hub-and-spoke models and strong hubs may still make sense for your environment.

11.5.5 Setting up Exchange 2000 for message switching

OK, so we've got Exchange 5.5 all set to pass all SMTP messages to Exchange 2000. Now we need to configure Exchange 2000 to do the right thing. There are a few things we need to keep in mind and a couple of interesting configuration changes we need to make to obtain the appropriate behavior.

Exchange 2000's recipient policies play a significant role in message routing, as we discussed in Chapter 10. Recipient policy configuration information is written to the IIS metabase; again, this is one of the functions of the System Attendant in Exchange 2000. Recipient policies determine which domains the SMTP virtual consider valid as inbound mail. Remember that the routing service is called no matter how a message enters the Exchange 2000 system (SMTP, MAPI, etc.), so the entries in the metabase determine whether a recipient is local (belongs to this organization) or gateway (the recipient doesn't belong to this organization).

Since an Exchange 5.5 recipient's SMTP domain (e.g., <user>@company.com) is the same as the primary SMTP address defined in the Exchange 2000 default recipient policy (e.g., @company.com), the categorizer thinks the Exchange 5.5 recipient is local despite the fact that no mailbox for this recipient exists in the Exchange 2000 organization. This will lead to an NDR and, as we all know, NDRs are a bad thing.

The magic that needs to be performed here is to make sure Exchange 2000 does not tag the Exchange 5.5 recipients as being local. This requires a change to the default recipient policy's primary SMTP address: specifically, changing the primary SMTP address to a nonexisting one to ensure that messages bound to the Exchange 5.5 organization are not stamped as local.

For local delivery the Active Directory lookup will provide mailbox store information, which will result in the message being sent to a local queue. If recipient policies will be used to generate SMTP addresses, a higher-priority recipient policy can apply the real SMTP address to Active Directory objects.

The connector to the Exchange 5.5 organization is configured as follows.

In the Exchange System Manager tool:

- Administrative Groups\Routing Topology\Routing Groups\<routing group>\Connectors\To Exchange\Properties\General tab
- Check Forward all mail through this connector to the following smart host.
- Fill the smart host with the Exchange 5.5 IMS server name or IP address enclosed in square brackets.
- Local bridgeheads: current server (bridgehead to the Exchange 5.5 organization).
- Administrative Groups\Routing Topology\Routing Groups\<routing group>\Connectors\To Exchange\Properties\Address Space tab.
- Add the following address spaces:

  Type: SMTP
  Address: *.company.com (if one or several subdomains are used)
  Cost: 1
  Type: SMTP

Address: company.com
Cost: 1
Connector Scope: Organization

- Check Allow messages to be relayed to these domains.

  The recipient policy is configured as follows.

  In the Exchange Management tool:

- Recipients\Recipient Policies\Default Policy\Properties\E-Mail addresses tab

  Note that a new secondary SMTP address must be created and promoted to primary, before the default one can be removed. At this point the This Exchange Organization is responsible for all mail delivery to this address box can be unchecked. (Although this box can be unchecked in this manner for the company.com SMTP address, doing this does not solve the routing problem.)

- New SMTP address: @bogus.company.com (for instance).

  Afterward, a higher-priority recipient policy can be defined with @company.com as primary secondary address; this will ensure that all mailbox-enabled Active Directory objects are configured with the appropriate SMTP address.

Changing the default recipient policy also breaks OWA, which relies on the recipient policy to properly map the SMTP address and locate the mailbox. The workaround to that problem is to add the bogus default SMTP address (bogus.company.com) as a secondary proxy address for each user allowed to use OWA. A nice side effect of this is that OWA can be limited to certain users only.

11.6 Configuring firewalls with front- and back-end deployments

This section discusses the configuration of firewalls for use with Exchange 2000 front- and back-end topologies, as well as some additional configuration information that may be required on front-end servers in these environments. The information in the remainder of this chapter, along with many ASP-specific setup scenarios, is also covered in the Exchange Hosting and ASP white papers available from www.microsoft.com.

11.6.1 Internet firewalls

In Internet scenarios, a firewall is required between the enterprise and the Internet. Certain TCP ports for a specific set of IP addresses need to be allowed to pass through the firewall. The best practice is to enable SSL for the various protocols and, taking that into consideration, Table 11.1 lists the ports required for front-end services.

11.6.2 Intranet firewall configuration

In some cases it may be desirable to further protect your environment by implementing a firewall between the front-end server and the internal network.

Basic protocols

Just as in the previous example of Internet firewalls, the front-end protocol ports must be open on the inner firewall. Since SSL is not used in communication between the front- and back-end servers, only the standard ports, listed in Table 11.2, are required.

Active Directory communication

To communicate with Active Directory, the Exchange front-end server requires LDAP ports to be open. Windows 2000 Kerberos authentication is also used, so the Kerberos ports must also be open, as shown in Table 11.3.

There are two sets of optional ports that can be opened in the firewall. The decision to open them depends on the policies of the organization. Each decision involves a tradeoff among security, ease of administration, and functionality.

Domain name service

For server names to be looked up correctly (e.g., to be converted from names to IP addresses), the front-end server needs access to either a DNS server or a hosts file that provides the mapping. In many Windows 2000 domains, Active Directory servers (i.e., Domain Controllers) function as DNS servers, so they should be accessible through the firewall over the DNS ports. Table 11.4 lists the ports required for access.

If these ports are not open in the inner firewall, you must create a hosts file for each mapping. The Windows 2000 TCP/IP stack uses the following file: `%SystemRoot%\System32\drivers\etc\hosts`. Edit this file to create

Table 11.1 *Ports Required to Be Open on the Internet Firewall*

Port number/transport	Protocol
443/TCP	HTTPS (SSL-secured HTTP)
993/TCP	IMAPS (SSL-secured IMAP)
995/TCP	POP3S (SSL-secured POP3)
25/TCP	SMTP

Table 11.2 *Protocol Ports Required for the Intranet Firewall*

Port number/transport	Protocol
80/TCP	HTTP
143/TCP	IMAP4
110/TCP	POP3
25/TCP	SMTP

Table 11.3 *Ports Required for Active Directory Communication and Kerberos*

Port number/transport	Protocol
389/TCP	LDAP to directory service
3268/TCP	LDAP to global catalog server
88/TCP	Kerberos authentication
88/UDP	

Table 11.4 *Ports Required for Access to DNS Servers—Use Hosts Files if These Ports Aren't Open*

Port number/transport	Protocol
53/TCP	DNS Lookup
53/UDP	

a name-to-IP-address mapping for every server that the front-end server might contact. This generally includes every Exchange 2000 server in the organization and each Active Directory or Global Catalog server that the front-end server might contact. Instructions for how to create the mappings are in the default hosts file. The most important thing about using a hosts file is to ensure that it is kept up-to-date when changes are made to the organization.

Service discovery and authentication

Windows 2000 uses RPCs to perform Active Directory service discovery and client authentication. To enable these features, RPC ports must be opened. Table 11.5 lists the required RPC ports.

Most firewall implementations restrict the type of traffic that can be sent into the corporate network. If certain RPC ports are not opened between the perimeter network and the corporate intranet, some front-end server features must be disabled or specially configured. First, without RPC access to the Active Directory servers, the front-end server cannot authenticate clients. This means that features that require authentication, including implicit logon and public folder tree access, do not work correctly. Public folder access is possible, but without being able to determine the identity of the accessing user, no load balancing is possible. When you configure a front-end server in such an environment, disable authentication and enable anonymous access. In addition, because Windows 2000 is unable to locate its Domain Controllers and Global Catalog servers without RPC service discovery, the Exchange front-end server must be configured with the names of these servers and their backups. There are registry settings available that, when set, can direct front-end servers to specific back-end servers, and ports, for authentication. When modifying the registry, it is important that you document what you have changed and be sure to keep the settings current as your environment evolves.

Table 11.5 *RPC Ports Needed for Service Discovery and Authentication*

Port number/transport	Protocol
135/TCP	RPC port end-point mapper
1024+/TCP	RPC service ports
445/TCP	Netlogon

11.7 Additional configuration considerations

11.7.1 Securing communication between client and front-end server

To secure data transmitted between the client and the front-end server, Microsoft recommends that the front-end server be SSL-enabled. In addition, to ensure that users' data are always secure, access to the front-end server without SSL should be disabled (this is an option in the SSL configuration). It is critical to protect the network traffic by using SSL when using basic authentication to protect the users' passwords from network packet sniffing.

You do not need to configure SSL on the back-end servers when using a front-end server, because the front-end server does not support using SSL to communicate to the back-end servers. You may configure SSL on the back-end servers for use by clients that are directly accessing the back-end server.

Note: Windows 2000 License Logging Service must be running on the front-end server when using SSL for more than ten simultaneous users. IIS does not allow more than ten simultaneous SSL connections unless this service is running.

11.7.2 Securing communication between front- and back-end servers

HTTP communication between the front- and back-end servers is not encrypted. In cases when the front- and back-end servers are maintained in at the same subnet, this is not a concern. However, if front- and back-end servers are kept in separate subnets and network traffic must pass over unsecured areas of the corporation, Microsoft recommends that this traffic be encrypted to protect passwords and data.

Windows 2000 supports IP Security (IPSec), an Internet standard that enables two servers running Windows 2000 to encrypt any traffic between them at the IP layer. This protocol can be used to secure the traffic between the front- and back-end servers. This kind of encryption affects the performance on both the front- and back-end servers. The precise extent to which it affects performance depends greatly on the type of encryption used.

Enable IPSec only if you have a thorough understanding of the workings of the protocol and its administration.

The Windows 2000 IPSec feature allows a server to encrypt any and all traffic. However, in this scenario, it is best to limit the encryption to only the HTTP traffic. The IPSec example in the appendix steps you through an IPSec configuration between two servers.

Do not use the included policy on the back-end servers. IPSec should be configured on the back-end servers so that they respond appropriately if a request for IPSec communication is received. However, they should not require that all communication from all clients be encrypted using IPSec. Windows 2000 has three included IPSec policy files. One of these—Client (respond only)—has the desired effect. With this policy enabled on the back-end server, the front-end server can use IPSec to communicate safely with the back-end server, while other clients (including MAPI clients such as Outlook 2000) and servers can communicate with the back-end server without needing to use IPSec.

When using IPSec in a perimeter network environment, you must make changes on the intranet firewall to support it. First, HTTP (port 80/TCP) is no longer required and should be blocked. Second, the IPSec negotiation port at 500/UDP is required. IPSec also requires IP identifiers 50 and 51 to be open on the intranet firewall.

IPSec encryption occurs after the application (e.g., Exchange 2000) has passed the request to Windows to send to the server. So, as far as Exchange 2000 is concerned, the request was made over HTTP using TCP port 80. However, before the traffic leaves the server, it is intercepted, encrypted, and sent over a separate channel (IP identifiers 50 and 51). Thus, the encryption is transparent to the Exchange 2000 applications running on each server, and the fact that these data never used port 80 is not an issue to these applications.

11.8 Summary

In this chapter, I've outlined some common additional configuration techniques. In the next chapter, we'll cover some tools commonly used.

12

Transport Service Tools

12.1 Introduction

This chapter describes some of the most useful tools that can be used day-to-day in your Exchange 2000 environment.

12.2 Monitoring message flow

If users are reporting missing e-mail or you suspect that there is a problem with message delivery or routing, use Message Tracking Center to determine whether a message is waiting in a queue or whether it has been sent. Message Tracking Center allows you to reference the message tracking logs stored on each server and view the history of sent messages. If the message does not appear in a tracking log, check the message queues, using the queue viewer tool, to see if the message is waiting in a queue for an available connection or for routing information before it can be delivered.

Message Tracking Center is located under the tools icon in Exchange System Manager. Once you expand the tools container, you can right-click on Message Tracking Center to begin tracking a message, as shown in Figure 12.1.

Once you've searched for the messages that meet your selection criteria, you can select an individual message and choose Message History to see the processing that has taken place on the specific message, as shown in Figure 12.2.

As you can see, the tracking log allows you not only to see where and when a message has been delivered, but it also shows how each component operates on a message. In the example in Figure 12.2 you can see that the message moved from one server to another (left to right) and was processed by all of the routing components we discussed in earlier chapters.

Figure 12.1 *Selecting messages to track.*

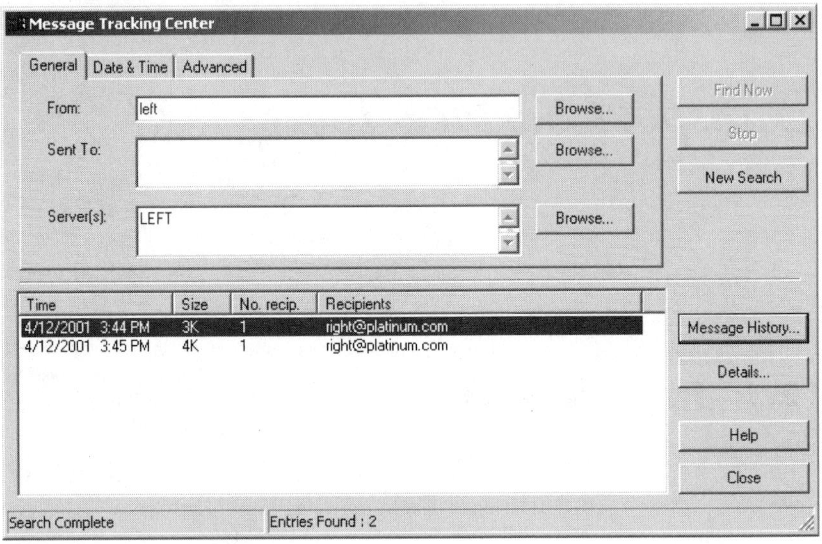

Figure 12.2 *Message history display.*

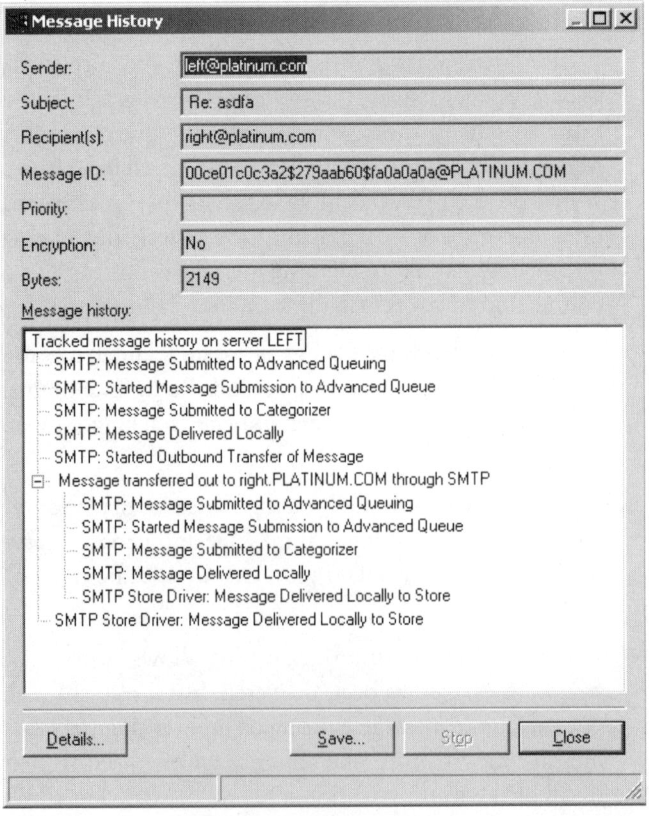

12.2.1 Messages tracked by Message Tracking Center

Message Tracking Center can track messages in Exchange 2000 organizations and mixed Exchange 5.5 and Exchange 2000 deployments. Message Tracking Center can also track messages going to or coming in from a foreign e-mail system, such as Lotus Notes. The path of a message that is forwarded after the message arrives at a foreign e-mail system cannot be tracked, but you can determine whether the message was delivered successfully. You must complete two main tasks when using Message Tracking Center. First, you must search for and select a particular message to track. Then, you can view the history of the message path. You can also save the history of the message flow to a text file for reference if message tracking logs are cleared.

Before you can use message tracking you must enable message tracking.

12.2.2 Enabling message tracking

Message tracking is implemented on a per-server basis. As Figure 12.3 shows, there is a checkbox on the server properties page that enables message tracking, as well as the logging and display of the message subject.

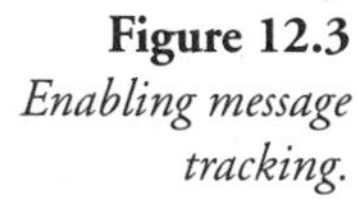

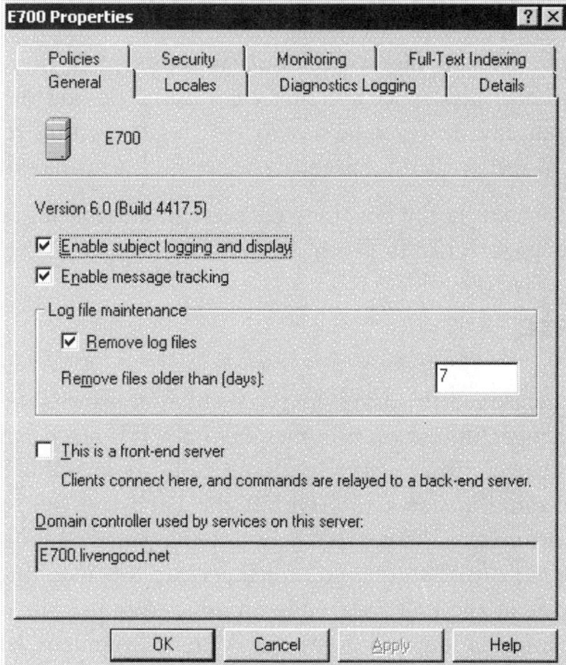

Figure 12.3 *Enabling message tracking.*

12.2.3 Manually reviewing message logs

If a user reports that a message was sent but never received, you can track the message by finding its history in message tracking logs. You can use the sender's e-mail address and server name to find the information using Message Tracking Center; however, if you cannot find a message in the search results, you can manually review the message tracking logs. Message tracking logs are stored in `Exchsrvr\servername.log`, in which *servername* is the name of your Exchange server. Each day, Exchange creates a new log that records the messages a server processes. Each daily log is named for the date on which it was created, with a format of `yyyymmdd.log`.

To review message tracking logs, proceed as follows:

1. To open a log file in the `Exchsrvr\servername.log` directory, use a text editor, such as Notepad. The log file has a .log extension, so you must browse for all file types. You can also import the log file into spreadsheets such as Microsoft Excel, or you can use it in custom applications.
2. To search for the missing message, using any information you know about the message, use the text editor.

12.2.4 Maintaining message tracking logs

If you allow log files to accumulate on the server, they can consume a large portion of disk space and affect performance. You should remove log files periodically; however, be sure to leave log files on the server long enough for you to review files if a problem occurs with your message flow.

You can specify how long the server maintains logs using the same properties page shown in Figure 12.3.

12.3 WinRoute

As mentioned in earlier chapters, the link state table that exists on every Exchange 2000 server is in memory only. It is not persisted to disk. Some of the characteristics of the link state table are viewable from the queue view tool and the status tool within the Exchange System Manager console. Unfortunately, the console does not give you a really good view of the link state table from an organizational perspective. Wouldn't it be nice to be able to look at the link state table on any server in your organization, capture that information, and in the case of an odd problem, have the ability to save

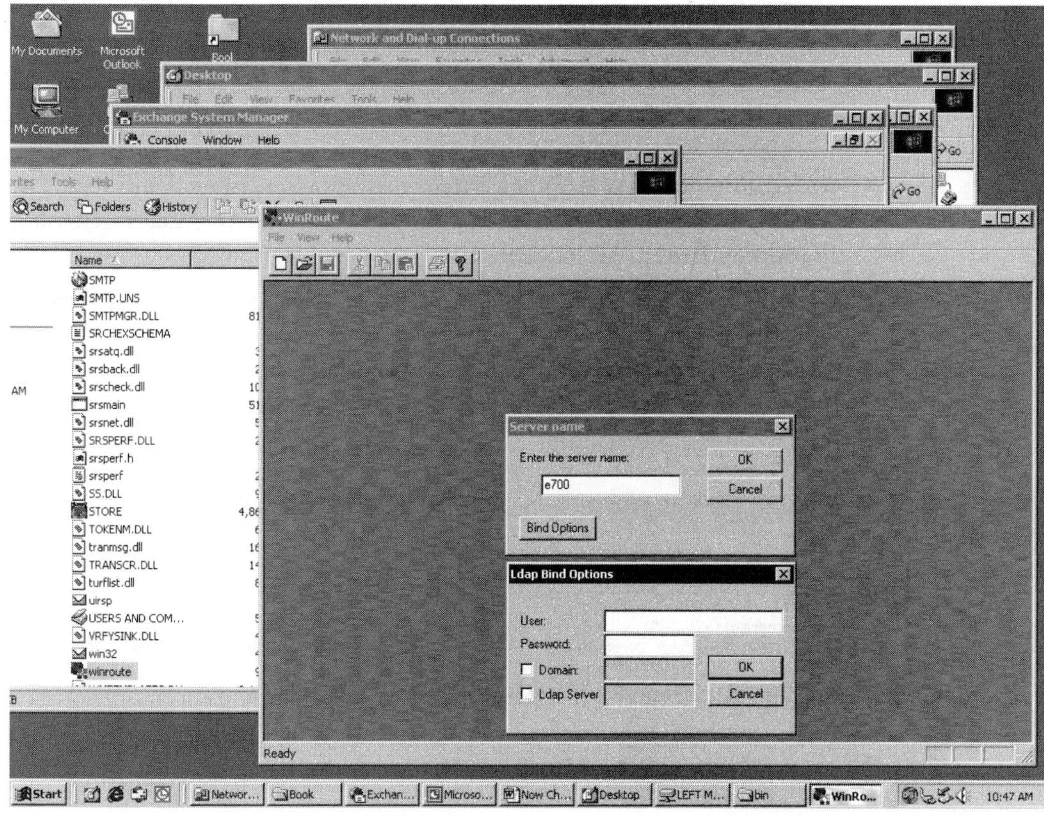

Figure 12.4 *Launching WinRoute.*

it to a file and send it to Microsoft's PSS organization? Well, that's exactly what WinRoute allows you to do. Even better, WinRoute is available on the Exchange 2000 distribution in `SUPPORT\UTILS\I386`.

At one point, to use WinRoute you had to copy the WinRoute executable to the `exchsrvr\bin` subdirectory before executing it, because it required exchange DLLs. That's not the case anymore, so you can run it from anywhere. So, launch the executable, enter a server name to connect to (as shown in Figure 12.4), and WinRoute will display the link state table associated with the server you connected to.

WinRoute works by connecting to an Exchange 2000 server and identifying itself as another Exchange 2000 server. When this occurs, WinRoute receives the link state table as if it were a real Exchange 2000 server within the organization.

The link state table exists in memory as data only and as a series of GUIDs. Once it receives the link state information, WinRoute uses Active Directory to decode the GUIDs into human-readable information. If you are using WinRoute to examine data from servers outside of your domain, you also have the capability to bind to a specific directory server to assist with the resolution of the GUID information presented by WinRoute. The LDAP BIND OPTIONS screen shown in Figure 12.4 is used to establish the appropriate LDAP binding.

As mentioned, one of the major benefits of WinRoute is the capability to save the link state information to a file and, potentially, send this file off to Microsoft for review if there are odd routing issues. It also gives you the opportunity to compare your configuration to what actually is being seen by Exchange 2000 routing.

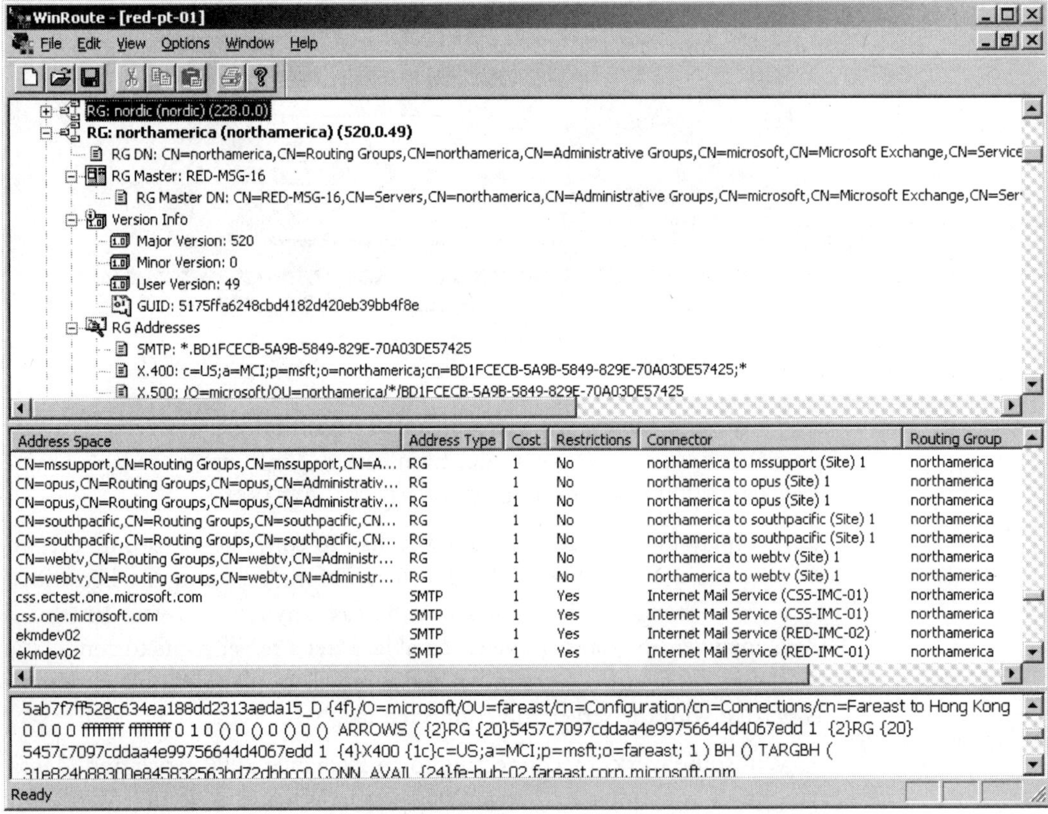

Figure 12.5 *WinRoute display.*

The display in WinRoute consists of three panes, as follows:

1. The top frame of the WinRoute display is grouped by routing groups. As you can see in Figure 12.5, each routing group expands to show information such as the Routing Group Master, link state version number, routing group addresses, connectors, and member servers.

2. The middle pane is focused on connectors. Specifically it focuses on address spaces, address types, connector names, cost, and what routing group and admin group the connectors belong to. This may be the most useful pane for most people. The display can be sorted on each column header by clicking the appropriate header, for example Address Type as shown in Figure 12.6.

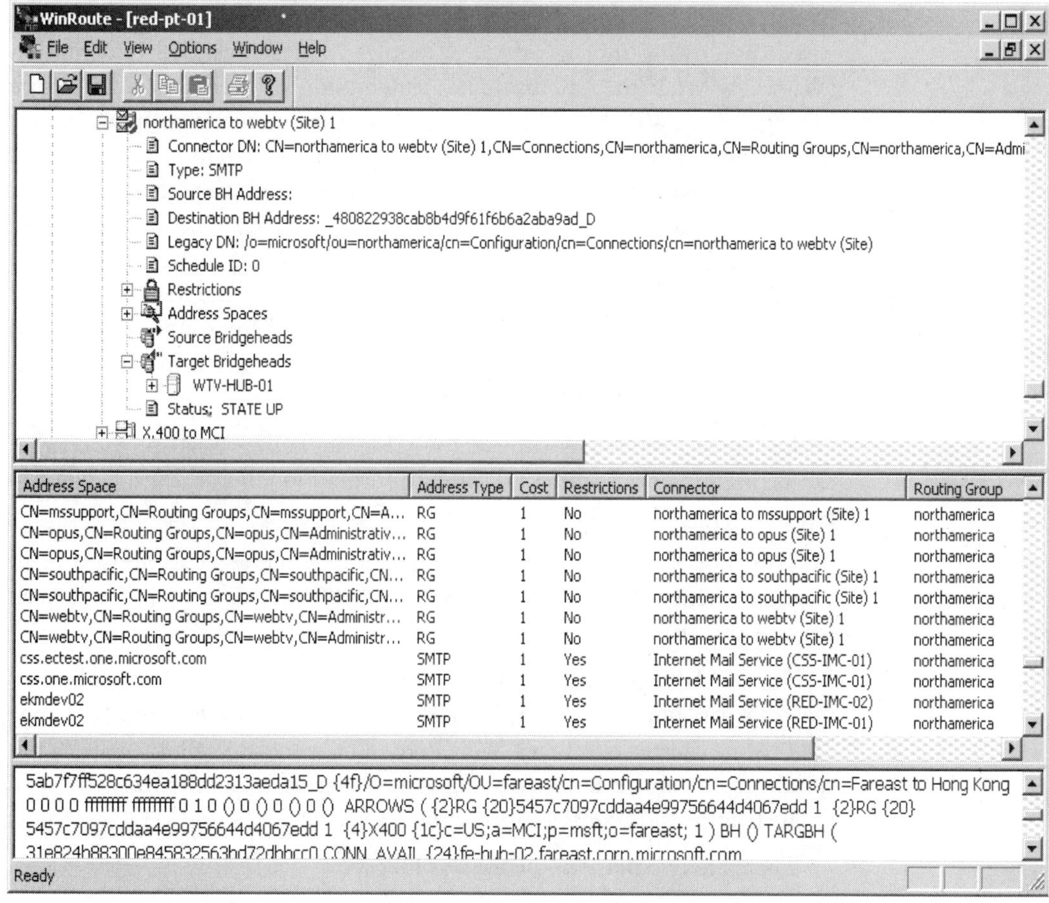

Figure 12.6 *Sorting by address type.*

3. The lower pane is the raw dump of the link state table. These data are used to map against Active Directory in order to show the human-readable data in the top and middle panes.

WinRoute will be an invaluable tool for environments with a large number of routing groups and connectors. One thing to keep in mind, though, is that the costs displayed in the middle pane are not cumulative costs to get to a particular connector; they are just the static cost assigned to the connector during configuration. The routing service uses these data to determine the least-cost path to any given connector at the time of message submission.

12.4 WMI monitoring tool

As part of the Exchange 2000 Resource Kit, Microsoft is delivering a Web-based monitoring tool based on Windows Management Instrumentation (WMI). WMI is the Microsoft implementation of Web-Based Enterprise Management (WBEM). WBEM provides uniform access to management information. This information includes the state of system memory, inventories of currently installed client applications, and other information about client status. WMI technology enables systems, applications, networks, and other managed components to be represented by using the Common Information Model (CIM) designed by the Desktop Management Task Force (DMTF). CIM can model anything in the managed environment regardless of data source location. (This definition comes directly from documentation available from Microsoft Corporation.)

Exchange 2000 Server supports WMI by including WMI providers that can be used to access status and other information about the Exchange system.

This tool is pretty clever actually and it does allow an administrator to view the queue lengths for many Exchange 2000 servers from a single Web page, as shown in Figure 12.7.

The WMI monitoring tool is located on the resource kit in a subdirectory called mailq. Within the readme file, this tool is called the Exchange 2000 Mail Queue Summary Web Page. The associated files in the mailq subdirectory can be used to build a Web page that summarizes the mail queue lengths for a configurable set of mail servers.

There are two parts to the tool, as follows:

1. The Crawler—a Visual BASIC script that is always running on the server used to display the information. This script collects the

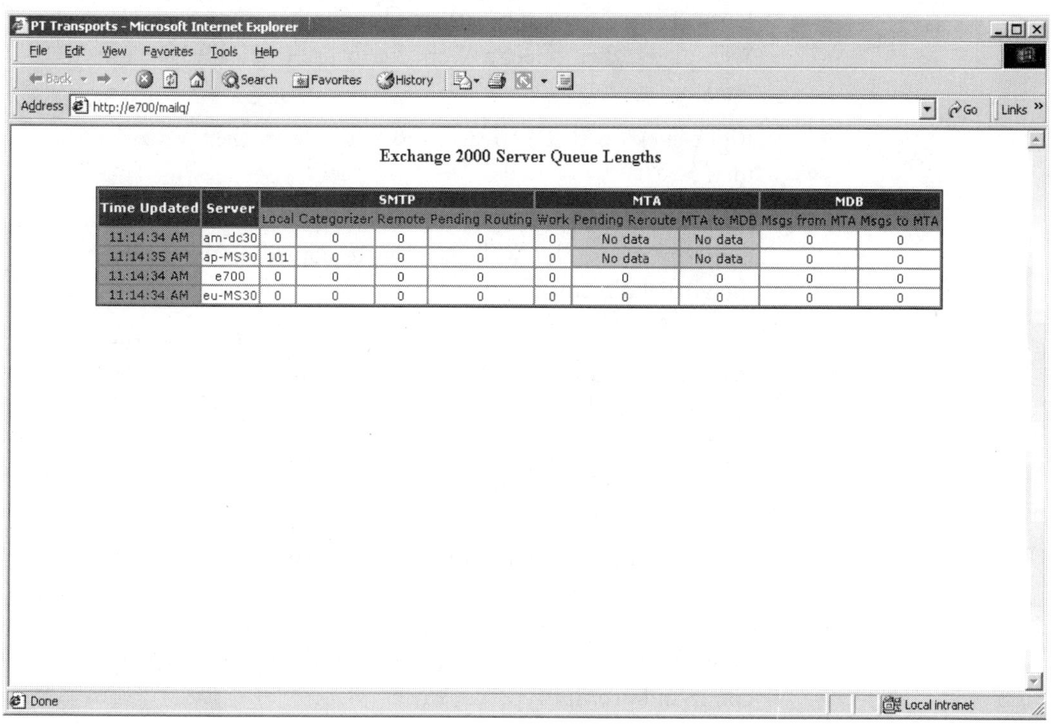

Exchange 2000 Server Queue Lengths

Time Updated	Server	SMTP				MTA			MDB	
		Local	Categorizer	Remote	Pending Routing	Work	Pending Reroute	MTA to MDB	Msgs from MTA	Msgs to MTA
11:14:34 AM	am-dc30	0	0	0	0	0	No data	No data	0	0
11:14:35 AM	ap-MS30	101	0	0	0	0	No data	No data	0	0
11:14:34 AM	e700	0	0	0	0	0	0	0	0	0
11:14:34 AM	eu-MS30	0	0	0	0	0	0	0	0	0

Figure 12.7 *WMI queue viewer tool.*

information from the servers to be monitored and writes that information to an XML file.

2. The Web pages—these are the Web pages that process the file generated by the Crawler and convert it into HTML.

12.4.1 Installation

WMI monitoring tool installation is as follows:

1. Copy the files in the Web subdirectory to the machine that will host the Web pages. To make things easy, copy the files into their own directory. I usually create a directory for the mailq tool called mailq and then create two subdirectories underneath it: web and crawler. So, in my case I usually copy the files into a directory called web. Whatever the name, this is the directory that will be used as the root of the virtual directory for the Web pages. Of course, now we've got to set up IIS to know about the directory.
2. Load the Internet Services Manager administration console.

3. Expand the root node in IIS and select the machine to host the Web pages, then select a Web site to use (typically, Default Web Site).

4. Right-click on the Web site, and select New, then Virtual Directory.

5. Follow the wizard; specify an alias (e.g., Mailq) and specify the directory where the Web pages were copied as the directory for the virtual directory.

6. Copy the files from the Crawler subdirectory to the same machine but a different directory. Again, in my case, I usually copy the Crawler data into a directory called crawler.

7. From the crawler subdirectory, edit the Globals.vbs file and enter the names of all of the servers you want to monitor. And, of course, your DNS will need to be able to resolve the server names in order for this to work. Once you've edited the Globals.vbs file, run go.wsf using CScript and specify the location of the directory of the Web files as the only parameter. If the directory name contains spaces, use double quotes around the name—that is, from a command prompt type `cscript go.wsf "D:\MailQ Web\"`. If the Web files were saved to D:\MailQ Web\, you must include the trailing `\`.

8. Ensuring that the Web server is running, surf to the appropriate URL—that is, http://*<machine name>*/*<alias>*/index.html, where *<machine name>* is the Web server, and *<alias>* is the alias specified when creating the virtual directory in step 5.

12.4.2 Use

Once everything is operational, the Web pages can be viewed by going to the URL created when the virtual directory was set up. The pages show the mail queue lengths in SMTP, X400 and in the store for the servers specified, as we saw in Figure 12.7.

At one point the tool read the servers from the serverlist.xml file in the Web directory. As of release to manufacturing (RTM), there doesn't appear to be such a file and editing the GLOBALS.VBS file works fine. Check the latest version of this tool on the resource kit, as it does appear to be evolving.

Other features include the following:

Sorting columns—data can be sorted by server name, time of data collection, or by any of the queue lengths. Simply click on the column header for the page to resort data.

Warnings—if the number of messages in a given category is above 2,000, the cell is colored red. If the number of messages is between 1,000 and 2,000, the cell will be colored yellow. All other cells will be colored white. This allows an administrator to see at a glance which servers may be having mail-flow problems. The XSL stylesheets can be modified to change this behavior if desired.

Old Data—the leftmost column on the table shows the time data for a given server were gathered. Under normal operation, this should have a white background. If data were not gathered today, then the background will turn beige. This might indicate problems with the

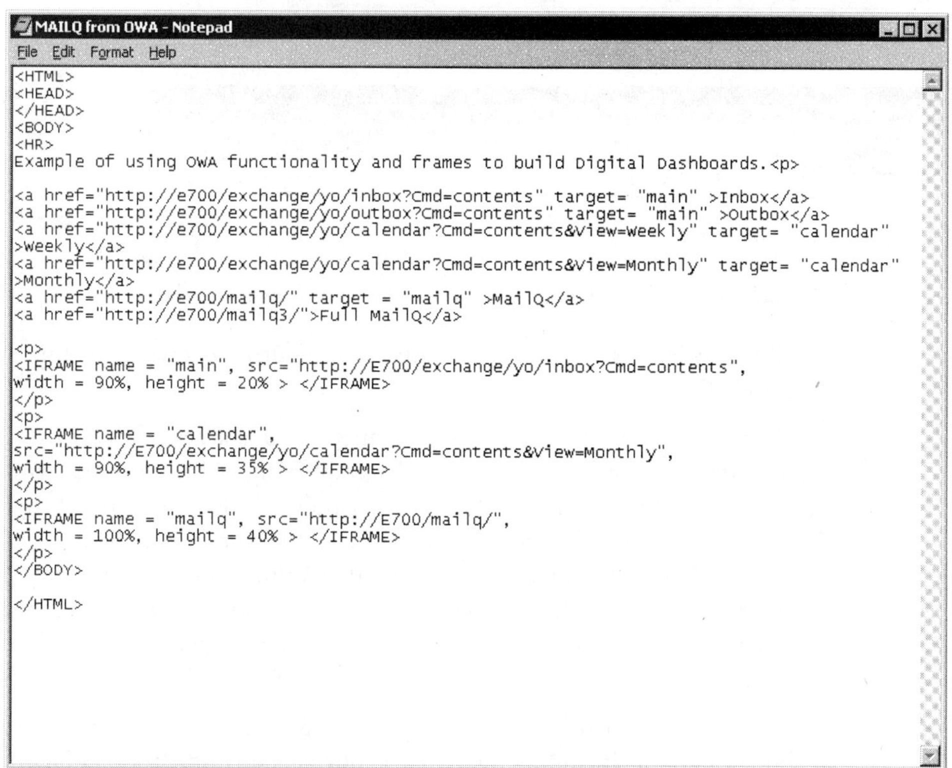

MAILQ from OWA - Notepad

File Edit Format Help

```
<HTML>
<HEAD>
</HEAD>
<BODY>
<HR>
Example of using OWA functionality and frames to build Digital Dashboards.<p>

<a href="http://e700/exchange/yo/inbox?Cmd=contents" target= "main" >Inbox</a>
<a href="http://e700/exchange/yo/outbox?Cmd=contents" target= "main" >Outbox</a>
<a href="http://e700/exchange/yo/calendar?Cmd=contents&View=Weekly" target= "calendar"
>Weekly</a>
<a href="http://e700/exchange/yo/calendar?Cmd=contents&View=Monthly" target= "calendar"
>Monthly</a>
<a href="http://e700/mailq/" target = "mailq" >MailQ</a>
<a href="http://e700/mailq3/">Full MailQ</a>

<p>
<IFRAME name = "main", src="http://E700/exchange/yo/inbox?Cmd=contents",
width = 90%, height = 20% > </IFRAME>
</p>
<p>
<IFRAME name = "calendar",
src="http://E700/exchange/yo/calendar?Cmd=contents&View=Monthly",
width = 90%, height = 35% > </IFRAME>
</p>
<p>
<IFRAME name = "mailq", src="http://E700/mailq/",
width = 100%, height = 40% > </IFRAME>
</p>
</BODY>

</HTML>
```

Figure 12.8 *Simple coding example that combines views.*

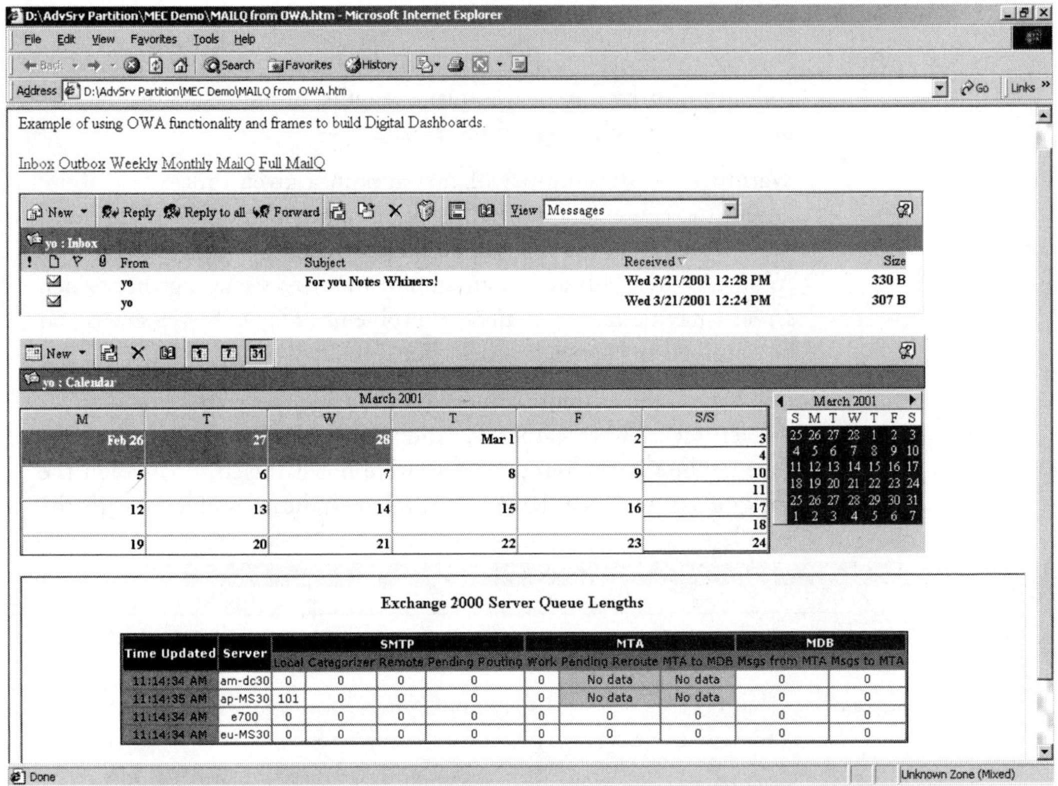

Time Updated	Server	SMTP				MTA			MDB	
		Local	Categorizer	Remote	Pending Routing	Work	Pending Reroute	MTA to MDB	Msgs from MTA	Msgs to MTA
11:14:34 AM	am-dc30	0	0	0	0	0	No data	No data	0	0
11:14:35 AM	ap-MS30	101	0	0	0	0	No data	No data	0	0
11:14:34 AM	e700	0	0	0	0	0	0	0	0	0
11:14:34 AM	eu-MS30	0	0	0	0	0	0	0	0	0

Figure 12.9 *"Digital dashboard" combining monitoring, calendaring, and e-mail.*

Web crawler—is it still running? Is it configured to output to the correct file?

Now, since nearly everything in Exchange 2000 is accessible via URLs, you can do some pretty clever things by combining WMI examples with standard capabilities of the product. For example, wouldn't it be really cool if we could use a Web browser to view our e-mail and monitor the messaging system at the same time? In fact, now that I think about it, wouldn't it be nice to finally quiet the complaints of the Lotus Notes crew, who always poke fun at Exchange for not being able to show the calendar and the inbox at the same time!

Well, it turns out that to do that with Exchange 2000 is so easy almost anybody can do it (including me). Take a look at the sample code in Figure 12.8 and see how easy this all is.

As you can see, there are only about nine lines of real code, and the first six do little more than build a set of menu choices. The next three lines are the heart of the display. In this example (see Figure 12.9), the inbox and calendar of a user called Yo appear first, followed by a display of the mail queue.

This type of access is perfectly feasible and will probably be quite common as VPN access, or other secure access from the Internet to internal systems, becomes more prevalent.

12.5 Protocol logging

With all of the communications between servers and the heavy use of SMTP, having the ability to see the exchange of protocol handshaking between servers is advantageous. Exchange 2000 has the ability to perform protocol logging on a per virtual-server basis.

To enable protocol logging for SMTP, you must first open the property pages of the virtual server, as shown in Figure 12.10, and select Enable logging as well as establishing the log format.

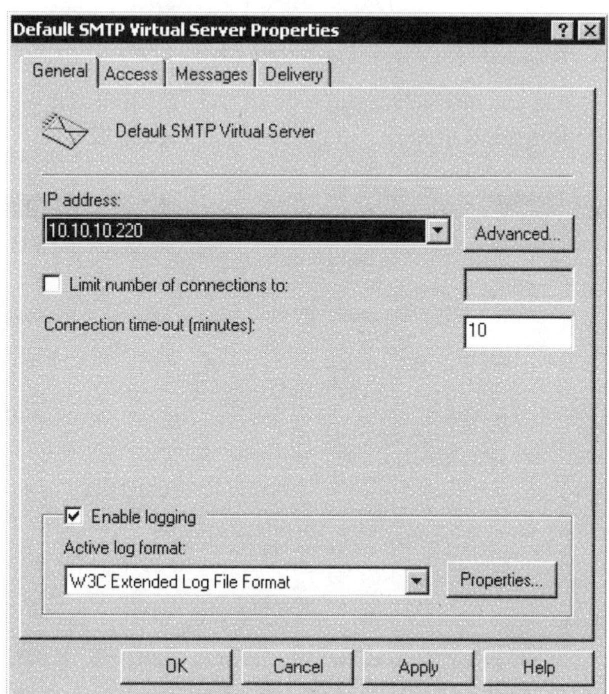

Figure 12.10 *Enabling protocol logging on an SMTP VS.*

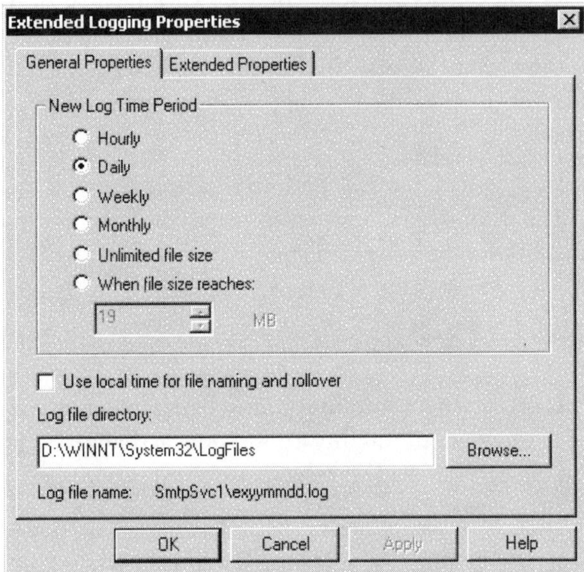

Figure 12.11 *Selecting log rollover criteria.*

Along with enabling logging, you can also define when log files get rolled over. To establish a new log period you must click on the Properties button in Figure 12.10. From there you will be able to select rollover characteristics, as shown in Figure 12.11.

You can also select the type of information that will be logged by using the Extended Properties tab shown in Figure 12.11.

ex010413 - Notepad

File Edit Format Help

```
#Software: Microsoft Internet Information Services 5.0
#Version: 1.0
#Date: 2001-04-13 11:17:24
#Fields: date time cs-username s-sitename s-computername sc-bytes cs-bytes
2001-04-13 11:17:24 e700 SMTPSVC1 E700 45 9
2001-04-13 11:17:24 e700 SMTPSVC1 E700 39 27
2001-04-13 11:17:24 e700 SMTPSVC1 E700 26 24
2001-04-13 11:17:24 e700 SMTPSVC1 E700 130 1130
2001-04-13 11:17:24 e700 SMTPSVC1 E700 67 4
2001-04-13 11:20:22 e700 SMTPSVC1 E700 45 9
2001-04-13 11:20:22 e700 SMTPSVC1 E700 38 26
2001-04-13 11:20:22 e700 SMTPSVC1 E700 31 29
2001-04-13 11:20:22 e700 SMTPSVC1 E700 130 1131
2001-04-13 11:20:22 e700 SMTPSVC1 E700 67 4
2001-04-13 11:20:22 OutboundConnectionResponse SMTPSVC1 E700 118 0
2001-04-13 11:20:22 OutboundConnectionCommand SMTPSVC1 E700 4 0
2001-04-13 11:20:22 OutboundConnectionResponse SMTPSVC1 E700 43 0
2001-04-13 11:20:22 OutboundConnectionResponse SMTPSVC1 E700 20 0
2001-04-13 11:20:22 OutboundConnectionResponse SMTPSVC1 E700 232 0
2001-04-13 11:20:22 OutboundConnectionResponse SMTPSVC1 E700 38 0
2001-04-13 11:20:22 OutboundConnectionCommand SMTPSVC1 E700 12 0
```

Figure 12.12 *SMTP protocol logging (view 1).*

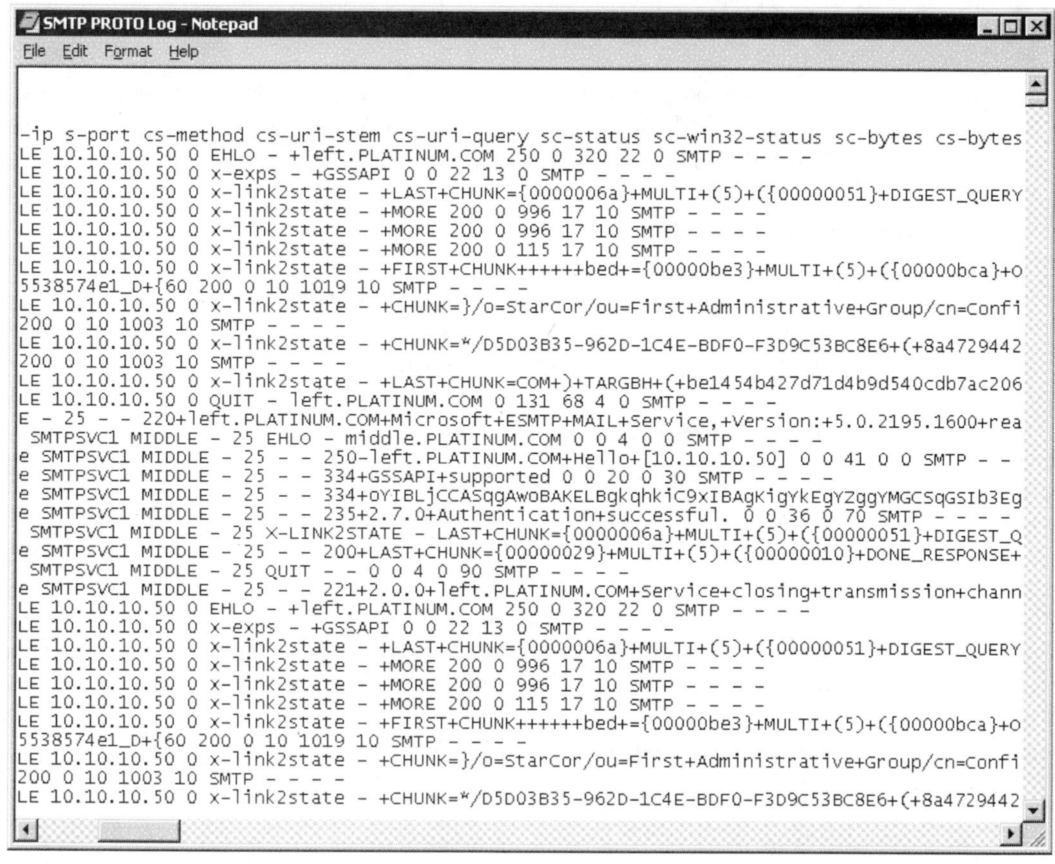

Figure 12.13 *SMTP protocol logging (view 2).*

Once configured, the protocol logging will be written to a file; in the case of Figure 12.11 the file will be `D:\WINNT\System32\LogFiles`. Views of this file can be seen in Figures 12.12 and 12.13.

You can see from Figure 12.13 that Exchange 2000 does, in fact, pass link state information in normal message communications. The handshake begins as follows:

1. An EHLO command is issued.
2. Authentication takes place via the x-exps command.
3. X-link2state follows and this is the command that carries link state updates.

12.6 ArchiveSink

When enabled, ArchiveSink will allow you to view every message entering or exiting Exchange 2000. This includes MAPI and non-MAPI messages. This sink should be used with caution, since it will use up a lot of disk space.

12.6.1 Description

ArchiveSink is a transport sink that basically archives all messages coming in and out of a platinum server. It basically hooks onto two transport events—OnMessageSubmission and OnPostCategorize.

OnMessageSubmission

All messages submitted to the transport via SMTP, the information store, or other sinks will trigger this event. Theoretically this event can be raised only once per message. Hence it can be archived only once. This event is raised before the routing or categorizer events and therefore the recipients will be in the same form as they were upon the original submission of the message, before distribution list expansion, as an example. These are what I refer to as PreCat messages—messages submitted prior to categorization.

OnPostCategorize

This event was designed to capture the message after the categorization. Categorization of a message basically means looking up the recipients and sender in the DS. It is also where the expansion of DLs is handled. Messages could possibly trigger this event one or more times. This case can only happen when messages (already cateogrized) stuck in a queue are reenumerated. When recipients are Internet bound (via entering SMTP addressing directly on the TO: field or via SMTP contacts), Internet message formats administered on the Exchange 2000 server require special content handling. For this case, the categorizer bifurcates or spawns new messages from the original message and moves these recipients into them. These new messages also trigger this event.

12.6.2 Other features

Other features include the following:

1. For debugging purposes, dumps P1 (envelope) recipients in the message
2. By default, ignores archiving of public folder and system messages

Source files are checked into ($TRANSMT)\test\msgcat\catsinks\archivesink. They can also be found in \\tdsrc\xxxxtest\msgcat\catsinks\archivesink.

Setup

Regsvr32 archivesink.dll is used for setup. The following text describes the important archiving control settings.

Archiving controls

When registered, archiving is on by default. It will then archive all messages to the system temp folder. For most Windows 2000 machines, the default location is %windir%\temp.

The following default settings also apply:

- Only OnMessageSubmission (PreCat) messages are archived.
- System messages are NOT archived (e.g., public folder, replication messages, etc.).
- Dump P1 recipients is enabled.

By registry key settings

If registry key settings are present, then more flexibility of control can be achieved. You need to set the following registry keys:

```
[HKEY_LOCAL_MACHINE\Software\Microsoft\Exchange\
ArchiveSink]

"Smtp Inbound"="d:\\ArchiveSink\\Smtp Inbound"

"Mapi OutBound"="d:\\ArchiveSink\\Mapi Outbound"

"Enable Smtp Inbound"=dword:00000001

"Enable Mapi Outbound"=dword:00000001

"Enable PreCat"=dword:00000001

"Enable PostCat"=dword:00000000

"Dump P1"=dword:00000001
```

With these keys, you can turn on/off archiving on SMTP inbound or MAPI outbound or both.

Note: Any registry key setting will override all default settings.

Caveats

UNC paths are not supported—Create File fails.

Registry settings changed on the fly are not picked up—restart of IISAdmin service will cause the changes to take effect.

If all these registry keys is absent, archiving is, by default, at %windir%\temp.

If archival of system messages are required, add this key also—Archive System Messages, which is a dword registry value, and set it to 1.

12.7 Performance monitor counters

Microsoft has incorporated performance counters for nearly every element of each component in Exchange 2000. Obviously your environment may require monitoring counters different from the ones we'll show here; however, if using Perfmon is new to you, the following text will give you a good starting point.

Figure 12.14 is a screen shot from Performance Monitor that shows most of the counters we'll discuss regarding message transfer.

12.7.1 Transfer service Perfmon counters

The following counters, available in Performance Monitor, can help you analyze the performance of your transfer service. There are many more counters available, but the ones that follow represent the core counters you should monitor on your system(s) from a transport perspective.

Information Store Driver

Current messages from MSExchangeMTA

Current message to MSExchangeMTA

MSExchangeMTA

Work Queue Length

MSExchangeMTA Connections, PendingRerouteQ

Queue Length

Process

% Processor Time

SMTP Server

Categorizer Queue Length

Local Queue Length

Local Retry Queue Length

Messages Currently Undeliverable

Messages Pending Routing

Messages Received/sec

Messages Sent/sec

Remote Queue Length

Remote Retry Queue Length

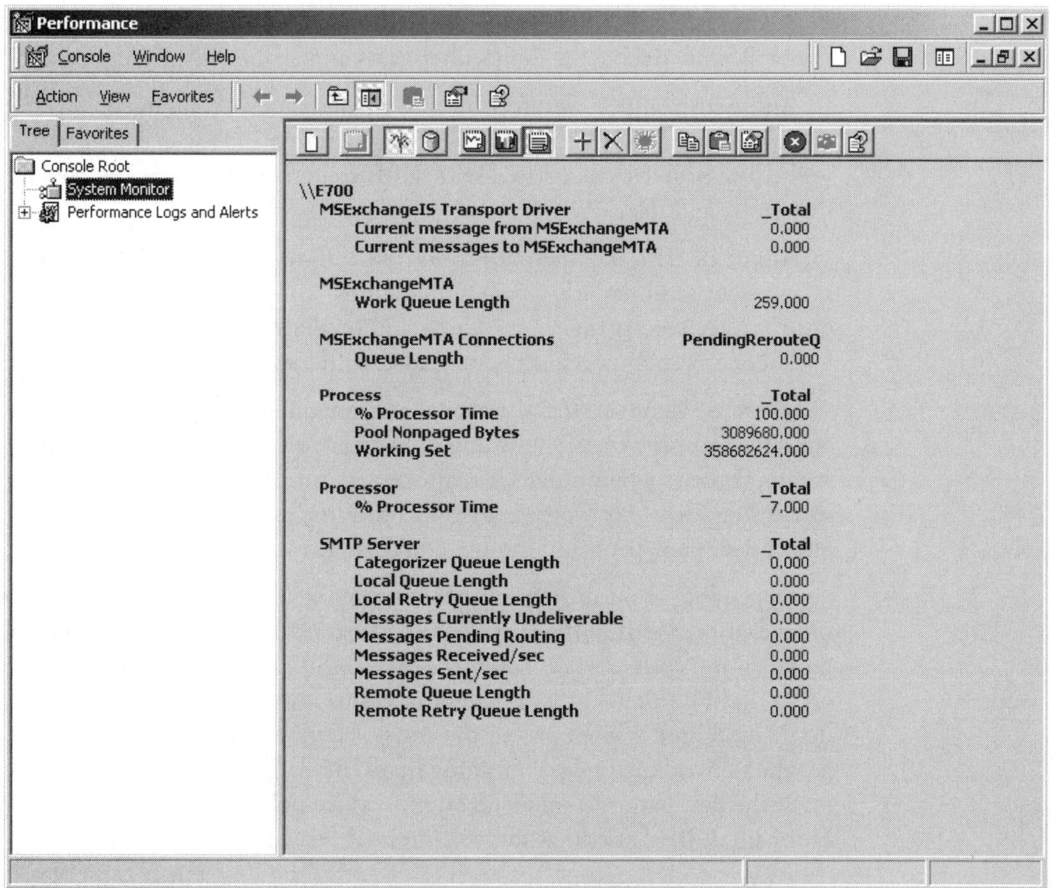

Figure 12.14 *Perfmon counters.*

12.8 Unsolicited Bulk E-mail (UBE)

The following information was gathered from various people at Microsoft when discussing what their direction and thoughts were in terms of spam or UBE protection. Some of the capabilities involve the messaging service directly, while others involve mechanisms associated with DNS. Some of the protective measures have been discussed, from a setup standpoint, in earlier chapters of this book.

There is no method that can insure 100 percent UBE protection. A reliable solution involves using authenticated SMTP, which is available with Exchange 5.5. Unfortunately, only a few other mail servers support this extension. Requiring this for every incoming connection would damage interoperability with other servers and clients.

Another critical point is logging. Antispam/antirelay local log information will allow tracing the events afterwards and enable further actions.

Antispam features are probably the single biggest requirement for ISP accounts. Nevertheless, they are a strong requirement for corporations as well. Core problems associated with UBE stem from the very low cost on the sender and the real costs on the recipients and their hosts.

Although UBE is sometimes compared with traditional bulk mail, there is an essential difference: Spam shifts almost all the costs of the message onto the recipients, their mail hosts, and/or the relay hosts. The Internet backbone is also unnecessarily overloaded with lots of messages.

There are some social and personal costs involved with UBE as well. The constant fear of irreversibly getting one's name on a mailing list has caused many people to avoid using UBE altogether. Similarly, the act of having to sort through cleverly worded UBE in order to find actual personal e-mail has caused many people not to use e-mail to its fullest potential.

Depending upon their specific business model, Internet mail hosts handle the costs of UBE differently. If the destination host is an Internet service provider, the costs of UBE are borne by the ISP's users. This cost is passed on to the ISP's users through higher prices or lower levels of service. If the destination host is an employer, the costs of UBE are often taken out of the general networking budget, meaning that UBE causes lower company profits. If the destination is someone offering a free public mail service (such as Hotmail), UBE causes that someone to offer less service to subscribers.

UBE sent over the Internet backbone causes delays for all Internet users. Further, because most UBE senders use mailing lists that have outdated addresses on them, many messages are rejected (bounced), causing the intended destination host to send a return response (NDR), which wastes more bandwidth.

Massive traffic directed toward one host might lead to denial of service. An attempt to do a mass mailing causes the queues to fill up and there is processing overhead. Most recipients usually receive e-mail from two kinds of senders: other people and mailing list agents. A mailing list agent (MLA) is a software program that acts like a recipient but does special processing upon receiving e-mail: It resends the e-mail to a list of recipients. Hence an MLA is a special form of e-mail relay. Most MLAs are controlled by people, but some are completely automatic and involve no human intervention or decision making. Because agents are sending mail to a lot of recipients in an automatic mode, a high risk of spreading UBE is involved.

Mail relaying is one of the biggest problems, since you don't have to authenticate when you submit mail to a server. This allows users to inject junk using any SMTP server. RFC 821, which defines the Simple Mail Transport Protocol, does not include verification of the authenticity of the FROM address in a mail message. This means that unscrupulous Internet users can create messages and impersonate, or spoof, the FROM address. Not only can they misrepresent themselves to the recipient who actually gets the mail, they can also dupe unsuspecting SMTP servers into sending mail for them.

Mail relaying done through a server can lead to blackholing. If an ISP gets a ton of junk from your server, as in the case of a spammer setting up a loop where 1,000,000 mail messages get directed through your system, chances are that the attacked ISP will set its servers' filters so that none of the mail from the latter ISP gets through, hurting legitimate users.

What we see today is only the tip of the iceberg. Most companies are afraid to advertise by means of UBE because of the bad name they would get. But the situation is likely to change in the near future, with the big names coming into e-business. While today you get only junk advertisements (XXX, FREE MONEY!!), you'll soon start getting UBE that some people might find useful (e.g., sales announcements at Sears, huge discounts for new Jaguars). We might even see voluntary content labeling coming on the scene.

Most of the spam today comes in bulk, the same message addressed to millions of recipients. New spamming techniques allow personalized pollution (Dear John Doe), making it even harder for automated systems to distinguish between legit and junk mail.

The key to a successful UBE control policy is a complete set of server events. Exchange 2000 contains a complete Event Model that can be used for UBE control. There are a few UBE-related controls that can be set on SMTP virtual servers, as discussed in the following text. However, taking advantage of the event model to make your environment bullet-proof will involve writing some code.

12.8.1 Relay control

An administrator can specify a list of incoming remote IP address/mask pairs that are allowed (or denied) relay capability. Within this list, actual domain names can also be specified. If domain names are specified, a reverse DNS lookup is performed on each incoming connection, and, if the resolved domain name appears on the configured domain name list, the connection is allowed (or denied if so configured) relay capability.

Relay must be enabled for the local host, hosts belonging to the same domain, and authenticated sessions. The default for new installed servers is to have the relay switch disabled.

12.8.2 Authenticated SMTP

Functionality related to authentication of users submitting mail was added to the Exchange IMS for Exchange 5.5 in order to satisfy customer requirements for a large account. This functionality is propagated into the new architecture of Exchange 2000, and Microsoft is reexamining what it's doing with respect to authentication to make sure it has the best possible story.

Exchange 2000's SMTP service follows the SMTP AUTH RFC, which provides the framework for verifying the identity of the submitting user. That document defines an SMTP service extension (ESMTP) whereby an SMTP client may indicate an authentication to the server, perform an authentication protocol exchange, and optionally negotiate a security layer for subsequent protocol interactions. The new verb added to SMTP is AUTH—syntax: AUTH mechanism (initial-response). This draft has changed since the 5.5 implementation of it, adding an AUTH keyword to the MAIL FROM: command, which carries the authenticated user's identity along with the message. This optional AUTH parameter allows cooperating agents in a trusted environment to communicate the authentication of individual messages. A server may treat expansion of a mailing list as a new submission, setting the AUTH parameter to the mailing list address. Microsoft may add this, both for interoperability with other vendors and as a middle ground between rejecting nonauthenticated mail and doing no authentication at all.

Note: The MS clients—Outlook 98/2000, Outlook Express—need to support the same authentication mechanism as the server. The same holds true for third-party clients such as Eudora. At this time they do not.

12.8.3 Blackhole lists

A blackhole list can be used in the configuration of somebody's own network or mail relay toward the goal of limiting theft of resources by spammers. This step must not be taken lightly—a blackhole creates intentional loss of connectivity for anyone who chooses to use it. A possible way of approaching this would be to provide some sort of a validating mechanism for the entries, filtering the information at synchronization time.

To implement a protection mechanism based on such a list, several approaches are possible: use one of the publicly maintained, real-time blackhole lists—for example, the list maintained by MAPS, LLC (see http://maps.vix.com/). Such a list can be interrogated in disconnected mode (inquiry—a DNS lookup is performed against the list) or connected mode (transfer—the copy is maintained in sync with the original through DNS specific mechanisms). You can optionally maintain your own list, based on information you acquire from trusted sources (partners, etc.) or your own experience (previous spamming attacks).

Blackhole list capability is not part of Exchange 2000 out of the box, but it could be provided via a third party making use of the Event Service. So for, nobody has done this that I know of.

12.8.4 Message filtering

A model can be built to assess the probability that a message is really spam. Typically message systems use a limited set of features that provide a generic coverage of UBE. The most common features are subject-field parsing for a few phrases ("FREE MONEY," "XXX"), domain information (spam usually originates in domains whose names contain certain tokens—"sexy*.com"), and addressing mode (coming through a mailing list, on a TO: line with multiple recipients).

Probabilities allow for flexible, decision-theory filtering. This method qualifies a message as being either legit or spam with an associated probability. The filter can be fine-tuned by the administrator to reflect the required level of tolerance. For instance, let's say that you want all messages that are identified as being spam with a probability less than 90 percent to be deferred to another designated authority (person) for further analysis.

Performance is a critical issue. For sites with heavy traffic, processing overhead involved with message filtering could be too big a burden. Fancier processing can be deferred to the client side.

The rejected message is sent back together with a note explaining the reason for the action taken (Your message contains the token "FREE TICKETS," which caused our automated spam-protection mechanism to interpreted it as unsolicited commercial e-mail). If the expediter of the message was unfairly labeled as a spammer and his or her mail was legit, he or she can try resending the message after removing or altering the discriminating structure or the postmaster can be contacted to clarify the situation. Microsoft does provide message filtering as part of the product. So, for example, you can block messages "FROM:" a list of users.

12.8.5 Message marking

The problem you might encounter when you delete mail is that if you have mail that is mistakenly deleted, nobody really knows that it hasn't been delivered and then you have people questioning the reliability of the mail server. Another way of approaching suspected commercial messages is to label them on the server. The client software can handle messages afterwards based on this labeling. There is nothing currently in IMAP/POP that supports this, however.

If a message is determined potentially to be UBE, a simple solution is to tag the subject line with a predetermined construction (e.g., <SUSPECTED UBE>). The client can set rules afterwards to handle these messages in a way most appropriate to the way they work. Tagging a message is less intrusive than deleting the message.

Many companies wish to have some text indicating that mail received from the Internet is marked as a nontrusted source. Microsoft can differentiate between internal- and external-originated mail. The mark itself is subject to customizations. This information can be placed in the subject field, which makes it easier for the mail client to convey the information to the user, or it can be placed in the envelope and written as a message property. This can be accomplished via the Exchange 2000 event model.

Many companies wish to attach disclaimers to outgoing mail. Requirements are likely to vary widely here, depending on how the disclaimer is to be added to the message. Microsoft provides a sample of this at the MEC Web site, and this sample also makes use of the Exchange 2000 event model.

12.8.6 Throttling

Throttling means controlling different parameters associated with network activity and its volume. It consists of a set of tools that allow traffic control, traffic monitoring, and streamlining and regulating the server message flow.

For incoming traffic it's useful to keep track of the quantity of mail and the number of recipients a given SMTP FROM address is sending. It could, in fact, be either a denial of service attack or a broad UBE attack. Limiting the size of a message that can be accepted and the number of recipients per message can control these types of attacks. These throttling settings are set on the SMTP virtual server in Exchange 2000.

12.9 Summary

In this chapter, I've outlined some of the most useful tools that you can use to monitor your Exchange 2000 environment. While rudimentary, these tools can be invaluable. You should also consider using third-party monitoring tools.

Appendix: Lists of Events Generated by the ADC

Table A.1 provides a list of the sources, event IDs, symbolic names, and severity of events that can be generated by the ADC.

Table A.1 *List of ADC Event IDs and Symbolic Names*

Event	Symbolic Name	Severity
1	SYNCHRO_CATEGORY	
2	ACCMAN_CATEGORY	
3	AMA_CATEGORY	
4	SERVICE_CATEGORY	
5	LDAP_CATEGORY	
6	ADDRESS_LIST_CATEGORY	
8000	LRALOG_MSG	Informational
8001	MSG_SERVICE_STARTED	Informational
8002	MSG_SERVICE_STOPPED	Informational
8003	MSG_SERVICE_STARTING	Informational
8004	MSG_SERVICE_STOPPING	Informational
8005	MSG_SERVICE_BADREQUEST	Warning
8006	MSG_LDAP_OPENSESSION	Informational
8007	MSG_LDAP_CLOSESESSION	Informational
8008	MSG_LDAP_BIND	Informational
8009	MSG_LDAP_BIND_NULL	Informational
8010	MSG_LDAP_SEARCHWITHFILTER	Informational

Table A.1 *List of ADC Event IDs and Symbolic Names (continued)*

Event	Symbolic Name	Severity
8011	MSG_LDAP_SEARCHWITHFILTER_ATTR	Informational
8012	MSG_LDAP_SEARCH_RESULT	Informational
8013	MSG_LDAP_ADD	Informational
8014	MSG_LDAP_ADD_ATTR	Informational
8015	MSG_LDAP_MODIFY	Informational
8016	MSG_LDAP_MODIFY_ATTR	Informational
8017	MSG_LDAP_DELETE	Informational
8018	MSG_LDAP_ABANDON	Informational
8019	MSG_LDAP_NOTIFY_SEARCH	Informational
8020	MSG_LDAP_SEARCHWITHFILTER_ERROR	Warning
8021	MSG_LDAP_ADD_ERROR	Error
8022	MSG_LDAP_MODIFY_ERROR	Error
8023	MSG_LDAP_DELETE_ERROR	Error
8024	MSG_LDAP_INITPAGE_ERROR	Error
8025	MSG_LDAP_GETNEXTPAGE_ERROR	Warning
8026	MSG_LDAP_BIND_ERROR	Error
8027	MSG_LDAP_GC_BIND_ERROR	Error
8028	MSG_LDAP_MODRDN_ERROR	Error
8029	MSG_LDAP_REFERRAL_ERROR	Error
8030	MSG_LDAP_EXTENDED_ERROR	Error
8031	MSG_LDAP_OPENSESSION_ERROR	Warning
8032	MSG_LDAP_SESSION_ERROR	Error
8033	MSG_LDAP_SEARCH_ERROR	Warning
8034	MSG_LDAP_COMPARE_ERROR	Error
8035	MSG_SYNCHRO_MODIFYENTRY	Informational
8036	MSG_SYNCHRO_DELETEDIRSEARCH	Informational
8037	MSG_SYNCHRO_DELETEENTRY	Informational

Table A.1 *List of ADC Event IDs and Symbolic Names (continued)*

Event	Symbolic Name	Severity
8038	MSG_SYNCHRO_ADDENTRY	Informational
8039	MSG_SYNCHRO_ENTRY_ATTRVALS	Informational
8040	MSG_SYNCHRO_PROXYRPC_ERROR	Warning
8041	MSG_SYNCHRO_PROXYSOMEFAILED	Warning
8042	MSG_SYNCHRO_UPDATEDIRSEARCH	Informational
8043	MSG_SYNCHRO_DIRSEARCH_ATTRS	Informational
8044	MSG_SYNCHRO_DIRSEARCH_DNLIST	Informational
8045	MSG_SYNCHRO_UPDATETOMBENTRY	Informational
8046	MSG_SYNCHRO_UPDATEEXISTENTRY	Informational
8047	MSG_SYNCHRO_DELETEENTRIES	Informational
8048	MSG_SYNCHRO_NONTOMBSTONEDELETE	Informational
8049	MSG_SYNCHRO_TOMBSTONEDELETE	Informational
8050	MSG_SYNCHRO_ENTRYNOTEXIST	Informational
8051	MSG_SYNCHRO_ENTRYEXISTS	Informational
8052	MSG_SYNCHRO_NODELETEENTRIES	Informational
8053	MSG_SYNCHRO_IMPORTATTRS	Informational
8054	MSG_LDAP_UNBIND_ERROR	Error
8055	MSG_SYNCHRO_NOREPLICATIONAGENTDN	Error
8056	MSG_SYNCHRO_REPLICATESTART	Informational
8057	MSG_SYNCHRO_REPLICATESTOP	Informational
8058	MSG_SYNCHRO_REPLICATEABORTED	Informational
8059	MSG_SYNCHRO_SYNCREMTOLOCAL	Informational
8060	MSG_SYNCHRO_SYNCLOCALTOREM	Informational
8061	MSG_DSCONFIG_READREPLICATIONINFO	Informational
8062	MSG_DSCONFIG_OPENSESSION_FAIL	Error
8063	MSG_DSCONFIG_READ_ROOT_FAIL	Error
8064	MSG_DSCONFIG_READ_OBJECT_FAIL	Error

Table A.1 *List of ADC Event IDs and Symbolic Names (continued)*

Event	Symbolic Name	Severity
8065	MSG_DSCONFIG_SEARCH_OBJECT_FAIL	Error
8066	MSG_DSCONFIG_NO_NAMESPACES	Informational
8067	MSG_DSCONFIG_NAMESPACEINFO	Informational
8068	MSG_DSCONFIG_NEW_NAMESPACE	Informational
8069	MSG_DSCONFIG_DELETED_NAMESPACE	Informational
8070	MSG_DSCONFIG_NAMESPACE_ERROR	Warning
8071	MSG_DSCONFIG_SETREMOTELASTUSN	Informational
8072	MSG_DSCONFIG_SETLOCALLASTUSN	Informational
8073	MSG_ACCMAN_INVALIDCOMPUTER	Error
8074	MSG_ACCMAN_ADDUSERLOCALOK	Informational
8075	MSG_ACCMAN_ADDUSERREMOK	Informational
8076	MSG_ACCMAN_LOOKUPSIDERR	Error
8077	MSG_ACCMAN_ADDUSERLOCAL_ERROR	Error
8078	MSG_ACCMAN_ADDUSERREM_ERROR	Error
8079	MSG_ACCMAN_DELACCINVALIDSID	Error
8080	MSG_ACCMAN_DELUSERLOCALOK	Informational
8081	MSG_ACCMAN_DELUSERREMOK	Informational
8082	MSG_ACCMAN_DELUSERLOCAL_ERROR	Error
8083	MSG_ACCMAN_DELUSERREM_ERROR	Error
8084	MSG_AMA_MAPTABLE_ERROR	Error
8085	MSG_AMA_STARTAMAOK	Informational
8086	MSG_AMA_STOPAMA	Informational
8087	MSG_AMA_LOCALTOREMATTRMAX	Informational
8088	MSG_AMA_LOCALTOREMATTR	Informational
8089	MSG_AMA_REMTOLOCALATTRMAX	Informational
8090	MSG_AMA_REMTOLOCALATTR	Informational
8091	MSG_AMA_REMTOLOCALOBJ	Informational

Table A.1 *List of ADC Event IDs and Symbolic Names (continued)*

Event	Symbolic Name	Severity
8092	MSG_AMA_LOCALTOREMOBJ	Informational
8093	MSG_AMA_OBJECTNOTFOUND	Informational
8094	MSG_AMA_DESTOBJNOTFOUND	Informational
8095	MSG_AMA_OBJNOATTRS	Informational
8096	MSG_AMA_ATTRFILEEXCEPTION	Error
8097	MSG_AMA_CREATEATTR_ERROR	Error
8098	MSG_AMA_CREATEOBJ_ERROR	Error
8099	MSG_AMA_NOLOCALTREE	Informational
8100	MSG_AMA_NOOBJECTCLASS	Informational
8101	MSG_AMA_NOREMTREE	Informational
8102	MSG_AMA_ATTRNOTFOUND	Informational
8103	MSG_SERVICE_INSTALLED	Informational
8104	MSG_SERVICE_REMOVED	Informational
8105	MSG_SERVICE_NOTREMOVED	Error
8106	MSG_SERVICE_CTRLHANDLERNOTINSTALLED	Error
8107	MSG_SERVICE_CREATESRVCFAIL	Error
8108	MSG_SERVICE_FAILEDINIT	Error
8109	MSG_SYNCHRO_IMPORTFAILURE	Error
8110	MSG_DSCONFIG_SETREMLASTUPDATETIME	Informational
8111	MSG_DSCONFIG_SETLOCLASTUPDATETIME	Informational
8112	MSG_DSCONFIG_UNKNOWN_AUTH_PACKAGE	Error
8113	MSG_DSCONFIG_DYNAMIC_LOAD_DLL_ERROR	Error
8114	MSG_DSCONFIG_DYNAMIC_ENTRY_POINT_ERROR	Error
8115	MSG_DSCONFIG_NT_API_ERROR	Error
8116	MSG_DSCONFIG_SYNCNOW	Informational
8117	MSG_SYNCHRO_BADIMPORTCONTAINER	Error
8118	MSG_SYNCHRO_BADEXPORTCONTAINER	Error

Table A.1 *List of ADC Event IDs and Symbolic Names (continued)*

Event	Symbolic Name	Severity
8119	MSG_AMA_INVALIDATTR	Warning
8120	MSG_AMA_INVALIDCONVERSION	Warning
8121	MSG_SYNCHRO_MISSINGMUSTCONTAIN	Warning
8122	MSG_SYNCHRO_INVALIDATTRIBS	Warning
8123	MSG_SYNCHRO_DELETINGMUSTCONTAIN	Warning
8124	MSG_SYNCHRO_BAD_CONFIG	Error
8125	MSG_ALDG_ADDRESS_LIST_NEW	Informational
8126	MSG_ALDG_ADDRESS_LIST_MODIFY	Informational
8127	MSG_ALDG_ADDRESS_LIST_DELETE	Informational
8128	MSG_ALDG_CHANGED_OBJECT	Informational
8129	MSG_ALDG_EVAL_OBJECT	Informational
8130	MSG_ALDG_ADD_TO_OBJECT	Informational
8131	MSG_ALDG_REMOVE_FROM_OBJECT	Informational
8132	MSG_ALDG_CALC_ABORTED	Informational
8133	MSG_ALDG_CALC_COMPLETE	Informational
8134	MSG_ALDG_Q_REQUEST	Informational
8135	MSG_ALDG_NO_RULE	Informational
8136	MSG_ALDG_CRUDE_LOG_FOR_NOW	Informational
8137	MSG_SYNCHRO_BAD_CA_VERSION	Error
8138	MSG_SERVER_UNAVAILABLE	Warning
8139	MSG_SYNCHRO_STALE_TIMESTAMP	Warning
8140	MSG_SYNCHRO_DELAYING_GROUP	Informational
8141	MSG_SYNCHRO_NO_MUTEX	Error
8142	MSG_SERVICE_UNHANDLED_EXCEPTION	Error
8143	MSG_CA_UNHANDLED_EXCEPTION	Error
8144	MSG_SERVICE_MEM_EXCEPTION	Error
8145	MSG_SERVICE_UNHANDLED_EXCEPTION_DETAILS	Error

Table A.1 *List of ADC Event IDs and Symbolic Names (continued)*

Event	Symbolic Name	Severity
8146	MSG_SYNCHRO_ERROR_EXCEPTION	Error
8147	MSG_LDAP_MODRDN	Informational
8148	MSG_SYNCHRO_SUMMARY_STATISTICS	Informational
8149	MSG_AD_SERVICE_DISABLED	Informational
8150	MSG_AD_SERVICE_NO_THREADS	Informational
8151	MSG_AD_SERVICE_NO_CONFIG	Warning
8152	MSG_AD_SERVICE_NO_SERVICES	Informational
8153	MSG_AD_THREAD_UNREC_ERROR	Error
8154	MSG_AD_THREAD_RESTART_FAILED	Error
8155	MSG_AD_THREAD_TERMINATED	Informational
8156	MSG_AD_THREAD_STARTING	Informational
8157	MSG_AD_THREAD_WAITING_SCHED	Informational
8158	MSG_AD_THREAD_RUNNING_SERVICE	Informational
8159	MSG_AD_THREAD_CHECK_SCHED	Informational
8160	MSG_ALDG_NO_CHANGE_REQ	Informational
8161	MSG_ALDG_EXCEPTION_WHILE_PROCESSING	Error
8162	MSG_ALDG_THREAD_WAITING_NEXT_TRAN	Informational
8163	MSG_ALDG_THREAD_NEXT_TRAN	Informational
8164	MSG_ALDG_THREAD_IDLE_SHUTDOWN	Informational
8165	MSG_ALDG_EXCEPTION_AL	Error
8166	MSG_ALDG_FAILED_TO_MODIFY	Warning
8167	MSG_ALDG_MODIFIED_USER	Informational
8168	MSG_ALDG_FAILED_TO_MODIFY_USER	Warning
8169	MSG_ALDG_GOT_ALL_UG_CHANGES	Informational
8170	MSG_ALDG_GOT_ALL_AL_CHANGES	Informational
8171	MSG_ALDG_AL_CHANGE_SKIPPED	Informational
8172	MSG_ALDG_CEVT_CYCLE_FAIL	Error

Table A.1 *List of ADC Event IDs and Symbolic Names (continued)*

Event	Symbolic Name	Severity
8173	MSG_ALDG_SVC_CHANGES	Error
8174	MSG_ALDG_AL_CHANGE	Informational
8175	MSG_ALDG_UG_CHANGE	Informational
8176	MSG_AD_SERVICE_SHUTDOWN	Informational
8177	MSG_ACCMAN_LOGON_FAILURE	Warning
8178	MSG_SYNCHRO_TARGET_SCHEMA_INVALID	Error
8179	MSG_SYNCHRO_DELETION_FILE_OPENFAILED	Warning
8180	MSG_START_SYNC_WAITING_PERIOD	Informational
8181	MSG_RESUME_SYNC_WAITING_PERIOD	Informational
8182	MSG_SYNCHRO_INVALID_LINK	Warning
8183	MSG_SYNCHRO_IMPORTFAILURE_SECOND	Error
8184	MSG_SYNCHRO_PASSWORD_EXPIRED	Informational
8185	MSG_SYNCHRO_PASSWORD_SHORTAGE	Warning
8186	MSG_SYNCHRO_PASSWORD_SET	Informational
8187	MSG_SYNCHRO_PASSWORD_LSA_READ_ERROR	Error
8188	MSG_SYNCHRO_PASSWORD_LSA_WRITE_ERROR	Error
8189	MSG_ADCI_START	Informational
8190	MSG_ADCI_STOP	Informational
8191	MSG_ADCI_BINDINGS	Informational
8192	MSG_ADCI_LISTEN_FAIL	Error
8193	MSG_ADCI_EPREG_FAIL	Error
8194	MSG_ADCI_USEALL_FAIL	Error
8195	MSG_ADCI_REGAUTH_FAIL	Error
8196	MSG_ADCI_REGIF_FAIL	Error
8197	MSG_SYNCHRO_GC_OPEN_FAIL	Informational
8198	MSG_SYNCHRO_GC_OPEN_SUCCESS	Informational
8199	MSG_SYNCHRO_GC_DEMOTED	Warning

Table A.1 *List of ADC Event IDs and Symbolic Names (continued)*

Event	Symbolic Name	Severity
8200	MSG_SYNCHRO_GC_UNSUPPORTED_AUTH	Warning
8201	MSG_SYNCHRO_DSBIND_FAILED	Warning
8202	MSG_ADCI_START_FAIL	Error
8203	MSG_ADCI_STOP_FAIL	Error
8204	MSG_SYNCHRO_STORE_DELETION_FAILED	Warning
8205	MSG_AMA_IMPORTRULES_ERROR	Error
8206	MSG_SYNCHRO_LSA_NO_PASSWORD	Error
8207	MSG_SYNCHRO_NO_DEL_FILE	Error
8208	MSG_SYNCHRO_FAILED_LOG_DISABLE	Error
8209	MSG_SYNCHRO_DISABLE_OBJECT	Informational
8210	MSG_SYNCHRO_DISABLE_FAIL	Error
8211	MSG_SYNCHRO_DISABLE_EX_OBJECT	Informational
8212	MSG_SYNCHRO_FAILED_LOG_EX_DISABLE	Error
8213	MSG_SYNCHRO_CANNOT_FIND_DC_FOR_DOMAIN	Error
8214	MSG_AD_SERVICE_NO_DOMAIN_SPECIFIED	Error
8215	MSG_AD_SERVICE_RUNNING_DOMAIN_CHECK_FSMO	Informational
8216	MSG_AD_SERVICE_COMPLETE_DOMAIN_CHECK_FSMO	Informational
8217	MSG_AD_SERVICE_ADDING_NEW_DOMAIN_SERVICE	Informational
8218	MSG_AD_SERVICE_SUCCESSFUL_NEW_DOMAIN_SERVICE	Informational
8219	MSG_AD_SERVICE_FAILED_NEW_DOMAIN_SERVICE	Error
8220	MSG_AD_SERVICE_DELETING_SERVICE	Informational
8221	MSG_AD_SERVICE_SUCCESSFUL_DELETE_SERVICE	Informational
8222	MSG_AD_SERVICE_FAILED_DELETE_SERVICE	Error
8223	MSG_SYNCHRO_CONFLICTING_ATTRIBUTE	Warning
8224	MSG_SYNCHRO_CONFLICTING_ATTRIBUTE_REPLICATION_FAILED	Error
8225	MSG_SYNCHRO_BEGIN_UNMERGED_CLEANUP	Informational
8226	MSG_SYNCHRO_FINISH_UNMERGED_CLEANUP	Informational

Table A.1 *List of ADC Event IDs and Symbolic Names (continued)*

Event	Symbolic Name	Severity
8227	MSG_ADCI_ACCESS_DENIED	Warning
8228	MSG_ADCI_ACCESS_GRANTED	Informational
8229	MSG_ALDG_UNSUPPORTED_POLICY_GROUP	Error
8230	MSG_ALDG_EXTERNAL_PROVIDER_EXCEPTION	Error
8231	MSG_ALDG_EXPROV_PERM_FAILURE	Error
8232	MSG_ALDG_EXPROV_WRONG_VERSION	Error
8233	MSG_ALDG_EXPROV_CALLING_PROVIDER	Informational
8234	MSG_ALDG_EXPROV_ERROR	Error
8235	MSG_ALDG_EXPROV_PROVIDER_CALL_COMPLETE	Informational
8236	MSG_ALDG_EXPROV_MAX_EXCEPTION	Error
8237	MSG_ALDG_EXPROV_LOADED	Informational
8238	MSG_ALDG_EXPROV_UNLOADED	Informational
8239	MSG_ALDG_EXPROV_STARTED	Informational
8240	MSG_ALDG_EXPROV_STOPPED	Informational
8241	MSG_SYNCHRO_DELETEBRANCH	Informational
8242	MSG_SYNCHRO_NOCLEARTEXT	Error
8243	MSG_SYNCHRO_INVALID_LINK1	Warning
8244	MSG_SYNCHRO_INVALID_LINK2	Warning
8245	MSG_SYNCHRO_INVALID_LINK3	Warning
8246	MSG_SYNCHRO_INVALID_LINK4	Warning
8247	MSG_ALDG_EXPROV_RESTART_AFTER_FAIL	Error
8248	MSG_LDAP_NOTIFY_RETURN	Informational
8249	MSG_DUPLICATE_SERVER_TRACKING	Informational
8250	MSG_DSCONFIG_NT_API_ERROR_CODE	Error
8251	MSG_AL_DSCONFIG_READ_OBJECT_FAIL	Error
8252	MSG_AL_DSCONFIG_SEARCH_OBJECT_FAIL	Error
8253	MSG_AL_DSCONFIG_NO_NAMESPACES	Informational

Table A.1 *List of ADC Event IDs and Symbolic Names (continued)*

Event	Symbolic Name	Severity
8254	MSG_AL_DSCONFIG_NAMESPACEINFO	Informational
8255	MSG_AL_DSCONFIG_NEW_NAMESPACE	Informational
8256	MSG_AL_DSCONFIG_DELETED_NAMESPACE	Informational
8257	MSG_AL_DSCONFIG_NAMESPACE_ERROR	Warning
8258	MSG_AL_SYNCHRO_REPLICATESTART	Informational
8259	MSG_AL_SYNCHRO_REPLICATEABORTED	Informational
8260	MSG_AL_DSCONFIG_OPENSESSION_FAIL	Error
8261	MSG_AL_DSCONFIG_SYNCNOW	Informational
8262	MSG_AL_SYNCHRO_BAD_CONFIG	Error
8263	MSG_AL_SYNCHRO_NO_MUTEX	Error
8264	MSG_AL_SYNCHRO_ERROR_EXCEPTION	Error
8265	MSG_CONFIG_MISSING_DXA_LOCAL_ADMIN_ATTR	Warning
8266	MSG_CONFIG_MISSING_REMOTE_CLIENT_ATTR	Error
8267	MSG_SYNCHRO_TIMEVETO_DELETION	Informational
8268	MSG_SYNCHRO_USERVETO_DELETION	Informational
8269	MSG_SYNCHRO_DELETE_ENTRY_SPECIAL	Informational
8270	MSG_LDAP_TRANSACTION_FAILED	Error
8271	MSG_SYNCHRO_REPLICATED_OBJECT	Informational
8272	MSG_SYNCHRO_NOT_REPLICATING_OBJECT	Warning
8273	MSG_SYNCHRO_NO_REPL_INTERFOREST	Warning
8274	MSG_SYNCHRO_NO_REPL_DELETED	Warning
8275	MSG_SYNCHRO_NO_REPL_READ_ONLY	Warning
8276	MSG_SYNCHRO_NO_REPL_NOT_BRIDGEHEAD	Warning
8277	MSG_SYNCHRO_NO_REPL_LATENCY	Warning
8278	MSG_SYNCHRO_NO_REPL_CONVERTDN	Warning
8279	MSG_SYNCHRO_NO_REPL_OBJECTCLASS	Warning
8280	MSG_SYNCHRO_NO_REPL_CONFLICT	Warning

Table A.1 *List of ADC Event IDs and Symbolic Names (continued)*

Event	Symbolic Name	Severity
8281	MSG_SYNCHRO_NO_MASTERACCOUNTSID	Warning
8282	MSG_SYNCHRO_NO_REPL_NO_REASON	Warning
8283	MSG_CONFIG_CANT_MODIFY_PT_OBJECT_IN_55	Warning
8284	MSG_ALDG_NO_ADDRESS_LIST	Warning
8285	MSG_SYNCHRO_NO_REPL_MB_TO_CONTACT	Warning
8286	MSG_SYNCHRO_NO_REPL_CR_TO_MB	Warning
8287	MSG_SYNCHRO_NO_REPL_INTERORG_NOTBRIDGE	Warning
8288	MSG_SYNCHRO_NO_REPL_INTRAORG_DIFFORG	Warning
8289	MSG_SYNCHRO_NO_REPL_INTRAORG_NOINFO	Warning
8290	MSG_SYNCHRO_NO_REPL_INTRAORG_SAMEORG	Warning
8291	MSG_SYNCHRO_NO_REPL_WRITEABLE_SITE	Warning
8292	MSG_SYNCHRO_GENERIC_MAPPING_FAILURE	Warning
8293	MSG_SYNCHRO_SUCCESSFULLY_IMPORTED_OBJECT	Informational
8294	MSG_SYNCHRO_BAD_ATTR_DELETE	Warning
8295	MSG_LDAP_RENAME_ERROR	Error
8296	MSG_LDAP_RENAME	Informational
8297	MSG_CONFIG_PUT_SERVER_IN_ROUTING_GROUP	Informational
8298	MSG_CONFIG_MASTERED_OUT_OF_55	Warning
8299	MSG_CONFIG_NO_MAPI_PUBLIC_STORE	Warning
8300	MSG_CONFIG_HOME_SERVER_NOT_REPLICATED	Warning
8301	MSG_CONFIG_CANNOT_DETERMINE_CORRECT_RG	Warning
8302	MSG_CONFIG_NEW_FILE_VERSION_ON_TARGET	Warning
8303	MSG_CONFIG_SITE_PROTOCOLS_NOT_REPLICATED	Warning
8304	MSG_CONFIG_PROTOCOL_TYPE_NOT_REPLICATED	Warning
8305	MSG_CONFIG_MISSING_REQUIRED_ATTRIBUTES	Warning
8306	MSG_CONFIG_MISSING_TARGET_ENTRY_IN_AD	Warning
8307	MSG_CONFIG_DELETIONS_NOT_REPLICATED_TO_AD	Warning

Table A.1 *List of ADC Event IDs and Symbolic Names (continued)*

Event	Symbolic Name	Severity
8308	MSG_CONFIG_MASTERED_OUT_OF_ACTIVE_DIRECTORY_NO_TARGET_DN	Warning
8309	MSG_CONFIG_MASTERED_OUT_OF_ACTIVE_DIRECTORY	Warning
8310	MSG_CONFIG_PRIVATE_STORE_DELETION_NOT_REPLICATED	Warning
8311	MSG_CONFIG_NON_MAPI_PUBLIC_STORE_NOT_REPLICATED	Warning
8312	MSG_CONFIG_DELETIONS_NOT_REPLICATED_TO_55	Warning
8313	MSG_CONFIG_DONOT_REPLICATE_RGC_IN_SAME_AG	Warning
8314	MSG_CONFIG_DONOT_REPLICATE_GWART_FOR_OSMIUM_RID_SERVER	Warning
8315	MSG_ALDG_ENTRY_DACL_PROTECTED	Warning
8316	MSG_ALDG_CONTAINER_DACL_PROTECTED	Warning
8317	MSG_ALDG_RETRY_DACL_PROTECTED_FAILED	Warning

Table A.2 describes each ADC event and provides an explanation and possible recovery action.

Table A.2 *ADC Event Description and Explanation*

Event	Description	Explanation	User Action
1	Replication		
2	Account management		
3	Attribute mapping		
4	Service Controller		
5	LDAP Operations		
6	Address List		
8000	%1.		
8001	The service was started.		No user action is required.
8002	The service was stopped.		Usually, no user action is required. If the service was shut down unexpectedly due to errors, start the service manually. If the service will not start, check the event log with Event Viewer for more details about related errors. If the service continually shuts down due to errors, contact Microsoft Product Support Services.
8003	The service is starting.		No user action is required.
8004	The service is stopping.		No user action is required.
8005	The service received an unsupported request.	The Service Control Manager has returned an invalid request.	If the problem persists, contact Microsoft Product Support Services.
8006	Opening LDAP session to directory %1 on port %2. %3		No user action is required.
8007	Closing LDAP session to directory %1. %2		No user action is required.
8008	Binding to directory %1 as user '%2'. %3		No user action is required.

Table A.2 *ADC Event Description and Explanation (continued)*

Event	Description	Explanation	User Action
8009	Binding to directory %1 as service account. %2		No user action is required.
8010	Searching directory %1 at base '%2' using filter '%3'. %4		No user action is required.
8011	Searching directory %1 at base '%2' using filter '%3' and requesting attributes %4. %5		No user action is required.
8012	Search of directory %1 at base '%2' returned %3 objects. %4		No user action is required.
8013	Adding entry '%1' to directory %2. %3		No user action is required.
8014	Adding entry '%1' to directory %2. Attributes are %3. %4		No user action is required.
8015	Modifying entry '%1' on directory %2. %3		No user action is required.
8016	Modifying entry '%1' on directory %2. Modifications are %3. %4	This message is logged whenever Active Directory Connector (ADC) modifies a directory entry.	No user action is required.
8017	Deleting entry '%1' on directory %2. %3	This message is logged when the Active Directory Connector (ADC) deletes an object in the directory.	No user action is required.
8018	Abandoning request '%1' on directory %2. %3		No user action is required.
8019	Requesting LDAP notification for base '%1' on directory %2. %3		No user action is required.
8020	LDAP Search of directory %1 at base '%2' using filter '%3' was unsuccessful. Directory returned the LDAP error:[0x%4] %5. %6	If the accompanying Lightweight Directory Access Protocol (LDAP) message refers to LDAP_OTHER, the directory service may be out of disk space.	Check network connectivity. Verify the user name, password, and port address are correct, and try again. If the problem persists, verify that the remote Exchange server is configured to support LDAP.

Table A.2 *ADC Event Description and Explanation (continued)*

Event	Description	Explanation	User Action
8021	LDAP Add on directory %1 for entry '%2' was unsuccessful with error:[0x%3] %4. %5	If the accompanying Lightweight Directory Access Protocol (LDAP) message refers to LDAP_OTHER, the directory service may be out of disk space.	Check network connectivity. Verify the user name, password, and port address are correct, and try again. If the problem persists, contact Microsoft Product Support Services.
8022	LDAP Modify on directory %1 for entry '%2' was unsuccessful with error:[0x%3] %4. %5	If the accompanying Lightweight Directory Access Protocol (LDAP) message refers to LDAP_OTHER, the directory service may be out of disk space.	Check network connectivity. Verify the user name, password, and port address are correct, and try again.
8023	LDAP Delete on directory %1 for entry '%2' was unsuccessful with error:[0x%3] %4. %5		Check network connectivity. Verify the user name, password, and port address are correct, and try again. If the problem persists, verify that the remote Exchange server is configured to support Lightweight Directory Access Protocol (LDAP).
8024	LDAP Search Initial Page on directory %1 at base '%2' with filter '%3' was unsuccessful. Directory returned the LDAP error:[0x%4] %5. %6	The Connection Agreement may be requesting too many objects based on the configuration setting of the target directory, or the target server may have failed.	Check network connectivity. Verify the user name, password, and port address are correct, and try again. If the problem persists, verify that the remote Exchange server is configured to support Lightweight Directory Access Protocol (LDAP).
8025	LDAP Get Next Page call on directory %1 for pagesize %2, was unsuccessful with error:[0x%3] %4. %5	The Connection Agreement may be requesting too many objects based on the configuration setting of the target directory, or the target server may have failed.	Check network connectivity. Verify the user name, password, and port address are correct, and try again. If the problem persists, verify that the remote Exchange server is configured to support Lightweight Directory Access Protocol (LDAP).

Table A.2 *ADC Event Description and Explanation (continued)*

Event	Description	Explanation	User Action
8026	LDAP Bind was unsuccessful on directory %1 for distinguished name '%2'. Directory returned error:[0x%3] %4. %5	Lightweight Directory Access Protocol (LDAP) allows you to query and manage directory information using a TCP/IP connection.	Check network connectivity. Verify the user name, password, and port address are correct, and try again. If the problem persists, verify that the remote Exchange server is configured to support LDAP.
8027	The LDAP Bind to the global catalog on %1 with credential '%2' was unsuccessful. The Directory returned error:[0x%3] %4 %5		Either promote to a global catalog the Active Directory Server that the Connection Agreement points to, or modify the Connection Agreement to point to a global catalog.
8028	LDAP ModifyRDN on directory %1 for entry '%2' was unsuccessful with error:[0x%3] %4. %5	If the accompanying Lightweight Directory Access Protocol (LDAP) message refers to LDAP_OTHER, the directory service may be out of disk space.	Check network connectivity. Verify the user name, password, and port address are correct, and try again.
8029	LDAP Referral on directory %1 for entry '%2' was unsuccessful with error:[0x%3] %4. %5		
8030	LDAP Extended result on directory %1 for entry '%2' was unsuccessful with error:[0x%3] %4. %5		No user action is required.
8031	Unable to open LDAP session on directory '%1' using port number %2. Directory returned the LDAP error:[0x%3] %4. %5	Lightweight Directory Access Protocol (LDAP) allows you to query and manage directory information using a TCP/IP connection.	Check network connectivity. Verify the user name, password, and port address are correct, and try again. If the problem persists, verify that the remote Exchange server is configured to support LDAP.
8032	LDAP Session result on directory %1 for entry '%2' was unsuccessful with error:[0x%3] %4. %5		

Table A.2 *ADC Event Description and Explanation (continued)*

Event	Description	Explanation	User Action
8033	LDAP search result on directory %1 for entry '%2' was unsuccessful with error:[0x%3] %4. %5	If the accompanying Lightweight Directory Access Protocol (LDAP) message refers to LDAP_OTHER, the directory service may be out of disk space.	Check network connectivity. Verify the user name, password, and port address are correct, and try again.
8034	LDAP compare result on directory %1 for entry '%2' was unsuccessful with error:[0x%3] %4. %5		
8035	Successfully modified entry '%1' on directory %2. %3		No user action is required.
8036	Searching EXPORT directory on directory '%1' for 'deleted' entries. Search base is: %2, filter is: %3. %4		No user action is required.
8037	Successfully deleted entry '%1' on directory '%2'. %3		No user action is required.
8038	Successfully added new entry '%1' on directory '%2'. %3		No user action is required.
8039	Completed the transaction... %1 %2		No user action is required.
8040	Server '%1' could not generate e-mail addresses for entry '%2'. Was unsuccessful with error:[0x%3] %4. %5	Active Directory Connector (ADC) could not contact the System Attendant service on the Exchange server.	Make sure that the Exchange server domain has trust with the Windows 2000 computer domain and that the Exchange server's service account shares the same domain as the Windows 2000 computer.
8041	Server '%1' could not generate some e-mail addresses for entry '%2'. Was unsuccessful for type(s): %3. %4	A unique e-mail address could not be generated based on the entry name. The Exchange 5.5 server service account may be in a domain different from the Windows 2000 server.	In the Add-ins or E-Mail Address Generator container, select the connector or address generator being accessed. On the General tab, verify that the specified DLL file is not corrupted and exists in \Exchsrvr\Add-ins or \Exchsrvr\Address in the proper directory on the server.

Table A.2 *ADC Event Description and Explanation (continued)*

Event	Description	Explanation	User Action
8042	Searching EXPORT directory on directory '%1' for new or changed entries. Search base is: %2, filter is: %3. %4		No user action is required.
8043	Directory search requested attributes: %1. %2		No user action is required.
8044	Search of EXPORT directory returned %1 entries: %2. %3		No user action is required.
8045	CImportDir::UpdateEntry, Destination entry marked as deleted, Adding new entry:(Server:%1, Entry distinguished name:%2). %3		No user action is required.
8046	Update existing entry '%2' on directory '%1'. %3		No user action is required.
8047	%1 directory entries were deleted since last replication: %2. %3		No user action is required.
8048	Using 'Non-Tombstone' deletion method, the following entries will be deleted: %1. %2		No user action is required.
8049	Using 'Tombstone' deletion method, the following entries will be deleted: %1. %2		No user action is required.
8050	Entry '%1' does not exist in IMPORT directory. %2		No user action is required.
8051	Entry '%1' already exists in IMPORT directory. %2		No user action is required.
8052	No directory entries were deleted since last replication. %1		No user action is required.
8053	Attribute values for entry '%1' in IMPORT Directory: %2. %3		No user action is required.

Table A.2 *ADC Event Description and Explanation (continued)*

Event	Description	Explanation	User Action
8054	LDAP Unbind on directory %1 was unsuccessful. Directory returned error:[0x%2] %3. %4	If the accompanying LDAP message refers to LDAP_OTHER, the directory service may be out of disk space.	Check network connectivity. Verify the user name, password, and port address are correct, and try again. If the problem persists, verify that the remote Exchange server is configured to support LDAP.
8055	Could not read Replication Agent distinguished name from registry. Cannot begin replication. %1		
8056	Starting replication for Connection Agreement '%1'.		No user action is required.
8057	Finished replication for Connection Agreement '%1'.		No user action is required.
8058	Stopped replication for Connection Agreement '%1'.	Synchronization was canceled.	No user action is required.
8059	Replicating from remote directory '%1' to local directory '%2'. %3		No user action is required.
8060	Replicating from local directory '%1' to remote directory '%2'. %3		No user action is required.
8061	Reading configuration information on directory '%1' using entry '%2'. %3		No user action is required.
8062	Could not open LDAP session to directory '%1' using local service credentials. Cannot access Connection Agreement configuration information. Make sure the server '%1' is running. %2	Active Directory Connector (ADC) could not gain access to Windows 2000 Domain Controller.	Make sure the ADC service account has permissions to read its configuration information from the Active Directory.

Table A.2 *ADC Event Description and Explanation (continued)*

Event	Description	Explanation	User Action
8063	Could not read the root entry on directory '%1'. Cannot access configuration information. %2		Verify network connectivity. Attempt to read attributes on the directory. Make sure the ADC (Active Directory Connector) service account has permissions to read its configuration information from the Active Directory.
8064	Could not read entry '%1' on directory %2. Cannot access Connection Agreement information. Make sure that service was installed properly. %3	Active Directory Connector (ADC) could not find its service object.	Make sure the ADC service account has permissions to read its configuration information from the Active Directory.
8065	Could not search under entry '%1' on directory %2. Cannot access Connection Agreement information. %3	Active Directory Connector (ADC) could not find the Connection Agreements container or does not have permissions to read the container.	Make sure the ADC service account has permissions to read its configuration information from the Active Directory.
8066	Object '%1' on directory %2 has no Connection Agreements defined.		No user action is required.
8067	Object '%1' on directory %2 has the following Connection Agreements defined: %3		No user action is required.
8068	Found new or changed Connection Agreement '%1' on directory %2.		No user action is required.
8069	Connection Agreement '%1' was deleted or had its owning service changed on directory %2. Shutting down thread for this Connection Agreement.		No user action is required.

Table A.2 *ADC Event Description and Explanation (continued)*

Event	Description	Explanation	User Action
8070	The Connection Agreement '%1' on directory %2 could not be loaded due to an error. Make sure that the Connection Agreement is configured properly.	There may be a network problem, or you may not have the appropriate permissions to perform this operation, or the Connection Agreement may be configured incorrectly.	Check network connectivity and the Connection Agreement configuration. If the Active Directory Connector (ADC) service account does not have the appropriate permissions, ask someone with administrative permissions to modify them. If the problem persists, restart the ADC service.
8071	Setting Remote last USN value to: %1. %2	The Unique Synchronization Number (USN) is monotonically increasing value; after every directory update the current USN is stamped on the modified object (by the directory) and then the USN is incremented.	This message requires no action and is informational only.
8072	Setting Local last USN value to: %1. %2		No user action is required.
8073	Could not add Windows 2000 user account, the computer name supplied is invalid. %1	The computer name has been entered in error.	Enter a valid server name and try again.
8074	Added Windows 2000 user %1 on local computer.		No user action is required.
8075	Added Windows 2000 user %1 on computer %2. %3		No user action is required.
8076	Could not retrieve security identifier(SID) for given account. %1	A user may no longer exist. Security identifiers (SIDs) are unique numbers that identify users who are logged on to the Windows 2000 security system. A security ID can identify an individual user or a group of users.	Verify this user exists on this domain. If the problem persists, create the Windows 2000 user account or delete the mailbox from the remote server.

Table A.2 *ADC Event Description and Explanation (continued)*

Event	Description	Explanation	User Action
8077	Could not add Windows 2000 user %1 on local computer. %2	Data may have been entered in error.	The account specified must have Change access to the Exchange directory. Verify the connection agreement account being used has the appropriate permissions to perform this task.
8078	Could not add Windows 2000 user %1 on computer %2. %3	Data may have been entered in error.	Verify the connection account has the appropriate permissions to perform this task. The account specified must have Change access to the Exchange directory.
8079	Could not delete Windows 2000 user account, invalid security identifier(SID). %1	The account may have been deleted and recreated. This action creates an account with the same name but a different security identifier (SID), which Windows 2000 views as a different account.	Run the User Manager program to manually delete the account.
8080	Deleted Windows 2000 user %1 on local computer. %2		No user action is required.
8081	Deleted Windows 2000 user %1 on computer %2. %3		No user action is required.
8082	Could not delete Windows 2000 user %1 on local computer. %2		
8083	Could not delete Windows 2000 user %1 on computer %2. %3		Verify the connection account has the appropriate permissions to perform this task and that the Windows 2000 user exists.
8084	Could not load mapping table. %1		Verify that the Active Directory Connector (ADC) account has permission to read the Connection Agreements and all of their attributes. If so, restart your computer and try again. If you still get this message, create a new Connection Agreement.

Table A.2 *ADC Event Description and Explanation (continued)*

Event	Description	Explanation	User Action
8085	Started attribute mapping agent. %1	As part of the replication process, a mapping table is generated.	No user action is required.
8086	Stopped attribute mapping agent. %1		No user action is required.
8087	Mapped local attribute '%1' to remote attribute '%3'. Local attribute value: %2, Remote attribute value: %4. %5		No user action is required.
8088	Mapped local attribute '%1' to remote attribute '%2'. %3		No user action is required.
8089	Mapped remote attribute '%1' to local attribute '%3'. Remote attribute value: %2, Local attribute value: %4. %5		No user action is required.
8090	Mapped remote attribute '%1' to local attribute '%2'. %3		No user action is required.
8091	Mapped remote object '%1' to local object '%2'. %3		No user action is required.
8092	Mapped local object '%1' to remote object '%2'. %3		No user action is required.
8093	Could not find object: %1. %2	The object does not exist.	
8094	Could not find destination object: %1. %2		
8095	Object has no attributes, object is: %1, destination object is: %2. %3	The attribute tree is empty or all attributes in the attribute map are turned off.	Turn on all attributes in the attribute map, if they are turned off.
8096	File Exception %1, occurred handling attribute mapping file: %2. %3		
8097	Could not create new attribute.	The Connection Agreement attribute map is corrupted.	Create a new Connection Agreement. If the problem persists, uninstall and then reinstall MSADC (Microsoft Active Directory Server).

Table A.2 *ADC Event Description and Explanation (continued)*

Event	Description	Explanation	User Action
8098	Could not create new object.	The Connection Agreement attribute map is corrupted.	Create a new Connection Agreement. If the problem persists, uninstall and then reinstall MSADC (Microsoft Active Directory Connector).
8099	Cannot find object class, local tree is empty. %1		If the problem persists, create a new Connection Agreement or try to reinstall the ADC.
8100	No mapping configured for object: %1		
8101	Cannot find object class, remote tree is empty. %1		If the problem persists, create a new Connection Agreement or try to reinstall the ADC.
8102	No mapping configured for attribute: %1	Attributes are a list of mappings between NT and Exchange 5.5 object attributes.	No user action is required. Currently there is no way to configure the attributes to be replicated. In the future you will be able to modify the list of attributes on an object to be synchronized through the Synchronization Agreement Properties page.
8103	The service was installed successfully.		No user action is required.
8104	The service '%1' was removed successfully.		No user action is required.
8105	The service '%1' could not be removed.	This message is logged when an uninstall of the ADC fails. The service account may not have the appropriate permissions to perform this task.	Verify that the service account has administrative privilege on the specified computer.
8106	The control handler could not be installed.		Note that the service account has administrative privilege on the specified computer. Check the event log with Event Viewer for more details about related errors.

Table A.2 *ADC Event Description and Explanation (continued)*

Event	Description	Explanation	User Action
8107	Could not create Windows 2000 Service object.	Setup has failed. This message is the last in a series of errors that occurred during setup.	Review all related event messages and try again. Note that the service account has administrative privilege on the specified computer.
8108	The initialization process failed.		Review the Event Viewer for related entries to determine the cause of this failure.
8109	Could not import the entry '%1' into the directory server '%2' in the first attempt. %3	There may be a network problem or the import failed for another reason. The Active Directory Connector (ADC) will try once more to import.	Check the event log for additional information. Check network connectivity.
8110	Setting remote last update time value to: %1	As a part of the directory service configuration, the last update time is written to the header.	This message requires no action and is informational only.
8111	Setting local last update time value to: %1	As a part of the directory service configuration, the last update time is written to the header.	This message requires no action and is informational only.
8112	The authentication package value (%1) is not supported on server %2. Check the Connections tab on the Connection Agreement. %3	The type of authentication being used is not supported on the specified server. The credentials cannot be processed.	On the Connection tab of the Synchronization Agreement property page, modify the authentication options for logging onto the Windows 2000 server. Possible options are: Basic, Basic using SSL, NTLM, and NTLM using SSL. Verify the directory service on the remote server is running. Check the port number. Then try again.
8113	The service could not be initialized because the necessary file %1 could not be found. Make sure that the operating system was installed properly.	Active Directory Connector (ADC) could not find the file, or the DllMain entry point returned an error upon loading the DLL.	Check the file version and verify that its location is in your executable path.

Table A.2 *ADC Event Description and Explanation (continued)*

Event	Description	Explanation	User Action
8114	The service could not be initialized because the necessary entry point '%1' could not be found in the file %2. Make sure that the operating system was installed properly.	Active Directory Connector (ADC) could not find the file or the entry point within the file to initialize this service.	Check the file version and verify that its location is in your executable path.
8115	The Win32 API call '%1' returned an error. The service could not be initialized. Make sure that the operating system was installed properly.	This is an operating system–level error.	Perform the user action specified in the message.
8116	The Connection Agreement '%1' has been signaled to start replication immediately.		No user action is required.
8117	Could not locate the import container %1. Make sure that the configured container exists, or that the account in the Connection Agreement has permissions to access the container. Replication stopped for this Connection Agreement. %2		Perform the user action specified in the message.
8118	Could not locate the export container %1. Make sure that the configured container exists, or that the account in the Connection Agreement has permissions to access the container. Replication stopped for this Connection Agreement. %2		Perform the user action specified in the message.
8119	The schema map in the Connection Agreement '%1' contains an invalid attribute: %2	The schema is missing an attribute, which the Active Directory Connector (ADC) expects to find.	No user action is required. If the problem persists, contact Microsoft Product Support Services.
8120	Syntax conversion from syntax type %1 to syntax type %2 is not allowed. %3	The syntax of an attribute cannot be converted.	Contact Microsoft Product Support Services.

Table A.2 *ADC Event Description and Explanation (continued)*

Event	Description	Explanation	User Action
8121	The entry with distinguished name '%1' will not be written to the directory because it is missing the following mandatory attributes: '%2'. %3		Add the required attributes, and ensure that the attributes are enabled in the schema map. Verify that Active Directory Connector (ADC) has permissions to read the attributes from the source directory.
8122	The entry with distinguished name '%1' will not be written to the directory because it has invalid attributes: '%2'. %3	ADC could not write the proposed attributes to the directory.	Disable the invalid attributes in the schema map.
8123	The entry with distinguished name '%1' will not be written to the directory because it is trying to delete the mandatory attributes: '%2'. %3	Active Directory Connector (ADC) cannot remove the attribute specified because the target directory requires that the attribute exist.	No user action is required.
8124	Processing of the Connection Agreement '%1' has been stopped due to an invalid configuration. Check the event log for more information.	This message follows a previous, related message. That message will usually indicate a missing import or export container or that the Connection Agreement was created or modified by a different version of Active Directory Connector (ADC).	Correct the information on the Connection Agreement.
8125	New address list '%1' found with rule '%2'. %3		No user action is required.
8126	Address list '%1' modified with rule '%2'. %3		No user action is required.
8127	Address List '%1' deleted. %2		No user action is required.
8128	Found change to directory object '%1'. Evaluating address list rules. %2		No user action is required.
8129	Evaluating directory object '%1' against address list '%2' rule '%3'. %4		No user action is required.
8130	'%1' added to '%2'. %3		No user action is required.
8131	'%1' removed from '%2'. %3		No user action is required.

Table A.2 *ADC Event Description and Explanation (continued)*

Event	Description	Explanation	User Action
8132	Received request to stop calculations on '%1'. %2		No user action is required.
8133	Calculations complete on '%1'. %2		No user action is required.
8134	Queuing request to process '%1'. %2		No user action is required.
8135	No rule set on '%1', skipping. %2		No user action is required.
8136	'%1'. %2		
8137	This version of ADC cannot run the Connection Agreement '%1'. Either upgrade ADC on this server, or change the ADC service on the General tab to a different server.		Make sure that the Connection Agreement was created using the Windows 2000 version of Active Directory Connector (ADC). ADC cannot run Connection Agreements created by other versions of ADC.
8138	The server '%1' is not available. Check for network problems and make sure that the server is running. All directory updates to or from the server cannot be replicated unless the server is available. %2		Perform the user action specified in the message.
8139	The target object '%1' was modified after the source object '%2'; consequently, the following set of updates will not be applied to the target object. If this warning persists, make sure that the time is correctly set on both the source and target servers. %3 %4	The service will not replicate changes from the source object to the target object if the target object has been modified more recently than the source object.	Ensure that the clocks on the source and target servers are synchronized.
8140	Delayed processing of group/distribution list: '%1' %2	To replicate objects as quickly as possible, distribution lists and groups are delayed until after users, mailboxes, custom recipients, and contacts have been replicated.	No user action is required.

Table A.2 *ADC Event Description and Explanation (continued)*

Event	Description	Explanation	User Action
8141	The operating system has run out of resources. The Connection Agreement will shut down and then restart. If this problem persists, try restarting the service or the server.	Other applications running on the system share resources. This is a Windows-level error that indicates a shortage of resources for all applications.	Perform the user action specified in the message. Reduce the load on resources by restricting any other unnecessary applications from running on the server.
8142	The service threw an unexpected exception.		Restart the service. Verify that there is enough disk space and memory. If the problem persists, contact Microsoft Product Support Services.
8143	The Connection Agreement %1 threw an unexpected exception.		Review related event logs to determine the appropriate action.
8144	The service threw an out of memory exception.		Increase the swap file size, close some other applications, or restart the service. If the problem persists, contact Microsoft Product Support Services.
8145	Exception %1 was raised at address %2.		Restart the service. Check for sufficient disk space and memory. Check that the target directory and source directories are running. If the problem persists, contact Microsoft Product Support Services.
8146	An operation on server '%1' returned [0x%2] %3. The Connection Agreement %4 stopped.		Restart the service. Check for sufficient disk space and memory. Check that the target directory and source directories are running. If the problem persists, contact Microsoft Product Support Services.
8147	Changing the relative distinguished name of entry '%1' to '%2' on directory %3. %4		No user action is required.

Table A.2 *ADC Event Description and Explanation (continued)*

Event	Description	Explanation	User Action
8148	Synchronization summary for Connection Agreement '%1' --- %n [Destination Server: %2] %n [Start Time: %3] %n [End Time: %4] %n [Number of entries processed successfully: %5] %n [Number of adds: %6, Number of modifications: %7] %n [Number of entries failed: %8]		No user action is required.
8149	The service has been disabled.		No user action is required.
8150	Cannot start service threads. Retry after 1 minute.		Perform the user action specified in the message.
8151	Cannot read service configuration. Retry after 1 minute.		Perform the user action specified in the message.
8152	No services currently configured for server '%1'.		No user action is required.
8153	Function %1[%2][#%3] had an unrecoverable error.		Contact Microsoft Product Support Services.
8154	Function %1[%2][#%3] had an unrecoverable failure on restart attempt.		Contact Microsoft Product Support Services.
8155	Function %1[%2][#%3] terminated with code: %4.		No user action is required.
8156	Function %1[%2][#%3] starting.		No user action is required.
8157	Thread #%1: waiting for next running schedule. %2		No user action is required.
8158	Thread #%1: running service. %2		No user action is required.
8159	Thread #%1: checking for running schedule. %2		No user action is required.
8160	No change required for %1. %2		No user action is required.
8161	Exception occurred while processing '%1'.		Contact Microsoft Product Support Services.

Table A.2 *ADC Event Description and Explanation (continued)*

Event	Description	Explanation	User Action
8162	Thread #%1: waiting for next Address List transaction. %2		No user action is required.
8163	Thread #%1: received next Address List Transaction. %2		No user action is required.
8164	Thread #%1: shutting down automatically since idle. %2		No user action is required.
8165	Exception occurred while processing Address List '%1' against user/group: '%2'.		Contact Microsoft Product Support Services.
8166	Could not modify Address List '%1' for user/group: '%2'. %3		Review the event logs. No user action is required.
8167	Modified user/group: '%1'. %2		No user action is required.
8168	Could not modify user/group: '%1'. %2		Review the event logs to determine the cause of the failure of the modification. No user action is required.
8169	Retrieved all user/group changes under: '%1'. %2		No user action is required.
8170	Retrieved all address list changes under: '%1'. %2		No user action is required.
8171	Address List change calculation of '%1' skipped since we are doing full recalculation of users. %2		No user action is required.
8172	Could not initialize scheduled change event cycle, will retry later. %1		Contact Microsoft Product Support Services.
8173	Could not commit changes to service '%1'.	This message usually indicates a problem accessing Active Directory (AD). Or, the service could be down or busy. It may also indicate that the Address List service is either down or busy.	Verify that Active Directory is functioning properly. The system will automatically retry.
8174	Processing change to Address List '%1'. %2		No user action is required.

Table A.2 *ADC Event Description and Explanation (continued)*

Event	Description	Explanation	User Action
8175	Processing change to user/group '%1'. %2		No user action is required.
8176	Received request to shut down service '%1'.		No user action is required.
8177	Could not add Windows 2000 user %1 on the primary Domain Controller %2, due to a logon failure. %3	The logon could fail if the Connection Agreement had permissions to administrate Exchange but not the Windows 2000 domain. It could also fail if the Domain Controller was down.	Verify that the user name and password are correct and that they have the required permissions, and try again.
8178	The directory schema on server '%1' is missing the following attribute types required for Connection Agreement '%2' to work properly: '%3'. Make sure that the directory service on '%4' was restarted after the Connection Agreement was created. If it was, either the Connection Agreement is not configured properly or the directory service on the server was reinstalled after the Connection Agreement was set up. Please recreate the Connection Agreement.		Perform the user action specified in the message.
8179	Unable to create or open the transaction file '%1' for writing a deleted entry. If the file exists, make sure that it's writable by the service, else make sure that the parent directory is writable and that the disk is not full. %2		The transaction file is in the same directory that Active Directory Connector (ADC) is installed in. User account and passwords are shown on the Connection tab in the Connection Agreement Properties dialog box. Make sure that these credentials allow writing, the file is writable, and the disk is not full.
8180	The Connection Agreement '%1' has paused the replication after %2 seconds. The replication will resume in %3 seconds.		No user action is required.

Table A.2 *ADC Event Description and Explanation (continued)*

Event	Description	Explanation	User Action
8181	The Connection Agreement '%1' is resuming its replication.		No user action is required.
8182	The service was unable to add the member '%1' to the group '%2'. This is because the group is a Universal Distribution group and it is not allowed to have Domain Local groups as members. %3	By default, ADC (Active Directory Connector) creates universal groups. Universal groups can have any object as a member. However, the Windows 2000 administrator can choose to create a global group. Global groups cannot have universal groups or domain local groups as members. Exchange does not have this restriction. So, if the Windows 2000 global group is to replicate to Exchange, and the Exchange administrator adds a unversal group to the global group, then the change cannot replicate back to Windows 2000.	Consider alternative architectures where this grouping is not necessary.
8183	Could not import the entry '%1' into the directory server '%2' in the second attempt. %3	If an imported entry fails, Active Directory Connector (ADC) will retry once. This message is logged after the second attempt fails.	Inspect the user entry that failed for any values that might prohibit its entry—for instance, an e-mail address that would produce a conflict.
8184	The password for the credential %1 has expired after %2 days without use.		Update the password on the Connection Agreement.
8185	The following credentials had their passwords removed because of shortage in the LSA Private Store. If you have a Connection Agreement that is still using one of these passwords, go to the Connection Agreement Property and reset the password. %1		Perform the user action specified in the message.
8186	The password for the credential %1 was set successfully. %2		No user action is required.

Table A.2 *ADC Event Description and Explanation (continued)*

Event	Description	Explanation	User Action
8187	The following error has occurred when trying to read a password from the LSA Private Store. Error number: %1. Description: '%2'. %3	ADC (Active Directory Connector) could not read the credential information. This message resulted from a Windows 2000 error.	Review any related Windows 2000 entries in the event log for further information.
8188	The following error has occurred when trying to write a password to the LSA Private Store. Error number: %1. Description: '%2'. %3	ADC (Active Directory Connector) could not read the credential information. This message resulted from a Windows 2000 error.	Review any related Windows 2000 entries in the event log for further information.
8189	Active Directory Connector RPC Interface started successfully.	Active Directory Connector (ADC) successfully established an RPC connection.	No user action is required.
8190	Active Directory Connector RPC Interface stopped successfully.	Active Directory Connector (ADC) Remote Procedure Call Interface allows server credential information to be stored securely.	No user action is required.
8191	Active Directory Connector RPC Interface is available on the following RPC end points: %1	ADC Remote Procedure Call Interface allows server credential information to be stored securely.	No user action is required.
8192	Active Directory Connector RPC Interface failed when trying to listen for RPC requests. Services handled by this interface will not be available. Error from RPC subsystem: %1.	Some services will still be available without an RPC connection. Services that are not available without RPC include password and credential modification.	This may be caused by a shortage of Windows resources or by corruption of resources used by Active Directory Connector (ADC). Restart ADC. If this fails, reboot the computer.

Table A.2 *ADC Event Description and Explanation (continued)*

Event	Description	Explanation	User Action
8193	Active Directory Connector RPC Interface failed when trying to register end points for RPC requests. Services offered by this interface will not be available. Error from RPC subsystem: %1.	Some services will still be available without an RPC connection, while others are not. Services that are not available without RPC include the ability to modify Connection Agreement passwords and credentials. This may be caused by a shortage of Windows resources or by corruption of resources used by ADC (Active Directory Connector).	Try restarting ADC. If this fails, try restarting the computer.
8194	Active Directory Connector RPC Interface failed when trying to use all network transports to accept RPC requests. RPC interfaces might not be available on all network transports. Error from RPC subsystem: %1.	Some services will still be available without an RPC connection, while others are not. Services that are not available without RPC include the ability to modify Connection Agreement passwords and credentials.	Verify network connectivity and restart Active Directory Connector (ADC). If this fails, restart the computer.
8195	Active Directory Connector RPC Interface failed when trying to register which authentication methods it will accept. RPC requests may be incorrectly denied even though they are authenticated properly to the server. Error from RPC subsystem: %1.	Some services will still be available without an RPC connection. Services that are not available without RPC include password and credential modification.	This may be caused by a shortage of Windows resources or by corruption of resources used by ADC. Restart Active Directory Connector (ADC). If this fails, reboot the computer.
8196	Active Directory Connector RPC Interface failed when trying to register itself with the end point mapper. This RPC interface will not be available. Error from RPC subsystem: %1.	Some services will still be available without an RPC connection. Services that are not available without RPC include password and credential modification. This may be caused by a shortage of Windows resources or by corruption of resources used by ADC.	Restart ADC. If this fails, restart the computer.

Table A.2 *ADC Event Description and Explanation (continued)*

Event	Description	Explanation	User Action
8197	Could not open Global Catalog port on server '%1'. Attempting to find alternate Global Catalog. %2	This occurs when a Connection Agreement is made with a server that is not a Global Catalog (GC). Each time the Active Directory Connector (ADC) encounters a server that is not a Global Catalog server, it logs this event.	Verify that the Connection Agreement points to a Global Catalog server and that there is a Global Catalog server in the Active Directory site to which this server belongs.
8198	Opened Global Catalog port on server '%1'. %2		No user action is required.
8199	The service could not find an active Global Catalog for the domain that contains server '%1'. It will not be able to find objects outside of the domain. %2	Global Catalogs (GCs) have been turned off, or the Global Catalog server may be down. Some objects will not be available for synchronization or replication until this is corrected.	Verify that the Global Catalog (GC) server is running and that GCs are turned on.
8200	The service could not search for a Global Catalog Domain Controller on server %1 because the Windows 2000 interface for this information does not support the "Basic (Clear Text)" method. Change the Authentication method for the Windows 2000 server on the Connection Agreement. %2		Perform the user action specified in the message.
8201	The service could not bind to server %1. Please check the credentials supplied. %2	While searching for a Global Catalog, Active Directory Connector (ADC) found a Domain Controller to which it could not bind due to credential problems.	Verify that the credentials on the Connection Agreement have sufficient permissions to access replication information on the server.

Table A.2 *ADC Event Description and Explanation (continued)*

Event	Description	Explanation	User Action
8202	Active Directory Connector RPC Interface failed to start.	This message may be preceded by other related messages. Some services will still be available without an RPC connection. Services that are not available without RPC include password and credential modification. This may be caused by a shortage of Windows resources or by corruption of resources used by ADC	Restart ADC. If this fails, restart the computer.
8203	Active Directory Connector RPC Interface failed to stop.		Restart the server. If the problem persists, contact Microsoft Product Support Services.
8204	When deleting the Store Mailbox from '%1' on server '%2' the operation failed with the following error code: %3. %4	An attempt to delete the mailbox store failed.	Verify that the mailbox store service is running. If the service is running, manually delete the mailbox store.
8205	Error loading import rules. %1		
8206	Couldn't find the password for the credential '%1' in the LSA Private Data. If this problem persists after 15 minutes, try to reset the password in the Connection Agreement properties. %2		Perform the user action specified in the message.
8207	Source object '%1' was deleted. No file exists for recording deleted objects, so target object '%2' will not be affected. Make sure there is enough disk space and this Connection Agreement has permission to write to the path where log files are stored. %3	The Active Directory Connector (ADC) requires more disk space to write the log file.	Perform the user action specified in the message.

Table A.2 *ADC Event Description and Explanation (continued)*

Event	Description	Explanation	User Action
8208	Unable to disable target object '%1' because an error occurred while adding the object to disable log file '%2'. Make sure there is enough disk space and this Connection Agreement has permission to write to the log file. %3		Perform the user action specified in the message.
8209	Successfully disabled target object '%1' and added the object to deletion log file '%2' because the source object '%3' was deleted. %4		No user action is required.
8210	Source object '%1' was deleted. Attempt to disable target object '%2' failed. %3		Check the event log for related errors.
8211	Source object '%1' was deleted. This Connection Agreement is configured to not replicate deletions, so target object '%2' will not be deleted. The target object has been successfully added to deletion log file '%3'. %4		Manually delete the target object.
8212	Source object '%1' was deleted. An error occurred while adding target object '%2' to disable log file '%3'. Make sure there is enough disk space and this Connection Agreement has permission to write to the log file. %4		Perform the user action specified in the message.
8213	Couldn't find an accessible writable Domain Controller for domain '%1'. %2		Use System Manager to verify that the domain name on the Recipient Update Service is correct.
8214	Invalid domain name specified for service '%1', cannot process changes %2		Use System Manager to verify that the domain name on the Recipient Update Service is correct.

Table A.2 *ADC Event Description and Explanation (continued)*

Event	Description	Explanation	User Action
8215	Running Domain Change FSMO Check on '%1' %2		No user action is required.
8216	Completed Domain Change FSMO Check on '%1', '%2' new domain services created, '%3' domain services deleted %4		No user action is required.
8217	Adding new domain service for domain: '%1' as '%2' %3		No user action is required.
8218	Successfully added new domain service for domain: '%1' %2		No user action is required.
8219	Failed to add new domain service for domain: '%1' %2		Contact PSS.
8220	Deleting domain service: '%1' %2		No user action is required.
8221	Successfully deleted domain service: '%1' %2		No user action is required.
8222	Failed to delete domain service: '%1' %2		Contact PSS.
8223	The service cannot add the mail address %1 to %2 because this address is already assigned to %3 %4		Assign the object a different address or change the address of the other object using the address.
8224	The service cannot replicate %1 because too many of its attributes conflict with other objects. %2		
8225	Searching for unresolved references in naming context '%1'. This CA will resolve all references to existing objects. %2		No user action is required.
8226	Completed search for unresolved references in naming context '%1'. %2		No user action is required.

Table A.2 *ADC Event Description and Explanation (continued)*

Event	Description	Explanation	User Action
8227	A client did not have the correct rights to access the ADC password interface.		Verify that the use is authorized to access the Active Directory Connector (ADC) password interface. If so, modify the user's permissions.
8228	A client has successfully connected to the ADC password interface.		No user action is required.
8229	Unsupported or unloadable policy group: '%1'. %2		Contact Microsoft Product Support Services.
8230	Exception occurred while calling policy group provider for '%1':'%2'. %3		Contact Microsoft Product Support Services.
8231	Permanent failure reported by policy group provider for '%1':'%2', error=%3. Taking provider off line. %4		Contact Microsoft Product Support Services.
8232	Invalid policy group provider version for '%1':'%2'. Taking provider off line. %3		Contact Microsoft Product Support Services.
8233	Calling policy group provider '%1':'%2':'%3'. %4		No user action is required.
8234	Error reported by policy group provider '%1':'%2', error=%3. %4		Contact Microsoft Product Support Services.
8235	Completed call to policy group provider '%1':'%2':'%3'. %4		No user action is required.
8236	Maximum allowed exceptions occurred while calling policy group provider for '%1':'%2'. Taking provider off line. %3		Contact Microsoft Product Support Services.
8237	Loaded policy group provider for '%1':'%2'. %3		No user action is required.
8238	Unloaded policy group provider for '%1':'%2'. %3		No user action is required.

Table A.2 *ADC Event Description and Explanation (continued)*

Event	Description	Explanation	User Action
8239	Started policy group provider for '%1':'%2'. %3		No user action is required.
8240	Stopped policy group provider for '%1':'%2'. %3		No user action is required.
8241	The entry '%1' and all corresponding child entries (if any) have been deleted successfully from the directory server '%2'. %3		No user action is required.
8242	The authentication type Clear Text is not supported by this service. Please use the Active Directory Connector Management tool to change the authentication type for this Connection Agreement. %1	Active Directory Connector (ADC) does not support LDAP Clear Text authentication method.	Change Connection Agreement to authenticate using another method.
8243	ADC was unable to add the member '%1' to the group '%2'. This is because the group is a Domain Local Security group and it is not allowed to have other Domain Local groups as members. %3		Change the group type from a domain local security group to domain global or universal. For more information about security groups, see the Windows 2000 on-line documentation.
8244	ADC was unable to add the member '%1' to the group '%2'. This is because the group is a Global Security group and it is not allowed to have other groups as members. %3		Change the group type from a global security group to a universal security group. For more information about security groups, see the Windows 2000 on line documentation.
8245	ADC was unable to add the member '%1' to the group '%2'. This is because the group is a Global Distribution group and it is not allowed to have Domain Local groups or Universal groups as members. %3		Change the group type from a global security group to a universal security group. For more information about security groups, see the Windows 2000 on line documentation.

Table A.2 *ADC Event Description and Explanation (continued)*

Event	Description	Explanation	User Action
8246	ADC was unable to add the member '%1' to the group '%2'. This is because the group is a Universal Distribution group and it is not allowed to have Domain Local groups as members. %3		Change the group type from a universal security group to a global security group. For more information about security groups, see the Windows 2000 on line documentation.
8247	Address List Service is restarting this instance because policy group provider '%1':'%2' returned a fatal error. %3		Contact Microsoft Product Support Services.
8248	LDAP notification search returned no results. Return code [0x%1] %2. %3	A problem occurred while reading changes to connection agreements.	Check the status of the Domain Control server.
8249	%1 = %2		
8250	The Win32 API call '%1' returned error code [0x%2] %3. The service could not be initialized. Make sure that the operating system was installed properly.		Perform the user action specified in the message.
8251	Could not read entry '%1' on directory %2. Cannot access Address List information. Make sure that service was installed properly. %3	A permissions problem may have occurred.	Verify that the Address List service has permissions to read the object.
8252	Could not search under entry '%1' on directory %2. Cannot access Address List information. %3	A permissions problem has occurred.	Verify that the Address List has the correct permissions to access the object.
8253	Object '%1' on directory %2 has no Address Lists defined.		No user action is required.
8254	Object '%1' on directory %2 has the following Address Lists defined: %3		No user action is required.
8255	Found new or changed Address List '%1' on directory %2.		No user action is required.

Table A.2 *ADC Event Description and Explanation (continued)*

Event	Description	Explanation	User Action
8256	Address List '%1' was deleted or had its owning service changed on directory %2. Shutting down thread for this Address List.		No user action is required.
8257	The Address List '%1' on directory %2 could not be loaded due to an error. Make sure that the Address List is configured properly.		Perform the user action specified in the message.
8258	Starting replication for Address List '%1'.		No user action is required.
8259	Stopped replication for Address List '%1'.		No user action is required.
8260	Could not open LDAP session to directory '%1' using local service credentials. Cannot access Address List configuration information. Make sure the server '%1' is running. %2	The directory may not be available or the name of the Domain Controller could be incorrect in the service.	Check the status of the directory and verify that the Domain Controller name is correct in the Recipient Update Services.
8261	The Address List '%1' has been signaled to start replication immediately.		No user action is required.
8262	Processing of the Address List '%1' has been stopped due to an invalid configuration. Check the event log for more information.		Review the event log for more information. Delete and recreate the Address List service as a possible fix, but be aware that this increases the resources on the Domain Controller.
8263	The operating system has run out of resources. The Address List will shut down and then restart. If this problem persists, try restarting the service or the server.		Perform the user action specified in the message. If the problem still persists, contact Microsoft Product Support Services.

Table A.2 *ADC Event Description and Explanation (continued)*

Event	Description	Explanation	User Action
8264	An operation on server '%1' returned [0x%2] %3. The Address List %4 stopped.		Delete and recreate the Address List that caused the error. Be aware that this action is resource intensive. It may overload network traffic and CPU utilization on the Domain Controller.
8265	The target object '%1' will be missing the dxaLocalAdmin attribute because the ADC was unable to map the original value (%2) from the source object. %3	The Active Directory Connector will log this message while replicating the MSMail DXA objects (DXA-Site-Server, Remote-DXA or DX-Requester) if it is not able to map the dXALocalAdmin attribute.	Manually change the target object.
8266	Replication of the source object '%1' failed because the ADC was unable to map DXA-Remote-Client attribute (original value '%2') to a target object in the Active Directory. %3	The DXA-Remote-Client attribute is a critical attribute on a DX-Requestor or Remote-DXA object, and the requester or remote DXA cannot function properly without this value. When Active Directory Connector (ADC) is not able to map this attribute from the source object, it does not allow the replication of the object.	Make sure you have a user Connection Agreement that is replicating the recipient specified by the DXA-Remote-Client attribute to Active Directory. Make sure the recipient replicates to Active Directory and then force a full replication on the configuration Connection Agreement.
8267	The entry '%1' was not deleted because it was modified after the source entry. %2	Active Directory Connector (ADC) will not delete objects in cases where the target is newer than the source.	Manually delete the object or wait for it to replicate back in next cycle.
8268	The entry '%1' was not deleted because it is a user-enabled account. %2	Active Directory Connector (ADC) will not delete enabled user accounts.	Manually delete the user account.
8269	The entry '%1' was deleted because it will be recreated as a different object class. %2	Active Directory Connector (ADC) deletes and recreates an object when the source object changes from a mailbox-enabled to a mail-enabled user or vice versa.	No user action is required.
8270	LDAP returned the error [%1] %2 when importing the transaction %3 %4		Check the event log for related messages.

Table A.2 *ADC Event Description and Explanation (continued)*

Event	Description	Explanation	User Action
8271	Successfully replicated the object '%1' to object '%2'. %3		No user action is required.
8272	ADC is deliberately not replicating %1. %2	Active Directory Connector (ADC) has been explicitly configured not to replicate this kind of change.	Change the configuration of the Connection Agreement if you want to replicate this kind of change. If not, no user action is required.
8273	This CA does not allow back replication. As a result, the ADC cannot replicate %1 to %2. %3		
8274	ADC could not replicate %1 to %2 because the target object is deleted. %3		No user action is required.
8275	ADC could not replicate %1 to %2 because the target object is not writable %3	ADC (Active Directory Connector) is attempting to replicate to a system object or an object in a different naming context that is not writable.	Replicate to a different object.
8276	ADC could not replicate %1 to the target directory because this CA is not a primary connection agreement. %2	If the Connection Agreement is not a primary Connection Agreement, then ADC (Active Directory Connector) will not create new objects.	Change the primary bit on the Connection Agreement, or take no action.
8277	ADC could not replicate %1 to the Active Directory because the object came from the configured Active Directory, yet the ADC cannot find it in Active Directory. This can happen if the ADC is configured to use multiple DCs, and the DCs are out of sync with each other. The ADC will try to rereplicate the object. %2	The security ID (SID) on the object indicates that it came from this domain, but ADC (Active Directory Connector) cannot find it in the domain.	Try again. If the problem persists, modify the SID on the source object to a valid account.
8278	ADC could not replicate %1 to the target directory because it could not convert the DN. %2		Contact Microsoft Product Support Services.

Table A.2 *ADC Event Description and Explanation (continued)*

Event	Description	Explanation	User Action
8279	ADC could not replicate %1 because it could not convert the object class %2	ADC (Active Directory Connector) cannot find a mapping for this object class.	Contact Microsoft Product Support Services.
8280	ADC could not replicate from %1 to %2 because there are too many similarly named objects in the target directory. %3	ADC (Active Directory Connector) could not create a unique name for the object.	Manually rename the source object.
8281	ADC could not replicate the msExchMasterAccountSid to %1 because this SID is already on the object %2. %3	Exchange requires each object to have a unique security ID (SID).	Assign the SID to the desired object and change SID on the other object.
8282	ADC could not replicate from %1 to %2 %3		Review the event log for related messages.
8283	ADC will not replicate entry '%1' to the Active Directory because the target object '%2' should be administered using the Exchange Server 2000 administration snap-in only. ADC will also force a back replication of the target entry in order to overwrite any modifications made in the Exchange 5.5 directory. %3		Perform the user action specified in the message.
8284	We couldn't find the Address List Root, which is located in the Exchange Service entry under the attribute addressBookRoots. This might have been caused by a permission problem. %1		To check permissions of the server, use ADSI Edit or LDP support tools available on the Windows 2000 compact disk. Check if the server has access to CN=Microsoft Exchange, CN=Services, CN=Configuration, DC=.

Table A.2 *ADC Event Description and Explanation (continued)*

Event	Description	Explanation	User Action
8285	ADC will not replicate from %1 to %2 because both objects are not mailbox enabled. The source object is a mailbox. The target object is either a Contact or a mail-enabled user. If this is a problem, consider making the Connection Agreement an Interorganizational Connection Agreement. %3		Perform the user action specified in the message.
8286	ADC will not replicate from %1 to %2 because the source object is a Custom Recipient but the target object is a mailbox. If this is a problem, consider making the Connection Agreement an Interorganizational Connection Agreement. %3		Follow the instructions in the message.
8287	ADC will not replicate %1. Even though this is an Intra-organizational Connection Agreement, it is not a primary Connection Agreement to the target directory, Consequently, over this CA, ADC is not allowed to create new objects. %2		Change the primary agreement, or take no action.
8288	The ADC will not replicate %1. The current connection agreement is not a primary Connection Agreement, and %1 came from a different organization. As a result, ADC is not allowed to create a new target for this object. %2	If the Connection Agreement is not a primary Connection Agreement, then ADC (Active Directory Connector) will not create new objects.	Change the primary agreement, or take no action.

Table A.2 *ADC Event Description and Explanation (continued)*

Event	Description	Explanation	User Action
8289	The ADC will not replicate %1. The current connection agreement is not a primary Connection agreement, and ADC cannot determine the name of the source organization. As a result, ADC is not allowed to create a new target for this object. %2	If the Connection Agreement is not a primary Connection Agreement, then ADC (Active Directory Connector) will not create new objects.	Change the primary agreement, or take no action.
8290	The ADC cannot replicate %1. The site that the object belongs in is read only on the connected Exchange 5.5 Server. If another Connection Agreement can replicate this object to a 5.5 server in the correct site, then ignore this message. %2		Perform the user action specified in the message. If you do not have a Connection Agreement that will work, create a new one to a server that can replicate this object.
8291	The ADC cannot replicate %1 because it does not have a legacyExchangeDN for the site it belongs in. %2	Active Directory Connector (ADC) recognizes that the object belongs in a particular site but cannot determine what it should be named.	Wait for the recipient update service to stamp the object with its distinguished name, and then try again.
8292	The ADC cannot replicate %1 because it failed to map the entry. %2		Review the event log for other related messages.
8293	Successfully imported the object '%1'. %2		No user action is required.
8294	The %1 attribute is not present on the import object %2. This can happen when ADC does not have permissions to see all links. Please ensure that the ADC has Read permissions to the all of the source directory, including the Microsoft Exchange Configuration container. %3		Perform the user action specified in the message.

Table A.2 *ADC Event Description and Explanation (continued)*

Event	Description	Explanation	User Action
8295	LDAP Rename on directory %1 for entry '%2' (to '%3') was unsuccessful with error:[0x%4] %5. %6		Try again or wait for Active Directory Connector (ADC) to retry. If the problem persists, manually rename the object.
8296	Renaming entry '%1' to '%2' on directory %3. %4		No user action is required.
8297	ADC will attempt to add the server '%1' to routing group '%2'. %3		No user action is required.
8298	ADC will not replicate entry '%1' to the Active Directory because the target object '%2' should be administered using the Exchange Server 2000 administration snap-in only. Any changes applied to the object in the Exchange 5.5 directory will get overwritten the next time the Active Directory object replicates back to the Exchange 5.5 directory. %3		Perform the user action specified in the message.

Table A.2 *ADC Event Description and Explanation (continued)*

Event	Description	Explanation	User Action
8299	ADC will not replicate the private information store '%1' because it was not able to find the corresponding MAPI public store object in the Active Directory. %2	Every Exchange 5.5 mailbox store points to a public folder server (Home-Public-Server attribute). The corresponding attribute on an Exchange 2000 private store is called msExch-HomePublicMDB and points to a public store object (instead of pointing to a server object). When ADC (Active Directory Connector) replicates a 5.5 mailbox store to the AD (Active Directory), it tries to map the Home-Public-Server setting to the NT5 DN (distinguished name) of a MAPI public store under the server specified. If ADC doesn't find a MAPI public store corresponding to the 5.5 setting, it logs this message.	Make sure the public store object for the specified public folder server exists in the Active Directory (Active Directory). If the public folder server is an Exchange 5.5. server, investigate why the public store object did not replicate to the Active Directory. You may also try performing a full replication on the configuration CA (Connection Agreement) and see if it replicates over. If the public folder server is an Exchange 5.5 server, investigate if the MAPI public store for that server was deleted. If you conclude that the Exchange 5.5 mailbox store object is pointing to the wrong public folder server, just repoint the mailbox store to a different public folder server (which has a corresponding MAPI public store object in the AD), and the new value should replicate over to the Active Directory during the next replication cycle of the configuration CA.

Table A.2 *ADC Event Description and Explanation (continued)*

Event	Description	Explanation	User Action
8300	ADC will not replicate the entry '%1' to the Active directory because it was not able to find the home server (corresponding to the %2 attribute on the source object) in the Active Directory. %3	Most connectors are homed on a particular server (usually specified by one of Home-MTA, Home-MDB, or Responsible-Local-DXA attributes). While replicating a connector object from 5.5 to the Active Directory, if the ADC is not able to map the home server setting for the connector to a target DN in the Active Directory, it will not replicate the connector. This is done because the home server setting determines which routing group to put the connector into, and if we can't find the home server in the target directory, we can't find the correct routing group to put the connector into. The failed object is put on the retry list and it usually succeeds on retry.	If the failed connector hasn't yet replicated over to the Active Directory, try doing a full replication on the configuration CA so that the object specified by the home server setting replicates over to the Active Directory successfully, which in turn will enable the connector to replicate over also.
8301	ADC will not replicate the connector '%1' because it was not able to determine the correct target routing group for the connector. %2	While replicating a connector object from the Exchange 5.5 directory to Active Directory, Active Directory Connector (ADC) was not able to determine the correct target routing group for the connector, and failed to replicate the object. This failure can occur if the home server for the connector is not part of any routing group. It can also occur if the home server on the connector changed, so that the original and the new routing groups are in two different administrative groups.	Investigate the cause of the conditions outlined in the explanation and try to rectify them.

Table A.2 *ADC Event Description and Explanation (continued)*

Event	Description	Explanation	User Action
8302	ADC will not replicate entry '%1' to '%2' because the target object has a higher file version than the source object. %3	In Exchange 5.5, the Addr-Type objects that describe the proxy address generation DLLs reside at the site level, while in Exchange 2000 these objects reside at the organization level. When ADC (Active Directory Connector) replicates these objects, if an object of the same type is in the target Active Directory and if it has a file version higher than the source object, the ADC will not replicate the source object.	No user action is required.
8303	ADC will not replicate entry '%1' because site-level protocol settings are not replicated from the Exchange 5.5 directory to the Active Directory. %2	The ADC (Active Directory Connector) only replicates server-level protocol settings from Exchange 5.5 to the AD(Active Directory) but since site-level protocol settings are also exported out of the 5.5 directory, Active Directory does not replicate these objects.	No user action is required.
8304	ADC will not replicate entry '%1' because protocol settings for this protocol type are not replicated from the Exchange 5.5 directory to the Active directory. %2	Active Directory Connector (ADC) only replicates three protocol types: Internet Message Access Protocol version 4 (IMAP4), Postoffice Protocol version 3 (POP3), and Network News Transfer Protocol (NNTP). For all other server-level protocol type objects—for example, Lightweight Directory Access Protocol (LDAP)—this message appears.	No user action is required.
8305	ADC will not replicate entry '%1' because the following required attribute(s) are missing from the source entry: %2. %3		Determine why the required attributes are missing from the source entry and rectify the condition.

Table A.2 *ADC Event Description and Explanation (continued)*

Event	Description	Explanation	User Action
8306	ADC will not replicate entry '%1' because it cannot find the target entry '%2' in the Active Directory. The target entry needs to be present in the Active Directory in order to replicate the source entry. %3		Determine why the target entry is missing from the target directory and rectify the condition.
8307	ADC will not replicate entry '%1' because it does not replicate deletions of object class '%2' from the Exchange 5.5 directory to the Active Directory. %3		No user action is required.
8308	ADC will not replicate entry '%1' to the Exchange 5.5 directory because the target object should be administered using the Exchange 5.5 administration program only. Any changes made to the object in the Active Directory will get overwritten the next time the Exchange 5.5 object replicates back to the Active Directory. %2		No user action is required.
8309	ADC will not replicate entry '%1' to the Exchange 5.5 directory because the target object '%2' should be administered using the Exchange 5.5 administration program only. Any changes made to the object in the Active Directory will get overwritten the next time the Exchange 5.5 object replicates back to the Active Directory. %3		No user action is required.

Table A.2 *ADC Event Description and Explanation (continued)*

Event	Description	Explanation	User Action
8310	ADC will not replicate deletion of private store object '%1' to the Exchange 5.5 directory because there are existing private information stores on the same server in the Active Directory that map to the same target object '%2' in the Exchange 5.5 directory. %3		No user action is required.
8311	ADC will not replicate entry '%1' to the Exchange 5.5 directory because only MAPI public store objects are replicated to the Exchange 5.5 directory. %2		
8312	ADC will not replicate entry '%1' because it does not replicate deletions of object class '%2' from the Active Directory to the Exchange 5.5 directory. %3		No user action is required.
8313	ADC will not replicate entry '%1' to the Exchange 5.5 directory because it does not replicate routing group connectors between two routing groups in the same administrative group. %2		No user action is required.
8314	ADC will not replicate entry '%1' to the Exchange 5.5 directory because the routing calculation server for the administrative group is an Exchange 5.5 server. %2		No user action is required.

Table A.2 *ADC Event Description and Explanation (continued)*

Event	Description	Explanation	User Action
8315	The service could not update the entry '%1' because inheritable permissions are not propagated to this object. The inheritable permissions may be disabled because the object belongs to a Windows 2000 administrative group or the inheritable permissions were disabled explicitly by an administrator. %2		
8316	The service could not update the entry '%1' because inheritable permissions have been explicitly disabled to all objects within the container '%2'. In order for this object to be mail enabled properly, you will need to enable inheritable permissions on the security tab for this container so that the permissions can be propagated correctly to the entry that the service is trying to process. %3		
8317	The service could not update the entry '%1' because inheritable permissions may not have propagated completely down to this object yet. The inheritance time may vary depending on the number of Active Directory objects within the domain and also the load of your Domain Controllers. To correct this problem, verify that the Exchange permissions have been propagated to this object and then force a rebuild for the Recipient Update Service on this domain. %2		

Glossary

This glossary lists definitions for terms associated with Exchange 2000, including terms for equipment, software, operating systems, organizations, and general computer networks.

Access control—A mechanism for limiting use of some resource to authorized users.

Access Control List (ACL)—A data structure associated with a resource that specifies the authorized users.

Access provider—A company that provides its customers a service whereby they can access the Internet. The user normally connects to the access provider's computer via a modem using a dial-up connection.

Active Directory—The Windows 2000 directory service. Active Directory consists of a forest, a domain, and organizational units.

Active Directory Connector (ADC)—The service that replicates information between the Exchange 5.5 Directory Service and Active Directory. ADC uses Connection Agreements to define configurations for replicating mailboxes, custom recipients, and distribution lists.

Active Directory Users and Computers—An MMC (Microsoft Management Console) snap-in that allows administrators to manage objects in the domain.

Administrative Group—A collection of Exchange Active Directory objects that are grouped together for the purpose of permission management. An administrative group can contain policies, routing groups, public folder trees, monitors, servers, conferencing services, and chat networks. The administrative group defines the administrative topology of an organization.

ADO (Active Data Objects)—A programming layer built on top of OLE/DB that allows high-level programming languages such as Visual BASIC and VBScript to access an underlying data store through a common query language.

ADSI (Active Directory Services Interface)—A directory service abstraction interface that allows COM-compatible programming languages such as Visual BASIC, VBScript, JavaScript, C, and C++ to make common directory calls to an underlying directory service. ADSI providers include LDAP, NDS, Bindery, and Windows NT (SAM).

ADSI Edit—A Windows 2000 utility found in the Windows 2000 Support Tools directory that allows suitably privileged administrators to view and modify objects and attributes in the Active Directory.

API (Application Programming Interface)—This is program code that allows the application program to interact directly with the operating system.

ASP (Application Service Provider)—The latest rendition of service providers that focuses on in-house applications: business-to-business (B2B) e-commerce, Enterprise Resource Planning (ERP), and e-procurement are examples.

Authenticate—To determine that something is genuine; to reliably determine the identity of a communicating party.

Authentication—The process of reliably determining the identity of a communicating party.

Authorization—Permission to access a resource.

Bandwidth—The bandwidth is basically the maximum speed at which data can be transmitted between computers in a network.

BDAT—An SMTP command for transferring binary data. The BDAT command provides a higher-efficiency alternative to the earlier DATA command, especially for voice. The BDAT command provides for native binary transport of messages. Compliant implementations should support the binary transport using the BDAT command.

BINARYMIME—The SMTP BINARYMIME keyword indicates that the SMTP server can accept binary encoded MIME messages. Compliant implementations may support binary transport indicated by this capability. Note that support for this feature requires support of chunking.

CCITT—Comité Consultatif International Téléphonique et Télégraphique was an international committee based in Geneva that set standards for the whole world on telecommunications. The functions of this committee have now been taken up by International Telecommunications Union (ITU).

CGI—Common Gateway Interface Scripts are used by Internet programmers to perform basic functions such as counting the number of times a Web page is accessed.

Chunking—The SMTP chunking keyword indicates that the receiver will support the high-performance binary transport mode. Note that chunking can be used with any message format and does not imply support for binary encoded messages. Compliant implementations may support binary transport indicated by this capability.

Cleartext—A message that is not encrypted.

Client—Something that accesses a service by communicating with it over a computer network.

Client/server—Client/server distributes the processing of a computer application between two computers the client and the server—the principle being to exploit the power of each. The client is normally a PC. The application program will access data and perform processing on the server; using data obtained via the server, more processing tasks will be performed on the client.

Collaboration Data Objects (CDO)—An application programming interface that allows users and applications high-level access to data objects within Exchange. CDO defines the concept of different object classes, including messages, posts, appointments, and tasks.

Combination server—A server that acts as both a front-end server and a standard server. Clients can connect directly to this server and get user data from a store hosted on this computer, or they can be proxied to another standard server or combination server.

Connection agreement—An instance of synchronization between part of the Exchange 5.5 Directory Service and Windows 2000 Active Directory.

Connector—A component that enables message transfer and directory synchronization between Exchange and other messaging systems.

Contact—A contact is a representation of a mail-enabled user and is not a security principal. Contacts are stored in the Active Directory and are very similar to Exchange 5.5 custom recipients. This is not to be confused with Outlook contacts, which are entries in the user's mailbox for contact items. Outlook contacts do not replicate or move over to the Active Directory.

Delegation—Giving some of your rights to another person or process.

DHCP (Dynamic Host Configuration Protocol)—A standard method for assigning IP addresses automatically to the devices on a TCP/IP network. As a new device connects, the DHCP server assigns an IP address from a list of available addresses. The device retains this IP address for the duration of the session; once the device disconnects, the IP address becomes available for use again.

Directory service—A service provided on a computer network that allows one to look up addresses (and perhaps other information) based on names.

DNS (Domain Name System)—The naming convention defined in RFC 1033. DNS names are often referred to as Internet addresses or Internet names.

Domain—A group of computers that is part of a network and share a common directory database. A domain is organized in levels and is administered as a unit with common rules and procedures. Each domain has a unique name.

Domain Controller—In a Windows 2000 Server domain, this is a computer running Windows 2000 Server that manages user access to a network, including logging on, authentication, and access to the directory and shared resources.

Domain tree—A collection of domains that have a contiguous name space, such as microsoft.com, sample.microsoft.com, and example.compaq.com. Domains within the forest that do not have the same hierarchical domain name will be in a different domain.

DSAccess—This is the common API used by the Exchange 2000 components to get to the directory. DSAccess performs cache to speed repetitive operations such as recipient lookup done during the reception of a message.

DSProxy—Proxies the MAPI client directory requests to an Active Directory GC. This is used for pre-Outlook 2000 MAPI clients. The Outlook 2000 client connects to the GC following referral to the most appropriate GC by Exchange 2000. The next release of Outlook will not use MAPI RPC for DS requests.

.ELM— File extension used to identify a mail message in the Store. Stands for Exchange Message Link and can be seen when you access a Store item via a URL or via the IFS.

EMO—Exchange Management Objects, used for Exchange 2000 scripted management.

Epoxy—Epoxy is the former name, and Popper's favorite for what is now called ExIFS. It is a high-performance interprocess communication interface based upon a queued-shared memory. It is mainly used between IIS and the Web Store. The queuing mechanism allows IIS to push commands and get results from the Store. This interface is asynchronous. Note that the bulk of inbound and outbound messages are done through IFS, but Epoxy is still required for property and file handle interchange. Epoxy can be monitored through the MS Exchange Epoxy set of counters, which is only available on internal builds.

ESM—The Exchange System Manager snap-in for MMC. This is the interface for managing system components and configurations. Unlike the Exchange Administrator in prior versions, ESM is not used for most user-oriented activities. These are now in the Active Directory Users and Groups MMC snap-in.

Event log service—A collection of databases used by Windows and applications to record events that occur while the system is running. You can use event logs to gather information about hardware, software, and system problems, and to monitor security events.

Event sink—A piece of code that activates upon a defined trigger, such as receiving a new message. The code is normally written in any COM-compliant programming language, such as Visual BASIC, VBScript, JavaScript, or C/C++. Exchange supports the transport, protocol, and store event sinks.

Event Viewer—The application used to review the events that have been recorded in the event logs. The Event Viewer displays these types of events: error, warning, informational, success audit, and failure audit. Using the event logs in Event Viewer, you can gather information about hardware, software, and system problems, and monitor Windows 2000 security events.

Extensible Storage Engine (ESE)—The module that accesses and controls the Exchange databases.

Fault tolerance—The ability of a system to respond to an event, such as a power failure, so information is not lost and operations continue without interruption.

FE/BE (Front-End/Back-End) servers—Front-End/Back-End servers are used to host protocols (Front-End) and store information (Back-End). FE servers' proxy protocols and redirect commands to BE servers. A Combination Server is a server that hosts an Exchange Store and can proxy protocols toward a different Exchange store server. Therefore, POP services are proxied and redirected to the POP service on the back-end server. The Epoxy layer does not distribute across multiple servers. Multiple front-end servers create redundancy for client access. They are load balanced by the means of WLBS or DNS Round-Robin, or Cisco's Load Director. Typically, FE servers do the directory lookup to locate the user maildrop. FE may cache information to avoid returning to the BE server. For instance, when a message is received by the SMTP service, the WIN32 file handle used to write to the STM file is kept in a cache, in case a POP or IMAP user claims it farther down the road.

Firewall—A combination of hardware and software that provides a security system to prevent unauthorized access from the Internet to an internal network or intranet.

Five Star—One who enjoys the finer things in life, including pens, watches, wines, food, clothes, hotels, and supersonic travel. Also one of the Exchange 2000 Academy Tutors and coauthor of this book.

Forest—A collection of domains and domain trees. The implicit name of the forest is the name of the first domain installed.

Fully qualified domain name (FQDN)—A DNS domain name that has been stated unambiguously to indicate with certainty its location in the domain name space tree. Fully qualified domain names differ from relative names in that they are typically stated with a trailing period (.)—for example, prop.spinfast.com, to qualify their position to the root of the name space.

Gateway—A translator between different mail systems. When a message is sent from one mail system to another, the gateway filters information specific to the originating mail system. Then it attaches information that the second mail system needs to deliver the message and sends the message. If a gateway has been added to an Exchange organization, you may find a gateway address list in the Address List.

Global Catalog (GC)—A server that holds a complete replica of the configuration and schema naming contexts for the forest, a complete replica of the domain naming context in which the server is installed, and a partial replica of all other domains in the forest.

Global Domain Identifier—Exchange uses the X.400 global domain identifier in a relay environment. The global domain identifier consists of the country ADMD and PRMD name of the remote MTA. It is used for inserting trace elements and can be used for troubleshooting an unsuccessful relay attempt. It is also used to prevent message looping in wide area messaging environments.

Globally unique identifier (GUID)—A unique number that identifies a Dynamic Link Library (DLL) file. The GUID is generated when the DLL is registered.

Group—In the context of security, a named collection of users, created for convenience in stating authorization policy. It can be either a security principle or a distribution group.

Hosted organization—A hosted organization is a collection of Exchange services (including, but not limited to, protocols and storage) operating to emulate a single Exchange virtual server. These services can span multiple physical machines. Typical implementations of a hosted organization are protocol farms or outsourced e-mail/collaboration services.

IETF (Internet Engineering Task Force)—A standards body whose focus is protocols for use in the Internet. Its publications are called Internet RFCs (Requests For Comments).

IFS—(Sometimes referred to as ExIFS—the name of the driver is exifs.sys.) The IFS (acronym to be sorted out—IFS stands for Installable File System) is a Win32 file system interface to the Web store, probably more to the STM content than the EDB content. IFS is a way for consumers of the store to flush data much more rapidly than through the Epoxy interface, which can have some limitation on the chunks of data you can pass between the components. When accessing information in the store, the store will return via Epoxy a file handle to the consumer—for example, TransmitFile() or WriteFile(). One of the purposes of IFS is to reduce memory copies and disk I/O for inbound and outbound messages. This allows the protocol servers to retain the abstraction one message per file, even though the actual contents are stored in a single NTFS file (the STM file), handled by the Store process. Typically, the Store creates IFS handles for outbound messages and IIS creates IFS handles for inbound messages.

IMAIL—IMAIL is a property parser. It gets the basic properties that are required for Exchange to provide many of its features (such as indexing).

In Exchange 5.5, IMAIL was the Store component that handled protocol access for IMAP4, POP3, and HTTP.

Internet—When not capitalized, it means a connected collection of computer networks. When capitalized, the Internet refers to the large and still growing network that started as the ARPANET, a research network funded by the U.S. Department of Defense.

ISO (International Organization for Standardization)—An international organization tasked with developing and publishing standards for everything from wine glasses to computer network protocols. It has defined standards for computer networking, known as the Open Systems Interconnection (OSI) protocol.

ISP—Internet Service Provider. A company or organization that offers consumers or companies access to Internet services. The services offered are typically Web, e-mail, and netnews (nntp). The companies offering these services, at the high end, are usually telcos.

LAN (Local Area Network)—A method of interconnecting multiple systems in such a way that all transmissions over the LAN can be listened to by all systems on the LAN.

LDAP—Lightweight Directory Access Protocol. A standards-based protocol that can be used to interact with conformant directory services.

Legend, The—An inspiring and exceptionally talented individual who encouraged and drove the entire Exchange Academy Tutor Team. And I'm serious about that.

LRA—LDAP Replication Agent handles the replication of user and configuration information between the Exchange DS and the Active Directory.

LSA—Link State Algorithm is a mechanism for Exchange 2000 to update routing information.

MAC—Message Authentication Code or Mandatory Access Controls. (And if that isn't enough, it also stands for medium access control in data link layer networking jargon, where it has nothing to do with the security sense of access control.)

Maddog—One who is not funny, but also the leader of the Exchange 2000 Academy Tutors, who challenged, inspired, encouraged, humored, indulged, and motivated us to the extreme.

Mailbox-enabled object—A mailbox-enabled object is a Windows 2000 object that has one or more mailboxes associated with it. By definition a mailbox-enabled object is also mail-enabled. Users and groups can be mailbox enabled but contacts cannot be.

Mailbox information store—The part of the information store that maintains information.

Maildrop—The maildrop identifies the server and the database hosting a user mailbox. The maildrop for a particular user is stored in the Active Directory user object.

Mail-enabled object—A mail-enabled object is a Windows 2000 object that has at least one e-mail address defined. Users, groups, and contacts can be mail enabled. In a pure Windows 2000 environment, objects are mail enabled only.

MDB—Mail Database, also known as the Store! Includes the EDB and STM files that support one another. A single MDB is normally identified as public or private depending on the type of data that it stores. Some Microsoft folks do not like this name and prefer to use something like virtual database.

Message Transfer Agent (MTA)—An Exchange component that routes messages to other Exchange MTAs, information stores, connectors, and third-party gateways.

Messaging Application Programming Interface (MAPI)—A standard interface that Exchange and Microsoft Outlook components use to communicate with one another.

Mooner—One who abstractedly wanders or gazes about, as if moonstruck, but also the nickname of one of the Exchange 2000 Academy Tutors who is far too smart, but whom we love and cherish dearly.

Name space—In Active Directory, a domain defines the unit of name space. This is the logical collection of resources that can be managed as a single unit.

Naming context—A self-contained section of a directory hierarchy that can have its own properties, such as replication configuration. Active Directory includes the domain, configuration, and schema naming contexts.

OLE/DB—An API that allows low-level programming languages such as C and C++ to access dissimilar data stores through a common query language. Data stores such as those in Exchange 2000 and SQL Server allow for OLE/DB access, thus making application development easier and faster.

Outlook Web Access—An Exchange feature that allows users secure access to their mailboxes through a Web browser. It is intended for UNIX and Macintosh users and for fortunate people without access to PCs.

Oz/Os—Abbreviation for Osmium, the project code name for Exchange 5.5. Also often spoken or written as Oz.

Permission—Authorization for a user to perform an action such as sending mail for another user or posting items in a public folder.

PEZ—Particular points and places within the Platinum Product Architecture that, when manipulated carefully, will make the product not just shudder, but scream. More information can be found from Popper.

Pipelining—The SMTP pipelining keyword indicates ability of the receiving server to accept new commands before issuing a response to the previous command. Pipelining commands dramatically improve performance by reducing the number of round-trip packet exchanges and makes it possible to validate all recipient addresses in one operation. Compliant implementations should support the command pipelining indicated by this keyword.

PKI (Public-Key Infrastructure)—A comprehensive set of required functions providing public-key encryption and digital signature services.

Policy—A collection of configuration settings that is applied to one or more Exchange Active Directory objects of the same class.

Popper—One that pops, but also one of the Exchange 2000 Academy Tutors who positively empathizes with technology, especially processors and disk IO subsystems. But again, one whose support and insight we've come to adore and rely on.

Ports—Not exactly a glossary term, but here are some common port numbers:

25—SMTP

110—POP3

119—NNTP

389—LDAP

3044—Link status within a routing group

3268—GC listens for forest-wide LDAP queries

Property Promotion—Internet content (SMTP, IMAP, or POP messages) is stored natively in the STM file database (as a MIME stream). However, for folder browsing, a few properties of the Internet message (e.g., date sent/received, from field, subject, etc.) are promoted to the EDB database to allow folder browsing and views of the Internet message. The promoted properties are duplicated from the MIME content.

Protocol farm—A protocol farm is a collection of protocol virtual servers (SMTP, NNTP, IMAP, POP, and HTTP-DAV) operating to provide a single protocol service for the purposes of scalability and redundancy. These virtual servers can span multiple physical machines. To the outside world (e.g., clients), a protocol farm looks like a single protocol virtual server. Transparent to the client, a particular virtual server is selected via round-robin DNS or a hardware device (such as Cisco's Local Director).

Proxy server—A firewall component that manages Internet traffic to and from a LAN and can provide other features such as document caching and access control.

Pt—Abbreviation for Platinum, the project code for Exchange 2000 Server.

Public folder—A folder that you and your coworkers can use to share a wide range of information, such as project and work information discussions about a general subject and classified ads. Public folders can have forms for posting information and views for finding and organizing information. Access permissions determine who can view and use the folder. Public folders are stored on computers running Exchange.

Public folder replication—The process of updating identical copies of a public folder on multiple computers running Exchange.

Public information store—The part of the information store that maintains information in public folders.

Recipient—A recipient is a Windows 2000 object that is either mail enabled or mailbox enabled. A recipient can be a user, group, or contact.

Remote procedure call (RPC)—Standard protocol for client/server communication; a routine that transfers functions and data between client and server processes.

Resource—A Windows 2000 Active Directory object that can be scheduled and is commonly used for conference rooms and shared equipment. A resource may have an Exchange mailbox.

Rick—A close supporter of the Exchange 2000 Academy Tutor team, who was always there for us when we needed him.

Role—A group of permissions.

Router—A device that forwards and directs data communications between networks.

Routing—The process of transferring and delivering messages.

Routing group—A collection of Exchange servers in which messages are sent directly from one server to another.

Routing Group Connector—A connector that specifies the bridgehead servers between two routing groups, as well as the connection cost, schedule, and other configuration properties.

RPC—*See* remote procedure call.

RPCINTF—The interface to the Store that MAPI is based on. RPCINTF is the best way to get to the store and is the basis for the Epoxy integration with the Store

Schema—The metadata that describe the use of objects within a given structure.

Schema attributes—Properties that describe Exchange directory objects.

Security context—An aspect of Windows 2000 that controls the kind of access a user, process, or service has to system services.

Server—Some resource available on the network to provide services such as name lookup, file storage, or printing.

Shark—The nickname of one of the Exchange 2000 Academy Tutors whose perseverance, ingenuity, and cunning made us all jealous.

S-MIME (Secure Multipurpose Internet Mail Extension)—S-MIME is a standard for encrypting and digitally signing e-mail.

Snorkel—A breathing apparatus used by skin divers, consisting of a long tube held in the mouth, but also the nickname of one of the Exchange 2000 Academy Tutors and coauthor of this book.

SRS—Site Replication Services. A component of Exchange 2000 that presents itself as a 5.5 Directory Service on an Exchange 2000 server.

Storage group—A collection of Exchange databases on an Exchange server that share the same Extensible Storage Engine instance and transaction log. Individual databases within a storage group can be mounted and dismounted.

Store—The generic name given to the storage subsystem on an Exchange server.

TLH (Top-Level Hierarchy)—This is the term used to describe multiple public folder hierarchies. MAPI clients can only see one TLH (All Public Folders) but other (Web) clients should be able to see all. Also known as Public Folder Root, Public Folder Virtual Root, Public Folder Root.

Trust relationship—The relationship between two domains that makes it possible for a user in one domain to access resources in another domain.

UPS (Users Per Server)—One goal of Exchange 2000 is to increase the UPS.

User—A user is a Windows 2000 security principal. A user may optionally have an Exchange e-mail address and/or an Exchange mailbox.

User account—Contains information such as the user name, password, group, membership, and permissions.

User class—A logical collection of chat users whose membership is based on one or more criteria, such as their chat client protocol (e.g., IRC) or their IP address. User classes allow you to protect your chat server and its users from flooding and other types of attacks.

User name—A unique name that is assigned by the administrator to each Exchange user. Use this name to address messages.

Virtual server—A virtual server is an instance of one of the protocol services (e.g., POP3, IMAP4, HTTP, NNTP, and SMTP) with a defined set of IP address/port combinations and an independent collection of configuration properties. When a client connects to the IP address/port combination of a virtual server, the configuration properties of that virtual server will be used unless overridden on a per-user basis. There can be multiple virtual servers per machine. A virtual server is registered to IIS and consists of an IP address and port pair (e.g., 10.1.1.1, 110 to support POP). If you wanted to support POP over SSL, you would need to register a second virtual server for port 993 (10.1.1.1, 993).

Virus—A piece of computer program that replicates by embedding itself in other programs. When those programs are run, the virus is invoked again and can spread further.

VSI—Virtual Server Instance of a particular IIS-based service—for example, SMTP. Therefore, there may be zero to many VSIs on one physical Platinum Server box. VSIs communicate with one another via TCP connection.

Web store—Common name for the Web-enabled Exchange 2000 store.

Whack-whack—A term employed primarily by Microsoft to describe the occurrence of two left-leaning oblique characters typically found at the beginning of a UNC. *See also* Legend.

Windows 2000 groups—A group is a collection of any object of the Active Directory. Possible objects are users, contacts, and computers. There are two types of groups: security group and DIstribution group. Security group can be used to allow/deny access to resources. Distribution group has no security principal and is used as Distribution List in Exchange. Groups can have different scopes: Universal, Global, Domain local.

WLBS (Windows Load-Balancing Services)—A set of services available from Windows NT that enables load balancing across multiple front-end servers. WLBS handles a domain name that clients connect to. Based on the FE server's load, it resolves the domain name to the least loaded server. It also maintains context. A client that connects to an FE server will use the same server for the remainder of the connection. WLBS is available only on Windows 2000 Advanced Server

WMI (Windows Management Instrumentation)—SMS 2.0 uses WMI to collect information from the hardware. WMI also stands for Windows Monitor Interface—an interface that monitoring tools can use to gather info from providers. Providers supply a schema definition and manage the objects in the schema. Examples are Perfmon, Event Viewer, and Exchange Monitors.

Index